NOTHING EVER HAPPENED

VOLUME TWO

DAVID GODMAN

AVADHUTA FOUNDATION
BOULDER, COLORADO

NOTHING EVER HAPPENED

ISBN 0-9638022-3-2

CONTENTS

HARDWAR, RISHIKESH

After his retirement in 1966, Papaji travelled extensively all over India, rarely staying in one place for more than a few weeks. However, once he had arranged and attended the marriages of his children in January, 1967, he felt an urge to spend more and more time in Rishikesh and Hardwar, the pilgrimage towns in northern Uttar Pradesh that are located at the place where the River Ganga leaves the foothills of the Himalayas and enters the plains. The towns are close to each other, with Rishikesh being twenty-four kilometres further upstream than Hardwar.

For most of my life I have been travelling to Rishikesh and Hardwar and spending time there. When I was a child my parents took all the family to Hardwar for the summer holidays. For most of my life I adjusted my schedule so that I could spend one or two months there every year. When I had no other commitments, I would spend much more time there. Sometimes I stayed on for years.

These are holy places People have been meditating in Rishikesh and Hardwar, by the banks of the Ganga, for thousands of years, and many have won enlightenment there. These are the places I always like to return to when I have had long or extensive trips to meet devotees.

After performing the marriages of my son and daughter at Agra and Delhi, I decided to leave my family and relatives once and for all. It was clear that my duties had been fulfilled. I felt no desire to continue the role of a householder.

I decided to go to Rishikesh and live the life of a *sadhu*. I wanted to live by the Ganga, and I wanted to be alone. I moved into a cave that was located near the main ashrams of Rishikesh. As it was very close to the waterline, on several occasions the water level rose, flooding my cave. I didn't care. When it was too wet to stay in the cave, I moved out to a nearby banyan tree that had a good, strong platform around it. The tree and the cave were not far away from the ashram of Maharishi Mahesh Yogi, the man who started the T.M. [Transcendental Meditation] movement. In those days, this ashram was his headquarters.

Papaji tried out several other caves in the neighbourhood. In one of them, located near a waterfall about fifteen minutes' walk from the Ganga, he not only had to contend with the weather and the primitive living conditions, he also had to deal with the local animals who shared his water source.

For some time I tried out a nice cave that was located in the forest. About halfway to Phool Chatti on the old Badrinath pilgrimage road there is a stream that flows into the Ganga. About one kilometre upstream, away from the Ganga, there was a nice waterfall that had a cave adjacent to it. I lived there for some time.

In those days there were still many tigers around. The nearby stream was the only safe source of water for all the animals in the forest, so they all used to come there. There were also bears and elephants in the neighbourhood, and they too occasionally came to have a good drink. I could watch them from my cave without disturbing them. We lived together very peacefully. The elephants used to come and bathe under the waterfall because they liked the pressure of the falling water on their backs. They would suck up vast amounts of water with their trunks and then squirt it against their bodies. Sometimes they would shake their trunks as they were blowing out the water. When this happened I would also get a shower while I was sitting in my cave.

I only had one close encounter with a tiger. I was down by the pool when a tiger came to have a drink. He looked at me with evident curiosity before beginning his drink. I got the feeling that he had just had a good meal, so he was more interested in drinking than in eating me.

It was around this time that Papaji had an interesting

experience in which all his past lives appeared before him. This is the account he gave of it in the Papaji Interviews *book:*

I was quietly sitting by the banks of the Ganga in Rishikesh between Ram Jhula and Lakshman Jhula, watching the fishes moving through the water. As I sat there I had an extraordinary vision of myself, the self that had been 'Poonja', in all its various incarnations through time. I watched the *jiva* [reincarnating soul] move from body to body, from form to form. It went through plants, through animals, through birds, through human bodies, each in a different place in a different time. The sequence was extraordinarily long. Thousands and thousands of incarnations, spanning millions of years, appeared before me. My own body finally appeared as the last one of the sequence, followed shortly afterwards by the radiant form of the Maharshi. The vision then ended. The appearance of the Maharshi had ended that seemingly endless sequence of births and rebirths. After his intervention in my life, the *jiva* that finally took the form of Poonja could incarnate no more. The Maharshi destroyed it by a single look.

As I watched the endless incarnations roll by, I also experienced time progressing at its normal speed. That is to say, it really felt as if millions of years were elapsing. Yet when my usual consciousness returned, I realised that the whole vision had occupied but an instant of time. One may dream a whole lifetime but when one wakes up one knows that the time that elapsed in the dream was not real, that the person in the dream was not real, and that the world which that person inhabited was not real. All this is recognised instantly at the moment of waking. Similarly, when one wakes up to the Self, one knows instantly that time, the world, and the life one appeared to live in it are all unreal. That vision by the Ganga brought home this truth to me very vividly. I knew that all my lifetimes in *samsara* were unreal, and that the Maharshi had woken me up from this wholly imaginary nightmare by showing me the Self that I really am. Now, freed from that ridiculous *samsara*, and speaking from the standpoint of the Self, the only reality, I can say, 'Nothing has ever come into existence; nothing has ever happened; the unchanging, formless Self alone exists'.

7

That is my experience, and that is the experience of everyone who has realised the Self.

A few years later, when I was staying in Paris, someone showed me a copy of the *Nirvana Sutra*. I read it and found that the Buddha had had a similar experience.

Early in 1993 I was watching a cricket match on TV in Papaji's house. One of the fielders dived for a ball, slid across the grass and ended up with a bright green stain down the front of his shirt. Papaji laughed, but while he was laughing he was suddenly reminded of another vision he had had on the banks of the Ganga. He began to talk about it in a lighthearted way.

'I had a green body once, just like this man. It was large, translucent and very beautiful. I was living on a different planet in another part of the universe. I saw it in a vision I had in Rishikesh.

'I felt that I had lived on this planet for a very long time. I also got the feeling that it was a planet where jivas *went to in order to use up all their good karma. It was a place where everyone seemed to be endlessly enjoying himself.'*

'Was anybody meditating there?' I asked. 'Was anyone trying to get enlightened?'

'No,' he replied. Then he paused, became more serious, and continued speaking.

'I have lived on different planets and I have visited many others in visions. This world we are in now is the only one I have seen in which people are striving for freedom and attaining it. You don't know how lucky you are.'

When I started work on this book, I asked him for more information. He repeated the story for me and added a few extra details.

I was living in Rishikesh, spending most of my time on the banks of the Ganga. I felt my body undergoing some kind of change. It became very subtle and transparent. Around me there were many other 'people' who had the same kind of subtle body. I looked into the sky and found that I was in a completely different part of the universe. There was a different sun in the sky, maybe more than one because there was no night. It was a strange world

Rishikesh: the Ganga flowing under Ram Jhula.

in which no one slept or awoke. We were awake all the time. Though the vision only lasted a few seconds, I knew that I had spent an enormously long time in this place.

I realised that it was a different planet. I reasoned that there must be many other planets with intelligent beings on them, and that as one moves from life to life, one can also move from world to world.

Though I could not deny that the vision took place, afterwards the thought came to me that it might have been a projection of the imagination. It's possible I heard some story like this when I was young and that the sudden memory of it caused it to manifest.

Papaji's ascetic, cave-dwelling period came to a temporary end when he was offered a room in one of the main ashrams in Rishikesh.

When I was hungry I would often go to buy *pooris* at the Gita Bhavan shop, because they sold cooked food at cost price to pilgrims for four months every year, from June to September. On

9

one of my visits the manager of Swarg Ashram Trust called out to me because he said he was curious to know who my Guru was.

I told him, 'My Guru is Sri Ramana Maharshi from Tiruvannamalai in South India'.

The manager had never heard the name before, which was surprising because the Maharshi is well known in ashrams all over India. We spoke for a while and during the course of our conversation he told me that he was a retired engineer from Madhya Pradesh.

After a few minutes he turned to me and said, 'He must be a great Master. Whenever I see you, you are alone and keeping very quiet. As I watched you, a thought occurred to me: "When I eat a Duseri mango from Malihabad near Lucknow, I know from the taste that it must have come from a great orchard. I have never visited those orchards, but I can tell from the taste of one mango that the orchard must be a good one. In the same way, I can judge this man's Master from the disciple I see before me." I have watched you behave. I can tell that you must have had a very great Master.'

He went on to tell me about the *sadhus* he looked after in his own ashram.

'We have three hundred *sadhus* living here in *kutirs* [small huts or rooms for monks]. We provide free food to all of them. The ashram kitchen can easily feed all these people. The *sadhus* stand in line, waiting for their food, and while they are waiting, devotees often bring them sweets to eat. In winter, devotees bring blankets for them, and some even give them Rs 100 each in case they want to go on a pilgrimage. These *sadhus* are spoilt. They don't appreciate what is being done for them. Some of them even abuse the gifts and the hospitality they are given. They accept the blankets even if they don't have any need for them. Afterwards, they sell them at half price to raise money. Others take home the food we give them and recook it in pure butter to make it taste better. These people don't need free handouts. Many of them are already rich from receiving presents every day from pilgrims.

'But it is my job to look after all these people. I have to take care of them all out of the small donations we receive. I don't encourage new people to come, but in your case I will be happy to make an exception. I can see that you are different. If you want a room, I can give you a permanent place. You can even eat in my house, the one that is allotted to the manager.'

I accepted a room in the corner of his ashram. It was so close to the Ganga, I could see visitors throwing coins into the waters from my window. However, after a few months there I suddenly felt an urge to go to Vrindavan and so I left. After that I didn't go back to Rishikesh for a while. I went on to Sri Ramanasramam instead.

A new pattern was emerging. After his initial spell of extreme asceticism, followed by a few months in an ashram, Papaji began travelling again. From this time on Papaji punctuated his long stays in Rishikesh with trips to Vrindavan or visits to his devotees in various parts of India. He also occasionally made long trips to some of the more inaccessible parts of the Himalayas. One journey was particularly memorable:

I once read an article about the aftermath of the great battle that is the culmination of the *Mahabharata*. It was a very destructive war. When it was over, the Kauravas were all dead and the countryside had been devastated. The Pandava brothers emerged victorious in the war on account of the help that Krishna had given them. Years later, after Krishna himself had passed away, the Pandavas decided that they no longer wanted to remain on earth. It held too many bad memories for them. The five brothers set off together in the direction of the Himalayas because they wanted to walk to heaven. There was supposed to be a gateway in the mountains that connected the two worlds. It was a dangerous route that took them to very high altitudes. One by one all the brothers died except for Yudhistara, who was accompanied by a stray dog that had adopted him. At the end of the march only the two of them, Yudhistara and his dog, reached the heavens.

The magazine described this expedition and gave a map that indicated the probable route of the Pandava brothers. I was intrigued by the idea that there might be a gateway between the earth and the heavens, intrigued enough to follow the route myself to see if it were true.

If I hear about some new method or technique, I immediately try it out for myself. Right from my childhood this has always been one of my habits. I am not satisfied with secondhand information. I like to try things out for myself to see if there is any merit in them.

Once, for example, I heard about a *sadhu* who was living on a diet of mud from the Ganga, and apparently surviving quite well.

I thought to myself, 'Why should I run around buying vegetables and cooking food if this is all that is needed to keep the body alive? I will try out this diet to see if it is possible.'

So, for one month I lived on mud and leaves that fell from the trees. It didn't work for me because within a few weeks I got very sick. I consulted a *sadhu* about this and asked him if I should carry on with this diet.

He said, 'You are only torturing your body by doing this. The human body is a temple of God. You have to keep it in good condition, for if the body is sick then one cannot meditate. The ancient *rishis* knew how to live properly. They ate sattvic foods and stayed healthy.'

I accepted his advice, gave up this practice and went back to eating a normal diet. All this took place around 1944 when I had a job, working for the army in Madras.

Anyway, when I heard that it might be possible to walk to heaven, and get there in one's physical body, I immediately decided to check out the route to see if it were possible.

In the beginning it was easy. I just followed the main pilgrimage route to Devaprayag, the confluence of the Ganga and the Alaknanda rivers. While I was walking along the banks of the Ganga it began to rain. As it was late at night, I started to look around for some shelter. There didn't seem to be any point in going any further that day. After a few minutes of searching I found a little hut with an old *baba* inside. I put my head in the door and enquired very politely if he would be willing to let me sleep in his hut for the night.

Since he looked as if he was about to prepare his evening

meal, I told him that I was willing to go to the nearest shop to buy some provisions for him. People like this often don't keep much food with them. Not wanting to be an unnecessary burden on him, I volunteered to go out in the rain to buy enough food for both of us to have a good meal

He accepted my offer and told me that I was welcome to eat and sleep with him.

I did the shopping, he did the cooking, and afterwards we ate together on the bank of the Ganga. We were sitting there at about 10 p.m. when I noticed another little hut about ten feet higher than his, away from the river.

When I asked him about it he said, 'I built that place so that I would have somewhere to live when the Ganga floods. The hut I use now goes underwater when there is a big flood. You can sleep there tonight. There is no danger from the river. We can have one hut each. Someone sent me some money to build this extra hut. I have been living here for thirty-six years, but this is the first year that I have had an extra place to move into when the river floods. I am from Bengal. Some people from that place sent me money so that I could live a little more comfortably. They send me twenty rupees a month to live on.'

This man had renounced the world to live an ascetic life by the banks of the Ganga. In his thirty years of living there he seemed to have accumulated nothing more than a few cooking pots. Furniture was non-existent.

When I went to sleep in his spare hut I discovered that there was nothing there except a coarsely woven sack that had been filled with sand. The sack looked as if it was meant to be used as a pillow. My bed was a patch of levelled sand from the Ganga. I tried the pillow out, but it didn't feel comfortable. It was too hard. I don't know if you have ever tried to sleep with a pillow like this. It doesn't give way when you put your head on it; it just feels like a rock.

I lifted the pillow up, thinking that it would be more comfortable to use my arm to rest my head on. Underneath I found a magazine which had photos of nude women in it. The *sadhu* must have been keeping it there, out of the sight of his usual visitors.

Earlier that evening, while we had been eating dinner together, he had said, 'I have been a bachelor all my life. I am the eldest son, and all my other brothers have long since married. I renounced the world a long time ago and I have not been back to my village for more than thirty years. My family knows that I am here. Occasionally I get messages from them via pilgrims who are on their way to Badrinath, but other than that I have no contact with my old life.'

This is what happens to most *sadhus*. They dress up in orange and tell everyone that they have renounced the world. They even make a good living out of looking pious and holy, but inside they have not renounced their desires. What is the point of running away to live like a *sadhu* by the Ganga if you bring all your desires and attachments with you? This *sadhu* would have been better off staying at home and getting married, as his brothers had done. Suppressing one's desires, pretending that they are not there, is a fraudulent way to live. No benefit comes from it.

I left the *sadhu* the next morning and travelled on to the high Himalayas on the north side of Badrinath. It was there, many days later, that I had a far more interesting encounter.

I was walking along a path at a great altitude. There were glaciers all around me. Since it was not a place where anyone lived, I was a little surprised when I saw a tall young man approach me from the opposite direction. As we were the only two people in the area, we stopped to exchange a few pleasantries. During the course of our conversation he asked me what I was doing in such an inaccessible spot. I told him about my desire to follow the Pandavas' route to heaven. When he found out that I was spiritually inclined, he asked me if we could sit for a while because he wanted to consult me about a problem he had had for some time.

'I am the son of a sub-postmaster from Jammu Tawi,' he began. 'I went to school there, but studying academic subjects didn't interest me. I ran away from school ten years ago and never went back to my native place. Since then I have travelled to many places, including other *lokas* [heavenly worlds].'

This sounded interesting. I asked him how he had done his travelling, and he replied that he had acquired a *siddhi* that enabled

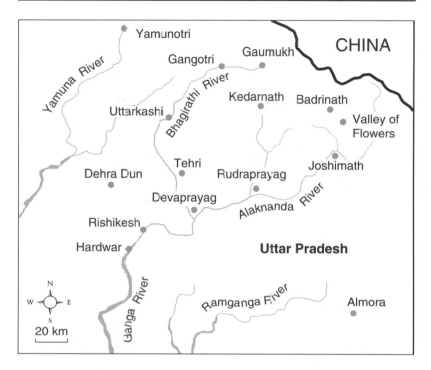

him to travel virtually anywhere in the universe.

'I had an aptitude for *kundalini* yoga,' he said. 'When I ran away from school, I started to search for a yoga teacher I could train with. I was first directed to Vishnu Prayag. Someone there told me to go on to Narada Hill, a place where Narada is supposed to have performed penance. On the other side of that hill there is a place where many *siddhas* live. I found one and persuaded him to accept me as his disciple.

'I mastered everything he had to teach me. I seemed to have a natural aptitude for learning these things. I learned to levitate; I learned how to make my body appear in different places at the same time; I learned how to summon up deities such as Durga and Lakshmi and ask boons from them. From Saraswati I earned the boon of being able to speak in any language and to understand even what plants and rocks are saying. I even know how to travel to other worlds.'

I found this hard to believe. Thinking that he was just

15

boasting, I decided to test his claim that he could speak in any language. His native language was Dogri, he said, but he offered to speak to me in any language I knew. I asked several complicated questions in Persian, Kannada, Tamil, Marathi, Gujarati, Sindhi and Konkani, and to each question he gave a fluent answer, with perfect pronunciation and vocabulary. I was impressed and a little more inclined to believe some of his other claims. I then asked him to levitate for me. This is a difficult *siddhi* to attain, but a very easy one to demonstrate. He agreed and a few seconds later his body was rising from the ground and moving around in all directions. Though levitation is mentioned as one of the *siddhis* one can attain through the practice of Patanjali's yoga system, this is the only man I have met in my whole life who actually proved to me that he could do it. Many people who have done Transcendental Meditation claim that they have learned to fly after doing a *siddhi* course, but all they can do is bounce up and down with their legs crossed. This man went up in the air and stayed there. When he wanted to go to the left, he went to the left, and when he wanted to go to the right, he moved to the right. He had complete control of his flying movements in all directions.

He floated down to the ground and we resumed our conversation.

'That's very interesting,' I said. 'But you are only doing what every bird in the sky can do. What else can you do?' I wanted to provoke him into showing some of his other tricks.

'I can bilocate,' he said, obviously annoyed that he was failing to impress me. Then, without any further prompting from me, he manifested his body in two different places.

'I can even do more than two,' he announced. And before my eyes he split himself up again and appeared in several different places on the ground in front of me.

'Not bad,' I said, 'but one body is enough for me. This one body gives me more than enough trouble. Why should I multiply my troubles by having five or six? And how long will these bodies last? Will you live six times as long by having six bodies? I don't think so. When one body dies, all the others will die as well.'

'Some of my powers are very practical and useful,' he replied.

'I will show you. What would you like to eat?'

I looked around. We were many miles from any settlement. There was no vegetation in sight, and he didn't have any bag with him that might contain food.

'Where are you going to get food from?' I asked. I had been living on the roots and leaves that the local people ate. There was no other food available in that area.

'I have another *siddhi*,' he said. 'If I want food, I can have it delivered here. A goddess has given me this boon. I call on her, tell her what I want, and it instantly materialises in front of me.'

I ordered a dish which is a speciality of Varanasi and within a few seconds it materialised in front of me. I tasted it and had to agree that it tasted just like the best of its kind that was served in Varanasi.

'What else can you do?' I asked. This man was proving to be a very entertaining interlude on my pilgrimage. I wanted to see what other feats he had managed to master.

'I can travel to other planets and I can move around freely in all the astral worlds except one. Whenever I go to Brahma Loka and try to get in, the guardians of the gate deny me access. This is the only place in the universe that I am unable to visit. My guru had the same problem. He couldn't get in there either. The *dwarpallas* [doorkeepers] always stopped him. This Brahma Loka is a place of no return. Once one has entered, one never returns again to the world of *samsara*. It is a place that enlightened people alone can enter, and neither my guru nor myself has reached that state.'

Though he had been willing to demonstrate his *siddhis*, he was not an arrogant man. He knew that there was more to life than supernatural tricks.

He continued to talk, telling me, 'My guru told me that these *siddhis* are not the highest accomplishment. He said that these powers come from the mind only, and that *jnana*, or true knowledge, is the highest accomplishment.

'My guru told me, "It is very hard to find a man who can pass on this highest knowledge. I don't have this knowledge, and I have never met anyone who has. It is a very rare accomplishment. I have taught you everything I know, but I cannot give you this final knowledge because I don't have it myself. After I die you should leave this place and look for a man who can show you what *jnana* is."

'My guru died two years ago at the age of ninety-two. Since his death I have been travelling throughout the country, searching for such a person. I even attended a Kumbha Mela, hoping to find someone who could teach me. I met many yogis, but none of them was a *jnani*, a man who had this final knowledge. I told all the people I met that I had learned all these *siddhis*, and I demonstrated the truth of my claim to them. Whenever the yogis saw the powers I had, they would always ask me to teach them how to perform similar feats. These things cannot be taught in an afternoon. If I thought that people were serious I would tell them that they should accompany me to the high Himalayas and stay with me for many years. None of the people I met was willing to make this kind of commitment, so I have never passed on my knowledge to anyone else.

'My search has so far proved to be fruitless. I have no disciples to pass my knowledge on to, and I have yet to find anyone who has the power to grant me this *jnana* that my guru told me to look for.'

I have done all these yogic practices myself, and I have met many other people who have done them. They are useful for performing tricks to impress other people with but they will not free you from bondage. They will not cut off the endless cycle of suffering.

I noticed that the yogi had a special stick with him, and that he treated it with great respect. Curious to know what significance it held for him, I asked him what it was.

'This was given to me by my guru,' he said. 'The power and knowledge he transmitted to me are in this stick. As long as I have it, I have the same power as my guru.'

'This stick is obstructing your enlightenment,' I told him. 'You are attached to the power and the knowledge that you think you have derived from it. If you truly want this *jnana* that you say you desire so much, you will have to renounce your stick and all the powers that go with it. I can help you, but I am not going to do anything until you throw your stick in the river.'

He must have believed me because, after considering the consequences for a few seconds, he threw his stick into a fast-flowing stream that was running a few yards away. His precious stick was instantly washed away. After it had gone, I asked him to demonstrate any of his *siddhis* to me. He was so convinced that his power was tied up in the stick, he couldn't perform even the simplest yogic feat without it.

After witnessing his repeated failures I told him, 'That was your power. It came and it went. It was not permanent. You accomplished it in time and it ended in time. Now I will show you something that has nothing to do with time. I will show you something that you cannot lose or throw away. I will show you your own Self.'

I was confident that I could do it because I could see from his face that he was a pure man who was ready for such an experience. He was proud of his accomplishments, but any man in his position would have been. He had been to see all the great yogis in India, but none of them had mastered the *siddhis* that he had.

'Sit quietly in front of me,' I said.

We sat facing each other, looking deeply into each other's eyes. I gave him a special look, a look I have rarely given to anyone else.

He got it in a moment. In this eternal moment he shouted, 'I got it! I got it! I am! I am *Brahman*, seated in the Heart of all beings, directing the activities according to their previous karmas! When the karmas cease, all will merge in me!'

He was very excited by his new discovery. It is a wonderful moment when one discards what is temporary and unreal and finds within oneself what is true and permanent. People respond in different ways. This man reacted by shouting his joy as loudly as he could.

When he had calmed down a little I asked him if he was satisfied.

'Is there anything else you want or need?' I asked.

To my surprise he said 'Yes'.

Then he went on to explain: 'My guru told me, "If you ever

find a man who can give you this *jnana*, you must serve him for the rest of your life. Even a lifetime of service will not be sufficient to repay him for this supreme gift."

'I now realise the truth of this advice. Now you have shown me who I am, I want to repay you by serving you till you die.'

In those days I was a fit, able-bodied man who didn't need anyone's assistance for anything. I particularly didn't want people following me around because I always preferred to have the freedom to go where I wanted to, without having anyone follow me. I liked to spend long periods alone, and I couldn't have done this if I had had people following me around all the time, trying to serve me.

I told him, 'I don't need any service from anyone. I am perfectly capable of looking after myself. You can do whatever you like now. Your work is finished. Stay here if you want to. Now that you have been granted this knowledge, other people may start coming to you for guidance.'

We sat silently for a while before we parted. I carried on with my expedition; he just sat at the place of our meeting. We had been in a place where one could see for miles in all directions. After I had walked for about half an hour, I looked back and saw him still sitting in the same place, looking in my direction. After a few more minutes walking, I disappeared from his view. We never saw each other again.

This is one of Papaji's favourite stories and he has told it many times. After one such telling I asked him, 'The various lokas that the yogi talked about, are they real places? Is there really a place called Brahma Loka that only enlightened beings can enter? Have you ever been there?'

He replied, 'There are many places that science knows nothing about. This loka is created by the Super Mind. The desire of the yogi manifests subtly as these worlds, and he can go there to enjoy them. All worlds, however subtle, are only projections of the mind. If there was a desire in me to go to such places, then I could go and enjoy them, but there is no desire. When there is no desire at all, these worlds don't even manifest.'

20

Papaji then went on to describe his final adventure on the road to heaven:

A few days later, at an even higher altitude, I had an even stranger meeting. As I rounded a corner, I saw Siva and Parvati ahead of me. It looked to me as if they were playing a game of dice together.

Siva looked up, smiled at me and then told Parvati, 'A good devotee has come. Let us receive him properly.'

She spread a bearskin on the ground and invited me to sit on it. When I had been comfortably seated, she went off and began to prepare some *payasam* for me. This is a kind of sweet porridge that is eaten in the South. I ate it with relish. It had a heavenly, unforgettable taste. Whenever I recollect this incident, the same taste reappears in my mouth. Even decades later, the taste is still there.

After enjoying both the *payasam* and their company, I decided to return to the plains. Coming to the high Himalayas in search of heaven, I had found Siva and Parvati and had been personally served by them. That was enough for me. I didn't feel a need to press on with my journey. I retraced my steps until I ended up at Joshi Math, the ashram of one of the Sankaracharyas. I stayed there for a few days in Annapurna Cave because I needed some time to rest after my arduous walk. This cave is the place where it is said Adi Sankaracharya wrote *Vivekachudamani* and his commentaries on the *Upanishads*. It is also the place from where he sent out his four disciples to teach: Sureshwaracharya to Sringeri, Pedampada to Dwarka Peetam, Hastamalaka to Badrika Ashram, and Trotakacharya to Jagannath Puri.

Papaji embarked on another investigative expedition in the same area sometime in the 1950s. A devotee of his had given him a copy of Autobiography of a Yogi *by Paramahamsa Yogananda. In this book the author traces his spiritual lineage back to an ageless yogi called Babaji who occasionally still manifests to his disciples. Yogananda claimed that Babaji was thousands of years old and that throughout that period he had been occupying a perpetually young body. Papaji felt a desire to investigate this claim by travelling to the Himalayas to see if he could find the elusive Babaji.*

He went to a deserted place to the north of Badrinath and called out, 'Babaji, if you really exist, please appear in front of me!'

A few seconds later a form materialised in front of him. The two men looked at each other for some time, but no words were exchanged.

Papaji later told some of his devotees in Lucknow, 'As I looked at his eyes, I got the distinct impression that I was standing in front of Sukadev, the ancient rishi. If this were really so, he would have been thousands of years old.'

When I asked Papaji about his meeting with Babaji, he surprised me by saying, 'I have never met Babaji. Some people in the 1950s tried to say that I was Babaji, but I never encouraged them to do so.'

Papaji has never claimed that the man who manifested in front of him near Badrinath was Babaji, even though that was the name he called out. Someone definitely appeared, but Papaji does not seem to believe that it was the man whose name he called.

Though the two expeditions – to find the route to heaven and to look for Babaji – did not accomplish their initial objectives, they did lead to interesting spiritual encounters. One other trip, in search of an equally improbable goal, was wholly unsuccessful. It took place in 1966, shortly after Papaji had resigned from his job in the mining industry.

Dr Dattatreya Bakre and I went on a trip to Rishikesh. He wanted to go to Devaprayag to perform the *shraddha* ceremony for his ancestors. These ceremonies are traditionally performed at the confluence of the Alaknanda and Bhagirati rivers. I went with him and asked if I could also perform this ceremony for myself.

He said, 'This is possible, but when you do it, it is an act of renunciation. When the ceremony is over, you should not enter your house again. And after your death, your son Surendra will not have to do it again because it has already been done. It is rather like taking *sannyasa*. You become a non-person and sever all your connections with your family.'

When the ceremonies were over, I asked the doctor to go back to his place alone because I wanted to go on a trip by myself. I had read many years before that there was a secret place in the Himalayas where many *rishis* lived in a special ashram. They apparently spent their time continuously chanting the *Vedas*. I had come across this place in a magazine called *Mastana Jogi* that I had read in Lahore many years before. The account was written by a man who claimed that he had been taking a bath at Har-ki-Pairi in Hardwar when he suddenly felt himself being lifted in the air and carried towards the high Himalayas. He descended into what looked like a huge fire. As he was engulfed by the flames, he felt that his whole body was being purified in some way. There was no physical burning. Emerging from this fire, he saw many *rishis* seated in a cave in front of him. In describing them he said that they had long grey hair, bushy eyebrows and very wide, red eyes.

The *rishis* clearly hadn't had a visitor for a long time. They looked at the man and asked him what *yuga* it was. There are four *yugas* in a *kalpa*: *satya, dwapara, treta* and *kali*. Each of these lasts for thousands of years.

The *rishis* told him that they were going to stay in that place, chanting the *Vedas*, until the end of the *kali yuga*, the last *yuga* of the current *kalpa*. When the end of the *yuga* came near, they all planned to go down to the plains to Kashi [Varanasi]. They were waiting for the *mahapralaya*, the moment of cosmic dissolution. At that moment, they said, there will be the complete destruction of every being on the face of the earth.

This story had always intrigued me. I wanted to know if there really were *rishis* in the Himalayas who had been there for thousands of years. I travelled all over the area indicated by the article, but I couldn't find any trace of the cave or the *rishis*.

In the late 1960s Papaji began to encounter foreigners who were coming to Rishikesh in search of enlightenment. One of the first to meet him was a Belgian woman called Geneviève Decoux, whom he later renamed Meera. This is her account of how she came to meet him in December, 1968.

I had a very happy childhood in Africa, but when I came to Belgium to attend secondary school and university I began to be affected by a profound dissatisfaction for all the things life seemed to be offering me. The questions 'What's life? What is the purpose of life?' nagged at me all the time, and my inability to find any satisfactory answer made me increasingly unhappy. I was desperate to find a solution because I knew my well-being depended on it. Then, while I was studying for a second-year philosophy exam that I was taking as part of an archaeology degree course, I came across Socrates' famous dictum, 'Know yourself'. It struck me with such force, I knew I had found the answer to my question.

I dropped out of university the same day, went home and told my mother, 'I have to find a wise man like Socrates. I have heard that India is the place to find such people. I intend to go there as soon as I can. I don't intend to come back until I have found a Master who can show me who I am.'

Though I was only twenty years old at the time, my mother made no objection to my plan. I think she saw how determined I was and probably knew that nothing she said would make any difference to my decision.

Over the next few days I begged and borrowed enough money to make the trip. Within a week I set off on my search, equipped, I remember, with little more than a bottle of wine and a bag of bread and onions to eat on the way. I had told my mother not to tell my father till after I left because I knew he would try to stop me. As I was not yet twenty-one, he had a legal right to prevent me from taking such a trip. My mother helped out by telling him that I had gone to stay for a few days at a friend's house. She only let him know what was really happening on the third day after my departure.

I had very little money so I hitchhiked to Istanbul and then followed the hippie trail that went from there to India.

I stopped for some time in Afghanistan and spent two to three months with a Sufi who lived in the mountains near Kabul. However, when I eventually decided that this was not the Master I was looking for, I travelled on to India and arrived there around August, 1968.

I started enquiring about gurus as soon as I got out of the train at Delhi station and was immediately inundated with the addresses of dozens, located in all parts of India. Somehow, I had no urge to check out any of the names that accumulated on my list. Instead, I decided that if I was destined to meet a Master, it would happen at the right time in the right place. I automatically assumed that I would recognise this Master as soon as I saw him.

Since many of the ashrams and gurus I had been told about were in the Himalayas, I decided to go straight to Rishikesh and let events unfold by themselves. On my arrival I found accommodation at Swarg Ashram and immediately fell in love with the Ganga. I began to live a very simple life there, spending much of each day walking up and down the banks of the Ganga, either at Rishikesh or Hardwar, in the hope of meeting my elusive Master.

On one of my trips, while I was wandering around near Sapt Sarovar, which is a little upstream of Hardwar, I found a man called Chandra Swami who was living alone on an island in the middle of the Ganga. I had a feeling that he might be a saint who was worth staying with, so I started to visit him every day. He initiated me by giving me a mantra, which was a new departure for him. He had never initiated either a woman or a foreigner before.

I went there regularly over a period of two months but at the end of that period I decided, 'I have had enough of listening to other people's teachings. I want to find out for myself what truth is. I will live by myself and wait for truth to reveal itself to me.'

I left Swarg Ashram and moved into a cave nearby. In the weeks that followed I spent most of my time meditating or bathing in the Ganga. At lunch time I would take *bhiksha* [free food] from the ashram. I say 'meditation', but it wasn't anything formal. I just sat quietly and watched what was going on inside me. I lived like this till the beginning of December. My visa had expired but I had no intention of leaving until I had achieved what I had come for.

Though I was living a simple life, I still needed money occasionally. At some point in December I found that I was down to my last rupee. I decided to go to the Lakshmi Hotel and spend this rupee on a cup of tea. In those days I had one book, a collection of poems by Kabir. I took it to the hotel and read it as I sipped my tea.

As I was sitting there reading a man came up to me, stood in front of the table and said, 'Do you need any help in understanding these poems, my dear child? Perhaps I can help you.'

I had had enough of people trying to help me so I made up a story to get rid of him: 'No thank you. I am doing a course at Sivananda Ashram. If I need any help I can ask the people who live there.'

The man seemed very gentle. He repeated his offer and added, 'If you need me you can find me every morning at 5 a.m. by the banks of the Ganga'.

Two nights later I had a very clear dream. It was so clear it may have been a vision of some sort. The face of this man appeared before me and said, 'Perhaps I am the man you are searching for'.

The following morning I decided to look for him at the place where he had said he could be found. As he had said, he was there, sitting by the river. He began to laugh when he recognised who I was, but it was a kind and friendly laugh. In between his laughs he asked me to sit down next to him.

After his laughter had subsided, he turned to me and asked, 'What do you want? Why have you come to see me?'

I was very naive in those days. In a very dramatic way I exclaimed, 'I want cosmic consciousness, and if there is anything more than that, I want that as well!'

This provoked another outburst of laughter.

'And what are you doing to try and get it?' he enquired when his laughter had died down again.

'I meditate.'

'Then show me how you do it,' he demanded.

I closed my eyes and tried to meditate in front of him. I don't remember how long my eyes were closed but after some time I suddenly decided to open them again. I looked around me and saw the sky and the Ganga. In that moment of looking, something clicked. Something that was so simple and obvious made itself known to me. Though it was very vivid, it was not a dramatic explosion of any kind. It was more like a quiet dawning of knowledge, of suddenly becoming aware of something that had always been there.

I looked at him but all I could say was, 'It's so simple, it's so simple'. I bowed at his feet and knew that I had found the Master I had been looking for. I didn't acknowledge him as my Master simply because he had given me this experience. There was something else. As I looked at him there was this strong feeling that I had known him for a very long time and that I had just temporarily forgotten who he was. Along with this strange feeling there was a strong attraction. I wanted to spend all my time with this man. I didn't want to let him out of my sight. His next words, therefore, came as a big shock to me.

'You can go now. You have got what you came for. You can go now.'

I was horrified. After months of arduous searching and practising I had finally found my Master. He had given me this remarkable experience and now he wanted to just walk out of my life. I begged and begged but he refused to let me stay with him. It felt like I was stumbling into and out of some crazy Zen story.

He finally pushed me away, saying, 'I have to go now. If you ever need me, I will find you again.'

After he left I realised that I knew absolutely nothing about him. I didn't know his name; I didn't know what town he was from; I didn't know where he was going next; and I didn't even know where he was staying in Rishikesh. The only fact I knew was that at 5 a.m. in the morning he could sometimes be found sitting by the banks of the Ganga on this particular stretch of the river.

I walked back to my cave near Swarg Ashram. Though I was disappointed at having lost track of my Master in this way, I was still in an ecstatic state. There was a strange perfume in the air that I couldn't identify. The experience I had had with him seemed to be final and complete. I felt that there was nothing more that he could give me, but at the same time I had this gnawing, nagging desire to be physically near him, to be in his company all the time. Eventually, though, my ecstasy swept away all traces of my disappointment. It filled me so completely, I started running and dancing. I ran into the nearby forest and began to hug and kiss all the trees there. I felt a complete oneness with everything around me and I wanted to express my love by hugging everything I saw.

Later on I sat down and addressed the problem of how to get to see this man again. 'This man appears occasionally by the side of the river,' I thought. 'Though he said 5 a.m., he may come back at any time. If I don't watch this portion of the river constantly, I may miss him. I have to find a place where I can keep this part of the river bank under constant observation.'

I looked around and saw a nice big tree that was right next to the river. Sitting under its shade I found I had a good view of the place where my Master might come. I went back to my cave, collected my meagre belongings and began to live under the tree itself. The ecstatic state obliterated all the hardships of living outdoors. It was not difficult to live like this in a pilgrimage centre such as Rishikesh. I was wearing orange, the traditional colour of *sannyasins*, so the local people showed me a lot of respect, even though I never spoke to them. I only had one dress. When it was time to wash it I had to stand up to my waist in the river and scrub it while I was wearing it. At night I had one blanket, which was just enough to protect me from temperatures that went down to three or four degrees centigrade at night.

In the beginning I would go and take *bhiksha* from one of the ashrams because I had no money to buy my own food, but when the local people saw that I was spending most of the day meditating under this tree, some of them started to support me. I would open my eyes after a period of meditation and find a plate of food in front of me. I never found out where the food was coming from, or who was feeding me. I walked, I swam in the Ganga and I meditated, but most of the time I just sat under the tree and watched the people coming and going along the river bank. I knew that sooner or later my Master would return.

Eight months later he finally did. One evening I was sitting meditating under my tree when I suddenly felt an urge to open my eyes and look in a particular direction. He was walking towards me with a smile of recognition on his face. He had been away from Rishikesh for those eight months, visiting his devotees in other parts of the country, but now he had come back to spend time by the Ganga again.

When the subject of this story came up during the course of my research, Papaji commented, 'I recognised the fire in her, the fire for freedom. That fire is very rare. I don't see it on many faces, but after one look at this girl I could see that she had fully dedicated her life to finding freedom.'

Papaji didn't know that Meera was waiting patiently under her tree. He only found out when he returned to Rishikesh after his eight-month absence:

When I came to Rishikesh from Lucknow, I crossed over the river by boat and sat down on a bench under a shady tree, facing the cool flowing waters of the Ganga. Next to me sat a couple from Gujarat who pointed to a girl by the river bank and said, 'This girl is the only female *sadhu* we have seen in Rishikesh'. It was the same girl I had met in the Lakshmi restaurant. They told me that she only had one dress and one towel and that she spent all her time sitting under her tree, meditating.

The woman from Gujarat told me, 'Once, when she went out for a walk, my husband tucked some money under the cloth where she sat. When she returned and found the money, she just threw it in the river and went back to her meditation.'

Meera continues with her story:

He still wouldn't let me follow him, but he reassured me that he would come to see me every day under my tree. From that day on, he appeared every day at about noon with a bowl of food, sat next to me while I ate and answered all the spiritual questions I had been saving up for him. I told him about the experience I had had at our first meeting and how the bliss that accompanied it had enabled me to pass eight months in a beautiful, peaceful state, even though I had had no physical comforts. I told him that though the ecstasy had worn off after a few months, it had been replaced by an intense feeling of peace. I had had many unusual experiences while I was meditating so I gave him details of all the things that had happened to me. He listened very attentively to everything I told him and made positive comments about most of the things I said. It was only during these early meetings that I found out his name was Poonja, that he had a family in Lucknow and that he spent a lot of time travelling around India, visiting his many devotees.

One day he showed up very early, so early in fact, he had to wake me up. He was accompanied by one of his devotees whom he had previously introduced as Baldev Raj. The two of them seemed to spend most of their time together in Rishikesh.

Baldev Raj was one of Papaji's Lucknow devotees. He and Papaji had lived very near to each other when they were boys but they didn't meet until the 1960s. Both of them came to Lucknow in the 1940s as refugees and settled in different parts of the city.

Papaji told me that during the late sixties and early seventies Baldev Raj had so much devotion towards him, his face began to change until it began to bear a remarkable resemblance to Papaji's. He went on to explain that when the mind is full of love for a particular form, the body and the face can transform themselves into an image of the beloved. In this particular case the transformation was quite startling: Papaji has said that Baldev's wife once mistook him for her husband and gave him a hug.

Something similar happened to Meera during the first few months she was with Papaji. He commented on this phenomenon in a letter he wrote to Sri B. D. Desai a few years later. The subject arose because Papaji had noticed that Sri Desai's handwriting was beginning to resemble his own:

When I saw your letter dated 3rd December, addressed to Sewan Jee, the handwriting on it absolutely resembled that of mine. Everyone here [Lucknow] believed it was my letter that had been addressed to Sewan Jee. Only Meera could smell the true meaning, that one's handwriting can come to resemble that of the Master's if a free flow of devotion is centred on the Heart of the Master. Meera told me that something similar had happened to her three years ago. A *sannyasin* whom she knew very well came up to her while she was bathing in the Ganga and asked her, 'Where is Meera?' When Meera identified herself, the *sannyasin* was

Papaji, pausing on a
walk to Phool Chatti.
Meera's head is in
the background. The
photo was taken
soon after their
second meeting
in 1969.

shocked at the change he saw.

He said, 'You have grown so much like your Master, I didn't recognise you. Your physique and even your sex seem to have changed.'

Baldev Raj is approximately the same age as Papaji, is about the same height, and comes from the same part of the country, so it was not too hard for him to come to resemble Papaji. Meera, then blonde and twenty, must have undergone an extraordinary transformation in order to be unrecognisable to someone who knew her well. She now continues her story:

That day when he woke me up early, he invited me to come walking with him and Baldev Raj. We went to Phool Chatti, which was not such an easy walk then as it is nowadays. It is a little ashram about six kilometres north of Rishikesh on the bank of the Ganga. This was the first time he let me spend a whole day with him. I found out that he was living in one of the local ashrams because he said that I could come there and visit him whenever I wanted to. From that time on I spent a lot more time with him. In addition to bringing me food at midday, he would often visit in the mornings and evenings, and if he didn't, I had a standing invitation to go and spend time with him in his ashram room.

This idyllic life continued for about one and a half months. At the end of that time Papaji shocked me by saying that he was leaving to go on a trip to the South and that I couldn't go along with him.

I asked him why not and he replied, 'I always travel alone when I go on these journeys. There are times when I need to be by myself. I have never travelled with foreigners before when I go on these trips.'

I could no longer contemplate life without him, so I begged and begged until he eventually relented. When he finally agreed, he made me sign a 'contract' that he wrote in his notebook. It specified that if he ever asked me to leave during his travels, I would promise to go without quarrelling or arguing. I happily signed. I would have signed anything to stay with him.

Next morning we took the little boat across the river, because there was no bridge in those days, and caught a train which took us to Vrindavan.

There was another reason for Papaji's reluctance. He told me, 'Vrindavan is not the place for meditation, it is the place for devotion. I told her this at the time, but she didn't care. She still wanted to come with me. I let her come, but I made her promise that she would go back to Rishikesh whenever I asked her to.'

Papaji now takes up the story of what happened next:

After arriving in Vrindavan, I wanted to visit the Sri Ranganatha Swami Temple with Meera, but the doorkeeper had been instructed not to allow foreigners inside. He was quite stubborn in obeying his orders. A man who had already had *darshan* inside the temple saw me arguing with the *chowkidar* [watchman] and intervened. He took us to the secretary of the

Papaji in Hardwar in the early 1970s. Baldev Raj is on the extreme left; Sumitra, Papaji's younger sister, whose stories featured prominently in the 'Early Life' chapter, is on the right. On either side of Papaji are Sumitra's daughter and the daughter's husband.

ashram and explained to him that we wanted to go into the temple and have *darshan* of the deity. The secretary was kind and polite, but he explained to us that the constitution of the temple forbade foreigners from entering. He was opposed to this policy, he said, but meanwhile, he had to enforce it since he was employed by the temple to do so. He had a proposal to change the constitution, but so far the trustees of the temple had not discussed it or voted on it. To show us that he was sympathetic to our cause and that the refusal was beyond his control, he offered us accommodation in a VIP guest house. We found out later that this palatial establishment had only previously been used by government ministers who were visiting Vrindavan. He said we could stay as long as we liked, and he arranged to have breakfast, lunch and dinner served to us in our rooms.

When I spoke to Meera about this incident, her recollection was that they actually managed to get into the temple and have darshan:

He took me to this big temple but the man at the gate refused to let us in. Papaji refused to accept 'No' for an answer and had heated discussions with several officials of the temple. Somehow, I think he ended up casting some kind of spell on them because after an hour or so he convinced them that I was a brahmin, even though I had blond hair and couldn't speak a word of any Indian language. Not only did we get in to see the deity, we were also offered accommodation at a VIP guest house whose previous tenant had apparently been the Prime Minister. We didn't even have clean clothes to change into, but somehow we ended up being treated like royalty.

The moment I set foot in Vrindavan I had a flash of recognition. Though I had never been there before, it all looked so familiar. As I walked down the streets, I knew what was coming up round the next corner.

I had never been exposed to the *bhakti* tradition before. I had meditated to get enlightenment, but I had never heard about the saints who had lost themselves in devotion to God. Papaji took me to all the places associated with Krishna and told me many stories about the gods and the saints. I took to it like a fish to water. Within a few days both of us were behaving like ecstatic *bhaktas*. I was singing and dancing in the streets, while Papaji was having innumerable visions of his beloved Krishna.

On our arrival Papaji had told me, 'I am taking a big risk in bringing you here. This is not a place of meditation, it is the place of devotion. I don't know if this is suitable for you, and I don't know what will happen to us here.'

We both had a wonderful ten days there, and I don't think he ever regretted his decision to bring me with him.

I talked to Meera about his ecstatic behaviour in order to get a better idea of how it manifested:

34

David: Was he exhibiting much *bhakti* when he was with you in Vrindavan?

Meera: Yes, he had a lot of visions. He was in ecstasy for most of the time. He had a completely different face, a face I had never seen in all the months I had known him in Rishikesh. I was very impressed.

David: What did he look like when he was having these visions? How could you tell?

Meera: Externally, everything stops. He stops registering anything that is going on around him. Then, after some time, his body starts to shake a little. Sometimes tears will start to trickle down his face.

David: Eyes open or eyes closed?

Meera: His eyes would mostly be open, but when the ecstasy got too much for him, he would close them. Tears would flow and sometimes he would laugh uncontrollably. He has a most peculiar laugh when he is in ecstasy. It is not like his ordinary laugh at all.

If his eyes were open, there would be an extraordinary beauty in them. He himself was seeing God, and while he was seeing that vision, there would be a reflection of that divinity in his eyes.

David: Did he describe what he was seeing while he was seeing it, or did he only talk about it afterwards?

Meera: He liked to share his visions by talking about them later, but he never talked about them while they were happening. There would often be a long period of silence after the vision ended. At that time he would still be overpowered by the experience and be unable to speak. Perhaps an hour or so later he would begin to relive the experience by describing it.

David: What kind of thing was he seeing? Can you remember a few examples?

Meera: It depended on where he was, or what he had been talking about. Because we were in Vrindavan, the place of divine love, his visions usually took the form of Krishna in the embrace of divine love with his *gopis* [female devotees]. That was a recurring image with him. But when he told me devotional stories about Tulsidas and Kabir, he would start having visions of these saints. When we went to places which were associated with Krishna's life, he would have visions of the events that happened there thousands of years ago. He was extraordinarily open to all the *bhakti* currents that were flowing in the air there. Somehow, he would tune into them and they would manifest physically in front of him. The whole of Vrindavan is saturated with the *bhakti* of the pilgrims. Master just tuned into this vast accumulation of holy thoughts, and the thoughts manifested before him as visions.

These visionary experiences could happen at any time. Sometimes they occurred while he was sitting in his room, sometimes when we were out walking, and sometimes even during the middle of a conversation.

David: Was he embarrassed to have other people watch him when he was like this? I sometimes get the feeling that he likes to hide his *bhakti*. He doesn't like to display it in public.

Meera: Yes, if there are a lot of people around, or people he doesn't know, he might try to hide it. But if he is with a small number of people he knows well, he doesn't seem to mind.

David: Do you think he brought on these experiences deliberately, or did they just happen to him?

Meera: Oh no, it was never deliberate. He always seemed surprised when they came. It looked to me as if the experiences were coming to him unasked. They would dance on him for a while and then depart.

Papaji concurs with Meera by saying that the whole atmosphere in Vrindavan is saturated with the bhakti *of the Krishna*

36

bhaktas *who have been congregating there for thousands of years. One amusing story that Papaji often tells illustrates his point very well:*

I once travelled from Hardwar to Vrindavan on the all-night bus. It takes about twelve hours and arrives at 6 a.m. One of my fellow-travellers got off the bus and started to walk down the road. After a few steps he encountered a woman who was sweeping the streets very vigorously. She was surrounded by a big cloud of dust. The man called out to her and asked her to stop sweeping while he walked past because he didn't want to get dirt on his clothes. She obliged him by stopping for a few seconds while he walked past. I was walking behind him.

As I drew level with the woman she said to me, 'That man must be new here, or he must have come for some other business. The people who really know the sanctity of this soil don't ask me to stop sweeping. On the contrary, they lie on the dirt and ask me to sweep some of the soil on their heads. And then they pay me five or ten rupees for doing it. This man doesn't know how holy everything is here.'

I will return now to Papaji's and Meera's pilgrimage to Vrindavan. Papaji enjoyed the luxury of the VIP guest house for a few days before deciding to move to a room that was a little less ostentatious. He decided to see if there were any rooms at the nearby ashram of Pagal Baba. Pagal is Hindi for 'mad'.

I showed Meera all the important places in Vrindavan. She told me that she felt as if she had lived there before because even the smallest lane was familiar to her. She was in such an ecstatic mood, she began to dance through the streets like Mirabai. Many devotees who had come on a pilgrimage to the town joined her and followed her as she danced her way up and down the streets.

I decided to move out of the VIP guest house and take a smaller room. I went to see Pagal Baba, a crazy swami of the town, and asked for accommodation because I knew he had several rooms in his ashram. The *baba* welcomed us warmly and immediately offered me a Commander's Navy Cut cigarette, a great luxury in those days. The *baba* was a chain smoker, and this was his favourite brand. He used to sleep for days at a time so we were lucky to catch him awake. As I said, he gave us a good welcome and asked one of his secretaries to give us a room.

In order to get Meera's account of the months she spent with Papaji in Rishikesh and Vrindavan, I interviewed her one after-noon while he was asleep. All the stories I have related so far came from this initial interview. At 4 p.m. Papaji woke up and came out for tea. We didn't tell him what we had been talking about but he seemed to know.

He told Meera, 'You didn't tell the story of the baby at Pagal Baba's ashram. Tell him about the baby with the big head.'

Meera had completely forgotten about this incident, but with a little prompting from Papaji she remembered the following details:

We had moved to the ashram of this man Pagal Baba who was a well-known saint of Vrindavan. Though he was a chain smoker and seemed to act in a very eccentric way, he was very kind and generous. He seemed to fall in love with Master straight away. Though he had never seen either of us before, as soon as we walked in, he was calling out instructions, telling his assistants to put us up and to look after us properly. The rooms were smaller than the previous ones, but the hospitality was just as good.

One day a couple walked into the ashram with a very sick baby. We could see that it was seriously ill because its head was swollen up to about twice its normal size. I don't know what the problem was. Maybe it was a tumour, or just water on the brain. Anyway, we soon found out that the parents had been told that the condition was untreatable, so they were taking it to all the saints they could find in the hope of getting a miraculous cure. I remember one of them said that the child was only expected to live a few more weeks. Since Pagal Baba was not there at the time, the baby was brought in to us. The mother put the baby on Master's lap and then disappeared with her husband. We thought that perhaps they had gone to arrange some food for the baby, or had gone looking for a bathroom.

After a few minutes Master suddenly became suspicious. He called out to me, 'Quick! Go and see where they are! Go and see what's happening!'

I rushed out and found the mother getting into her car. It looked to me as if they were both about to drive away, leaving us with the baby. I told her to come back and take her baby with her. She apologised and said that she had completely forgotten about the baby because she was in such an agitated state. Personally, I think that she felt that leaving the baby with a saint was the best thing she could do with it. Master handed the baby back to them and they all left a few minutes later.

One month later she came back with sweets, garlands and a healthy baby. We were not there at the time; we only heard this story later. The baby had defied the doctor's prognosis and had suddenly got better.

I asked Master if he had done anything and he said, 'No. They just had a strong faith that something would happen if they brought their baby to a saint, and so something happened. If your faith is strong enough, any kind of miracle can happen.'

I asked Meera if Papaji had joined her as she danced through the streets of Vrindavan. The question was prompted by reports I had received from other people who had seen Papaji dancing in ecstasy. A swami from Rishikesh called Balayogi fondly remembers him dancing down the road there in the early seventies, occasionally taking bites out of a karela-*stuffed chapati that was rolled up in his hand. It must have been an extraordinary sight, for at that time Papaji would have been about sixty years of age and probably weighed about 80 kg.* Karela *is the Hindi word for 'bitter gourd', a small and very bitter member of the squash family.*

Meera told me that she had never seen him dance, so such occurrences could not have been common. There was one occasion, though, which he rarely talks about, when he danced in Vrindavan with Krishna and Mirabai, a famous Krishna bhakta *who lived several hundred years ago. Papaji often tells Mirabai's*

*life story in his satsangs, usually emphasising the fact that she was
a princess who gave up her family and her royal surroundings in
order to pursue her passion for Krishna. I asked him about the
dancing incident and received the following answer:*

From early childhood I was strongly attached to Krishna. I
had this strange idea that he could only be seen by a woman
because in all the stories I read he was only revealing himself to
the *gopis* of Vrindavan. I had some special women's clothes made
that I wore whenever I wanted Krishna to appear. I also bought
jewellery to go with the clothes. I would make myself up, wear the
jewellery and clothes, and sing to Krishna with an *ektara*, a one-
stringed instrument, on my lap. I had seen a picture of Mirabai in
this position, and Krishna seemed to appear to her when she sang
to him, so I thought, 'Maybe I should try it and see if it works'.

Then I read the complete life of Mirabai. On several occasions, when she had danced before Krishna, Krishna appeared
before her. I thought, 'This is something else I can try if I want
Krishna to appear'.

Once, when I was in Vrindavan, I closed the door of my room
and danced the whole night. Krishna appeared, and so did Mirabai.
The three of us danced together for hours. The ecstasy of this holy
dance was all-consuming. In the weeks that followed, wherever I
looked, I only saw Krishna and Mirabai dancing.

*For Papaji, dancing is only truly beautiful if it is a manifesta-
tion of no-mind. He has said, 'When I look at people singing and
dancing before me in satsang, I don't just listen to the words or
look at the movements, I look to see where the singing and dancing
are coming from. If the words and movements come from the mind,
then to me it looks and sounds ugly, even if the person performing
is a skilled, accomplished professional. But if the singing and
dancing come from the Heart, from the place of no-thought, then
the performance is always beautiful to me, even if the singer is out
of tune or the dancer clumsy.'
When he speaks in this vein he often illustrates his point by
narrating two stories of dancers he saw many, many years ago.*

I once saw a man dancing on the bank of the Kaveri River in South India. He seemed to be dancing by himself.

I thought to myself, 'Who is he dancing for?'

When there is a performance like this, there is usually an audience to watch it. I looked around but I couldn't see anyone. It was a very deserted place in which uninhabited forests touched the river banks. He was dancing with his eyes closed, not caring if anyone saw him or not. It was a beautiful, unselfconscious dance by a man who was spontaneously expressing his inner joy. I had never seen a dancer like this before. I was so touched by his performance, I wanted to go up to him and speak with him, but he was lost in his inner world. Once or twice his eyes opened, but he didn't see me, even though I was in his field of vision. His eyes were open but he was not seeing anything. None of his attention was externalised. Sensing the inner beauty that was manifesting as the physical movements, I left him alone to continue the enjoyment of his dance.

I have seen many dance performances, both in the West and in India, but I have never seen a professional dancer who had the beauty that this man had. There was a smell, a taste in this man's exhibition that cannot be got merely through practising.

I saw another man putting on a show like this. It was a long time ago, in 1945, when I was still living in Madras. I was visiting a Siva temple there when I saw this man dancing. He also was not aware that he was dancing. He danced the whole day and the whole night. People were putting food in his mouth but he wasn't even aware that he was being fed. He had touched an inner beauty and that beauty gave him the energy to dance beautifully for hours together. This was not just some man jumping around in ecstasy. He had all the right steps, all the right movements, so he must have trained in the usual way. But, through his devotion to Siva, he had learned to transcend the limitations of the body and the mind. Through his intense *bhakti* to Siva he had learned to dance the way Siva dances. That is, with no mind and with no awareness of the body. When you are in love with your own Self, this is the best art. This is the best way of expressing it.

41

After ten days in Vrindavan, Papaji decided to go back to Lucknow to collect some money from his bank. He had originally planned to go to Ramanasramam, but when he arrived in Lucknow he changed his mind. Meera takes up the story again:

When we arrived in Lucknow, I was immediately introduced to Master's parents. His mother seemed to me to be a very strong lady. She seemed to be the guru of several ladies who came to listen to her *bhajans*. I couldn't speak to her because she only knew Punjabi, but there was a nice atmosphere in her home. The whole house seemed to be full of *bhakti*. Master's father spoke excellent English. There was a quiet dignity about him, but he rarely spoke to anyone.

I had never seen Master with devotees before, except for the time I had spent with him and Baldev Raj. In Lucknow I was surprised to discover that he was a Guru for many people. When it became known that he was in town, a constant stream of people began to visit him wherever he was staying. In those days there was no special time for satsang. He would see people whenever they turned up.

In Rishikesh he had been speaking to me in a purely advaitic way. In Lucknow it changed to a more traditional *bhakti* approach. He would talk about the lives of the saints and give explanations of verses from texts such as the *Ramayana* or the *Gita*. Master seemed to adapt his teaching to the differing inclinations of the people who came to see him. There was no fixed message for everyone.

In those days he was very self-sufficient. He would often cook for himself and he loved to go out shopping to buy vegetables for the family's meals. I watched him vigorously bargain for the best price and I noticed that he always tested and checked each vegetable before he put it into his bag. If he was preparing anything in the kitchen, he would often invite me in and give me a few cookery lessons.

At other times, if there were no visitors, he would just sit quietly or read out loud from the *Bhagavatam*. He loved that book very much. Once, when he was in Hardwar, he decided to read the whole book out loud to the Ganga. He sat in a deserted spot and read her a portion every day until the whole book was finished.

There are several versions of the Bhagavatam, *but the one that Papaji liked the most was one translated by Eknath, a famous saint. Papaji once gave a commentary on this work that was recorded on tape by an Austrian scholar, Bettina Baumer. It was apparently so good, she said she would transcribe the talk and get it published. She took the tapes back to Varanasi, where she was working as a lecturer, but they were stolen. Her room was locked at the time, and nothing else of value went missing.*

When news of the loss was communicated to Papaji, a devotee remarked, 'You didn't really want this to be published, did you?'

He shook his head and said 'No'.

Papaji read the Bhagavatam *to the Ganga while he was sitting on an island near Sapt Sarovar, just north of Hardwar. He would wade across to the island each day and spend several hours there. On one of his trips he encountered some naked young men who were speaking Urdu to each other:*

I greeted them in Urdu and talked to them for a few minutes.

One of them saw my copy of the *Bhagavatam* and asked me if it was the *Koran*.

'Yes, yes,' I replied.

They were Muslims and they were assuming I was also a Muslim since I had talked to them in Urdu. I didn't want to upset them by telling them that it was a Hindu scripture.

'What are you doing here?' I asked, 'And why are you sitting around with no clothes on?'

'We are rickshaw drivers,' one of them answered. 'We live on the other side of Hardwar. Every morning we catch the first bus and spend all day here, just sitting around with no clothes on. The Hindu pilgrims who come to the ashrams in Sapt Sarovar hear that there are naked yogis sitting on this island, so they wade across the river to see us. When we see them coming, we sit in *padmasana* and pretend to be in *samadhi*. It's a good business because the pilgrims always leave money for us. In winter, when there are no pilgrims and the weather is cold, we put our clothes on and go back to our rickshaw business at the other end of town. However, we make far more money doing this than working in our rickshaws.

Meera now continues with her account of her trip with Papaji:

After we had spent some time in Lucknow, he cancelled his trip to Ramanasramam, deciding instead that we should go back to Hardwar and Rishikesh. On our arrival, he took a room in one ashram and I took a room in another that was nearby. We spent most of the time wandering around, taking long walks or just sitting by the banks of the Ganga. Sometimes we would walk so far we would sleep outside in the forest or by the river and only return the following day. On a few occasions we stayed away for days. It was a very free and easy life, living close to nature. Since there were no other devotees who needed Master's attention at that time, he was free to wander around and do whatever he liked.

When we were out of town we would cook, camp and eat by the side of the Ganga. I would collect firewood from the forest every morning and put it out in the sun so that it would be completely dry before lunch. The food was always very simple. For weeks together we would live on a diet of potatoes, *raita* [curd and raw vegetables], and cracked wheat. We carried a cooking pot wherever we went and Master always had little packets of sugar and tea in his pockets. If we were on a walk and needed a tea break, Master would sit down and pull out his packets. That would be a sign for me to hunt around for firewood to brew up some tea.

We never took plates or cutlery with us. When it was time to eat, Master would select a couple of flat stones and serve the food on them. We would always eat with our fingers. He was very particular about choosing the right stone. Sometimes he would spend fifteen minutes by the river picking up and rejecting potential plates.

These were ecstatic days for me. There was a simple, peaceful joy in that life that I had never had before.

At some point during this period Papaji and Meera decided to get married. Papaji must have been aware that he was flouting both tradition and the law when he went ahead with this ceremony since Vidyavati, the woman he had married around 1930, was still alive and living in Lucknow. Historically, there have been many instances of Hindu men taking second wives, but in recent times such marriages were deemed to be socially unacceptable unless the first wife was unable to bear children. The practice was actually made illegal in the 1950s when the Indian government passed an act of parliament that clarified and codified traditional Hindu practices that related to marriage, divorce, inheritance, etc. Because of the pluralistic nature of Indian society, the state allows different religions to have their own unique laws on such matters.

Papaji had never had a close or intimate relationship with Vidyavati. Though he had always been willing to support her financially, from the 1950s onwards, he didn't spend much time in the family home in Lucknow. Often, when he did return to Lucknow, he would prefer to stay with his parents or with devotees who had houses in other parts of the city.

Though Vidyavati must have witnessed many extraordinary transformations in the satsangs that took place in her home, she never really believed that her husband was qualified to be a Guru. She would occasionally speak about the wonderful silent presence that Ramana Maharshi had, but she never made such remarks about Papaji's satsangs. She dutifully served the unending stream of devotees who came to his door at all hours of the day and night, but she never seemed to regard her husband as anything more than an exasperating and occasionally irresponsible provider of her household needs.

I asked Papaji about this side of his life:

Question: What did your family, and particularly your wife, think of your wandering lifestyle? How many of them treat you as just another member of the family, and how many regard you and relate to you as a *jnani*?

Papaji: None of my family accepted my behaviour. My wife in

45

particular was very unhappy about it. In her opinion, I wasn't behaving in a responsible way. From the early 1940s onwards, I had always put my spiritual activities first. I had resigned my commission in the army to look for a Guru who could help me to see God because I thought that this was the most important thing in the world. My wife didn't see it that way. From her point of view, I wasn't working to support her or my family. Instead, I was wandering around India, spending all our money on a fruitless search for a Guru who could help me. She never really understood or sympathised with my passion for God. She just thought that I was being self-indulgent and lazy.

Whenever I would come home she would get angry with me and demand to know who was going to support her and the children if I didn't bother to work.

'How are you going to educate them? How are you going to feed them? How are you going to get them married if we don't have any money? No family will want them once they find out that their father is unemployed and is wasting all his time and money on endless pilgrimages.'

I would tell her, 'Everything will be taken care of. Don't worry. God is looking after us. He will give us what we need.'

Answers like this just made her even more angry.

While I was collecting material for this part of the book, I asked Papaji if he wanted to give an account of his marriage to Meera. He gave the bare facts but declined to explain or elaborate on them in any way.

We decided to get married while we were in Hardwar. I took Meera to the Arya Samaj temple and requested the priest there to perform the ceremony. He wasn't sure that he was permitted to marry Indians to foreigners, so he asked me to get written permission from the Indian Home Ministry and the Belgian embassy. I knew that getting these papers would be a long, complicated process, so we decided to perform our own ceremony on the banks of the Ganga. After obtaining a copy of the marriage service, I took Meera to the banks of the river and performed the service myself.

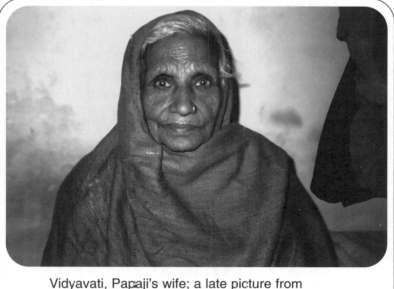

Vidyavati, Papaji's wife; a late picture from around 1990. Vidyavati passed away in 1992.

We made the approved vows to each other, put garlands around each other's necks, and then took a bath in the Ganga as a final act of consecration.

Though this may sound like a private exchange of vows, it is a binding ceremony for Hindus. Marriage ceremonies may be long and elaborate, but they can also be short and simple. A wedding ceremony that merely involves an exchange of garlands and vows is legally acceptable in India.

When I asked Meera about this event she confirmed Papaji's story and said that they reaffirmed their vows on subsequent occasions when they were alone together on the banks of the Ganga.

The marriage to Meera upset many of Papaji's Indian devotees, many of whom stopped coming to see him. I have never heard Papaji say what prompted him to embark on this course of action, but on several occasions I have heard him say that he has no ability to choose what he should do or what he should not do, since these faculties are no longer present in him. This is what he had to say in 1994 when he was speaking about how people behave after enlightenment:

There is nothing to do and nothing not to do. What can you do in this state? Nothing. Whatever you do after enlightenment is just a reaction to the circumstances around you. 'Should I do this, or should I do that?' are questions that arise in an unenlightened mind. When there is no mind, the question cannot even arise. The Self will make the body perform various actions and all those activities will be correct and perfect because they are prompted by the Self. Mind will not intervene to decide whether or not some course of action is correct or not, because mind will no longer be there. Enlightenment ends all debates about behaviour. Problems of conduct and morality are problems of the decision-making mind. They do not arise in the Self at all. This is hard to understand because understanding cannot penetrate or encompass what I am talking about. This state cannot be described, cannot be imagined, and cannot be touched.

I will return now to Papaji's activities in Rishikesh in the late 1960s.
When Papaji first settled down in Rishikesh after his retirement, it was a quiet, conservative town, but its character changed dramatically a couple of years after he moved there. Papaji himself describes what happened:

In the late 1960s a swarm of westerners, mostly young boys and girls, invaded Rishikesh. They looked like *sadhus,* and some of them even behaved like *sadhus.* They had long hair and beards, they wore *tilaks* and *rudraksha* beads, and they even spent time meditating by the banks of the Ganga. Professor Timothy Leary, the man who popularised LSD in the 1960s, visited Rishikesh and announced that it was 'heaven on earth'. Word of this spread in the West, and soon the town was invaded by a mob of LSD-taking and hash-smoking hippies. Within a year foreigners began to outnumber Indians in some of the ashrams.

During this period I was spending most of my time sitting by the banks of the Ganga. Several of these people approached me to tell me how wonderful LSD was. Some of their experiences were quite impressive. One boy who had taken LSD before he came to see me described his experience while he was under the influence of the drug. Though he had no spiritual background, some of the things he was saying sounded as if they were coming straight from the *Upanishads*. Other people told me that during their trips they entered some kind of superconscious state in which they spontaneously found that they had a knowledge of all the world's scriptures.

'What happens when the drug wears off?' I asked.

'The experience goes away about six hours after we take the pill, but when it goes, we just take another dose.'

I told them that they shouldn't depend for their happiness on transient states or on chemicals whose effects were only temporary. I explained to them that there was a happiness that was permanent, that was not dependent on any external cause.

'If you find this happiness,' I said, 'you will never need to take another pill to keep it or get it back. It will be there all the time.'

Not many of them were interested in what I had to say.

Some of the hippies lived in an enormous cave a few miles out of town. It was north of Rishikesh on the road to Vasishta Guha. I visited them in 1969. About twenty people were living there with an elderly foreign man they said was their guru. He was wearing some kind of gown and looked like a monk. He was telling them all how to meditate and how to get enlightened, and his instructions included taking large, regular doses of LSD.

When the hippies first invaded the area, no one knew what LSD was. In fact, it was such an obscure drug, it wasn't even illegal to possess it or use it. When the Indian government finally passed a law outlawing its possession and use, the hippies got their supplies by getting their friends abroad to soak part of their letters in a liquid form of the drug. When the mail arrived, the hippies would eat their letters to get high.

I noticed that LSD seemed to suppress the appetite. The hippies in this cave could go for days without eating as long as they had regular doses of LSD. One of their group would go to Lakshman Jhula to get an enormous pot of tea, and that would keep them all going for a day. They would sit around for hours, trying to meditate under the influence of this drug. Their teacher would intervene occasionally to give them instructions on what they should be doing. They tried to get me to take LSD once but I refused. I was curious enough to want to hear about their experiences, but I didn't need one of their little pills to make me happy.

I talked to several of the young boys who were living there about what happened when they took the drug. Several of them talked with great authority about the mystical states they had entered. They gave very impressive reports. I couldn't reject the experiences, but I did emphatically reject the means they utilised to get them. Their teacher taught them that LSD was a short cut to enlightenment. I don't believe this. It can give interesting, temporary experiences, but anything that is temporary is not enlightenment.

Initially, most of the ashrams in Rishikesh welcomed these new visitors. They looked like *sadhus* and many of them were genuinely interested in meditation and enlightenment. The problem was, they didn't know how to behave properly. They made a lot of noise in their rooms and disturbed their neighbours. They would sleep together in the nude in places where they could be seen; the girls would take nude baths in the Ganga, and many of them were not vegetarians. Rishikesh and Hardwar are sacred to the Hindus. It is actually illegal to sell or consume meat or drink liquor within the municipal limits of these two towns. The new visitors did not respect this rule, or any other rule. Many of them were importing packaged or canned meat from abroad and were then littering the roads with the empty cans and packages. When the locals read the labels and saw what the foreigners were eating, there was a wave of resentment against them. Many of the ashrams closed their doors to these people because they weren't observing or respecting the traditional sattvic lifestyle of *sadhus*.

Some of the hippies turned out to be genuine seekers. They gave up their outrageous behaviour, stopped taking drugs and integrated themselves in the life of some of the big ashrams. I saw several ex-hippies doing very well at Sivananda Ashram, Ved Niketan and Gita Ashram, but these people were exceptions.

The hippie invasion got worse when Maharishi Mahesh Yogi began to attract famous westerners such as the Beatles and Hollywood movie stars. Because none of these newcomers knew how to behave, the police eventually had to be called in. Too many people were disturbing the peace and breaking the local laws. The police clampdown caused a massive exodus of hippies. The ones who were interested in meditation either went off to the hills to be by themselves, or took off to other ashrams in India. Some went to Ganeshpuri to be with Swami Muktananda, some to Monghyr in Bihar, to the ashram of Swami Satyananda. Others ended up with Neem Karoli Baba in Vrindavan or with Maharishi Mahesh Yogi. The man who helped Timothy Leary to popularise LSD, Richard Alpert, ended up with Neem Karoli Baba, who gave him the name Ram Dass.

I met Ram Dass in 1990 when he came to one of my satsangs in Lucknow. I talked to him about LSD and found that he still had positive thoughts about it.

First I said to him, 'I have heard that one should only take LSD three times, and even then only under the guidance of an expert. If it is not taken like this, it can make you go mad.'

Ram Dass replied, 'In that case I must be completely mad because I have taken it over three hundred times. It didn't harm me and I still believe it's an aid to enlightenment.'

'I don't think that's so,' I replied. 'I have watched many people take this drug, and hundreds of others have told me that they have used it at one time or another. None of them ever got enlightenment through taking it.'

One of Ram Dass' students came on another occasion and asked me if he could take LSD during my satsang. He was a boy from Los Angeles.

'The satsang will be much more intense if I take it,' he said. 'That has been my experience on previous occasions.'

I told him he could do whatever he liked. 'Sit in that corner,' I told him, 'and don't tell anyone else what you are doing. Let us see what happens.'

51

He sat through the whole satsang with his eyes closed. We tried to wake him up for lunch but no one could rouse him. He seemed to be in a semi-conscious state.

After we had cleared away all the food and washed the dishes, Gopal, one of the boys who was working in my house, went up to him and said, 'You have to leave now. I am going out to buy vegetables for tonight. I am going to lock up the house so you have to go.'

The boy was very upset. 'How can you talk about vegetables at a time like this? I am almost enlightened. I just need a few more minutes. Leave me alone and let me get enlightened.'

I let him sit there for some time, but after half an hour had passed without any sign of his getting enlightened, I asked one of my devotees to load him into a rickshaw and take him back to town, to his room in the Carlton Hotel. He was incoherent and utterly incapable of looking after himself. On the way there he kept collapsing on the back of the rickshaw driver. The devotee who took him home had to support him for the whole journey.

Some people have reported having very good experiences on LSD. Others lapse into states like this boy, while some seem to go completely mad. I encountered one boy who fell into this third category while I was staying in an ashram in Rishikesh. He was called Joseph and he was staying in a room near mine. We sometimes went swimming in the Ganga together. He was a nice English boy, about nineteen or twenty years old.

One night I heard a lot of screaming coming from outside my room. Sometimes it sounded like a wolf howling. In the morning the swami who was in charge of the ashram came to me to complain about this boy. He had apparently spent the whole night sitting up a tree, shouting, screaming and howling. Since this swami didn't speak any English, he wanted me to tell the boy that he could no longer stay in the ashram. I went to look for Joseph to find out what had happened to him.

'I took some LSD,' he said, 'because I wanted to meditate. Soon afterwards I noticed that there were many monkeys around my room. I had the feeling that they were waiting for a chance to get into my room to steal all my food. I thought, "I have to be

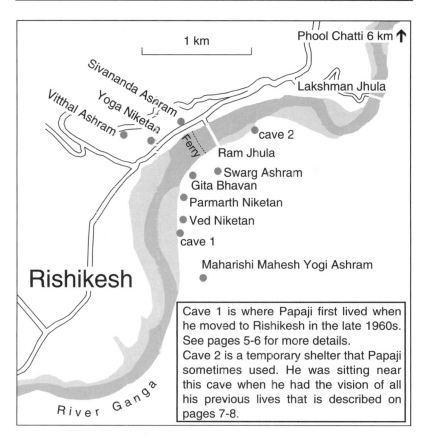

1 km

Phool Chatti 6 km ↑

Sivananda Asram
Yoga Niketan
Vitthal Ashram

Lakshman Jhula

cave 2

Ram Jhula

Swarg Ashram
Gita Bhavan
Parmarth Niketan
Ved Niketan
cave 1

Maharishi Mahesh Yogi Ashram

Rishikesh

River Ganga

Cave 1 is where Papaji first lived when he moved to Rishikesh in the late 1960s. See pages 5-6 for more details.
Cave 2 is a temporary shelter that Papaji sometimes used. He was sitting near this cave when he had the vision of all his previous lives that is described on pages 7-8.

prepared for them". I climbed up the tree where they were sitting and started imitating their noises. I was chattering and screeching and jumping up and down on the branches. I even tried hanging from the branches for a while. Within a short time I actually felt I was a monkey. I spent the whole night in the tree making monkey noises because I was convinced that I had turned into a monkey.

'One time I tried to jump from branch to branch, but I fell out of the tree. That was probably when he heard me screaming. The rest of the time I was just making monkey noises. I had initially decided to concentrate all my attention between the eyebrows during the trip and become absorbed in that place. Somehow, though, I got distracted and ended up concentrating on the monkeys instead.'

'The swami is very angry with you,' I said. 'Your noise kept him awake all night and now he wants to throw you out of the ashram. Because you weren't really responsible for your actions last night, I will try to help you to stay here. I will tell the swami a good story in Hindi, and I will tell you how to behave afterwards.'

I went back to the swami and told him, 'This boy was in ecstasy last night. He says you are a great enlightened being and somehow your power affected him very strongly. While he was in this state he climbed up this tree and started shouting, "This swami is so enlightened, so wise, so generous! He has given me a room in his wonderful ashram! I am so happy with him and the way he is treating me! I have never seen such a swami anywhere else in all the world!" This morning, when I went to see him to find out what had happened, I found him sitting in meditation, chanting your name.

'He likes you very much,' I continued, 'but he is also a little unhappy because he can't stay here any more. His money has run out and he will soon have to leave because he can no longer afford the charges here.'

This part of the story was true. The boy had run out of money and he was waiting for additional funds to come from his parents.

The swami was very happy to have found such a devotee. He said, 'All right, he can stay on here if he stops shouting at night. I won't charge him anything. He can eat all his meals with me.'

I went back to Joseph and told him that I had found him a free place to stay. 'All you have to do,' I said, 'is prostrate to the swami every time you see him. As long as you carry on doing this, he will be happy to give you free food and a free room.'

Meera watched Papaji deal with some of the hippies during these years. I asked her for her impressions:

He was very interested in them. Most of them had given up comfortable lives in the West to come to India to live primitively and to find new meanings for their lives. This intrigued him. Because they were looking for new directions and new perspectives, many of them were open to what he had to say. They were very eccentric in their ways, but Master seemed to appreciate this. He always seems to be entertained by people who are a little bit crazy. He was very gentle with them, but he also used to make fun of them. We had a lot of good satsangs with them, but they were never very serious. Too many weird things were going on.

In the beginning he never criticised them for taking drugs, but after a year or two, when he saw the damage it was doing to their minds and bodies, he would often encourage them to give up their drug-taking habits.

In one of his recent Lucknow satsangs Papaji remarked, 'There is one baba *in Hardwar who has been smoking* ganja *[cannabis leaves] all his life. He seems to thrive on it. I have seen him there every year for the last sixty years, and every time I see him he has a* chillam *in his mouth. The foreigners I met there didn't seem to have this same capacity to smoke all day without damaging themselves, so I started to encourage them to stop.'*

Meera now resumes her account of life with Papaji in the late '60s. In this section she speaks about the way that Papaji found and dealt with the genuine seekers who were beginning to appear in Rishikesh, looking for freedom.

Master never made any attempt to look for devotees, but he had some kind of inner radar that could sense if there was someone in the neighbourhood who could benefit from a satsang. We might be sitting by the river when he would suddenly feel an urge to go somewhere. He wouldn't say, 'There is somebody waiting for me in such-and-such a place,' he would just have a feeling that he should go to a particular restaurant or shop or ashram. On his arrival, or on the way there, we would meet some new seeker who needed guidance, and we would have a wonderful, spontaneous satsang. This was very nice for me because he hardly ever spoke when we were together, except for casual conversation about cooking or the things he saw around him. It was only when we met these new people that I began to realise what a marvellous teacher he was, and how direct and profound his teachings were.

He never knew why he was being sent to a particular

rendezvous. There would just be an inner voice that would prompt him to get up and start moving in a particular direction. At first it looked to me as if all these meetings were happening by chance, but I later came to realise that the Self was choosing the right moment to bring seekers into contact with the Master. That is what happened in my own case, and I saw it happen again on innumerable occasions in the years that followed. Master told me on several occasions that it was not his mission in life to have an ashram and be surrounded by hundreds of people. Instead, he had somehow been selected to give the final kick to seekers who were ready for a direct experience. The right people would be sent at the right time and Master's 'inner voice' would simply direct him to the place where they were. Master did have an ashram, but it was an invisible one. It was not on any map, but those who had a desire for freedom would find that their footsteps would be directed towards it.

One side effect of all this was that life could never be planned. Master might say, 'Let's go to such-and-such a place'. On the way there, without giving a word of explanation, he would suddenly veer off in a different direction. You couldn't ask him why he had changed his plan because he wouldn't know himself. He was just following inner instructions to be in a different place.

There was a beautiful economy in all this. He didn't have to waste his time with hordes of immature seekers, nor did he need to go looking for people who needed him. He would sit or walk by the river, relaxing and enjoying himself. If the call came, he would go, do his business and then come back to his spot by the river. There was a feeling that everything was perfect, that everything that was happening was being executed according to a divine plan.

Of course, once he started giving seekers these experiences, there were always people looking for him. Sometimes he would allow people to visit him, at other times he would shun all company. The same power that directed him to needy seekers could also make him invisible or unfindable if he didn't want to meet people. If people he didn't want to see were coming, that same inner voice would prompt him to be somewhere else when they arrived.

*When I asked Meera to give an example of a chance meeting
that a devotee had with Papaji, the first example that sprang to her
mind was a Frenchwoman called Sita.*

Papaji had disappeared for a few days, leaving me alone in
Rishikesh. While I was wandering around in the town, I thought I
saw an old friend from the West. I rushed up to her to greet her but
it turned out to be someone else. After I had apologised for my
mistake, I started up a conversation with her. This was unusual for
me. In those days I rarely spoke to anyone except Master. Within a
few minutes I found out that she too was a spiritual seeker and that
she had come to India specifically to look for her Master. Over the
next few days we became good friends.

*Papaji had gone to Lucknow, telling Meera that he had some
business there and that he would be back in a few days. After a
couple of days in Lucknow, he felt an urge to go south to visit
Ramanasramam. He bought a ticket but, as he relates in the next
story, he never boarded the train. Instead, he went back to
Rishikesh and met Meera's new friend.*

In 1970 I had a plan to go to Ramanasramam. In those days
the train service to the south was not very good. There was only
one bogie on the train that went all the way to Madras. And that
train only left once a week. I went to the train station to catch this
train and found out that the particular bogie that went to Madras
had somehow got detached from the train before its arrival in
Lucknow. Because nobody knew where this bogie was, and
because the next train with a bogie to Madras would not leave for
another week, I decided to go to Rishikesh instead. I already had
my bag with me, so it wasn't a problem. I just got on a different
train.

When I got to Rishikesh, I crossed the Ganga. I had no particular plans to stay anywhere. I was just thinking about which temple
or *dharamsala* I would go to when a girl came up to me and stood
in front of me.

'I want to speak to you,' she said.

'All right,' I said. 'Go ahead and speak.'

'Not right now,' she said. 'I have just bought some things in one of the shops. I have to pick them up and pay the owner. I will be back in a couple of minutes.'

A few minutes later she came back with a bag of nuts and introduced herself.

'I am a teacher and I live in Paris. I came here three days ago. I have a spiritual guide there. He is a Thai teacher who has been teaching me Buddhism.

'One day he told me, "I am not your real teacher. I am just your guide. You have another teacher who lives in India. He is an invisible teacher who has an invisible ashram. When you go to India, you will find him."'

We talked a little more and I found out that she had not been given any more details. She was not told the teacher's name, his address, or where she could find him. She was just told that she would find him in India.

Then she told me what happened next.

'There were exams in my school that I had to be present for. They were due about a month after my Thai teacher told me this, and I knew I had to attend. I asked for some leave and was granted it on the condition that I return from India before the exams were held. My principal told me that under no circumstances would she extend my leave to a date that would include the date of the exams. I was given a maximum of twenty days.

'I immediately flew to Delhi. I have never been to India before, so I had no idea where to look for spiritual teachers. I got into a taxi at Delhi airport and told the driver, "Take me to where the saints live".'

The taxi driver, sensing some good business, drove her to Rishikesh, a five-hour drive, and offloaded her outside the Sivananda Ashram. He took his money and went back to Delhi. She went inside, but there was no room available at that time because there was a special yoga course going on and all the rooms were full. They recommended the Transcendental Meditation headquarters on the other side of the river, so she went there instead. When I met her, she had been staying there for three or four days.

This was an interesting story but one thing puzzled me. 'Why are you telling me all this?' I asked. 'Why did you run out of your shop without paying and tell this story to a complete stranger?'

'Because you are the man!' she exclaimed. 'For the last thirteen years I have been dreaming about this man. Though I have seen you often in my dreams, it didn't occur to me that you were the one I had to meet in India. As soon as I recognised you, I came running out of the shop. Will you come to my place with me? I have a nice air-conditioned room in the Transcendental Meditation centre. There are so many things I want to talk to you about.'

'Not now,' I said. 'I am tired after an overnight journey. I want to have a bath in the Ganga and then I want to sleep a few more hours. You can come and see me in the evening.'

I fixed a spot for our meeting and then went off for my bath. That afternoon I had a long sleep in which I dreamed about the girl I had met early that morning. In the evening I told her about the dream.

'You were a young child about seven years old. We weren't in India because the houses didn't look Indian. It must have been some other country. It was somewhere I didn't recognise, somewhere I have never been before. I was calling you Sita in the dream because that seemed to be the right name for you.'

When I mentioned this name, she took out a pendant that she had been wearing round her neck.

'I bought this at an Indian exhibition in France two years ago. As soon as I saw it, I knew that I had to have it.'

I looked at the pendant and saw that it had 'Sita' written on it in Devanagari letters. She had been wearing it without knowing that her name had been engraved on it. That was the final proof for her. She then knew for certain that she had found her 'invisible' Master.

Sita wanted to stay with me permanently, but I didn't give permission. 'You have a job to go back to. You have promised to be back within twenty days. You cannot run away from your responsibilities like this.'

'I can get another job any time I want to,' she said. 'I have seven years' experience. It will be easy for me to get a job whenever I return.'

59

I told her, 'Looking after children is the right job for you. You are very intelligent and you are a good teacher. I can see that by looking at you. So many children are damaged because they don't get the right teachers when they are at school.'

'If you promise to come and see me, I will go back to France,' she said.

I gave her a promise and when I went to France a year or so later, I made a point of going to see her.

Now, who arranged this meeting? I was planning to go to Tiruvannamalai and this girl had work commitments in Paris. The power that arranges all these things sent me back to Rishikesh because it had also arranged that this woman would be there at that time for less than three weeks. And as soon as I walked into Rishikesh, she was there waiting for me. This was not an isolated case. I have been sent to many meetings like this.

Nor was she the only person to drop everything and fly to India because she had been summoned to a meeting with me. I was once visited by a Venezuelan maths professor who dropped everything and came to India as soon as he heard about me.

'One of my friends told me about you,' he said. 'He didn't know you himself. He had just heard about you from someone who had met you in Spain. As soon as I heard about you, I knew I had to see you. I took leave from my job and caught the next flight to India.'

What brought him here? When the time is ripe, the seeker gets the divine summons, drops everything and runs off in search of God. I have seen it happen many times.

The story of the maths professor will be given in a later chapter.

There is another meeting Papaji speaks about that begins in an identical way: a trip to Ramanasramam is cancelled because the bogie to Madras failed to arrive in Lucknow. Because of the similar beginnings I suspect that this next encounter is part of the same trip, and that it took place shortly after he met Sita.

I was planning to travel to Sri Ramanasramam, but when I

arrived at the station in Lucknow, I found out that my train had been delayed by an accident, and that no one knew when it might arrive. There was another train destined for Rishikesh on the next platform, so I embarked on that one instead.

Papaji has an almost legendary reputation for changing his travel plans at the last minute. His daughter, Sivani, once told me that whenever she travelled with him by train, she would never unpack any of the food she had brought until the train had passed at least one station. She had learned from experience that Papaji could start out on a long trip, change his mind a few minutes after departing, and get off at the next station. In one famous incident, his family came to Lucknow station to see him off on a long trip. When they returned home, they found that Papaji had arrived before them. He had left the train via the door on the opposite side of the platform and had then walked home, without bothering to tell any of the people who had come with him to the station.

After arriving in Rishikesh, I felt a sudden inexplicable urge to go to Badrinath. This place is 4,000 metres above sea level, and in winter it is extremely cold. I had no woollen clothes with me, but that didn't bother me. Though it was midwinter, I got on a bus and started on my journey. A few hours later, when the bus arrived in Rudraprayag, I felt an urge to get off the bus and spend the night there. I had one bag with me that I carried into a nearby restaurant. I thought I would eat there before looking for somewhere to stay. After my meal, when I came out to wash my hands, a man approached me and asked if he could speak with me. I asked him what he wanted.

He said, 'Please, let us sit at the bank of the Alaknanda River and speak there'.

He took me to the river and introduced himself as an engineer, working in M.E.S. [Military Engineering Services] at Pune. He had had a Guru, a man called Gulvani Maharaj, who had left his body about a year before. Before he died he had assured his disciple, 'You will realise your Self in this life'.

He looked at me earnestly. 'So far,' he said, 'I have not done it. But I cannot disbelieve my Master. I have full faith in his prophecy. He recently appeared to me in a dream, saying that I should go to Badrinath, even though the temple is buried in snow for the entire winter. In fact, the temple is not scheduled to open until the snow melts in the middle of May.

'I was in two minds about coming here because he had never asked me to perform any pilgrimages before. On the other hand, I could not reject the command of my dear Guru. So, I decided to go on one month's leave. I left four days ago and arrived here this afternoon. As I am an engineer, I have a room reserved in the officer's bungalow. When I entered this hotel and sat down to eat on that bench by the door, my Guru appeared to me, pointed you out and said, "This is the man you must speak to". I immediately asked if I could speak with you, and you agreed, even though your bag is still inside the restaurant. You must be the man I am supposed to meet.'

We went down the slope and sat on the *ghat*. After some time he turned to me and asked, 'Please tell me how to realise the Truth'.

I told him, 'You don't have to do any practice. You don't have to chant any mantras. You don't have to do any yogic *asanas,* and you don't have to go on any pilgrimages. You simply have to look within at your own Self. In no time at all you will see that you have been always free, but you didn't realise it before because you were always looking outwards.'

We looked deeply into one another's eyes. Suddenly, his whole body shook and tears flowed down his cheeks. He was not able to speak or walk, so I helped him to get up. He invited me to stay with him in the officer's bungalow and I accepted. The entire night he sat in a state of absorption, very still.

That was the end of Papaji's projected trip to Badrinath. Realising that he had been prompted to go on this unlikely expedition merely to meet this man, he cancelled his plan to go all the way to Badrinath and instead went back to Hardwar. The two men never saw each other again.

These two encounters – with Sita and the army officer – are typical examples of the way Papaji dealt with devotees during the period of his life when he was physically very active. He would appear in a devotee's life when the time was right, facilitate a direct experience of the Self in a single session, then disappear as mysteriously as he had appeared. For many years Papaji fiercely guarded his privacy and his independence. He rarely gave out his permanent address in Lucknow, and he avoided the problem of large crowds following him by keeping his travel plans to himself. If he decided to travel to a particular place in India, he would write to devotees in that area to inform them that he was coming. When the visit was over, he would either take off by himself for a while, or inform other people that he was planning to visit them. This strategy enabled him to be alone whenever he wanted to, and it kept the satsang groups down to manageable numbers. It was only in 1990, when ill health made it impossible for him to travel freely, that he settled down in Lucknow and allowed large numbers of people to gather around him.

When I asked Meera to give other examples of people who had had special meetings with Papaji, she cited a German man called Joachim Grebert. He came to see Papaji because Sita had talked to him about her own remarkable encounter. Though his initial meeting was less fraught with strange coincidences than the two I have just recounted, it is an interesting story that deserves to be told because Joachim played a key role in persuading Papaji to travel to the West a couple of years later.

This is Papaji's own account of their meeting.

This encounter happened during the time when I was living outside under a tree by the banks of the Ganga. It was near Maharishi Mahesh Yogi's ashram. I had no place of my own, not even a cave. The weather was nice, so I used to eat and sleep by the side of the river.

One day a young German man came and asked if I spoke English. I nodded. He said that he wanted to ask me some questions. Then, without waiting for permission, he gave me a long list. I answered all his questions, apparently to his satisfaction. He seemed to be deeply moved by some of the answers. During the course of our conversation he mentioned that he was the president of the T.M. centre at Köln in Germany and that he was currently with the Maharishi in his ashram. He underwent some kind of transformation during our talk because at the end of it he was ready to drop all his past, all his practices, and even his position with the Maharishi's organisation.

'I don't want to stay there any longer,' he informed me. 'I have found what I was looking for here. I don't need to go back. From now on I want to stay with you.'

'I have no place of my own,' I said, and I told him about the primitive conditions under which I was living. Even after discovering the facts, he still expressed a desire to stay with me.

Explaining his position, he said, 'I have asked Mahesh Yogi many times to answer the same questions I put to you today. I had many doubts and questions for which I wanted answers. But every time I asked him, he told me that I was not yet ready to receive the answers. I was told by him that I didn't have the maturity to comprehend the answers to these questions. This has been going on for a long time. Today you answered all my questions and my mind is now at peace. I came here with a busy mind, but now I have no thoughts at all. I never experienced this peace with Mahesh Yogi, or through following any of his practices. I want to leave that organisation and come to stay with you. Why should I stay in a place that doesn't give me any peace?'

The next day he turned up at my tree with all his baggage.

His departure was a matter of concern for the officials of his old ashram. It was soon learned that he had left the ashram to go and live with a *sadhu* on the banks of the Ganga. It is well known that most of the *sadhus* who live by the Ganga spend all their time smoking *chillams*. The people who ran the T.M. ashram automatically assumed that he had ended up with one of these *chillam*-smoking *babas*. They organised a rescue expedition to bring back their prodigal son.

A couple of days later the president of the ashram and four other people came to persuade the German boy that he should come back to their ashram.

After they had finished talking to him, he came up to me and said, 'These people from the ashram have come to take me back, but I don't want to go'.

I advised him to go back with them. 'I have no proper facilities for you here. I am just living under a tree. How long can you stay here with me?'

He wasn't willing to leave so I told him that he could carry on coming to see me if he wanted to. But first I suggested that I should talk to the officials of his old ashram so that I could at least assure them that I was not going to make their ex-student start smoking *ganja.*

They came and asked me many questions. In particular, they wanted to know what my teaching was.

In order to placate them I said, 'I have no teaching. I am just a devotee of Sri Ramana Maharshi who used to live in Tiruvannamalai, in South India.'

They were very hostile towards me. It wasn't my teaching or my lifestyle that bothered them. They were just afraid that I might continue to steal their own devotees from the ashram. They threatened me by saying that if I continued to live near their ashram, they would send people to attack me and beat me up.

Shortly after these events took place the Indian government banned foreigners from staying at the Maharishi's Rishikesh ashram. The government claimed that the foreigners were a security threat because some of them might be spying for their respective countries. The ban on foreigners is still in force. Papaji continues:

I didn't want to get into a fight with these people so I suggested to the German boy that we leave and go on a trip.

'Let's go to Sri Ramanasramam,' I suggested. 'We don't have to stay here and get into fights with these people.'

The next morning I told him that I had to go to Lucknow first because I didn't have enough money with me to make the trip to the South. The next day we both left Hardwar and went to Lucknow. On our arrival I didn't want to go and stay with my family, so instead we went to stay with a devotee who had provided me with a house to give satsang to my Lucknow devotees.

When news of his return spread in the city, Papaji found himself giving satsang to about sixty people. Joachim Grebert attended but soon found himself being lectured to by some of the Indian devotees. Papaji explains why:

We had been living very simply and primitively in Rishikesh and Joachim seemed to have forgotten about some of the basic rules of hygiene that city people observed. Because he looked a bit dirty to some of the Indian people, they started telling him that if he wanted to make progress spiritually he should purify both his mind and his body and keep them both immaculately clean. Joachim was a bit naive. He didn't know much about the Hindu tradition, even though he had been a T.M. teacher, so he took the instructions very literally.

He found a packet of Surf detergent in his bathroom and read the slogan 'Surf washes whiter' on the packet. Thinking that he could use it to clean his mind and his body, he tipped the whole packet into a bucket of water and drank as much of it as he could. He told me later that he felt contaminated and that he wanted to clean and purify his insides so he would be ready to receive the grace of the Master.

He started vomitting and eventually lost consciousness. Soon afterwards someone found him and brought me to him. I laid him on the floor, face down, with his belly on an earthen pot, and pressed his back to make him vomit up as much of the water as possible. I gave him hot milk to drink, but he vomitted that as well. I tried again, adding a lot of honey to soothe his stomach and his nerves, and this time he kept it down. In two or three days he was back to normal.

Papaji cancelled his planned visit to Ramanasramam and went back to Hardwar, taking Joachim and Baldev Raj with him. Joachim then had another accident that required Papaji's intervention. Meera describes what happened.

We were walking with Master in Rishikesh, accompanying him back to his room. It was late evening and we couldn't see where we were putting our feet. Joachim trod on a black snake and the snake responded by biting him in the leg. We weren't aware of what had happened until a few minutes later. By that time Master had gone inside his room, which he was sharing with Baldev Raj, and locked the door. I got Joachim back to his room and then rushed to tell Master what had happened.

Baldev Raj intervened and told Master, 'You have to help this boy. Your reputation is at stake. All the people here know that this boy used to be an important person in Maharishi's ashram. Now he has come to you, and immediately he gets bitten by a poisonous snake. If you don't do something to save this boy, everyone will say that the Maharishi has cursed him for leaving, and this is the result.'

Master made no comment on this but he agreed to come to see how Joachim was. He found the puncture hole through which the snake had injected its venom and began to draw a *yantra* [spiritual pattern or diagram] on the skin near the hole. Within a few minutes Joachim's condition improved, and within half an hour he seemed to be almost back to normal.

'Take him out for a walk,' ordered Master. 'Don't let him sleep tonight. Take him down to the Ganga and keep his attention engaged all night. Don't let him sit quietly. Entertain him and keep his mind busy.'

I took Joachim out and we had a hilarious night laughing and playing by the banks of the Ganga. The playing somehow washed out his mind as well as his body. The following day Joachim had no memory of being bitten, and no memory of Master's visit to him.

This was the first time I had seen Master cure a snake bite, although I had seen him deal with scorpion bites on several occasions. He had such a reputation for curing scorpion bites, the local people started coming to him as soon as they were bitten. There was a plague of scorpions that year [1970] in Rishikesh and we heard about people being bitten almost every day. Master would treat everyone the same way. He would take a metal-tipped pen or any object made of iron, such as a key, and then draw a special diagram on the skin close to where the bite was. Within a few minutes the patient would be free of pain and able to function quite normally. That year, when there were so many people being bitten, Master acquired a reputation for being a miraculous healer. The locals started calling him 'Scorpion Baba'. I have been told that even nowadays when he goes to Rishikesh, people from that period still recognise him and call him 'Scorpion Baba'. Master didn't like all these crowds gathering around him, so he slipped away from Rishikesh one night and didn't come back until his exploits had been mostly forgotten. After that I never saw him perform this cure again.

The yantra *that Papaji used was featured in an article that appeared in 1965 in* The Mountain Path, *the journal published by Sri Ramanasramam. In this article a woman called Ethel Merston described a* yantra *that was widely used by railroad workers to cure scorpion bites. The* yantra, *which looked like an elaborate figure four, had to be drawn near the wound with a metal object. No magical powers were needed, she said, for ordinary railway workers were regularly giving each other instant relief from the pain and the swelling of poisonous bites by using this* yantra. *No explanation for the curious phenomenon was offered, but I know of*

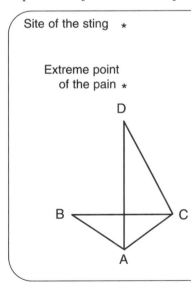

Site of the sting ✱

Extreme point of the pain ✱

D

B — C

A

The *yantra* that Papaji used to cure scorpion bites. The advice given in the article was as follows:
 Take any sharp object made of iron and draw this diagram in one continuous movement: A to B, B to C, C to A, A to D, and finally, D to C. After a few seconds, the pain-affected area should diminish. Keep making new *yantras* on the edge of the pain-affected area until it diminishes and disappears into the site of the sting. The whole process should only take a few minutes.

several people who have used the same yantra *with some success.
I asked Papaji for an account of his brief career as 'Scorpion
Baba'. He confirmed Meera's account and revealed that he had
once had another flourishing practice in a different part of the
state.*

We were staying in the Ved Niketan ashram in Rishikesh.
There were many black scorpions in the area at that time and many
pilgrims were being stung. The bites of these scorpions were
extremely painful. The pain usually lasted for about forty-eight
hours. Even the people who were staying in the Ved Niketan
ashram were being bitten. People began coming to me because I
could cure them without any medicine. News of this spread to
Swarg Ashram and other places. Every evening four or five people
would come, usually writhing in agony. They would be carried in
crying, but a few minutes later they would walk out smiling.

I was once staying in Nemisharanya. This is a famous
pilgrimage site where in ancient times eighty-four thousand *rishis*
performed *tapas*. The site of their *tapas* is a tank called Chakra
Tirth. It received its name at the end of the *Mahabharata* war
because this was the place that the *sudarshan chakra* [Krishna's
discus] fell on the ground and plunged deep into the earth.

Jagadacharya Swami Naradananda had arranged to hold a
massive vedic ritual there. Thousands of pandits were involved and
tents had been erected to accommodate one *lakh* [100,000] people.

I was on my way to attend one of the functions – a reading of
the *Gita* by Naradananda Swami – when I saw many people
walking in a procession. I stopped one of the men to ask where
they were all going.

He said, 'We are carrying the body of a man who has been
bitten by a large poisonous scorpion. There is no doctor in the area,
so we are rushing him to the nearest government hospital before
his condition deteriorates any further.'

I noticed a woman who must have been the sick man's wife.
She was crying and cursing the gods.

She beat her chest a few times and cried out, 'We have come
here on a pilgrimage! Why have you given us so much suffering?'

I went up to her and said, 'This is not a serious problem. If you will give me your permission, I can cure him in a few minutes. The nearest government hospital is forty miles away. You don't need to waste your time going all the way there.'

The other people in the group told her to ignore me.

'Don't stop and talk to people like him,' they said. 'We are wasting valuable time. We have to get him to hospital quickly. This man is just a quack. He will ask for money and then give some useless cure.'

I ignored their remarks and spoke again to his wife.

'I am only asking for one minute of your time. I am not asking for any money. What can you lose by letting me try?'

The wife reluctantly consented. I told the porters to lay the body on the ground. I could see that the affected ankle was black and swollen.

I drew a *yantra* near the wound and in less than a minute he was completely cured. Much to everyone's amazement, he stood up and started laughing. The wife wanted to give a gold necklace from around her neck while her husband tried to force Rs 1,000 on me. I refused to accept anything. All the people in the group wanted to know where I was staying in case they too got bitten. Word spread and after a few days I was seeing ten to twelve people every day. The area was infested with snakes and scorpions, so I never lacked patients. After about a month, though, when the crowds became too much, I left quietly and went back to Hardwar.

Though Papaji always maintains that he has no miraculous powers, it cannot be denied that seemingly miraculous things happen around him. I have talked to many of his old devotees and from them I get the impression that in the late 1960s and early 1970s extraordinary, inexplicable phenomena were happening in his presence almost every day. This is Meera's account of two such events:

We were living near Mahesh Yogi's ashram, camping under a huge tree. There were caves nearby which we also used occasionally. Sita, Joachim and a few others would come and join us there for a few hours every day.

At that time we were living on a diet of broken wheat. We ate it almost every day, cooking it with water over a wood fire. It was a big job getting the wood dry because the rain could start and stop at any time. Since it was the middle of the monsoon season, it usually rained at least once every day. When we started cooking there were only the two of us present, so I only put a little broken wheat in the pot. I had just got the fire going when there was a heavy downpour that drenched us and extinguished the fire. We ran for shelter under the tree. As we stood there, waiting for the rain to stop, we were joined by Joachim, Sita and a few other people who had walked from the town.

After the rain had stopped, I realised that we had no more dry wood stored anywhere. I told Master, who replied phlegmatically, 'Well that means no food today. Throw the wheat in the Ganga because it won't keep till tomorrow. It has been soaked so it will ferment in the water. At least we can give the fish something to eat.'

As I approached the pot, I noticed that steam was coming out, and when I took the lid off, I found the wheat had cooked itself during the rain. It had only been on the fire a few seconds when the rain came down.

I showed it to Master who just laughed and said, 'Very good, we can serve it to our guests'.

I obeyed, thinking that I would have to serve very small portions because I had originally only put in enough wheat for two people. However, when I served the food, there was a full portion for everyone, with plenty more left over in the pot. During the meal an Indian couple who were returning to Rishikesh from a walk in the mountains saw us eating and came to join us. Master invited them to eat and two more full portions were found in the pot.

There is one other story that I remember from this period. I think it happened a few days before or maybe a few days later. Master and I had gone for a long walk along the banks of the Ganga. Eventually we stopped and started to make preparations to cook our lunch. I noticed that Master was looking a little tired so I started hunting around for a nice flat stone for him to sit on while we prepared the food. Since there was nothing suitable on the beach, I went down to the edge of the Ganga to see if there were any suitable rocks that were slightly submerged in the water. As I stood there, peering into the water, a wooden stool floated down the river and beached itself right in front of us. It was the perfect size for Master to sit on.

I laughed and called out, 'Ganga has sent you a stool to sit on!'

Master looked and agreed that Ganga herself had found out about our needs and had supplied us with a seat. Though it was an unwieldy object to carry, we took the stool home with us and presented it to Master's mother on our next visit to Lucknow. She preserved it in her *puja* room as Ganga *prasad*.

Most people who were around Papaji for any length of time in the late sixties or early seventies can relate similar stories. I will just cite one more which came to my attention recently. Arno Wehmeier, an Australian devotee whose story will appear later, told me that while he was staying in Hardwar with Papaji, Meera tore her clothes. She requested Papaji to buy a needle and thread while he was out walking with Arno. Papaji forgot and on his return Meera mildly scolded him for not remembering. Arno recalls what happened next:

Papaji and I were sitting on the floor, cross-legged, facing each other. Meera, who was in an adjacent room, was calling through the open doorway, telling us both off for forgetting the needle and thread. Papaji's hands were resting on his knees with the palms upwards. As we sat there a needle and thread just materialised on the palm of one of his hands. The thread even matched the colour of the torn cloth. Papaji grinned and chuckled for a couple of seconds and then gave me the needle and thread to give to Meera. As I walked across the room he put his finger to his lips to indicate that I shouldn't tell her where it came from.

Papaji never made any attempt to produce these phenomena; they just seemed to happen by themselves. Though he has given no rational explanation for all these strange, miraculous occurrences, he did make the following comment a few years ago.

I sometimes wondered why all these strange things were going on around me. I didn't think I was in any way responsible for them. Then one day I thought, 'Maybe I have some subtle unconscious desire for things like this to happen, because whatever appears in this world is a manifestation of one's desires'. I didn't want to have such latent desires, so I made a firm resolve.

I said to myself, 'I don't want these things to happen around me any more'. After that they didn't happen so much, and eventually they stopped.

On one of his visits to Lucknow Papaji was approached by Om Prakash Syal, a graduate student at Lucknow University. Om Prakash describes their first meeting and some of the incidents that followed it:

I first encountered Papaji on 22nd November, 1969. I was on my way to post some letters at the railway station in Lucknow. It was about 7 p.m. and I was walking near the Railway Police Station. I noticed Papaji standing in a space in front of the station. Meera was with him, and so was an Indian man, but I can't remember his name. All three of them were standing there, looking as if they were waiting for someone. My guess turned out to be correct. I found out later that they had come to collect a woman called Bettina Baumer who was arriving on a train from Varanasi. I met her later. She was an Austrian girl who was doing a Ph.D. at Benares Hindu University in Varanasi. I don't know why Papaji was standing outside the station to wait for her. Most people wait on the platform when they go to greet someone.

I posted my letters and began to walk towards the western side of the station. I passed Papaji and carried on walking, but after about 100 yards I found I physically couldn't walk any further. I had to turn round and go back towards this complete stranger whom I had seen waiting outside the station. I didn't know why I was so attracted to him. There was nothing in his appearance that distinguished him from many of the other people who had come to the station that day. He was wearing ordinary street clothes and wasn't doing anything to attract anyone's attention. Still, I had to go back and have another look at him.

I walked past him again, without introducing myself. Because he was a complete stranger, I felt too embarrassed to walk up to him and ask him who he was. I walked another 100 yards and stopped again. The pull was still there. I had this perverse feeling that I couldn't just walk away from this man, even though I had never seen him before. Something was preventing me from moving more than 100 yards from him. I tried the same manoeuvre again and again. Each time I walked past him, I couldn't go more than 100 yards without stopping. And having stopped, some strange power would drag me back in his direction. This must have happened about five times. Each time I passed him, I felt that some power was being transmitted from his forehead into me. He wasn't looking at me or obviously directing any force towards me. It was just a feeling I had. Whenever I went near him, I had the distinct feeling that some energy was moving from him to me. I never guessed that he was some sort of yogi because he was wearing such ordinary clothes. The two people who were with him were also dressed very simply.

Finally, I could not resist the pull any more. I went up to him and said, 'Sir, I have walked past you five times, and each time I went past you I felt some power emanating from you. I don't know what you are doing to me, but I can't walk away from you. Every time I try, I find that I can't go more than 100 yards in any direction. Please excuse my interruption, but under the circumstances I feel that I have to know more about you. Please tell me who you are.'

Initially, Papaji just smiled at me without uttering a word. Then he looked across at Meera and the other man who was waiting with him. I found out later that he was a good devotee of Papaji's.

After a few seconds of silence Papaji began to laugh. 'This is a very pertinent question,' he said in between his laughs. 'But before I tell you about my identity, you must tell me yours.'

I had no objection to this. 'Sir, my name is Om Prakash and I am a postgraduate of Lucknow University. I live quite close to this place where we are speaking.'

This was the usual way to introduce oneself but Papaji was not satisfied with it.

'This is not your real identity,' he said. 'Tell me who you really are.'

This was very confusing for me. I had given him a proper introduction, but he seemed to be accusing me of lying to him.

I told him, 'I assure you that I am really the person I am claiming to be. I am Om Prakash; I am a maths graduate of Lucknow University, and I live near here.'

He shook his head. 'No, this is not your name. Tell me what your real name is!'

I didn't realise that he was giving me a philosophical interrogation. I was a complete ignoramus about all things pertaining to philosophy. I had studied maths at Lucknow University up to the postgraduate level but had few other academic interests. Though I performed the usual Hindu rituals, I had never bothered to go into any of the philosophical ideas that underpinned them. In my whole life up till then, it had never occurred to me that I was anyone or anything other than the person I believed myself to be.

Even though he had just accused me of not telling the truth, I still felt a very strong attraction towards him.

'Sir,' I said, 'if you will not tell me who you are, and if you will not believe that I am who I say I am, will you at least allow me to visit you occasionally? I feel a very strong attraction towards you and I want to renew our acquaintance.'

He refused to give me his address, even though I pointedly asked for it. He just looked at me and said, 'If it is destined to happen, then we will meet again'.

It had not been a very informative exchange for me, but I still felt overwhelmed by the meeting. There was something about this man that was irresistibly attractive. I think I can say that I fell in love with him the moment I saw him. At the end of our meeting I prostrated to him on the street. I didn't know that he was a holy man but I still did it because of the reverence and respect I felt for him. At a subconscious level something in me recognised his saint-liness and his greatness. There was also a spontaneous surrender to him. At the moment I approached him, I knew I would give this man anything he asked for, even my life if necessary.

At the time of our first parting I remember saying to him, 'I am willing to give you everything I have. If you ask for the last drop of blood in my body, I will happily give it to you. If this last drop of blood is of any use to you, please take it from me and keep it.'

I don't know what happened to me at that first meeting, and I don't know why I made this ridiculous offer. All I can say is that I melted and surrendered to this complete stranger to such an extent that I was willing to give him everything I had.

I can't speak about this in a rational way. I have been coming to see Papaji for twenty-six years now, and I still don't know why I come. Something keeps pulling me again and again. I can be sitting at home with my family when suddenly I get up and leave because I know I have to see this man again. I can't stay away from him; I keep coming again and again, but I never do it for any reason. It is just something I have to do. It's a mystery because there is nothing I want from him. I never go to him from any conscious motive. I just have an irresistible impulse to be in his presence again and again.

I met him again a few weeks later. I had been to Mahanagar to visit my maths teacher, Dr Mehra. I was cycling from his house in the direction of Nishat Ganj when I noticed Papaji walking along the bank of the Gomti River. I remember that he was wearing a white *dhoti*, folded up and tucked into his waistband, and a *kurta*. As soon as I caught sight of him, I felt a physical thrill in my body. I dismounted, ran up to him, and prostrated on the ground. My whole being was flooded with happiness.

Without my having to ask, he invited me back to his house. Not the house where he lived in Narhi; his parents' house, which was on the Gomti River. He was staying there at the time with Meera.

We went into the kitchen where Papaji asked Meera, 'Do you remember this man? He is the one we met at the train station a few weeks ago.'

Meera was delighted to see me. She started jumping up and down and even started doing a little dance in the kitchen.

Papaji invited me for lunch. I accepted immediately even though I had been suffering from various stomach ailments for a long time. I had to be careful about what I ate, but I didn't tell any of this to Papaji. I wasn't going to turn down an invitation to eat with him just because my stomach might suffer later. I was willing to put up with any amount of pain in order to have the privilege of eating with him.

He sat me down on the floor and put a banana leaf in front of me. A big South Indian meal was served to me. There was rice, *sambar*, *rasam* and some curd-rice. Papaji told me that he had cooked some of the food himself.

I ate all the food with great relish and never experienced any ill-effects afterwards. In fact, the meal effected a permanent cure. From that day on I never experienced these stomach problems again.

After lunch he casually remarked to me, 'I must introduce you to my Master. I want to show you my Master.'

I was thrilled at the prospect. I thought to myself, 'This man is so great. His Master must be at least as great as he.'

Papaji took me by the hand and led me into a different room. With an expansive wave of the arm he exclaimed, 'This is my Master!'

I looked around, but there was no one there. Then he threw himself full-length on the floor and prostrated before a photo of Sri Ramana Maharshi. This was my first introduction to his Guru and the first indication I ever had of just how devoted he was to his Master. He had not spoken about his Master in the past tense. For him, Sri Ramana was clearly a still-living presence.

There were other pictures there, many of them scenes depicting Krishna. I found out later that these belonged to his mother who was an ardent Krishna *bhakta*.

I had never heard of Ramana Maharshi. As I have already mentioned, I was very ignorant of spiritual matters. The only Guru I had heard about at that time was Sathya Sai Baba. I knew a little about him because he was famous.

I started to talk about Sai Baba and mentioned some of the miracles that he had performed.

Papaji immediately expressed his disgust for such behaviour. 'He is just a juggler! If you want powers like these, there are exercises you can do. And if you do them properly, you can get these powers within six months.'

Later that day I asked him if I could come and see him again. Now that I knew where he could be found, I wanted to come to see him as often as possible.

He replied, 'You must make up your mind what you want from life. If you want what I have to offer, then you are welcome. But don't come to see me unless you get your parents' approval and permission. Each time that you decide that you want to see me, ask your parents if you can come. Prostrate to your parents and ask their permission. If they don't give you that permission, then don't come.' From that day on, I tried to see him every day.

On the third or fourth time that I went to see him no one was there in the house except his mother.

'Where is he?' I asked.

'I think that he has gone to the train station to see off some foreigners who were here. I don't know when he will be back.'

At that time Bettina Baumer and Swami Abhishiktananda had been visiting him. I assumed that he had gone to the station to put them on the train for Varanasi. I checked the time. I knew what time the train left and I calculated that I just had enough time to meet him there. I raced to the train station and found him standing on the platform.

After he had seen off his guests, I approached him and said, 'My house is very near here. Would you like to come and visit? We can walk. It is not far.'

At first he refused, saying, 'No, we have to go for lunch'.

'But it's not far,' I replied. 'Just come for five minutes and see where I live.'

Seeing my eagerness, he accepted my invitation and came to look at my house. This was the first of many visits that he made. Eventually, he became such a frequent visitor, the house was almost a second home for him.

Papaji with Om Prakash in the early 1970s.

In those days I had a job, lecturing in Kanpur, but I managed to adjust my schedule so that I could see him every day. I would leave for Kanpur about seven in the morning so that I could reach there in time for my 9 o'clock class. I would finish my lecturing at 10.50 and then rush to the station to catch the 11 o'clock train back to Lucknow. Arriving in Lucknow at around 12.30, I would go straight to Papaji's house. I wouldn't even bother to go home first. I would reach his house around 1 o'clock and stay there for the rest of the day. If he didn't tell me to go home at the end of the day, I would sleep there as well.

About a month after I met him I decided that I should ask him for some spiritual teachings. I hadn't asked him any questions up till then, nor had he given me any advice or instructions. We would just sit together and pass the time of day. When he lay down, I would sometimes massage his legs, but that was the extent of our interaction. He never asked me to massage his legs. It was just something that I felt attracted to do, and he always allowed me to do it.

I felt very ignorant about spiritual matters and felt that it was time to get some kind of spiritual education from him. Papaji was lying on the ground, reading a book by Ram Tirtha. No one else was with us, so it seemed to be a good opportunity to ask him a few questions. In those early days I used to call him 'Swamiji', not 'Papaji'.

'Swamiji,' I began, 'I have been coming to you for some time now, but you haven't told me to do anything. You haven't given me any spiritual practice to do or asked me to study anything. Please give me some technique or method that will help me to attain enlightenment. I want to learn meditation. Please give me some mantra, or teach me some other method that will be suitable for me.'

He remained silent for about half an hour. I was sure that he had heard my question, but he didn't seem inclined to answer it. At the end of that half hour I repeated my question. Again there was no response. He remained silent for another half hour. I asked a third time and once more waited half an hour for an answer, but it never came. He wasn't sleeping. He was just sitting quietly with his eyes open, not looking at anything in particular.

Finally, out of frustration, I gently shook his shoulder to wake him from his reverie and said, 'Swamiji! I have asked you this question three times, but you are refusing to give me any kind of answer. If you don't want to give me any kind of advice, you can at least say so. You should at least speak to me and tell me that you don't want to answer my question.'

Papaji just smiled and said, 'Om Prakash, I did speak to you, but you weren't listening.'

This surprised me. I had been looking at him steadily for an hour and a half, waiting for an answer, and I could definitely assert that no sound had come from him.

I did not say this directly. I just looked at him and said, 'I did not hear it. Please tell me again.'

'Oh,' said Papaji, still smiling, 'then there must be something wrong with your eardrum.'

'How could I have missed your reply in circumstances like these? I am sitting next to you, eagerly waiting for your reply. I have just watched you for an hour and a half, and during that time I never saw your lips move and I never heard any sound.'

Then he said, 'You didn't listen properly. You say that I have not spoken to you. That silence in which I didn't speak was my answer to you.'

He sat there for a few minutes longer. He was in a special sitting position, one that Muslims often use. The legs are bent under one's body and one sits on the heels. In those days, Papaji used to sit like this quite a lot.

Finally, he pointed a finger at me and said, very sharply, 'Think when you must. Look when you must. Talk when you must. Otherwise, keep quiet!'

In those first few months I used to go to him every day. If I had not reached his house by about nine in the evening, he would come looking for me. He would start walking from his own house to find out why I had not come. I wasn't often late, and when I was, it was usually because my train was late.

Though he clearly expected me to come every day, he very rarely spoke to me. We would just sit together for hours in silence.

Occasionally he would say something practical, such as, 'Om Prakash, can you bring me some water,' or 'Om Prakash, fetch me some *paan*,' but that would be the extent of our interaction. I never asked any questions, and he rarely spoke about anything that was not related to his immediate personal needs. This was the way he behaved with almost everyone in those days. In the first twenty-one years that I knew him, that is to say, from 1969 to 1990, I don't think I heard him speak for more than a total of twenty-one hours. That's one hour per year.

Occasionally devotees would come to him for advice. He would listen and say something appropriate. But if no one was asking him anything, he would keep quiet. It wasn't that he was rude. He was just a very quiet man who only spoke when he had to. Nobody minded his silence because we all felt benefited by it. Most of the people who came to see him and sit with him in silence felt a little touched by his grace.

Let me give you an example. My parents were not happy that I was spending all my spare time with Papaji. In fact, I can say that they were very much annoyed. I once overheard them complaining about me.

'He is spending all his time with Papaji. He is not looking after us properly. We are his parents, but he doesn't want to spend any time with us any more. Every spare minute he has he spends with this man Papaji. He is our eldest son. It is his duty to stay at home and be with us.'

My father eventually went to Papaji to complain about my behaviour. But instead of voicing his complaints, he just sat there silently, without saying anything.

Papaji never looked at him or even spoke to him, but when my father returned home that day he said to me, 'Om Prakash, when I met Papaji today I felt as if I was sitting in front of my own father, or perhaps my own grandfather. I don't mean that there was some physical resemblance. I just had this feeling that I was in the company of one of the elders of my own family.'

After this visit my father stopped complaining about my behaviour. In fact, over the course of time he too began to have some faith in Papaji.

Eventually he asked Papaji, 'I can see that your *kundalini* has awakened. Can you please awaken my *kundalini* as well?'

Papaji just smiled and said, 'It will happen by itself'.

I must tell you something about that smile. For me, when Papaji smiles, it is not just an indication that he is happy or friendly. There is a penetrating power in it. When Papaji directs a smile at someone, there is a force or power in his gaze that goes right through to the Heart. The mind cannot withstand it. When the smile meets the mind, the mind has to give way. The entire garbage of the mind gets washed away the instant it comes into contact with that smile.

Whenever I visit Papaji I never want to leave. In all the years that I have been visiting him I have never wanted to say to him, 'Papaji, I have to go now. May I go home?'

So, it is always Papaji who has to say, 'Om Prakash, you can go now'. Only then will I be able to leave.

In the early years of our association he sometimes forgot to tell me to leave. Or perhaps he just wanted me to stay. If this ever happened, I would usually spend the night with him because, as I have just said, I could never tell him that I had to leave and go. On one such occasion I spent two consecutive nights at his house because on both evenings he omitted to tell me that I should go home. On the third day my father came to the house to find out why I had not come home. He was in a very angry mood when he arrived.

'My son doesn't even have the courtesy to tell me where he is or where he is going,' he began. 'What kind of son is this? He has no respect for us at all!'

Papaji told him, 'You say that you are the father of Om Prakash. In a way you are right. But I am also his father. You are the father who threw him into the womb of his mother. Fathers like these have caused Om Prakash to be born and reborn again and again. I am the father who has taken the responsibility of stopping him from entering another mother's womb. Please remember that I am also this boy's father.'

Some of Om Prakash's subsequent experiences with Papaji will appear in other parts of this book. Meanwhile, I will return to Papaji's activities in Hardwar and Rishikesh.

In the 1950s and '60s many of the foreigners who came to see Papaji had been sent by Swami Abhishiktananda, the French monk whose meetings with Papaji in South India were described in an earlier chapter. Swami Abhishiktananda himself continued to visit Papaji throughout the 1960s, either in Rishikesh or in Lucknow. Meera gives her impression of some of these meetings:

I met him for the first time in the late 1960s when I was staying with Master at Sapt Sarovar Ashram in Hardwar. Abhishiktananda at that time was living in a hut at Uttarkashi, only a few hours away by bus, so he often stopped off to see Master when he was travelling to and from places further south. Master had told me about him before I met him, so I knew all about him even before he arrived Abhishiktananda found Master to be a fascinating figure, but he was never really a devotee. He had an unwavering allegiance to Christianity and this prevented him from accepting Master's teachings and from regarding him as a Guru. Even so, he kept coming again and again, always with a long list of spiritual questions to ask.

Satsangs were good fun when he was around because he knew how to provoke Master into giving good answers. Though he was interested in mysticism and meditated a lot, he had a very intellectual approach to Christian theology and Hindu philosophy. He wanted to find some kind of common ground between Christianity and Hinduism and many of his questions were framed with this purpose in mind. Sometimes Master would humour him by discussing philosophy with him, but more often he would try to tell him that all ideas – both Christian and Hindu – had to be dropped. Master told him again and again that his attachment to his Christian ideas was preventing him from discovering the state that he was thinking and writing so much about, but Abhishiktananda could never accept this.

Satsangs around Master were never serious for very long. There would always be a lot of laughing and joking. Abhishiktananda sometimes complained that we were not being serious enough, and that we were laughing for no reason at all. This would just make us laugh even more. One time, when we were in Lucknow with him, Abhishiktananda had some kind of ecstatic experience as a result of something Master said to him. Without being aware of what he was doing, he tripped, fell over and landed with his face in a bowl of flour. We were all sitting in Master's kitchen at the time. When he emerged he was white all over. Of course, everybody laughed and laughed, so much so that Abhishiktananda got upset.

'I am not staying here any more!' he exclaimed angrily. 'I am going back to Uttarkashi to do some serious meditation. It will probably take me three months of meditation to recover from this one satsang!'

He carried out his threat and didn't appear again for many weeks.

Master would often have visions of Christ around this period and his descriptions of them fascinated and perplexed Abhishiktananda. He could never understand why Christ was so regularly appearing to this man who was making disparaging remarks about being too much attached to Christianity. I remember one vision particularly well. Master suddenly stopped what he was doing, lay down, pulled a blanket up to his chin and remained absolutely motionless for several hours. I had never seen him do anything like this before. When he came back to normal, he very slowly and deliberately described a cosmic vision of Christ he had just had in which Christ, looking as if he occupied the whole universe, was welcoming him with wide-open arms. I looked at Master's face as he described his vision and it completely melted as he narrated the story.

This particular vision probably appeared to Papaji in November, 1970, for on the 23rd of that month he sent the following letter to Swami Abhishiktananda:

...I wanted to read *Bhagwat*, but somehow I couldn't start. I left it and I saw Lord Christ standing in front of me physically, feet on the ground, but head extending beyond the skies. First his hands were resting on his chest, and then they extended at full length, beyond full length. Then he again folded them, bending them at the elbows. Finally, he moved forward to hold me. This lasted for about one hour. Afterwards I got up and went to the jungle, but the image persisted in my heart. Please explain in your own way.

Swami Abhishiktananda was unable to assimilate this vision into his world view. In his biography, written by Father James Stuart, Swami Abhishiktananda admitted that this report of the vision bewildered him. He could not understand how and why Christ had appeared to an advaitic Hindu in this cosmic form.
Meera continues:

Abhishiktananda was actually present when Master had a vision of Jesus and Peter by the banks of the Jordan River. Master described what he was seeing while Abhishiktananda gave a kind of commentary and explanation that was based on his knowledge of the Bible and the geography of the area.

Abhishiktananda was impressed enough to send or bring several other Christians to Master. There was a girl called Bettina Baumer who stayed with Master for several years, an Italian woman called Marina who saw him regularly in the 1960s, and a few others. Only one, Enrique Aguilar, was able to give up his Christian past. He came to India as a Benedictine monk, but under Master's influence, he quickly dropped his Christian ideas.

As Meera reported, Papaji would sometimes encourage Abhishiktananda in his quest to find parallels between Hinduism and Christianity, while at other times he would encourage him to drop all his Christian ideas completely. Here is an example of the former approach, taken from a letter Papaji wrote to him in November, 1970:

I have known quite a few Christian foreigners who came to me seeking Truth and who returned to the natural state in a short time. It shows that they prepared themselves by a Christian way before they came to me. I myself don't find any difference between a Christian thought and an upanishadic truth. I find an absolute parallel between *shlokas* from the *Upanishads* and verses from the Bible. But why even call them parallel? There must be two different things to be parallel. In truth, there is only one Divine thought whether it is Krishna speaking or Christ talking. They both spoke of ONE Father. *AUM* or AMEN.

With Loving Embrace,

H. W. L. Poonja

A good example of the opposite approach can be found in a story that I have heard Papaji tell on several occasions:

Swami Abhishiktananda and I were sitting by the banks of the Ganga near Rishikesh.

We had been sitting quietly, but suddenly he turned to me and asked, 'Ram, how far am I away from freedom?'

He always called me Ram, as did a few other people in those days.

Swami
Abhishiktananda

I replied, 'As far away as the sky is from the earth.'

I could see that he was disappointed by the answer.

'But what's wrong with me?' he asked plaintively. 'I have meditated for many years. I have done intense *tapas*. I have dedicated my whole life to this pursuit.'

'If you really want to be free,' I told him, 'I can tell you how to do it instantly. Why wait five weeks or five years? You have a bag with you. Throw this bag into the Ganga and I guarantee that you will be instantly free. Why don't you do it?'

It was a serious offer but he couldn't accept it. He had his Christian books in his bag, along with the equipment he needed to perform mass. I was telling him to throw his Christianity in the river, but he couldn't do it.

'I can't,' he said. 'I am committed to Christianity and I will never drop it.'

He must have written about this conversation because I found out years later that it was included in a film documentary of Abhishiktananda's life. Two actors were engaged to play our roles, and the dialogue was more or less the same one that I have just described.

Abhishiktananda eventually became disenchanted with Papaji and stopped coming to see him. Om Prakash remembers the following exchange that took place in Lucknow in the early 1970s:

I was sitting with both of them in Lucknow when Abhishiktananda said to Papaji, 'Ram, you are not the same Ram I first saw in 1953. You had so much power in those days. Now you seem to be very much changed.'

Papaji looked at him and answered, 'It is your spectacles which are seeing this change. You have put on new spectacles so you are seeing differently now. I am the same. I am always the same. If there has been any change, it must only be in the way that you are viewing me.'

Papaji had been telling Abhishiktananda to drop his Christianity for almost twenty years, without success. However, the Christian ideas spontaneously fell away when Abhishiktananda had a heart attack in Rishikesh that left him semi-paralysed on the street. In letters he wrote to his Christian friends soon after the event, he explained how, lying on the road, he had had a direct experience of the Self that demolished all his previous beliefs.

Who can bear the glory of transfiguration, of man's dying as transfigured; because what Christ is, I AM! One can only speak of it after being awoken from the dead.... It was a remarkable spiritual experience.... While I was waiting on my sidewalk, on the frontier of the two worlds, I was magnificently calm, for I AM no matter what in the world! I have found the GRAIL!...

The more I go on, the less able I would be to present Christ in a way which could still be considered as Christian.... For Christ is first an idea which comes to me from outside. Even more after my 'beyond life/death experience' of 14.7.73 I can only aim at awakening people to what 'they are'. Anything about God or the Word in any religion, which is not based on the deep 'I' experience, is bound to be simply 'nction', not existential.

Yet I am interested in no Christology at all. I have so little interest in a Word of God which will awaken man within history.... The Word of God comes from/to my own 'present'; it is that very awakening which is my self awareness. What I discover above all in Christ is his 'I AM' ... It is this I AM experience which really matters. Christ is the very mystery that 'I AM', and in the experience and existential knowledge all Christology has disintegrated....

What would be the meaning of a 'Christianity-coloured' awakening? In the process of awakening all this colouration cannot but disappear.... The colouration might vary according to the audience, but the essential goes beyond. The discovery of Christ's I AM is the ruin of any Christian theology, for all notions are burned within the fire of experience.... I feel too much, more and more, the blazing fire of this I AM in which all notions about Christ's personality, ontology, history etc. have disappeared.

Sometime during 1970 Papaji and Meera went to Lucknow and stayed for some time. While they were there they were visited by a Japanese teacher, a Professor Oshida. Papaji has told the story of their meeting many times. In the version that follows he narrates it to a Japanese woman who has just told him that she didn't want to postpone her enlightenment by thinking of it as an event that might happen in the future.

That's a very good attitude. If you want it now, you will get it now. Don't get stuck in the mind by thinking that you are going to make progress towards it and achieve it later. All these ideas are tricks to keep you unaware of what you are right now.

I have met several Japanese people like you. They heard about me in Japan and instantly decided to come to India. If freedom is what you really want, nothing will stand in your way. When you hear the call, you will answer it immediately.

A Japanese man, Professor Oshida was his name, once came to my house in Narhi and asked for me. One of my family told him that I was upstairs giving satsang and that he was welcome to participate.

At first he didn't want to come up because he only had one lung. The other had been surgically removed. His doctors in Tokyo had advised him against climbing stairs because they thought that the effort would be too much of a strain on his remaining lung.

Then he thought to himself, 'I have come all this way to see him. He is only a few metres away now. If I have to climb stairs to see him, then I will climb.'

You see, no postponement again. He could have waited until I came down, but he didn't want to. Not caring about the damage he might cause to his one remaining lung, he climbed up the stairs to see me.

He sat quietly for some time at the back, but after a few minutes he began to laugh. Within a few seconds of starting, he was laughing uncontrollably. For one hour he laughed without stopping.

At the end of the satsang I invited him to eat lunch with us. While we were eating he told me his story.

'I only have one lung,' he began, 'and my doctors have advised me to be very careful with it. I am not supposed to climb stairs and I am not even supposed to laugh. Activities like these that make the lungs work hard are supposed to be prohibited. If I laugh accidentally, I have to take some medicine.'

He showed me his x-ray, which he was carrying with him in case he needed treatment in India, and he also showed me the bottle of pills that he always carried with him.

This was the first time I heard that laughter was some kind of disease, and that there was even a medicine one could take if one unexpectedly caught it. In my experience, Japanese people don't laugh very much. Only a nation like this would call laughter a problem and invent a chemical antidote for it.

The professor was in a very happy mood. He clearly wasn't worrying about his disease any more.

'Today I climbed up your stairs, sat with you and laughed for one hour. I didn't feel any pain or strain. In fact, I feel as if I have grown a new lung. I haven't breathed as easily as this since the days when I had two perfectly good lungs. Laughing with you has been a very good treatment. I am going to ignore my doctor's advice. I am going to climb up your stairs every day and I am going to laugh with you as much as I can.'

When he went back to Japan a week later, his colleagues all wanted to know why he had gone to India and what he had got there. He told them about me and mentioned that I was a spritual teacher in the Hindu tradition.

His friends, who were all teachers themselves, immediately wanted to know what my teachings were. I think they were probably expecting some kind of philosophical lecture as a reply. Instead, the professor just started laughing.

His colleagues repeated their request, and again the professor began to laugh.

They started to get a little worried about him because they all knew that his doctors had forbidden him to laugh. They were also wondering about his state of mind after his trip to India because whenever they asked him about my teachings, he just started laughing.

Finally, when they asked again about the teachings, he replied, 'This laughter is the teaching. It is the best expression of what I have brought back from India.'

He wrote and told me about all this. That's how I came to hear about it.

Laughter is natural. Happiness is natural. But when you fill your head with thoughts, you can't laugh any more. When you get rid of all the thoughts, then the laughter and the happiness will come by themselves.

You can never find two doctors who agree with each other on medical treatments. They all read the same textbooks when they are studying at college, but when they begin to practise, they all start disagreeing with each other. The Japanese doctors thought laughter was bad because it put too much of a strain on the lungs. Recently I read that research in America had demonstrated that a laugh a day keeps the doctor away. I prefer the American medicine.

Professor Oshida never returned to see Papaji, but twenty-five years later Meera met him accidentally in Brussels:

I was walking down the street when I saw this Japanese man racing towards me. He looked familiar. As he embraced me in a big bear hug, I suddenly realised that this was the same Professor Oshida I had met in Lucknow around 1970. He was still laughing, and from the way he was behaving, I had to assume that he was still in perfect health. We had a wonderful meeting during which he told me how happy he had been since meeting Papaji.

Meera and Papaji returned to Rishikesh a few weeks later and resumed their usual routine of walking, swimming and meeting visitors. Some were serious seekers, but others were merely trying to cope with their malfunctioning mental processes. In the next section Papaji describes how he dealt with some of the people who came to him during this period.

For the last sixty years I have been travelling to Rishikesh and meeting many young people there. Sometimes they are very young. One girl I met there was only seventeen years old. I found out later that she was British and that she had come all the way from London by herself. Some of the Indians in the town mentioned her to me during one of my visits.

'Go and see that girl who sits down by the river. She sits there day and night without moving. Even when the sun is hot or when the rain is pouring down, she doesn't move. Even the so-called *sadhus* of this town are not doing *tapas* like this. We only go to the Ganga once or twice a day for a bath, but this girl spends her whole time there.'

I felt an immediate attraction towards her, even though I had not yet met her. When you have this kind of determination, the teacher will come to you. There is no need to go looking for him. I asked for directions and went and sat next to her on the bank of the Ganga.

'Have you come here with your parents?' I asked. I thought that this was the most likely possibility since she looked so young. I thought she might even be on her summer holidays from school.

'No,' she replied. 'I came here by myself from London. I finished school this year and decided to take a year off before I start college.'

'And what about your parents?' I asked. 'Did they allow you to come here to India by yourself?'

I thought she must have run away from home, for no Indian parents would give their seventeen-year-old daughter permission to travel halfway round the world by herself.

'Yes,' she answered, 'they agreed. They said that I could have one year in India before I start college.'

'So why did you come here?' I asked 'What made you choose this place?'

'I want enlightenment,' she answered, in a very determined way. 'I only have one year before I start college, so I don't want to waste any time. I am going to spend the whole year meditating by the banks of the Ganga.'

'How did you hear about Rishikesh?' I enquired. The town is quite well known in India but I didn't think that schoolgirls in London knew about it.

'One of my friends in London had parents who used to work in India. I knew I had to come to India for freedom, so I asked them where people in India went if they wanted to do some serious meditation. They told me about this place.'

I was impressed by her unwavering commitment. When you have this desire for freedom, and when you discard everything else in life in order to attain it, the gods themselves come to you and serve you.

She recognised that I had something to offer her because she asked me if I could help her to open her mind.

'Yes,' I replied, 'but it will only happen at the right time.'

I visited her regularly, took her out to eat in some of the local restaurants and invited her to come with me on the walks I took in the nearby hills. We had a pleasant time together for a few weeks, eating and walking together.

After some time I found out that her parents didn't even know where she was. She hadn't written to them since her arrival in India. I made her sit down and write a letter, and I also wrote a letter to them, informing them that they need not worry about her because she was in a good place and was being well looked after. For several weeks I treated her as if she were my granddaughter.

Eventually, she had the direct experience she had been seeking. After it had happened I told her, 'You don't need to stay here any more. You have got what you came for. Now you can go home and make your parents happy.'

She accepted my advice and left soon afterwards. This kind of thirst for freedom is very rare. It is very wonderful to see it occasionally on the faces of young people.

Some of the people I saw meditating in Rishikesh were so young I had to enquire how they had managed to finance their trips to India. Some had done jobs and some had been given money by their parents. One teenage girl I met had earned her money very quickly and very easily.

She seemed to be living very well. When I asked her where she got all her money from, she replied, 'I posed half-nude for a men's magazine. The money I received for that one picture will keep me in India for years.'

Around the same time I was visited by a Brazilian girl who looked a bit older. Maybe she was about twenty. She came up to me while I was sitting by the Ganga, presented me with some fruits and told me her story in broken English.

'I come from a rich family in Brazil. I came to India to meditate and ended up at Ved Niketan Ashram because none of the other ashrams I went to accepted foreigners. The swami there has given me a room. I have been there six months and though the swami is very nice to me, I no longer think he is an enlightened man. He looks after me well but I am not getting any teaching from him or any help with my meditation. I came to India for enlightenment but I now know that this man cannot help me to attain it. One boy who used to stay there left and came to see you. I saw him recently in the market and he said he was very happy with his decision. I also want to come and see you regularly, but there is a problem. My swami will not allow me to visit any other teacher or ashram. In order to come to see you today I had to tell him that I was going to the market to buy some fruit. He keeps my traveller's cheques and passport locked up in the ashram, so it will be difficult for me to leave. I feel a little bit sorry for him, and I also feel a desire to help him. If you can help me to attain enlightenment, I want to go back there and help him to attain it. I am only allowed out for one hour every day, so I cannot stay for long.'

I had seen many things in my life, but this was something new for me: a disciple who wanted to enlighten her guru. In the past it was the Gurus who gave enlightenment to their disciples. Now, in this Kali Yuga [the current epoch of time], everything is upside down and the students have to enlighten their gurus.

I told her, 'You didn't make a good choice in going to that place. You were new to India and you ended up at the only place that would accept you. Travel around a bit to places like Varanasi and see a little more of the country before you entrust your spiritual welfare to someone.'

'But the swami has taken all my money,' she said. 'How can I leave?'

'You said you came from a rich family. Write home and get some more. As soon as it comes, demand your passport and walk out.'

Many of the ashrams try to keep their devotees under their control by prohibiting them from visiting other teachers and institutions. In my years in Rishikesh I came across several other people who were being kept under virtual house arrest by one swami or another.

A woman named Suzanne from the south of France had been given my name by Yvan Amar, a French boy who had spent a long time with me. She had also been given the name of Chandra Swami, a teacher who had an ashram in Hardwar. She had gone there first and had been initiated by him. Suzanne wanted to visit me, but because she knew that Chandra Swami didn't like members of his ashram visiting me, she had to make her plans secretly. She had found out from the hotel in Hardwar where I sometimes stayed in those days that I was in Lucknow. Someone gave her my Lucknow address but she needed an excuse to visit me.

She told Chandra Swami, 'I have to go to Delhi to arrange my return flight. I will be back in a few days.'

She came to Lucknow on the Doon Express and turned up at my door at about 9 a.m. We had a very nice meeting. We talked for the whole day, right up till eleven that evening. I let her stay in our house overnight because she had nowhere else to go.

The next morning I took her a cup of coffee and enquired how she was. I asked because I could see she looked very happy.

'After you left yesterday evening I was immensely happy, blissful and quiet. Now there are no thoughts in my mind at all. There is just stillness and peace. Is this what you call freedom?'

Later that day she left to go back to Hardwar because she had promised her swami that she would only be away two days. She must have told some of her friends that she was planning a secret trip to Lucknow because when she returned she found that her room had been emptied. Her bag had been packed and it had been left under a staircase.

Not all the people who came to see me came for spiritual reasons. Many came to see me because they were depressed, mentally disturbed or even mad.

One man from New York came to see me because he claimed he had been haunted by a ghost for many years. He was a psychiatrist himself but no one in his profession had been able to help him. Finally, after many years of treatment, someone who knew me had suggested to him that I might be able to help. In those days I was living a little way up a mountain near Rishikesh in a house that had three rooms. He arrived there in a taxi and immediately began to tell me all about his problem.

'I am haunted by a female ghost. I cannot get rid of her. If I lie down I see her seated on my chest, with a dagger in her hand. When she is not trying to stab me, she is trying to strangle me. If I sit down to eat a meal, she sits next to me and tries to steal all my food. Everywhere I go, she follows me. She even followed me to India. When I went to buy my ticket, she was standing in line next to me. She also bought a ticket for the same flight. And when I boarded the plane and took a seat, she sat next to me for the whole flight. In Delhi she got into my taxi and came with me all the way here. She only disappeared as I approached your house. There must be something about this place that she doesn't like. Can I stay here with you? I will feel much happier if I can stay in a place where I know she is not going to appear.'

I agreed and let him put his bags in one of the empty rooms of my house.

'You can stay here for now,' I said. 'Sleep here tonight and tomorrow we can talk some more about your problem.'

That night at 1 a.m. he knocked on my door and said, 'She's come again! She sat on my chest while I was lying in my room. I don't want to stay there any more. Can I come and sleep with you?'

I let him in because he was too afraid to sleep by himself.

Over the next few days I tried to find out what could have caused this man's problem. He was definitely seeing a ghost, and the mere sight of it would make him terrified. He told me the same basic story several times without offering any clue as to how he got himself into this state. Finally, I decided to do a little investigation. I asked him to go to town to buy some fruits for us, knowing that this was an errand that would keep him away from the house for about two hours. While he was away I went through his bags to see if he was carrying any clues with him.

At the bottom of his bag, wrapped carefully in a silk cloth, was a photo of a young girl and what looked like a wedding ring. It was made of gold and had a diamond set in it. I had asked him many questions about his personal life, hoping to get some information about his problem, but he had never once mentioned a girl like this. I decided that this girl must somehow be connected with the problem.

Next time we talked about his trouble I asked him whom he thought the ghost might be. Could she be an ex-wife or an ex-girlfriend? He said he didn't know. I also asked whether he was married or whether he was living with his girlfriend. He said he was married, but when I asked him to talk a little about his wife, I realised she could not be the woman whose picture was in his bag. Eventually, when I realised I wasn't going to get him to talk about the mystery woman, I took the photo from his bag when he wasn't looking, showed it to him and asked who she was.

'I am sorry to do this,' I said. 'I tried to search your mind, but you wouldn't let me in, so I had to search your bag instead. I think that this is your ghost. Why don't you tell me who she is?'

Faced with the picture, he finally admitted that this was the girl who was haunting him. It was his first wife. Many years ago he had killed her while they were on a camping trip together because he had fallen in love with another woman. He had put poison in her coffee and disposed of her body in the river. He covered up his tracks quite well, for he was able to persuade all her friends, her relatives and even the police that she had just disappeared without trace. Images of the woman had been haunting him ever since. He had never admitted to anyone before that this girl was the ghost who was giving him so much trouble.

I could see that he was ready to put down his burden.

'It's time to give her up,' I said. 'Bring the picture and the ring down to the edge of the river and we will conduct a proper funeral service for her.'

I gave him some flowers to offer to the river and I told him to ask the ghost of his dead wife for forgiveness. After this brief ceremony I suggested that he sit quietly for half an hour, during which time he should meditate on the soul of the departed one.

'Wish her well,' I said, 'and send her on her journey. She is probably just as tired of you as you are of her. It's time for her to move on. Send her off with love and affection.'

At the end of the thirty minutes I asked him to throw the ring and the photo in the river. This was the real test. If he did it willingly and happily, it would mean that he had exorcised his own ghost. He threw them in the river without a moment's hesitation. He spent the next six months with me and when he went back to America he was completely cured. He wrote to me that he was living happily with his second wife and a daughter from the second marriage.

It is not good to carry heavy burdens like this. Guilty secrets can poison the heart and the mind. It is better to admit what one has done, apologise, take the consequences and move on. Carrying stories from the past like this just makes the mind sick.

Other people have come to me with minds that were just as sick. One Canadian boy was sent to me by a missionary in the late 1960s. He was about nineteen years old but his mind and his body had already been destroyed by drugs and excessive sex. When he told me how he had been living, I found it hard to believe that someone so young could destroy himself so completely by leading such a degenerate life. Someone had suggested that he spend time with me as a last resort because it looked as if he was heading for an early death. Young people are usually full of vitality but this boy looked completely drained. He had been deliberately destroying himself because I think he had a perverse inner desire to die. He actually told me that he had contemplated suicide on several occasions. I saw him regularly for a few weeks but he always seemed listless and lethargic. He didn't want to do anything, and sometimes he didn't even want to eat. His body was run down and he suffered from bouts of depression.

The boy wanted to end his old habits because he could see what was happening in his life, but there wasn't much I could do for him. What he needed was a healthy, wholesome lifestyle, good company and lots of physical exercise. I suggested that he go to work for Mother Theresa in Calcutta for a while, but he didn't think she would accept him. In those days she was hardly known outside India. I sent him off there with a letter of recommendation and she took him in, even though he looked very disreputable. He wrote to me a few weeks later, saying that he was happy to be involved with the work there.

The American psychiatrist and the Canadian boy had brought about their own troubles by behaving irresponsibly. Other sick people I met were victims of others' misdeeds. One girl came to see me after hearing about me in the Burmese Vihar in Bodh Gaya. She was a Buddhist and had spent a lot of time meditating in Thailand and Bodh Gaya. Though she was very sincere and meditated a lot, there was something about her mind that didn't seem quite right. I sensed a lot of fear and unhappiness in her that she wasn't willing to talk about. I eventually found out her story from a Frenchwoman who had stayed with her in Hong Kong and become very friendly with her.

When this girl was about thirteen years old she had asked her mother, 'Why don't I look like you? I am blonde and fair-skinned, but both you and daddy have black hair and a darker complexion.'

Her mother decided it was time to tell her the truth. 'We adopted you when you were a baby. Nobody knows who your mother was. The adoption agency told us that you had been left by the side of the street in a plastic bag. We have been looking after you since you were a few months old.'

This proved to be a very traumatic revelation for her. She began to feel unwanted and unloved and eventually ran away from her adopted parents, even though they were looking after her well. She sought refuge in Buddhism and ended up meditating for hours and hours every day. Her meditation blocked out the painful memories but it didn't cure the underlying problem. She needed love and affection and she needed to feel that the people around her cared and wanted her.

Her mind was injured. It couldn't open to me at first because she felt that she had been deprived of the love of her real parents. Her background and her obsessive thoughts about it were making her mentally ill. This kind of problem is not uncommon in the West. I have visited many countries and talked to thousands of seekers about their pasts. I am continually astounded by the numbers of westerners who tell me stories of the parental abuse they have suffered. It seems that one has to be lucky to be born into a good, loving family in the West.

On her second visit I made her live a more social life. Instead of letting her hide in her meditation, I kept her busy for most of the day. We went swimming in the Ganga together and I took her for long walks in the forest. I encouraged her to talk about her past in a relaxed way because I didn't want her to feel that it was a guilty secret that she should hide. The love and affection she received over those few weeks did more for her well-being than all her hours of forced meditation.

When she left she was in good shape. I told her, 'You don't need to carry the past around with you. It's not your business. Your mother behaved badly when she abandoned you, and for that she will have to suffer one day. But that is not your business any more. We have a tradition in India which says that if you attain liberation, the past generations of your family are blessed, wherever they may be. Instead of having antagonistic feelings towards your mother, bless her with your own enlightenment. She probably needs help just as much as you did when you came here.'

I am by nature a happy man, and I like to see people being happy around me. Most of the people I encounter, even the ones who are seriously striving for freedom, know how to laugh and enjoy themselves, but a few people I encounter are incorrigibly humourless. Nothing I do or say ever brings a smile to their face. I met several people like this in the years I lived in Rishikesh.

One man like this was from Mill Valley, California. He came especially to see me, so I took him around Rishikesh to show him the important places. I was in high spirits that day and thoroughly enjoyed all the sights that nature had to offer. I pointed out all the things I thought might interest him and explained some of the local customs so that he could understand some of the things that were going on around him. When you visit a new country, the activities of the people there are always entertaining and amusing, but this man remained sombre and serious throughout the walk. We ended up sitting by the banks of the Ganga. The lapping of the waves and the chirping of the birds induced such a feeling of well-being in me, I began to laugh. My companion clearly found my behaviour to be very odd, although he was too polite to say so.

After some time I turned to him and asked, 'Why are you so serious all the time? You are wearing a dead man's face. It looks so fixed and rigid, I don't think you could smile or laugh even if you wanted to.'

'You Indians can laugh for no reason,' he said, 'and nobody will do anything about it. In America, the kind of behaviour you have exhibited today would not be tolerated. If people sit in public places and start laughing for no reason at all, a policeman will come. People who behave like you run the risk of being carried off to the nearest mental hospital.'

He said this with a totally straight face. He probably thought that such people deserved to be locked up.

On another occasion I took a professor from Paris on a tour of Rishikesh. He also seemed to be a very serious man, but with him it was more a facade.

'Michel,' I said to him, 'you seem to be a very serious man. It's a nice day. We are sitting here by the Ganga and nature is putting on a wonderful show for us. The fish are jumping and the

---

101

birds are singing. Doesn't it all make you feel happy and peaceful? And if it does, why don't you show it a little more?'

Rather sadly he replied, 'I had to learn to be serious in order to do my job properly. I am a professor of philosophy. If I stood up in front of my students and laughed and giggled the way you have done today, who would take my lessons seriously? Philosophy is supposed to be a serious subject, so I have to look serious when I stand up and talk about it.'

'But I'm not your student,' I said. 'You can relax with me and show what you really feel.'

'It's hard,' he admitted. 'In our society we are conditioned to be serious for most of the time. Right from our childhood, if we don't behave in a serious way, our parents and elders tell us off for being too frivolous. We may be laughing inside, but we can't show it because somebody will always be on hand to criticise us. So we pretend, but after a while this habit of seriousness becomes so ingrained, we cannot stop it in order to relax and show our real character. We become imprisoned in this image that society expects of us. I think this has happened to me as well. Sometimes a desire comes up to express my joy and happiness in an extroverted way, but the ideas of acceptable behaviour that my society imposes on me prevent me from even trying. I think there are many people like me in the West. We all need to stay serious in order to keep our jobs and the approval of the people around us.'

Most of the stories I have so far told in this chapter have been about the foreigners Papaji encountered in Rishikesh or Hardwar. He was not neglecting his old devotees during this period, for he still periodically visited Londa, Bombay and Lucknow to see them, and they in turn occasionally visited him in Hardwar. The next story is about an ill-fated expedition that Papaji embarked on with a group of his Indian devotees. Papaji's earlier meetings with some of the members of this group were narrated in the previous chapter.

Some of my devotees from the South wanted to go on a pilgrimage with me to Badrinath. They had told me several times that they wanted to go on this trip with me because they wanted to see some of India's sacred places in the company of their Guru. I eventually agreed to go with them. Apart from myself, there were five others. One was Narayan Bakre, a doctor from Londa; another was a forest contractor from Belgaum; a third was a teacher; the fourth, B. D. Desai, worked in the accounts department of the Taj Hotel in Bombay; and the fifth, Kamlani, ran the canteen at the Londa railway station.

We travelled together from Karnataka to Hardwar, the place where all the buses leave for the pilgrimage centres in the Himalayas. It was the height of the tourist season and we couldn't get reservations on any bus for seven days. It didn't matter. We had plenty of time and there were lots of places to see in Hardwar and Rishikesh. During the week we bought all the things that we thought would be necessary for a trip to Badrinath. We needed a lot because we were also planning some side trips to neighbouring places such as the Valley of Flowers. The altitude in some of these places is over 5,000 metres so we made sure we had good boots, coats, umbrellas, etc. We also procured a large supply of non-perishable food because we knew that eating places were few and far between in the places we were intending to go. The doctor who was travelling with us bought special medicines which he said would be useful if any of us suffered from altitude sickness.

On the appointed day we assembled at the bus stand, tied all our bags to the roof and took our reserved seats. After a few minutes I announced to everyone, 'We are not going to Badrinath. Everybody get off the bus. We are staying here.'

The others were shocked. They had spent a week waiting for this bus, and within a few minutes of its departure I was telling them that I didn't want any of us to go on the trip.

They all wanted to know why, but I wouldn't give them any reason. I ordered the whole party to get off the bus and remove the bags from the roof. All the other people on the bus wanted to know why we were leaving, but I wouldn't give them any reasons either.

A *sadhu* wearing orange robes asked one member of our party why we were getting off and he replied, 'He is our Guru. We have all come on a pilgrimage with him from South India. We were planning to go to Badrinath with him, but now he has ordered us off the bus, saying that we are not going to go there. We have been waiting a week for this bus, but now he says we cannot leave on it.'

This swami, who had a long beard, said, 'Don't believe him, he's a lunatic! What kind of Guru would prevent you from going to a holy place like Badrinath? He's not a Guru, he's a fraud! Don't listen to him. Get back on the bus and ignore what he is saying.'

To make sure that none of my party went back on the bus, I handed in our tickets to the conductor and got a refund. He immediately resold them to some other people who were waiting nearby in the hope that there would be a last-minute cancellation.

Three of the five were happy to abide by my decision, but the doctor and the teacher still wanted to go. They had come a long way and they were disappointed to have their long-awaited pilgrimage cancelled at the last minute.

Seeing their disappointment, I proposed an alternative trip.

'Let's go to Kashmir instead. We can go to the Vaishno Devi Temple. We can also go and see the ice *lingam* in the Amarnath Cave.'

The Vaishno Devi Temple is one of the richest in India. On big festival days hundreds of thousands of people go there on pilgrimage. The ice *lingam* at Amarnath is equally famous. Situated in a cave high up in the Himalayas, it is a naturally formed *lingam*. In August every year, tens of thousands of people make an arduous trek to the cave to have *darshan* of the *lingam*. It is a walk of several days that ends at a height of about 12,000 feet.

We began to journey by train. At Amritsar two of the boys got down, saying that they wanted to have a cup of tea on the platform. Actually, they wanted to have a smoke but they didn't like to smoke in front of me. One of them bought a newspaper, *The Tribune*, and immediately found a story about a bus crash. It was the bus that we had been booked on. Forty miles out of Hardwar it had fallen into the Ganga, killing the thirty-eight people who were on board. Some of the group were still complaining about the cancelled trip to Badrinath, but when they read the newspaper, they suddenly got very quiet and didn't mention the subject again.

The next leg of the journey was by bus to a place called Katra. From there we had to walk up a steep mountain to get to the temple. We had *darshan* and then began the long journey back to Jammu. The return journey was a difficult one because it had been raining heavily and the road was in a bad state of repair. We had several narrow escapes.

At times it was so bad, one of the boys in our group started complaining, 'You have saved us from one bus crash, but now we are going to die in another!'

When we arrived at our destination, we discovered that the route we had travelled on was officially closed to buses. The government had banned bus traffic on the road until repairs had been made, but our driver ignored the ban and delivered us to our destination. These close encounters with death dampened the enthusiasm of our group for more adventures in high places. We decided not to go on the Amarnath pilgrimage because we were not equipped to camp out at high altitudes for several days. Instead, I proposed a trip to Varanasi and Chitrakoot.

This cancellation may have averted another disaster. That year, because of the exceptionally bad weather, forty pilgrims perished on the Amarnath pilgrimage.

Papaji continues with his account:

The boys in our group had already written to their families, saying that we were leaving for Badrinath on the day of the bus crash. As soon as the story was shown to me, I made them all write new letters informing everyone that we were all safe. The letters did not arrive in time. When I eventually got back to Lucknow, there was a big pile of telegrams awaiting me, all sent by relatives of the people who went with me. During our absence the relatives of our group had been ringing up my house every day, asking for news, but no one knew where we were. Many of them knew that we were scheduled to travel on the bus that crashed, but we were unable to get news to them for several days.

The bus crash took place in August, 1969. Papaji briefly

mentioned the incident in a letter he wrote to Swami Abhishiktananda after his return to Lucknow:

4th September, 1969
Lucknow

My dear friend,
I got your letter of 31st August. We had reserved our seats in a bus for Badrinath on 5th August. There were five others from Bombay who came along with me from Mysore. My inner voice forbade me to go by that bus as it was going to meet with an accident. I therefore cancelled the trip and instead went to Kashmir the same day.

The next day at Amritsar we read in the papers that the bus met with a fatal accident in which all thirty-eight pilgrims on board died.

In 1995 I spoke to Sri B. D. Desai about his recollections of this trip. He confirmed the version given by Papaji and added a few extra, interesting details.

The trip back from the Vaishno Devi Temple was a nightmare for everyone except Papaji because heavy rains had washed away portions of the mountain road. Even as we were driving along we could see the torrential rains eroding and washing away the road that we had to drive on. At times we were skidding on wet mud on the edge of vertical drops that went down hundreds of feet. At one time some of the wheels were hanging off the edge of the road. Papaji was the only one who seemed to be unconcerned. Whenever it looked as if we were going to plunge to our death, he would reassure us and tell us not to worry. By then I knew that he had already saved us from death once, so I had a strong faith that he would not allow us all to perish.

In his letter to Abhishiktananda Papaji claimed that it was an 'inner voice' that told him to cancel the trip to Badrinath. When I asked Sri Desai what he had said at the time, he told me that Papaji had been more explicit:

'He definitely said that it was a devi *[female celestial being]*

who appeared to him and told him to cancel the trip. She also told him that we should go to the Vaishno Devi Temple instead.'

I overheard Papaji and Sri Desai reminiscing about this incident on one of the latter's recent visits to Lucknow. On that occasion Papaji also agreed that it was a devi *who had given him the message.*

There is a tradition in India that a Guru can take away some of the karma of his devotees. That is to say, if a devotee is destined to have a serious accident, the presence or grace of his Guru can mitigate it to some extent. The karma still has to bear fruit, but it will manifest in a less severe way. Papaji no longer believes that he takes on the karma of his devotees, although he did have this idea for much of his teaching career. He does admit though, that the men in the group were destined to die in this bus crash, and he also admits that the accidents that several of them had shortly afterwards were karmic manifestations of the same destiny.

I was happy that they all returned to their families safe and sound, for I knew that all of them should have died in that bus crash. Because of this I was certain that they would have to face other accidents instead

The accidents started even before the trip was over.

After we had all had *darshan* of the deity at the Vaishno Devi Temple, we had to walk back to Katra, the village at the base of the mountain where pilgrims begin their final walking ascent. One of the boys, Dr Narayan Bakre from Londa, was still angry with me for cancelling the trip to Badrinath. He came on the trip with the intention of going to Badrinath, Kedarnath, Gangotri and Yamunotri, but in the end we visited none of these places. Because he was still angry, he didn't want to walk back with us on the normal route. Instead he said he would come back via a different path that had a reputation for being both narrow and dangerous. The other five of us took the usual path. At Katra we had to wait several hours for Dr Bakre to appear. During that time I got very anxious because I knew that something must have happened to him to cause him to be so late.

When he finally appeared, he ignored me and instead told his story to Sri Kamlani, the member of our party who ran a railway canteen .

'It was raining hard and the ground was wet and slippery. I fell off a narrow path into a deep valley. I thought I was falling to my death, but on the way down my foot caught in a tree. It broke my fall, but it also trapped my leg. I was suspended upside down in this tree for more than an hour. I shouted for help and eventually a party of returning pilgrims heard my cries and arranged a rescue. They criticised me very strongly for walking alone on this path. Its dangers are apparently well known to all the regular pilgrims.'

The drive from Katra to Jammu nearly resulted in another fatal crash. I was sitting on the side of the bus nearest the valley. At one point the tyres on my side of the bus slipped off the road and hung over a precipice. The driver very cautiously backed up and managed to get the bus back on the road. There were landslides everywhere and we only found out later that the road had been declared unfit for buses.

At Jammu Sri Desai came down with a high fever. He was in no condition to travel any further, so I sent him back to his family in Bombay. The rest of us went on to Varanasi, Allahabad and Chitrakoot. After some time I sent them back to their families, hoping that they would all be safe, but fearing that some of them still had accidents to come.

Dr Narayan wrote to me later to say that he had broken his leg in a motorbike accident, and Sri Kamlani reported soon afterwards that he was bedridden with a severe case of typhoid.

During all the years he spent in Rishikesh and Hardwar Papaji never had a place of his own. He either lived in ashrams, dharamsalas, *rented rooms or caves. Judging by the number of times he went to them, his favourite places to stay seemed to be Swarg Ashram, Vitthal Ashram, Dullichand Bhatia Bhavan, Arya Nivas and Sapt Sarovar Ashram. The last-named place, located just north of Hardwar, had been built by a man from Papaji's home town, so he was always welcome there.*

---

*Since Papaji never had a place of his own, he was never able
to accommodate the many visitors who came to see him. They
would have to make their own arrangements in nearby ashrams or
hotels. From the early 1970s onwards many of Papaji's Indian
devotees tried to persuade him to get a place of his own where
visitors could be accommodated. Though Papaji occasionally
showed interest in some of these schemes, none of them ever
materialised.*

*The following letters, written to Sri B. D. Desai in 1971 and
1972, indicate that Papaji seemed at one time to be definitely interested in having a place of his own:*

Though I am not interested to have such a big piece of land,
or have any such establishment, yet I am in favour of having some
small place, enough to make four to five rooms for a few very good
seekers who have one thought, one goal and one aim: to stay
together for a few days in a year in seclusion and to speak to each
other for mutual emancipation. I will let you know if I can find a
smaller plot than the one previously discussed so that we do not
have to approach anyone for money....

I am in search of a house that I will get on rent for six months.
Later, I will try to get a plot and build a few rooms on it. It will be
good for all of you to come here and stay as long as you choose. I
prefer the place outside the town [of Hardwar] near Kankhal. I
want your advice in this matter.... I am reading Tukaram's verses
and Eknath *Bhagwat* at the banks of Ganga every morning....

Please contact Mr Chitnis if he is still in Bombay and find out
more details from him about the land you mention in your letter. It
is better to have some place in Rishikesh where we can all meet
every year. In case he has left for Rishikesh, please give him my
address. Make more enquiries and even send someone to see the
place. Even though we don't need much land, if we get a forest
area, it can be acquired at a cheap price. Please find from him the
cost of it. My devotees could also share the cost if you take an
interest....

This is to inform you that I am leaving here [Lucknow] for Rishikesh to see the land you referred to. In case the plot is suitable I shall inform you and I will even stay there to complete the construction. I will rent a house at Rishikesh as I want to shift my parents so that they can stay permanently in Rishikesh on the banks of the Ganga till the end of their lives....

The planned purchase never happened. When Papaji's father died and Papaji himself accepted an invitation to travel to the West, the scheme was abandoned. During his absence from India another group of devotees from India launched a new project to find Papaji a permanent place in either Hardwar or Rishikesh. The following letter was circulated to all Papaji's Indian devotees:

Bombay

As has been brought to your kind notice already, a few devotees of our Master Sri Poonjaji Maharaj are humbly aspiring to establish a small living place for our beloved Master, in view of the fact that Master's health has been deteriorating and that He wishes to spend most of His days on the Holy banks of Mother Ganga.

It is also hoped that by having a common place of our own, we, the blessed servants of His Feet can meet Him at the place He likes most and that we can serve His Feet and also have the unparalleled company of Gangamata [Mother Ganga] and Himalayas, at a place of OUR OWN.

As you are aware, Master has never sanctioned the establishment of an Ashram so far. Not that He has suggested it now, but it is considering the urgent need for the Ashram due to reasons mentioned above, that we have sought to come out with a humble plan of having an ASHRAM of our own – that too at the foot of the Himalayas and at the banks of Gangamata [Mother Ganga]. Fortunately, the merciful Master has shown interest in a scheme and we are sure about His blessings on the venture.

In this connection, two of Master's staunchest devotees, one Sri K. K. Sharmaji and one Sri Phoolsinghji from Delhi, have, in association with one Sri Sitaram Panditji of Hardwar, been keenly looking for a place. One place called Muktidham, behind SWARGASHRAM at Rishikesh was seen by many of us and considered as the most suitable one. But it has now been observed that a bit of complication is foreseen in acquiring this site. Later, Sri Panditji, who stays at those places, considered a beautiful bungalow called NEELADHARA at Hardwar. Sri Panditji now informs that this place too may not come to our lot for certain reasons.

After describing the size and location of all the possible plots, along with the legal complications associated with each one, the letter continued:

Anyway, it is better to wait for the arrival of Rev. Masterji to seek his opinion and choice. For the time being, even if He comes with the foreign brethren, good arrangements are made, where He and the foreign devotees can stay peacefully, for 5-6 months till our premises take ground. Everything has been written to Him in detail....

Ever at His Holy Feet
Sitaram Pandit

Sitaram Pandit was a devotee from Goa who made regular trips to Rishikesh to an ashram called Sadhana Sadan. After a profound experience in Papaji's presence, he started this scheme to find a permanent place for Papaji. Like all other projects of its kind, it fell through.
Papaji himself has spoken of one other offer to provide him with a permanent place to stay:

I was once offered a cottage on the banks of the Ganga, along with a garden and a small house. They belonged to a Calcutta industrialist.

This man called me one day and said, 'I am an old man now. I want to go and stay with my sons. I want to put this property in your name.'

111

He also offered me a cook, two cows, and a man to look after them. I rejected this offer also.

So far as I have been able to ascertain, Papaji has never owned a building or a piece of land since his arrival in Lucknow in 1947. Prior to this, he was a part owner of the joint family property in the Punjab, but this was confiscated by the Pakistani government after Partition.

When I spoke to Meera about all the various schemes to build ashrams for him, she made the following comments:

In the 1970s plans like this would come up almost every year. Master would appear to play with the idea for a few weeks, but after some time he would lose interest and the plan would be dropped. I saw it happen so many times, I eventually came to the conclusion that he didn't really want a place at all.

Papaji confirmed this in an answer he gave in 1992 in response to a faxed invitation to visit Germany.

I was invited to Germany many years ago. As soon as I arrived someone tried to buy a house and start an ashram for me. I turned down the offer by saying, 'All this universe is my ashram! Its roof is the sky, the floor is this earth and the walls are this space! Will you buy this for me? If so, then I will surely accept.'

I have no desire for an ashram. I want peace and love for all beings in this world. There are no other desires. I am not interested in having an ashram. I am eighty years old. What would I do with an ashram now? People have offered me houses, ashrams, even islands. I was once offered a whole island. I don't want to be tied down to one place. All my life I have always taken my teachings from door to door. I have never really been interested in having a permanent place. I went to the people who needed me. They did not have to come looking for me.

During his many years in Rishikesh and Hardwar Papaji's dislike of ashrams was heightened by the experiences he had at the many spiritual centres in these two towns. He has a uniformly low opinion of all of them and makes no attempt to hide his contempt. I have heard him say on many occasions that the ashrams there are run by unenlightened businessmen who make their money selling fake spirituality to a credulous public.

On my first trip to Hardwar with him in 1993 he showed me a few places, without giving any information about them.

At the first one, when I asked, 'What goes on here?' he snorted in disgust.

'It's a honeymoon centre! Nice garden, nice rooms, good food and a beautiful view of the Ganga. What more does a couple need?'

At each place we stopped he made equally negative comments either about the head of the institution, or the way it was funded. I soon realised that it was his intention to show me how corrupt and spiritually bankrupt these places were.

In an earlier part of this chapter Papaji told the story of how a Brazilian girl got herself trapped in the ashram of a swami who took her money and forbade her from visiting other swamis. Papaji knew this man very well. When he talks about the fake swamis and the way they cheat their devotees, this man is often the first to spring into his mind.

In the early 1970s I often stayed at Ved Niketan Ashram. The swami in charge was a clever man who knew how to milk the maximum amount of money from his visitors. One of his former devotees told me that he had been a poor *jalebi* [sweet] maker in Aligarh and had switched to the swami business because it needed no work at all and produced much higher profits.

Many rich people come to Hardwar or Rishikesh with thousands of rupees in cash, hoping to earn some *punya* [spiritual merit] by donating it to a worthy cause. People who watch every *paisa* at home and at work come to Hardwar and spread their money around indiscriminately. Many swamis get rich by collecting money from such people.

One day a couple came to Ved Niketan and handed over a large package that obviously contained money. The swami asked me to count it for him. There were Rs 50,000 in the package. The swami was a little surprised because he had never met them before. After finding out how much money there was, he took me aside and asked me to look after them while they were in his ashram.

'Put them in the best room. Find out everything you can about them. They might have met me before somewhere, but if so, I have forgotten all about it. If I have met them before, and they start talking about what happened, it will be embarrassing for me if I have no idea who they are. I must have made a good impression on them at some time, otherwise they would not be giving me so much money.'

As I took them to their room, I started a conversation with them. I asked how long they had known the swami and they surprised me by saying that they had never met him before.

'So why did you walk in and give him Rs 50,000?' I asked. This was strange behaviour, even by Hardwar standards. The explanation they gave was quite interesting.

'We came here because we wanted to make a donation that would benefit the *sadhus* and pilgrims who visit Rishikesh. We went to Swarg Ashram first and noticed that *bhiksha* was being given to a long line of *sadhus*. That ashram is very well off. They have many rooms there and they have built *dharamsalas* on the main pilgrim routes to Badrinath, Gangotri and Yamunotri. We thought, "They don't need our money. They have plenty of their own."

'Next we went to Gita Bhavan, looked around and made some enquiries about what was going on there. They are publishing books, they run a large canteen, and they sell food to pilgrims at cost price. Their Gita Press is so well supported, they either sell their books at cost price or give them away for nothing. It looked like a well-managed place with lots of funds, so we decided they didn't need our money either.

'We checked out a few other places and found the same story everywhere. At Parmarth Niketan we found that they already have facilities to house thousands of people. They have a free dispensary and sell cheap milk to pilgrims. All this costs a lot of money, so somebody must already be supporting them in a big way. At the Sadhana Sadan we were told that they didn't even want donations. Someone there said, "We are supported by wealthy people from Delhi, so we don't need to take money from people who are passing through".

'Finally, we found this place. It looks very poor and run down. The walls and the roofs of some of the buildings have not even been completed, and I don't see any workers there. You must have run out of money before the building was finished. We both feel that this is the right place to give our money. We are giving this money because we want you to use it to finish your ashram.'

I went back to the swami's office and told him the full story. He was a smart man and he immediately realised that there was money to be made out of a half-completed ashram. He kept his ashram the way it was and spread the word that he needed funds to complete all his buildings. Over the next few months a succession of rich visitors came and donated money to complete the building work. He pocketed all the donations and the ashram stayed just the way it was.

Meanwhile, he decided that he could probably extract even more money from this couple. He called them to his office, thanked them very warmly and initiated them with a mantra.

Then he said, 'This money you have so generously donated will be used to construct ashram rooms. This is a very meritorious act that you have performed. However, you could get even more merit by performing a *pada puja* to me and offering *bhandara* [the act of feeding many people to honour a sage] in the traditional way. To do this properly you must invite 500 *sadhus* and give Rs 5 to each one of them. Then, since it is a *pada puja* to the guru, you also have to give *guru dakshina* [a gift of money to the guru]. In this case Rs 11,000 would be most appropriate. We can make all the arrangements here. If you give the money to my secretary, we will see that everything is done in the proper way.'

The couple handed over another Rs 13,500 without a word of protest. The *bhandara* was fixed for the following Friday. The swami asked me to deliver the invitations, but he only gave me fifty invitation cards. All of them went to swamis in the nearby ashrams. On the day of the feeding only forty of them turned up.

The swami explained to the couple that the 500 swamis were not coming in person. Representatives from each ashram, he said, had come and these people would carry all the food back to the *sadhus* in their respective ashrams. Only small amounts of food were dispatched and the swami made a large profit out of the meal. He even got away with charging Rs 21 a head to the swamis who showed up to collect food.

Seeing that the couple had still not made any complaint, the swami told them, 'What you have done so far is very good, but there is one more ceremony that you have to complete. Once you have done it you will definitely be assured of great happiness and good fortune. At the conclusion of a ceremony like this, you have to give *gupta daan* [an anonymous charitable donation]. You must put money in a bag and offer it secretly. Even I must not know how much is in the bag. It will go in our collection box anonymously.'

The couple obligingly went back to their room, filled a bag with rupee notes and dropped it in the ashram's donation box. During the lunch that followed the swami made an excuse to leave the room, raced off to count the money and discovered that he had made another Rs 25,000 out of them. He locked up the bag in his safe before returning to his lunch.

During the meal he said, 'I don't know what you have given but I am sure that it will bestow great blessings on you. Your life will be successful and after death you will be reunited in the heavens. To mark your great acts of charity I will construct a bench by the Ganga with your name on it. Pilgrims who bathe in the Ganga can rest there or leave their clothes on it while they bathe.'

This was the only expenditure the swami ever made with their money. He put up the bench and made an inscription which stated that it had been donated by Sri and Smt Govind Dass of Jayapur. The rest of the money went into his pocket.

The swami knew that pilgrims like to see their names inscribed on plaques, especially those which identify charitable donations. He made a very good business out of this. When people came to donate money to complete his half-finished ashram, he would accept their gift and have a plaque made with their names on it. The plaque would be prominently displayed for the duration of their stay, but as soon as they left it would be taken down. The swami didn't want prospective new donors to think that funds had already been donated. When the donors wrote to him to say that they were making another trip to Rishikesh, he would pull out their plaque and display it prominently. If these visitors arrived unexpectedly and wanted to know where their plaque was, he had an ingenious explanation for them. I saw him give it to a family from Delhi who had given Rs 2,000 the previous year to have a room constructed in the ashram.

'Officials from the Income Tax Department have been raiding the ashrams here in Rishikesh. They have been taking down the names and addresses of all the people who have made big donations. They send the names to the tax officials of the donors' home towns so that their income can be investigated. As soon as I heard what was happening, I rushed out and took your plaque down. You were lucky. Many rich people who gave money to other ashrams have been caught.'

The family he had cheated actually thanked him for being so clever. Over the years he collected money to have many rooms built, far more than were actually constructed, but all the donors had plaques, and whenever they came, their name would go up on one of the rooms.

What was he doing with all this money? I don't really know but I was told by someone who had known him for many years that he had a wife and three sons in Aligarh who farmed land there. He apparently sent a lot of the money to his farm to help run the family business. His wife often came to visit him, posing as a devotee. No one ever found out she was his wife.

Papaji knew about the antics of this swami because for some time he was working there as a kind of unpaid secretary. I asked Meera about this.

Yes, we were both staying in Ved Niketan Ashram for some time, and Master was doing all kinds of jobs for the swami. I felt very bad about this. We all knew what a rogue the swami was, yet Master was writing his letters, delivering his messages and even

driving him around in the swami's car. I think the swami was illiterate, so he couldn't write letters himself. All Master's devotees
wondered why he was acting as a kind of servant because everyone
knew how unspiritual and dishonest the swami was. At one time
Master even wanted me to prostrate to the swami to keep his ego
happy, but I drew the line at this.

I said, 'He is not my Master. I would rather prostrate to the
donkeys on the street.'

Master laughed and didn't insist. From then on, we were all
calling him 'Donkey Swami'.

I think Master was being entertained by the swami's outrageous and overt swindles. He has always liked colourful, eccentric
people and he seems to derive a lot of amusement from their antics.
I was often amazed at the company he kept and the kind of people
he liked to have around him. Stoned hippies, certifiable lunatics
and all kinds of cheats and thieves could find themselves
temporarily welcome in his company. One never knew whom he
would accept and whom he would reject.

As for this swami, I think Master actually enjoyed watching
him think up novel ways to deprive people of their money. He
didn't have much sympathy for the wealthy donors who got
cheated. I think he regarded them as undiscriminating fools who
deserved to lose their money.

Incidentally, Master cured me of hepatitis while I was staying
in this ashram. I contracted a bad case and at one point I thought I
might even die. I was yellow all over and I didn't even have the
strength to sit up in bed. When Master came to see me, I told him
how sick I was and how I thought I might even die.

'Nonsense!' he exclaimed, 'There's nothing wrong with you.
Get out of bed and come with me.'

He pulled me out of bed, took me to the nearest *paan* shop and
made me eat a banana and a leaf with some lime paste on it. Within
a few minutes all my symptoms went away. I had resigned myself
to having a few weeks in bed, the standard treatment for hepatitis,
but after this *paan*-shop cure I never had any more trouble from the
disease.

Though Papaji had a low opinion of all the swamis and gurus in Rishikesh, he was outwardly polite and friendly towards them. When he showed visitors around, he would often take them to the various ashrams where satsangs, lectures, recitations, bhajans, etc. were going on. Usually he would sit through the programme without commenting or interrupting in any way. These are Meera's comments:

If some famous saint or teacher came to town, he would always be interested enough to go and have a look. He had no desire to interact with them; he just seemed to want to have a good look at them. Ananda Mayi Ma was probably the most famous teacher in Hardwar in the years we were there. Master took me along to see her, and I know he took several other people who wanted to have her *darshan*. There was always a long line of people waiting to see her. Master would wait patiently in the queue and then stand silently in her presence. It was the same with all the other teachers he went to see. He would look at them in silence and then leave without introducing himself. Once he was back home, he might make a few uncomplimentary comments about whomever he had just seen, but while he was in his or her presence, he made a point of being quiet.

On one occasion, though, Papaji was persuaded by one of his devotees to ask a question at a lecture he was attending. Papaji himself explains how it happened:

I once went from Lucknow to Rishikesh to stay for one month. Sri Mittal, a friend of mine from Lucknow, came with me. It was the time of Guru Purnima, so all the ashrams were conducting satsangs to try to attract the maximum number of people. They all wanted to demonstrate the greatness of their respective *mahatmas*.

The Swarg Ashram Trust was conducting public readings of the *Ramayana*. The Gita Bhavan and Parmarth Niketan ashrams were competing by having recitations from the *Bhagavad Gita* and the *Srimad Bhagavatam.*

My friend and I went to the recitation of the *Bhagavad Gita* in the Gita Bhavan ashram. It was being held in their upstairs hall. The recitation had not begun when we entered. Instead, a man called Swami Purnananda was answering spiritual questions from members of the audience. Though he was a famous scholar and had a reputation for being a great saint, he was a very bad-tempered man. If people in the audience did not understand his answers, he immediately got very angry with them. My friend did not like to see him behave like this, so he asked me to ask him a question which he couldn't answer.

I didn't want to provoke him, so I just stood up and asked, very humbly, 'Swamiji, I have a question. Based on your own experience, can you tell me how a person behaves when he becomes a *jivanmukta* [liberated while still alive]? What is the behaviour of such a person?'

The swami was very quiet for a while, but then he said, 'I can't answer that question. I am not a *jivanmukta* myself, so I have no direct experience.'

My friend and I were both very happy to hear this answer because he spoke the truth. Though he was proud of his spiritual learning, he was honest enough to confess in public that he had not attained enlightenment. Standing there in front of thousands of people, he had a big reputation to protect because he was a well-known spiritual teacher. He could easily have given some answer from the scriptures to show off his knowledge. Instead, he was humble enough to say that he was not qualified to give an author-itative answer.

Om Prakash Syal, whose first meeting with Papaji was described earlier in this chapter, remembers two occasions when Papaji took him to see swamis. The first was on the outskirts of Lucknow and the second was in Hardwar.

When Papaji was in Lucknow he enjoyed going out on little expeditions to old devotees or to different parts of the city. On many occasions he invited me to go with him. One such trip, which took place over twenty years ago, brought me out to the area where

Satsang Bhavan is now located. In the early 1970s, the place that is now called Indira Nagar didn't exist. It was an area of agricultural land, not a suburb. The Bhutnath Temple was there, and it had a few shops surrounding it, but it was a small island of buildings in a sea of green fields.

The Bhutnath Temple was occupied by a *sadhu* who was well known all over Lucknow for his ability to materialise objects in much the same way that Sathya Sai Baba does nowadays. Several of Papaji's devotees had mentioned the *sadhu* in Papaji's presence, and these reports had aroused his curiosity a little.

One day Papaji said to me, 'Om Prakash, let's go and see this famous *baba* today. Let us see what he is really like.'

We travelled by rickshaw because there was no other public transport to Bhutnath in those days. The *baba*, who had heard that Papaji was a spiritual teacher himself, greeted us cordially and gave us a special seat in front of him. When everyone was ready, the *baba* gave us a demonstration of his powers. He held his hand out in front of us with the palm facing upwards. He wanted us to see that there was nothing on it. Then he closed his hand into a fist and blew across the top of his fingers. With a smile on his face he slowly uncurled his fingers and revealed some cloves and cardamoms that were resting on his palm. So far as I was concerned, it didn't look like a conjurer's trick. The hand was outstretched and in front of our faces for the whole of the performance. I don't see how he could have introduced anything into his clenched fist without our noticing it.

The *baba* offered the cardamoms and cloves to Papaji as his *prasad*.

Papaji pretended to be very impressed by this miracle. He told the *baba*, 'These are very holy cloves and cardamoms. This is such holy *prasad* I cannot touch it unless I wash my hands first. I must be in a pure and clean state to receive this offering. Please bring me some water so that I can wash my hands.'

The *baba* sent one of his attendants out to fetch some water. While we were waiting for it to arrive, Papaji was staring intently at the cloves and cardamoms that had just materialised. The water came and Papaji washed his hands very slowly, all the while looking intently at the spices which were still on the *baba's* hand. Then, without any warning, everything on the *baba's* hand vanished.

I saw the *baba* tremble as he watched his spices disappear. He had produced them inside a closed fist, so no one really knew how he did it – whether it was a conjurer's trick or a real materialisation. But when they disappeared from sight, they were out in the open, on top of his palm.

The *baba* realised that Papaji had somehow caused the spices to disappear, although Papaji himself never claimed that he was the one who had done it.

He told Papaji, 'You have a great power, just like me. I have been told that you travel to the West to teach foreigners. Next time you go, you must invite me. We can give performances together.'

Papaji just laughed. He promised he would invite him, but he never contacted him again. Papaji was never impressed by tricks of this kind and I often heard him criticise teachers who indulged in them to attract disciples, fame and money.

As an interesting postscript I should mention that this *baba* eventually found a far more profitable business to indulge in. When the city of Lucknow spread outwards, the land that the Bhutnath Temple controlled became very valuable. This *baba* sold the land off to property developers and then disappeared with the money. Most of the big shops in Bhutnath are built on land which this *baba* sold in the 1970s for a small fortune.

Papaji travelled a lot during the first twenty years that I knew him. He would rarely say where he was going or when he was coming back. He didn't like people to follow him around, so he didn't often tell people his plans or his destined addresses. If he was in India, his most frequent destination would be Hardwar or Rishikesh. He would always manage to spend a few months there every year, and on a few occasions I also went with him.

He never did much while he was there. He would go for walks, have a few baths in the Ganga, eat and sleep. Over the years he stayed in many different places, but trips on which I accompanied him, we always stayed at the Arya Nivas. He didn't mix much with other people while we were there. Usually, just the two of us would be alone together. I would bring him tea occasionally, and sometimes he would let me massage his legs, but for most of the time we would both be sitting quietly, doing nothing.

One night, as we were sitting in the Arya Nivas at about ten o'clock, I asked Papaji if he would like some hot milk to drink. In those days he often had a cup of hot milk in the evening before he went to bed.

'Yes, yes,' he said, 'you can go and get some.'

I took his steel *lota* [pot] and went out to look for some hot milk. As I was walking towards the milk shop I noticed that a bus was arriving at the Bhatia Lodge and that many people were disembarking from it. I saw a swami with them who looked familiar.

I went up to one of the passengers and asked him, 'Is this Haidakhan Baba?'

Haidakhan Baba was very famous in those days. He had thousands of devotees all over the country. The man I spoke to confirmed my guess.

Haidakhan Baba started to walk towards Har-ki-Pairi at the head of his followers. I felt an urge to follow him even though I was on an errand to buy milk for Papaji. The distance from Bhatia Lodge to Har-ki-Pairi is about two or three kilometres. We walked there very slowly. I forgot my original plan and it was not until about 1.30 a.m. that I realised that I had completely forgotten my errand for Papaji.

I retraced my steps as quickly as I could and arrived back at Arya Nivas around 2 o'clock. Papaji was still awake. He must have been sitting up, waiting for me.

'Where have you been?' he asked. 'Does it take four hours to buy a cup of milk?'

I explained what had happened. 'As I was going to buy the milk I met Haidakhan Baba and a group of his followers. I felt a strong urge to follow him, so much so that I completely forgot my original plan. I only remembered it again a few hours later. By that time I was sitting at Har-ki-Pairi with him, so it took some time to come back. I am sorry that I took so long. I had heard that he was supposed to be an enlightened being, so I followed him to see what he was like.'

Papaji made no complaint about my later arrival. He just said, 'All right. Tomorrow morning we will go and have a look at him. Now we can go to bed.'

The following morning we walked from the Arya Nivas to the place where Haidakhan Baba was staying. Papaji had asked me to point him out because he had never seen him before, but it wasn't necessary. As we approached the spot, Papaji immediately identified him because he was a swami at the centre of a large crowd. Papaji didn't make any attempt to introduce himself. He just stood at a distance and stared very intently at Haidakhan Baba for a period of about ten minutes. It was an unwavering, unblinking stare.

At the end of that period Papaji said, '*Chalo* [let's go]. It is too early for this man to come into the marketplace. He should do more *tapas* first. Let's go and have a cup of tea.'

We walked off to a neighbouring *chai* [tea] shop and the subject was never mentioned again.

In the early 1970s Papaji was quite interested in looking at other swamis to see what they were doing. He never confronted them directly. Usually, as he did with Haidakhan Baba, he would just have a look from a distance and then walk away, often without even introducing himself. Though I know he had a low opinion of virtually all the swamis in Hardwar and Rishikesh, he kept his views to himself and never interfered in what they were doing.

Sometime in the 1970s I received a letter from him, posted from Bombay. It said that he had had enough of visiting people who were claiming to be enlightened, and that he wouldn't do it anymore.

Though Papaji seems to have stopped visiting other teachers sometime in the late 1970s, they still continued to visit him. The following story, which Papaji has told on several occasions, probably dates from this period.

I was staying in the Arya Nivas Hotel at Hardwar when an eighty-year-old swami from Gujarat came to the reception desk and asked to know my room number. The manager informed him that I had left my room at 6 a.m. and had returned at 1 p.m. for lunch. He told the swami that I would probably go out at around 5 p.m. and return about five hours later.

The swami left without coming to see me, but the next day he came back and again asked the manager if I was in.

The manager said, 'Yes, he's in at the moment. He is staying in room number three, the one facing the Ganga.'

This time he came to see me and knocked at my door. When I opened it I found this swami standing there, clad in saffron robes and wearing a *rudraksha mala* around his neck. I saluted him, invited him inside, and offered him a seat in front of me.

He introduced himself by saying that he was a guru with thirteen ashrams in Girnar, Gujarat, Madhya Pradesh and Rajasthan. He also said that he was a yogi who taught the *Upanishads,* the *Vedas,* the *Gita* and the *Bhagavatam.*

'So,' he said, 'please do not speak to me about any of the above subjects, as it will be a waste of time. I have no questions to ask, unless you can speak of something that is not part of the yoga tradition and not mentioned in these books. I am a yogi myself and I have mastered the art of going into *samadhi* for long periods. You may have seen my photo in the newspapers because recently I was in an underground chamber in *samadhi* for forty days. The government in Gujarat found out in advance that I was planning to do this and tried to prevent me. They told me it was too dangerous. As a compromise we eventually agreed that I would do it with a doctor present and that one of the walls of the chamber would be made of glass so that I could be observed at all times.

'There is nothing you can teach me about yoga, and I am not interested in listening to a discourse on the scriptures because I teach them all myself. However, if you have something new to say, I will be happy to listen to you.'

He went on to tell me that he was currently on a pilgrimage to Badrinath and Kedarnath with eighty of his devotees. They were travelling there on two buses that he had hired.

He explained how he had come to hear about me. 'We are all staying at the Gujarat Mahila Mandir, on Kankhal Road. The founder of this ashram, Smt Shanta Ben, is one of my devotees.

She is the one who gave me your address.'

After he had finished telling me how important and famous he was, I told him, 'I agree to your conditions. I will not mention any book that you have read. I will not even talk about yoga, *kundalini* or any of these other things you are so interested in. I have something fresh and new to tell you but I cannot talk about it now because you have brought this enormous bag of ideas into the room with you. All these ideas belong to the past. So take this bag outside. Drop it outside the door and re-enter the room without it.'

He didn't understand what I was talking about, so I got up and started propelling him towards the door. When I had got him outside, I told him very firmly, 'You can come back in only when the garbage of the past, which you seem so fond of, has been left outside.'

He sat outside the room, looking very bewildered. I sat in my chair, looked at him through the doorway, and stared into his eyes. Neither of us spoke a word for a period of about fifteen minutes.

At the end of this time the swami suddenly leapt to his feet, rushed into the room and attempted to touch my feet.

I quickly moved his hands away and told him, 'This is not the tradition. I should be touching *your* feet, for three different reasons: first, you are my elder by twenty years; second, you are learned and I am illiterate; and third, you are a *sannyasin* whereas I am just a householder.'

'I understand your point of view,' he said, 'but if you won't let me touch your feet, will you at least tell me where you learnt this teaching? I have been teaching people for many years. I have read books on all the spiritual traditions, but I have never even heard of this technique. Where did you learn it?'

I didn't answer his question. Instead I changed the subject by asking him how he had heard about me.

'One of my students told me about you. She said, "If you are in Hardwar, ask around for him. He doesn't stay in any particular place. In fact, most of the time he isn't there at all because he likes to wander around in the Himalayas by himself. But if he is in town, you can probably track him down by asking at some of the ashrams and *dharamsalas*. Many people know him in Hardwar."'

Then he said, 'Something very different and very special happened to me today. When can I come back and see you again?'
'Why should you come back?' I asked. 'What more do you need? What has happened to you is quite enough. You don't need to come again.'

He was overcome with emotion. As he left, his body was still shaking uncontrollably.

The next day, the founder of the Mahila Samaj Mandir came and asked me, 'What have you done to this swami who was so proud of his knowledge? Many rich people – including high government officers – are his devotees. He came up to me and said, "This person did not even speak to me, but his silence removed all my garbage. He told me not to touch the past and as I looked at him I became free from it. No one has ever done this to me before."'

This woman looked very perplexed. She couldn't understand what had happened to this famous swami.

She continued: 'He has decided not to go on any pilgrimage. His devotees have already left without him. They are going to Badrinath and Kedarnath by themselves.'

This woman from the Mahila Samaj Mandir told me that the swami would return home the next day, because he had no more business in the Himalayas.

Many people come to see me with a head full of garbage. Garbage means everything they have collected in the past. None of this garbage is useful, so I tell them to throw it away. Many people want to have discussions about this garbage because they think that understanding it will somehow make it less smelly, less rotten. You can talk about garbage all day, but at the end of the day the garbage will still be garbage.

Instead I tell people, 'Don't touch it,' which means, 'Don't allow any thought of the past to arise in the mind. Come to me with a clean, fresh mind in which no thought of the past is arising.' If anyone can do this, one satsang will be enough to reveal the truth. Satsang means association with your own Self. When thoughts of the past don't arise, the Self reveals itself.

In the middle of 1971 Papaji accepted an invitation to travel to the West. Joachim Grebert, the T.M. teacher who had drunk the detergent to purify himself, bought him a return ticket to Köln, his home town, in Germany. He left India to make arrangements for Papaji to hold satsangs there.

Meera also left to go to Europe, but with some trepidation because both her passport and her visa had long since expired.

Master accompanied me to Delhi and put me on the plane. It was easy. No one bothered me at all. I was just thinking how lucky I had been when we arrived in Bombay. The international passengers had all their papers checked there. I didn't realise that the first leg of the journey would just be treated as a domestic flight. When they saw that my visa had expired two and a half years before, and that my passport was no longer valid, I was arrested. I begged and begged to be allowed to leave on my flight, but no one paid any attention to me. I was told it was a criminal offence to overstay and that I would probably be put in jail. I was really worried because I suddenly realised that I didn't even know Master's address any more. If I got into serious trouble, I would have no idea how to contact him.

Finally, one official came up to me and asked, very angrily, 'What have you been doing all these years in India?'

'Studying Hinduism,' I replied. I didn't want to drag Master's name into the business in case he also got into trouble, so I didn't say what I had really been doing. Then, for no reason at all, I put my palms together in a gesture of *'namaskar'* and began chanting verses from the *Bhagavad Gita* in the original Sanskrit. I don't know how it happened. It just felt as if some power had taken me over and was making me sing these verses. The whole office became quiet as everyone stopped to listen to my chanting.

Eventually, the man who had just been harassing me came up to me, flung my passport on the table in front of me and said, 'You can go, but don't do it again'.

On the way out he said, 'Most of us Indians don't know the *Gita* that well. You have not been wasting your time.'

I made it to the plane with about five minutes to spare. The flight was to Paris and another surprise awaited me when I disembarked. My father was waiting for me. I had not seen him for years, nor had I told him that I was coming. He had turned up because he said that someone had called him and told him which flight I would be on. Master, knowing that I would make it home on that flight, called my father to let him know I was coming.

In the period leading up to Papaji's departure for Europe, Parmanand, Papaji's father died in Lucknow. Before I give an account of this, I will move the clock back a little to an earlier incident in which several members of his family thought that Parmanand had died. To give the story a little context I should say that throughout his life Parmanand had been doing japa *of 'Sitaram' in order of get a vision of his favourite deity. Though Papaji had repeatedly told him not to look for images of gods that would appear and disappear, it was only in his final years that he accepted the wisdom of these remarks.*

Papaji now takes up the story:

One day, after a satsang in my house in Narhi, I paid a brief visit to see my father because he had been ill for some time. At that time my parents were living near the banks of the Gomti River on Butler Road.

In the two days that followed I could not manage to see him again because I was busy with a Zen teacher who had come to visit me, along with many other people.

At the end of those two days I was having my early morning bath when my sister, who had been nursing our father, started banging on my door.

I knew that something had happened because she was shouting, 'Come out at once! This is important! You can have your bath later!'

I couldn't think of anything that was so urgent that it couldn't wait till I had finished my bath, so I called back, 'What's the hurry? Can't it wait a few minutes?'

She was in no mood to argue.

She called through the door, with some agitation, 'Come out! Come out and I will tell you!'

The rickshaw she had arrived in was still waiting outside the house. She hustled me into the rickshaw, telling me on the way that my father had expired during the night. My mother, my younger brother, his wife and several other members of the family had already formed a mourning party at the house. My mother was upset that I hadn't been present at the moment of my father's death because there is a tradition that the father should die with his head in his oldest son's lap. My parents' house had been bolted from the inside because my mother didn't want anyone to come in and discover that her oldest son had not been present in the final moments.

During my absence, those members of the family who had been present had lifted his body onto the floor and performed the last rites by placing an oil lamp on his right palm. Then they left the body in a room by itself while they waited for me to arrive.

My mother gave me all the details of his final hours as soon as I arrived at the house. Everyone was crying as she recounted how her husband had finally passed away. They were still crying as she opened the door to show me the body. As we went into the room we all witnessed a most incredible sight. My father was sitting up in bed, shaking his walking stick in a very vigorous way. He seemed to be engaged in a fight with some invisible person.

He was shouting, 'Go away! Go away! I won't come with you! I am going to stay here!'

My mother almost fainted. She didn't know whether she was dealing with her husband, a dead man or a ghost.

'Who are you shouting at?' she called out when she had regained some control of herself.

My father calmed down a little and said, 'The gods and my forefathers came with garlands in their hands. They approached me and said, "The chariot is waiting outside. Come with us to the heavens."

'I refused to go. I said to them, "My son told me not to go to any heavens because, after one has spent a long time in these places, one has to incarnate again on this earth and perform *tapas* to get enlightened."'

My father was completely unaware that the last rites had

130

already been performed and that the oil lamp was still burning. We only told him later when it looked as if he had returned to his normal mental state.

My mother washed the floor and gave breakfast to my father. Many of the neighbours and all our friends came to see my father. They all wanted to see this man who had refused to go to heaven and who had had the strength to defy even the gods on his deathbed. I stayed for some time to make sure that he was fully restored to health.

When his father finally did die a few years later, Papaji was present at his bedside. In his dying moments Parmanand finally revealed to his son the extent of his faith in him. I have never heard Papaji speak of this final meeting with his father, but there is an eyewitness account from Om Prakash, the only other person who was present during this dramatic encounter.

In 1971 Papaji's father was seriously ill in a hospital in Lucknow. I think we all knew that he wouldn't live much longer. I accompanied Papaji to the hospital on what turned out to be the night before his father's death. It was the middle of the night, maybe around 2.30 a.m. Papaji's father was lying in a big ward that must have contained about fifty beds. I recollect that Papaji's father was lying about halfway down the ward. In his final hours he looked very frail and weak. He was being fed intravenously and his body seemed to be tied to the bed. We were told that the pain of the needles had irritated him so much, he had tried to pull them out. To prevent him from trying again, the doctors had ordered that his arms and legs be tied in such a way that he couldn't reach them. The doctors were also afraid that he would pull the whole intravenous apparatus down and smash it on the floor.

Papaji had been organising the visits to his dying father. He had allowed many people to come and pay their last respects, but he didn't permit any of them to stay for a long time with him. Papaji had somehow arranged things so that only he and I together could spend any amount of time there in the last few days.

On this last visit Papaji spoke to him about his forthcoming death in a very loving way.

'Father,' he said, 'I have the feeling that you are experiencing a lot of pain. This horse you have been riding all your life is very old and weak now. You must leave this horse and go. If you want, I can give you a new horse right now. It is no problem. There is nothing to be afraid of.'

'I am not a coward,' answered his father. 'There is nothing for me to be afraid of. I don't want a new body, but I know that I will have to leave this one soon. I know that I am on my way to see God, but I am not going there with any fear. When my time comes I will stand before him and say, "I am the father of that enlightened man who is now walking the earth. That man is the true controller of this universe. No one can judge me here. I am the father of the Lord of the Universe."'

Though his words were whispered and broken, there was a fierce pride in them. He knew that he had lived with God all his life and he was truly afraid of nothing that could happen to him after his death.

He was silent for a while, but after a few minutes a beatific smile lit up his face. He seemed to be having some visionary experience.

'Look! Look!' he cried. 'The gods are present even here! I can see them all! They are all moving around my son and worshipping him. All the cosmos is revolving around him. I can see it with my own eyes!'

What a beauty was contained in those eyes! Neither Papaji nor I could see what he was seeing, but the sight of his eyes alone was sufficient proof that he was witnessing some divine vision.

Finally, as the vision seemed to fade, he whispered, 'How blessed I am to witness this tiny portion of the kingdom of my son! Has any other father in this universe been granted a blessing like this?'

It was a great privilege to be a witness to this wonderful scene. Papaji's brothers and sisters were sitting outside the ward. Only Papaji and myself were present during these precious moments.

That was not the end of the revelations of that night. At about 3 a.m., while I was still sitting by the bed, Papaji blessed me with

Papaji's parents: Parmanand and Yamuna Devi.

a marvelous vision of my own. As I think about it now in order to describe it, it reappears before my eyes again as if it was yesterday, instead of more than twenty years ago. Papaji's father had described seeing a vision in which the whole cosmos, along with all its gods and goddesses, was revolving around his son. I now saw something very similar.

I saw innumerable gods and goddesses rotating around Papaji and Ramana Maharshi. Behind the deities, all the stars and planets were also rotating around this same centre. Papaji and the Maharshi were both wearing the kind of crowns that one sees in pictures of Indian kings. There was an intense golden light suffusing the whole scene. It was an ecstatic, blissful experience that completely overpowered me.

After some time I heard Papaji's sister Sumitra enter the ward. I heard her cry out, 'Om Prakash is about to fall! Catch him!'

Papaji rushed over to where I was sitting and caught me before I hit the floor. He pulled me back onto my feet, embraced me and then made me walk out of the ward. I didn't want to walk but Papaji forced me to keep moving. We went out of the hospital and walked up and down some of the deserted streets nearby. I wanted to dwell on the vision I had just had, but Papaji was determined to pull me out of it by discussing my programme for the next day. I had already told him that I had to go to Kanpur the following day to transact some business there. Papaji started to talk about what I would be doing there and forced me to concentrate on what he was saying. Slowly my mind returned to normal. After a few minutes of patrolling the streets and talking about the trivial details of everyday life, I was able to regain full control of all my faculties.

When I had sobered up sufficiently to engage in a sensible conversation with him, I said, 'Papaji, I don't really want to go to Kanpur tomorrow. After what I have witnessed tonight in your presence, I have a feeling that I should be quiet for a while in order to assimilate fully what has happened here today.'

Papaji disagreed. 'No,' he said, 'you have to keep your attention on the world for a while. Here are Rs 50 for your travelling expenses. Go home, take some rest while you can, and tomorrow go to Kanpur and transact all your business. Come back as soon as you can. I will see you again when you get back.'

Papaji's father died the next day while I was in Kanpur. I am still immensely grateful to Papaji for sharing this night with me and for showing me a rare and exquisite glimpse of his divine, cosmic form.

Papaji had already accepted an invitation from Joachim Grebert to make a trip to Germany. Thinking that his mother should not undergo a prolonged period of mourning while he was away, he volunteered to clear up all his father's belongings. During the tidying-up operation he made new discoveries that revealed the full extent of his father's devotion and admiration:

After my father died I had to leave for Köln because I had been invited there by some people who had lived with me in Hardwar and Rishikesh. At that time my mother was alone in her house by the Gomti. The thought suddenly came to me that she shouldn't be surrounded by all his personal possessions. I had a feeling that she would get over her grief better if I took away all the things in the house that were constantly reminding her of his presence.

I told her as politely as I could that I would be happy to take away all the old things in the house and replace them with new items that would not remind her too much of her deceased husband. She agreed to the idea. They had been married for sixty years, but she knew it was pointless to have a long period of morbid mourning.

With the help of a young boy whom I recruited, I threw away everything that was in his room. Afterwards, I cleaned out his *puja* room and got rid of all the statues, books, *malas*, etc. that were on the shelf where he did his *pujas*. There were only two things that my mother wanted to keep: a pocket edition of the *Bhagavad Gita* that he always kept with him, and his diary, which he called the 'Long Register'.

An Austrian girl, Bettina Baumer, was helping me to go through all his possessions. She was the one who found and opened the diary, but she couldn't read it because it was written in Punjabi, Urdu and Persian. I glanced through some of the pages and found a verse written by my father in Urdu. It said:

O stupid mind, why don't you keep quiet?
Don't you see your son?
Although he is a householder with children,
He is nevertheless a free man [*jivanmukta*].
Such a one is rare to find, even among *sadhus*.
He has neither greed nor attachment.
Shame on you!

Presumably, he was ashamed that he had not made more spiritual progress in his life, whereas his son, with all his worldly responsibilities, had become a *jivanmukta*. My father had never told me during his life that he held me in such high esteem.

In another place in the Long Register my father had written that he once spent fifteen minutes without any thought in his mind. During that period, he said, he was completely quiet. He wrote that the peace he had felt during those moments had never come to him before. Then, slowly, his mind began to come back again.

My father wanted to stay in this state of peace, but he didn't know how to hold on to it.

In his diary he wrote, 'How to check it? I shall ask my son. I have been going to other gurus, but I didn't recognise the greatness of my own son.'

On many occasions I had told my father to stop wasting his time by going to town and talking to worldly people.

Once, by way of a reply, he said, 'Look, my dear son, if God has been maintaining any account of the people who are very devoted to him, you will find the name of your father at the top.'

When the Austrian girl opened the *Gita,* she found an old photo of me that my father used to show to his friends. I only found out after his death that he used to show this picture to anyone who was interested, and then follow it up with a little lecture on how great I was.

I was surprised when Papaji told me that he only discovered the extent of his father's devotion and esteem after the latter died. Papaji's sister, Sumitra, told me that when Papaji was only twelve years old, Parmanand had stood up at a family meal and announced to everyone that his son was his Guru. Papaji seems to have no recollection of this incident. Nor does he ever mention the many devotees that Parmanand sent to him.

In the years that he lived in Lucknow Parmanand enjoyed spiritual and philosophical debates with other devotees. However, if he ever failed to convince his opponents on any particular point, he would send them off to Papaji because he knew that Papaji had a knack of showing people the reality that was the substratum of all mental thoughts and arguments.

With the exception of his mother, the other members of his family had a much lower opinion of Papaji's spiritual state. In the following story Papaji describes a meeting he had with his brother Kant in Hardwar.

My younger brother Kant used to work in the Income Tax

Department. He did very well there and retired with the rank of Commissioner. I was once staying in Hardwar when he paid me a surprise visit. On the day he came, there were about fifteen people sitting around me in Bhatia Bhavan, the place where I was staying. I invited him to stay with me, but he didn't want to. He had come to Hardwar for another reason.

'I have come to stay with a famous yogi,' he said. 'His ashram is by the Ganga, near the platform in front of the Chandi Devi temple. That's the place where the ferry boats stop. Do you know this man?'

I didn't know him personally, but I had heard all about him because there were big signs all over Hardwar, advertising his ashram and his miraculous powers.

'This yogi was recently in Bombay,' said my brother. 'I was introduced to him by a rich businessman. I liked him and spent quite a lot of time with him. We got on so well, he invited me to come and stay in his ashram here. That's why I have come. I need some help with my business affairs. I think that this yogi can improve my financial position.'

Some of the people who were sitting with me were amazed that my brother was looking for other yogis to help him.

One of them said, 'Don't you know that your own brother is a famous spiritual teacher? That is why we are all gathered here. Why don't you go to him with your problems?'

My brother was not interested in the kind of advice I gave out. He didn't want to keep quiet; he wanted to make lots of money. He had such a low opinion of my financial acumen, I would probably be the last person in the world he would consult about increasing his profits.

I knew that my brother had been experiencing some severe financial problems. He had purchased a rubber factory in the suburbs of Bombay that needed new machinery to make it profitable. My brother couldn't afford to buy all the equipment himself, so he took a partner. This partner made a big investment in return for a share of the company. Unfortunately, after some time, they disagreed about how much money the factory needed to make it profitable. The partner wanted a bigger investment and insisted that my brother put up an equal share of the money. When my brother refused to invest the money, saying that he couldn't afford it, his partner said that he no longer wanted to have a share in the company. He offered to sell his share of the factory back to my brother at the price he had paid for it, which was reasonable, but my brother didn't have enough money to buy him out.

This was a big problem for Kant. He had put all his spare cash into the factory in the hope that it would provide employment and an income for all his family. His oldest son was already working in the factory as a manager and his youngest son was also planning to start work there once he had passed his accountancy exams. Unless some more money appeared, the factory was in danger of closing down. Like many other credulous businessmen, Kant thought that tantric swamis could perform some mysterious rites for them which would increase their business and their income. He had come to Hardwar, hoping that this new swami would help him to get rich.

My brother was a confirmed materialist who believed that all activities could be evaluated in terms of how much money they generated. He often used to ask me why I wasn't making more money through my travels and teaching. Citing the examples of other gurus such as Muktananda, he would complain that I wasn't charging enough for my *darshan* or my teachings. He seemed to think that with a little more enterprise on my part, I could be a successful businessman-swami.

I have never charged for my teachings. No one has ever paid money to attend my satsangs. When people abroad invited me to come and teach in their countries, I would accept a free ticket and free accommodation from them, but I would never ask for money from anyone who came to me for teachings.

My brother often used to go to Muktananda's ashram in Ganeshpuri, so he knew how much money could be made in the swami business if one put a little effort into it.

A few stories about other members of his family will appear in some of the later chapters.

By the beginning of September, 1971, Papaji had

Kant, left; Papaji, right: Hardwar, 1975.

accumulated many invitations from devotees in several parts of Europe. However, he was initially reluctant to accept them. In one of his final letters from India, written to Abhishiktananda, he made the following comments

18th September, 1971
N. Delhi

I leave Lucknow on 27th September. I am not going to prolong this trip beyond Köln as I don't wish to see persons who are quite happy about whatever station of life they are placed in by the Lord.

139

Somehow I am pulled to Köln. The purpose of this pull is unknown to me; nor do I want to know.

I feel I am responding to the will of the Divine. Although the programme is finalised, my mind is so still, it can take any turn. I may even decide to stay here. Anyway, let me see everything that happens before me. Why should I tilt on this side or that side?

FOREIGN TRIPS, 1971-74

Papaji flew into Frankfurt airport on 28th September, 1971, and was greeted by his devotees in the traditional Indian way.

Many people I had known in India came up to me in the arrival lounge and prostrated full-length on the floor. Some of them also put garlands around my neck. This caused quite a stir because foreigners never greet each other in this way in the West. Some reporters, who were permanently stationed at the airport to get interviews with VIP arrivals, rushed up to us and started taking photos. They didn't know who we were, but we were putting on an interesting show for them.

One of the girls who had come to greet me laughed and said, 'They have never seen anything like this before. We will all end up getting our pictures in the papers.'

Prostrating to your teacher is a good tradition. The teacher himself doesn't care whether you prostrate or not, but by having this as a custom, it gives devotees an opportunity to reduce their egos and get rid of a little of their arrogance. When you prostrate with humility before your teacher, he takes on some of your defects, your faults, and in return gives you love and freedom. Even though this is a great bargain for the devotee, many west-erners still find it difficult to bow down in front of a teacher. Indians don't have this trouble. If they see their teacher walking down the road, they will happily throw themselves full-length in the dirt to lie prostrate at his feet. In my experience, foreign heads do not bend very easily.

I first noticed this when I was staying at Ramanasramam. Some foreigners privately confessed to me that they found it very difficult to prostrate before the Maharshi because such actions were not part of their tradition. In my opinion, this was just their arrogance. They were in the presence of the greatest saint that this century has produced, but their big egos refused to acknowledge this fact. Indian *maharajas* who ruled whole kingdoms would come and throw themselves at his feet, but the foreigners would just nod their heads or give a standing *namaskar* when they came in to greet him.

When India became a republic, Dr Radhakrishnan was installed as the first Vice-President. A few years later he was made President. He was one of the most eminent men in the country, but when he visited the Maharshi in the 1940s, he fell at his feet and made a full-length prostration. This is the way that all our rulers, except the British, showed their respect to our great enlightened beings.

Since Papaji has mentioned Dr Radhakrishnan's visit to the Maharshi, I will briefly mention a little-known incident that took place while he was there.

On the day prior to his visit a French scholar arrived at Ramanasramam and asked the Maharshi to explain what maya *is. The Maharshi ignored his question. About an hour later he asked again and was met with the same response. The scholar followed the Maharshi onto the hill during his evening walk and again asked for an explanation of* maya. *The Maharshi still didn't acknowledge the question in any way.*

When Dr Radhakrishnan arrived the following day, all the devotees went to the gate to greet him. He was brought to the hall where the Maharshi was sitting and, as Papaji has already mentioned, Dr Radhakrishnan made a full-length prostration on the floor. A few minutes later he was taken on a tour of the ashram by the manager. Everyone went with him, leaving only the Maharshi and the Frenchman in the hall.

When they were finally alone together, the Maharshi looked at the scholar and said, 'Yesterday you asked me three times what maya *is. People come here for liberation, but after some time, something or someone more interesting appears and they run after that instead. That is* maya.'

Papaji was taken from Frankfurt airport to Köln where he

was put up in a house that Joachim Grebert had specially prepared for him. Soon afterwards Papaji began to give daily satsangs there.

Joachim showed me around his large hall when I first went there. He had stored all the old furniture and thrown away many other things onto the footpath outside. Many changes had been made inside. The old wallpaper had been replaced with a more agreeable colour. All the pictures that used to hang on the walls had been removed, and all the literature that used to be on the tables and shelves had been taken away. Even the tables and shelves themselves had been thrown away. Joachim did not want to have anything from the past remaining. In the place of all the old furniture, cushions had been arranged on the floor so that visitors could sit around me in a cross-legged position. It was not a big place. About thirty people could sit there. On the first night I gave satsang there, so many people came, there was no room for them all. Many had to go away disappointed because they couldn't get in. Grebert wanted to buy me a bigger place on the banks of the River Rhine, but I refused. I have never been interested in acquiring property and ashrams.

People were coming from all over Germany to attend these satsangs. In the first couple of weeks I met visitors from München, Düsseldorf, Frankfurt and Berlin, as well as the local people from Köln. On weekdays most of the people in the satsangs would be from Köln, but at weekends devotees would come from all over Germany.

Joachim translated whatever I said into German because many of the people who came didn't know English. I soon realised, though, that he must have been adding comments of his own because his translations were always much longer than my original comments.

I told him, 'I speak for twenty seconds in English, but when you translate it into German it takes about two minutes. Why are you taking so long?'

'These German people have never come across teachings like yours before,' he replied. 'What you say is very clear, very simple and to the point, but if I just give a literal translation, I don't think most of the people here will understand what you are talking about. So, I add a few German spices to the words to improve the flavour of your talks. These spices make what you say more palatable for the Germans.'

This wasn't what I wanted. The original words of the Guru are very powerful. If you mix them up with extra comments and explanations, they lose their power. I explained all this to him.

'You don't need to go to the kitchen to cook up extra flavours for my talks. Just say what I am saying, without adding anything. If you translate literally and properly, the true import of what I am saying will be clear.'

Joachim couldn't do it. He said, 'But who will understand you here? If you say "You are already free," and I translate it literally, somebody will say "What does 'free' mean? What is he talking about?" So, I explain as I go along.'

I didn't agree with him, but I couldn't get him to change his habit. There is a power in the true teacher's words that touches the hearts of listeners who are ready for the teachings. Other people's explanations don't have the same effect.

Joachim was a nice boy, but he occasionally did very strange things. I have already mentioned the time he tried to drink a bucketful of detergent while we were in India together. After a few days of my stay in Köln, I witnessed another manifestation of his strange behaviour. I was resting in my room, waiting to be called for lunch, when I heard a series of loud bangs. My first thought was, 'It must be some car backfiring on the street,' but then I realised that the noise was coming from inside the house, not outside. I checked the window to make sure that the noise really wasn't coming from the adjoining road and then went into the living room to find out what had happened. There was a very strange drama being enacted there. Joachim, his mother and his father were all standing on the dining room table. Joachim was holding a rifle.

He called out to me, 'Check under the table to see if the rat is still there. I think I got it, but it may still be hiding under the table.'

He had been taking pot shots at a little rat that had been scurrying around his living room. In India everyone has rats or mice in

Joachim Grebert, Meera and Papaji in Köln, 1971.

his house, but their appearance in western homes seems to cause major outbreaks of panic and alarm. I looked under the table and found a dead rat on the floor. Thinking that they would not come down while the rat was still there, I picked it up by the tail, carried it to the window and threw it out. This simple act caused even more consternation among the family members.

'You shouldn't have touched it!' exclaimed Joachim. 'You don't know what kind of diseases it was carrying. Now we will have to take you to the doctor for some inoculations.'

I protested: 'It didn't bite me. It was dead. How can it make me sick? If there are some germs on my fingers, I can go to the bathroom and wash them off. Why do I need to see a doctor?'

They wouldn't listen to me. Joachim called up a doctor and made an appointment for me. Just to keep them happy I went along, thinking that he would just give me something like a tetanus shot in the arm. Instead the doctor insisted on injecting something in my buttock.

I told him, 'The rat didn't bite me there. Can't you find some-where else to stick your needle?'

This man didn't listen to me either. I ended up getting my

shots, along with a strong lecture on not touching animals that may be carrying lethal diseases. Different countries do things in different ways. This was my first introduction to German ideas of health and cleanliness.

Papaji had been exposed to the strange habits of many foreigners during his years in Rishikesh, but even so, his first few weeks in Germany produced many surprises:

One man who came to see me told me that he was a meditation teacher in Düsseldorf, a nearby city. He invited me to go and meet the members of his group. I went and found that he was charging DM 100 for each forty-five minute session that he led. He was quite honest with me, confessing that he was just running the centre as a business.

'Look at these people who come,' he told me, pointing at the people who were sitting on his floor with their eyes closed. 'None of them knows how to meditate, or even how to try. Some of them bring their girlfriends along and hold hands for the whole of the forty-five minutes. Some of them can't even sit still that long without a cigarette. They have to go out for a smoke in the middle of the session.'

Even at these prices thirty to forty people were coming to sit with him every week. When I asked him how he got so many people to pay so much money every week, he told me the secret of his success.

'I'm just a businessman,' he said. 'I don't know how to meditate myself, and I don't know how to teach others how to do it. I run this place as a business. When people come here I give them a spoonful of "holy water" and ask them to sit quietly in my presence for a few minutes. I put a sedative in the water beforehand, along with a chemical that will make them feel happy and peaceful for half an hour. They all take this mixture as *prasad* and then think that they are having wonderful meditations afterwards. Every week they come back for more, and every week I collect another DM 100 from each of them. It is a very good way to make money.'

I wasn't surprised he was attracting such a large group every week. I soon found that there was a great interest in eastern forms of meditation. I was not known in Germany, but fifty or sixty people would often come to my own satsangs, even though we didn't have space for all of them to sit down in one room. Most Germans work during the day, so my satsang hours were 7 to 9 p.m. From 9 to 11 p.m. I was available for anyone who wanted to have a private discussion on spiritual matters.

Though the crowds were impressive, not everyone came for spiritual reasons.

One girl telephoned me at my house in Köln and said, 'Can I come and see you? It is nothing to do with the meditation classes that you are conducting. It's a personal matter, but I think you can help me.'

I told her, 'We have sessions every evening from seven till nine. If you come half an hour early, we can talk.'

She arrived on time and told me what she wanted.

'There is a blond boy from München who comes to your meetings every weekend with his girlfriend. She is attending a drama college. I have a boyfriend myself. I have been living with him for the last seven years, but now I don't like him so much. He's from Düsseldorf. I think it's a good time to get rid of him. I have fallen in love with this boy from München. I want you to try to arrange a swap for me. Tell this girl, the drama student, that she can have my old boyfriend if she will let me have her present boyfriend. It will be a good exchange for her because this man from Düsseldorf is very handsome. I'm sure she will like him.'

This was something new for me. We don't have business deals like this in India: 'You give me your wife and I'll take yours.' The boy from München and his girlfriend were good students. I liked them very much. They came along to see me every week, and they asked good questions. I could tell that they were both serious spiritual seekers. I didn't think they would have anything to do with this girl's offer, but I saw no harm in introducing them to each other.

'I can introduce you,' I said to her, 'and you can make your own proposal. Let them make up their own minds what they want.'

'No,' she said, 'it will be better if I can see the boy by himself. Then, afterwards, I will take my boyfriend to the girl and introduce them. It will work better this way.'

She had an innocent face, so I was surprised that she was contemplating an exchange like this. I found out later that she was British, not German. Her parents had sent her to a medical college in Germany because they thought the quality of the education was better in German universities.

I told her, 'This boy from München is not likely to accept you until he gets to know you a little better. Why don't you attend some of the sessions here? He likes to meditate. If he sees that you are also interested in meditation, he may start showing some interest in you.'

She started to come but after a few days she fell in love with meditation instead. Her face became very beautiful and she began to sit for two or three hours every day in the room where I gave satsang. I gave her some work to do, helping the new people who came, and she soon forgot about the boy from München.

Though I had met many foreigners in Rishikesh in the preceding years, I was still occasionally surprised by the sexual habits and activities of the people I met in Germany. Girls of fourteen and fifteen were openly having sex with their boyfriends, and their parents didn't seem to mind. Some of them were even letting these young boys and girls sleep together in the family home.

In the house where I was living there were two teenagers: a girl about thirteen and a boy about eighteen, but I hardly ever saw them. They weren't there in the morning at breakfast time, and they weren't often there in the evening at dinner time. I asked their parents, my hosts, why they were absent so much.

'My daughter has a boyfriend and she goes to sleep with him at night. Our son has a girlfriend, so he often disappears to spend the night with her. They are sometimes here for lunch, but they don't often appear for breakfast or dinner.'

Their mother didn't seem to be worried that her thirteen-year-old daughter spent her nights in her boyfriend's bed. I kept quiet about it. It wasn't my family, and it wasn't my job to interfere. I just thought, 'This is Europe. Everything is different here.'

Every day I learned something new about German habits and customs. One morning I answered the phone and found myself talking to one of the devotees who usually came every day.

'I will be a little late today,' he said. 'My father has died.'

I offered to come and attend the funeral but he said it wasn't necessary.

'You don't need to,' he said. 'I am not even planning to go to the graveyard myself. The undertaker will take care of the burial, along with a few of his assistants.'

'But won't there be some kind of service or ceremony at the graveyard? Don't you have to attend that?'

'It's not necessary.' he said. 'I have paid the undertaker to do all that. He and his assistants will perform the ceremony without me.'

I had never heard of a funeral in which the family members subcontracted all the work to professional mourners, and didn't even bother to attend themselves. I changed the subject.

'When did he die? What did he die of?'

'Well,' he answered, 'he's not actually dead yet. The doctor said that he would probably die at around seven-thirty this morning, so I am making all the arrangements on that assumption. I hired the undertaker several days ago because I knew my father would die soon. The grave is already dug. Everything is ready.'

'But what if he doesn't die?' I asked. 'What will you do with the grave and all these mourners you have hired?'

'This doctor is very reliable,' he replied. 'If he says my father will die at seven-thirty. then that is what will probably happen. Anyway, I hope he is right because these mourners are very expensive. I am paying them by the hour, and I don't want them standing around all day doing nothing. We will have a big meal with all the relatives when the service is over, and then I will be able to come to satsang. I am just phoning to say that I will be a little late.'

He arrived at the time he had predicted and informed me that everything had gone according to plan. His father had died at the appointed hour and the body had been handed over to the undertakers for burial.

I hope his father really was dead, and that he didn't just hand over the body at the right time just to save money on the funeral. I say this because I was shown a story in a German newspaper about bodies that had been buried while they were still alive. A road that ran through a graveyard had been widened and some of the bodies had to be dug up and buried elsewhere. Some of the coffin lids were loose and the workers discovered scratch marks and kick marks on the inside of the coffin lids. Also, some of the bodies were not lying flat. The knees were bent in a position that indicated that the unfortunate occupants had been trying to fight their way out. This is the famous German efficiency: funerals are ordered while the victim is still alive, and the ceremonies are conducted as quickly as possible to save money on the hourly rates of the undertakers. In India we let people die naturally, in their own time, and then we attend all the services ourselves.

India is not a rich country but we show more respect to our family members. One day, while I was staying in Germany, I was told that a baby had been thrown away in a plastic bag on the street in front of our house. It was still alive. The mother just wanted to get rid of it. This wasn't an isolated example. Several foreigners have told me that they are still suffering emotional traumas because they were abandoned or thrown away by their parents.

Meera came from Belgium to help organise Papaji's satsangs in Köln. I asked her, in view of some of the stories he tells about his early days in the West, whether she thought Papaji was suffering from some sort of culture shock.

'Oh no,' she replied. 'I don't think he was ever really shocked. He had moved with some really weird people in Rishikesh, so he knew what to expect in the West. He had long since come to the conclusion that all foreigners were a little bit cuckoo. He wasn't judgmental or critical about their behaviour. He likes to be entertained, and the foreigners he met put on a very good show for him.'

After a few weeks in Köln, Papaji went to Belgium for a few days to meet Meera's family. On his return he decided to see some of his own relatives who lived in Berlin.

Papaji and Meera in Belgium: winter 1971.
Meera's mother's house is nearby.

My nephew had emigrated to Germany and opened a shop that sold Indian products. He married a local girl and settled down there. After some time his mother, my sister Sumitra, came to stay with him in Berlin. Since they were both in Germany at the time of my visit, I went to see them.

We had a nice Indian dinner together, after which we were served home-made *barfis* [crunchy sweets]. I was surprised to see Indian sweets so far away from India. Several other expatriate Indians had been invited to the meal. Though everyone there was an Indian, the conversation was all about Germany and German things. Sumitra's grandchildren were brought up as Germans and this cultural conditioning was so strong, they didn't like India at all when they were brought to see their other relatives in India.

When they arrived in Delhi for the first time, one of them said, 'Mummy, I don't like this country. The cows are shitting on the streets, there is a bad smell everywhere, and so much dirt and noise. Why can't we go back to Germany where it's nice and clean?'

They stayed about twenty days, but they didn't enjoy their visit.

After dinner we all went for a walk in the city because I wanted to see what it was like. I had heard a saying, 'Evening in Paris, night in Berlin'. I wanted to see why Berlin nights were so famous.

A few minutes into our walk I noticed that there were packages outside some of the shops. I asked my nephew why there were so many abandoned parcels lying around.

'Somebody must have ordered something during the day and not collected it. The shopkeeper puts items like this out on the street with the purchaser's name on it. The person who has ordered can collect it whenever it is convenient.'

This struck me as being a very strange way of doing business.

'But how does the shopkeeper get paid?' I asked.

'The customer will pay on his next visit to the shop.'

I had never come across such trusting people before. Nobody was stealing the parcels, and apparently the customers could be depended on to turn up later to pay their bills.

It was late in the evening, sometime after 10 p.m., but there were still many people roaming around. On one street we came across a girl who was laughing ecstatically on the footpath. I liked her very much. It always makes me happy when I see people laugh, especially if they are laughing for no reason at all. That's the best kind of laughter. But I didn't get to enjoy her laughter for very long because a few minutes later a police van drew up alongside her and two policemen jumped out. The girl was in ecstasy. She was laughing and occasionally stumbling on the footpath, but she wasn't causing any trouble to anyone. We were the only other people in her vicinity, and we certainly had no objection to her behaviour. In fact, we were enjoying it immensely.

One of the policemen went up to her and asked, 'Who are you?'

She giggled and said, 'I don't know'.

'Where have you come from?'

She laughed again and said, 'I don't know'.

'Where are you going?'

'I don't know.'

One of the policemen opened her bag and pulled out her

identity card. After looking at it for a few seconds, they picked her up, loaded her into the van and drove off with her.

'So,' I thought to myself, 'this is "night in Berlin".'

I couldn't understand the behaviour of these policemen. She had not been bothering anyone, nor was she disturbing anyone with her laughter. We were the only people near her, and we were all enjoying her performance.

The following day I asked one of my German friends why she had been arrested. After I had described the events of the previous evening, he looked very serious and said, 'She was misbehaving. In this country, this kind of behaviour is not allowed.'

Papaji has told this story many times in his satsangs. Usually, he offers no explanation for the girl's ecstatic laughter, but on one occasion he did confess that the girl behaved the way she did as a consequence of a spiritual experience she had had as they encountered each other on the footpath. I asked Meera, who was present on this occasion, what she saw.

We were walking along the streets, looking at the sights. It was late at night, but many places were still open. Master stopped and pointed out a beautiful young girl who was standing on the pavement. It looked to me as if she was waiting for her order at one of the fast-food shops that lined the street.

As he was pointing to her he said, 'Look at that girl standing there. What a beautiful, innocent face she has!'

Something about her puzzled or attracted him. He kept on looking at her very strangely, as if he were trying to look into her mind to find out more about her. He commented several times on her beauty and her innocence, and once remarked that he was astonished by her purity.

We eventually carried on with our walk but after a few steps we noticed that the girl was beginning to laugh. At first she was just smiling, but then she started giggling a little, and finally she abandoned herself to the full ecstatic laughter that Papaji describes whenever he tells this story. As he said, a police van eventually came and took her away because ecstatic behaviour in public places is definitely frowned on in the West. I think that Master was just looking at her mind to see what she was like inside, but the strong powerful look he gave her accidentally triggered off her outburst of laughter. She had a pure, innocent mind and it didn't need much to push her into a state of happiness and ecstasy.

Papaji returned to Köln but he did not stay there very long. A few days later he informed Joachim that he had a desire to meet with some Christian monks:

I told him that I had a desire to seek out people who might be enlightened, and I thought that Christian monasteries might be a good place to start. I was curious to know if Christianity was producing enlightened beings. It is best to judge religions and spiritual practices by their results. Though I knew it wasn't very likely, I thought that there might be a Ramana Maharshi or a Nisargadatta Maharaj living secretly and undetected in one of these institutions.

I asked Joachim to organise a programme for me that would include meetings with Christian contemplative monks. I wanted to see for myself what kind of experiences their religion and their practices were giving them.

The first trip was to Maria Laach, a famous monastery in northern Germany. Papaji met several of the monks there and had a very good satsang with at least one of them. Meera gave me her memories of the meeting:

We met the abbot who first invited us to attend one of the services. There was some beautiful chanting which Master seemed to enjoy. Later we were introduced to some of the monks. We had a very good satsang there because one of the people we were introduced to had a profound experience in Master's presence. I remember that he was well-informed, very learned and very intelligent, but in the satsang he let go of his impressive intellect and allowed Master to enter his heart. I could see from his face that he was melting in love. It was nice to see this man, who must have been a committed Christian, have such a profound experience in Master's presence.

Afterwards Papaji returned to Köln where he sent a report on his activities to Swami Abhishiktananda in India.

1st November, 1971
Köln

Yesterday Fr. Enomiya-Lassalle, a professor from a Tokyo university, came from Maria Laach to Köln to see me. He is conducting Zen meditation classes in that monastery. One of the fathers there suggested that he might be interested in meeting me. We discussed various subjects for six hours and then he left for Holland. He has read your books.

What you spoke about Europe may have been true some ten years ago but I find the trend of people is quite different today. The land of Lord Christ has forgotten who He is. They are proud to speak of Zen, Yoga and Krishna, although some are content merely to smoke hashish. There are some hippies here who don't smoke. They spend the whole night singing *'Hare Ram, Hare Ram, Ram Ram, Hare Hare'*. They are not really following Hinduism. They are just disgusted with society and the lifestyle here.

Some fifty to sixty people call on me every day, from eight in the morning till eleven at night. I am holding a meditation class from 7 p.m. to 9 p.m., and from nine till eleven each evening there are questions and private discussions.

All those who attended for twenty-five days have undergone a marvellous change. They are good seekers now. Some philosophers too have come to see me from München and other far-off places. Sometimes I like to talk about Lord Christ and the Bible with them, but they are hesitant and don't like it, but when they sit with their eyes closed and their legs crossed, they are happy.

In early November Joachim rented a car so that he could drive Papaji to Switzerland and Italy. On the way they visited a monastery at Niederaltaich in Bavaria where Papaji had a good meeting with one of the monks. Meera, who was present at the meeting, commented on the encounter in a letter she wrote to B. D. Desai:

That one Christian monk was really wonderful. We visited him in his own monastery in South Germany for some days. He is blessed. Master has given him HIS LOVE and his Heart. This monk is now 'caught', as all of us beautifully are, by HIM.

From Niederaltaich Papaji, Joachim and Meera drove to Lausanne in Switzerland where Papaji had accepted an invitation to visit the family of a boy who had stayed with him in Rishikesh.

When I lived in Rishikesh in the late sixties a young boy called Thierry, who was in his early twenties, came to see me. He was suffering from schizophrenia and hadn't responded to any of the usual treatments. As a last resort his parents had sent him to me because they had heard from someone in Switzerland that people around me sometimes got cured of chronic ailments. Thierry stayed with me for over a year, and when he went back to Switzerland he seemed to be perfectly normal. As a gesture of gratitude his parents invited me to stay with them in their house in Lausanne.

I knew that Thierry's family was rich but I was still surprised by their luxurious lifestyle. I was given a penthouse apartment on the shore of Lac Leman. Every hour or so the whole apartment would rotate through 360 degrees. When the apartment was pointed in the right direction, I spent a lot of time admiring the views of the lake through a pair of binoculars that Thierry's parents had lent me.

Thierry's father had earned his wealth by manufacturing cars. He had a big factory that employed thousands of workers, but he wasn't happy. He couldn't sleep at night because his business worries kept him awake.

He approached me one day and said, 'My son has told me all about you. He gives me lectures on knowledge, enlightenment and freedom, but I'm not interested in things like these. I just want to sleep at night. Can you help me? I take pills and I always have a couple of alcoholic drinks late in the evening to try and help me to sleep, but nothing seems to work. I just lie awake for hours, thinking about all the problems I will face at the factory the next day.'

Eating dinner in Thierry's house in Lausanne. The boy next to Papaji is Thierry's younger brother.

I thought this man just needed a break from his work and his worries so I told him, 'Come with me tomorrow and I will show you how to sleep. We will take your car, drive to the nearest forest, and then we will go for a long walk. When you are exhausted from the walk, we will lie down on the forest floor and have a good sleep. You won't need any drinks or pills. You just need to forget about your factory for a day and instead come out with me for a long walk.'

He agreed, but when I went to collect him at the appointed hour he said, 'I can't come. Something important has just come up in the factory. I need to be here.'

I tried again later but got the same answer. We never went for our walk, and while I was there, he never solved the problem of how to get a good night's sleep. He was a miserable and depressed workaholic whose wealth was giving him no pleasure or satisfaction, but he couldn't see that his schedule and his lifestyle were the cause of his problems.

One night this same man started a discussion with me at the dinner table. He had heard about the caste system in India and he wanted to tell me how much he disapproved of such artificial divisions.

'All people are equal in my sight,' he said. 'I don't believe that people should be divided by birth into these artificial categories.'

Just then one of the man's servants, a boy who did household cleaning, walked through the room. I pointed him out to Thierry's sister, a young girl of eighteen, and asked her if she would like to marry a nice boy like this.

'He's a handsome boy,' I said. 'He would make a good husband for you.'

She got very angry. 'I'm not going to marry someone like this. He's just a cleaner. When I marry, I will choose some rich handsome boy from my own class.'

I laughed and then spoke to her father. 'It seems you have a caste system here as well. Merchants here engage themselves in business, and when it is time for their children to marry, they find someone suitable from their own social and financial group. It is the same everywhere in the world: workers marry workers, and businessmen's children marry the children of other businessmen. You may not approve of it, but that's the way the world is.'

Thierry was told about my plan to visit monasteries and contemplative monks. He knew several in his area and soon arranged a few meetings for me. One was with a hermit who lived about forty kilometres away. We drove to see him but were told by his attendant that it was the wrong time to visit. I explained that I was a Hindu and that I had come all the way from India to meet Christian monks because I wanted to talk to them about their experiences. The attendant relented and said that he would try and get an interview for me. The door to the hermit's room opened and a great cloud of cigar smoke came out. It was so dense and malodorous, I couldn't enter the room.

'Could I meet him outside?' I asked. 'I don't think I could breathe for very long if I went in there with him.'

'Oh no,' replied the attendant. 'He never leaves his room. He stays in there all day with the doors and windows closed.'

'Well, could you open the windows and the doors when I go

in?' I asked. 'It would be nice to have some fresh air in there while we talk.'

Again the answer was 'no'.

'He likes the smoke to be in there. He smokes all day and for most of the night. He says it helps him to stay awake and alert when he meditates.'

This was a new kind of *pranayama* [breathing practice], one I had never come across before. In India the yogis insist on clean, pure air for their breathing exercises. This monk preferred cigar smoke, with all the doors and windows closed to enhance the effect. I went home without seeing him because I didn't want to fill my lungs with all his exhaled cigar smoke.

Thierry arranged for me to visit another monastery that was about eighty kilometres from Lausanne. In that place the abbot asked me to give a talk to his monks. I obliged him by giving them some of my thoughts on Christianity. I didn't think they would appreciate a lecture on *moksha* [liberation], or any other Hindu subject. After the talk was over, I had what I thought was a good talk with some of the monks who had attended.

About two or three days later I telephoned the abbot and asked him if I could come again because I had enjoyed my visit and my meeting with some of his monks. When someone else answered the phone, I explained who I was and asked to speak to the abbot.

'I'm sorry,' the voice on the other end of the telephone said, 'you cannot speak to him. He is sick.'

'Then can I talk to someone else?' I enquired. 'I would like to arrange another visit to your monastery.'

'No,' said the voice, 'everybody here is sick. You cannot talk to anyone.'

In India, when friends get sick, we always go to visit them.

I told the man on the phone, 'I'm very sorry to hear this. I will come at once to see how you all are.'

I couldn't imagine how everybody had suddenly got so sick, no one could even get to the phone. I thought to myself, 'Maybe they all got food poisoning from eating the same meal, or maybe they all came down with flu together'.

The voice on the phone suddenly sounded very alarmed.

'No! No!' he shouted. 'You cannot come here again.'

I thought that perhaps it was some kind of infectious epidemic, and that no one was allowed to visit.

'But what disease do you all have?' I asked. 'Is it so infectious that friends are not even allowed to visit?'

The man replied, 'It's not a physical disease. It's psychological and emotional. We are all in a very distressed state. After you spoke to us about Jesus and Christianity, we all got sick. We are not used to hearing talks like this. If you come here again we will probably all get even sicker.'

I couldn't remember saying anything offensive about Christianity. It had mostly been a talk about the love of God. Still, it must have offended the ideas of these monks because they were all still suffering three days later. By this time I had seen several monasteries and I had come to understand that these places were full of people who couldn't keep quiet. There were lots of services and rituals, but I had not found anyone who had a really quiet mind. In most of the places I had visited, the monks were busy working, distilling alcoholic drinks or manufacturing other products to make money for their respective monasteries. It was just like the outside world: lots of hard work to make money, and not much time left over to be peaceful and quiet.

I asked Meera, who also attended this particular talk, what Papaji had said that had offended the monks so much.

She laughed and said, 'It's true he talked about the love of God, but he also made it clear that rituals and the outer forms of religion are often a hindrance in an earnest quest for God. That's probably not the right line to take with monks because their whole lives revolve around various rites and rituals.'

After a few days with Thierry's family in Lausanne, Papaji moved on to northern Italy where he was taken to a monastery at Monteveglio, near Bologna.

As I was arriving I saw some robed men releasing partridges from cages. The birds flew about, enjoying their freedom. I asked the driver to stop the car because I wanted to find out who these kind people were. I thought that they must have purchased these birds in order to set them free in the forest. Some people in India do that when they see caged birds. I didn't know Italian so I asked my driver to find out who they were and what was going on.

The monks told him, 'This is an act of kindness. We don't like to keep the birds cooped up all the time, so we give them a chance to fly around for a while before we catch them and kill them. This way they have a more natural life. They live in a walled sanctuary here, so they have no chance of escaping. When we want to eat one, we come here and catch one.'

As I stood there I noticed six monks with long poles. They had come there to catch the birds that were to be eaten that day.

I went up to the monastery and was introduced to all the monks who lived there. Only one man, a Father Alphonso, spoke any English, but he was very fluent. He took us to their church where we witnessed a long mass. There was the usual procession up to the altar where the monks and nuns took communion. I had been told beforehand that I should not follow them because the bread and the wine were only given to baptised Christians. The mass seemed to go on for hours. It would have been nice to have been offered a piece of bread at the end of it because I was feeling hungry, but I knew that this bread was only fed to people who had formally accepted the teachings of the Catholic Church.

When the mass was over, we all gathered in one of the halls. I had been introduced to them as a spiritual teacher from India, so they wanted to ask me some questions. I thought that they would ask me something about Hinduism or enlightenment, but instead they wanted my interpretation of several biblical quotes. I told them that I would be happy to answer any question that they put to me. I had found from long experience that when people put questions to me about spiritual texts, an appropriate answer comes out of my mouth. These answers are not derived from any knowledge of the texts, or from any formal study of them. Instead, they just come from the Self. There have been several occasions when I have been able to give interpretations of verses and texts that had baffled even experts. When you allow the Self to speak, the right answer always comes out.

161

One of the senior monks began the interrogation: 'Why did Christ cry on the cross? Why did he call out, "My God! My God! Why hast thou forsaken me?"'

I had been asked this question before by some other Christians. It is my belief that God the Father was deliberately severing the relationship between Himself and His son so that Jesus could be free of all ideas of relationships at the moment of His death. However, I had found from experience that Christians tend to get agitated when I say this. So, on this occasion I gave a different answer which I thought would be more appropriate for the circumstances.

Christians like to regard themselves as sheep, being herded by a divine shepherd. They never think of themselves as lions who are free to walk wherever they please. So, usually, when I talk to orthodox Christians, I give them sheep answers because I know that lion answers will upset them. Since I was a guest of these people, I didn't want to offend them too much. I can't remember exactly what I said, but I do remember that on this occasion even my sheep answers upset them.

Many more questions followed: 'What is your opinion of the virgin birth? Why did Jesus' disciples abandon him in his final hours? Why did Peter himself deny that he was a follower of Christ? Why did God put Jesus through such unnecessary suffering? Why, for example, did He allow him to drag his heavy cross to the place of his execution?'

The questioning was quite aggressive, but I gave a reply to each of the points that was raised. My answers did not satisfy them because I could provide no authoritative, documented support for them.

If I gave an unusual answer, someone would say to me, 'What authority do you have for that statement? Where is that statement written?'

They were the sort of people who would only be willing to accept my answers if I could prove that they were in agreement with some ancient text or interpretation. For them, the Bible was the final authority, and if I disagreed with anything that was written there, they were unwilling to accept my views.

The discussion was getting quite heated. They were demanding some authority for my statements, and I was merely telling them that my own experience was sufficient authority.

At one point I told one of them, 'The Bible is not a book. You should not call it a mere book. It is the transmission of the Father's words to the Son. It is not just a collection of words that you can argue about. It is a direct transmission from God.'

This seemed to strike a sudden chord with one of the old monks who had not joined in the discussion at all. He left the room and came back a few minutes later with a large, ancient, Greek book.

He read out some portions from the book and translated them into English and Italian for me and the other monks. His words were a verbatim repetition of what I had been saying at various stages of the discussion. Even the comment about the Bible not being a book was there. Everyone stopped arguing with me and went through the book with the old monk. Eventually they had to agree that what I was saying could be backed by a recognised authority. They were all astonished that I could make these statements because they knew that I had not studied Greek, nor did I have any background in Christian theology.

I went to bed early, but the monks stayed up to go through this old book. A few hours later Father Alphonso came in to see me to tell me that almost everything that I had said that evening could be found in this old book. I had never read it before because it was in Greek. In fact, I can't even remember what it was called. But somehow I was able to quote large portions of it in order to satisfy these scholars that what I had said was true.

Unlike many other monasteries, this particular one was not run exclusively from donations given by ordinary Christians. Some of the inhabitants had been educated professionals who had saved up some money before they became monks. I met ex-professors and ex-lawyers there who had given large amounts of their earlier earnings to the monastery. It was an old monastery that had been founded several hundred years before, but conditions were still very primitive. The monks were deliberately trying to live a very simple life even though there were ample funds available for their upkeep. They carried their own water from a nearby well, using tractors to move large amounts at a time. Also, they used candles instead of electricity. However, their poverty was contrived. It was probably costing them more money to burn candles than it would to pay the electricity bill. And if they had installed tap water, they could have saved on the expense of having a tractor carry water all day. They were actually wasting a lot of money on a primitive lifestyle because they thought that such a way of life was spiritually beneficial.

I stayed there for a few days. At the weekend a young woman came to talk to some of the monks. The abbot held her hand for a long time while he was greeting her. I think these weekend visits were the only times he ever got to touch a woman. Then all the other senior monks came and greeted her in the same way. They all managed to hold her hand for about twenty seconds while they were saying 'hello' to her. Since she was a pretty girl, everyone wanted to hold her hand.

I thought to myself, 'Maybe my turn will come soon,' but it didn't happen. The monks, who had to make up for seven days of being deprived of a woman's touch, kept her to themselves. I wasn't even introduced.

There was one very amusing incident at this monastery. I had been talking about some of the great saints of Hinduism to some of the people there. Not to be outdone, one of them went off and produced an Italian book that contained short biographies of Christian saints. They were read to me via the translator. One of the stories sounded very familiar, so familiar in fact, I found it hard to suppress my laughter.

'This one is very interesting,' I remarked. 'Is this saint still alive?'

'Oh no,' they replied. 'it says here that he died a long time ago.'

'This is my life story,' I said. 'Some of the names have been changed, but this is very definitely the story of my own life. All the events that happened to this man happened to me, and in the same order they are written here.'

I found out later what had happened. Swami Abhishiktananda

had written an account of my life and had sent it to several of his Christian friends in Europe. One of them had changed some of the names for this Italian version and had then placed the story in mediaeval Europe. In the process he also claimed that I was a Christian saint.

Papaji began his investigations into Christianity with a fairly open mind, but his experiences in European monasteries convinced him that this religion was not producing enlightened beings, and had no capacity to do so. Nowadays when he is asked about Christianity, he usually launches into a fierce assault on the mental conditioning that Christianity imposes. The following attack, dating from 1994, is typical:

Virtually everyone in this world lives like a sheep. The whole population of this world consists of flocks of sheep who are herded by different shepherds. I am not joking when I say this. The founder of Christianity is called 'the good shepherd' by the sheep he is controlling.

What is the function of a shepherd? It is to make sure that the sheep in his charge do not stray away from the flock. There are five or six big shepherds in the world, and each one has a flock that numbers in the millions. These shepherds are the founders of the world's main religions. All the sheep are branded or painted with identification marks so that the shepherds know which flock each one belongs to. What are these marks? They are the ideas and beliefs that the shepherds impose on all the members of their own flock. Sheep are very docile animals. They have a group mentality and don't think for themselves. Instead, they just follow the sheep in front and do whatever they are doing.

Looking after millions of sheep is a big job, so the shepherds need lots of dogs to keep their flocks under control. And who are these dogs? They are the priests who run around barking, making all the sheep of their own group move in the approved direction.

Once in a while a sheep will rebel. He will look at the dogs and the other sheep and think to himself, 'I don't want to live like this. I want to be free. I want to walk my own way.'

These rare sheep sneak off when the shepherd is not looking and follow their own path. They have an inner sense that enables them to follow the scent of true freedom. Some perish, some get afraid and return to their flock, but a very few walk on undaunted and reach the goal.

I don't think the sheep who stay in the flocks ever attain true liberation. They live and die following the instructions and promptings of the shepherds and the dogs. The church masses, the rituals, the prayers and so on are specially designed to make you think how wonderful the founder of the flock is and how lucky you are to be in his group.

These big shepherds tell their sheep: 'You may be miserable now, but if you move in the way that the dogs make you go, we promise you that you will be happy after you die.'

What a gigantic fraud all this is! Why should you wait till you die to be happy? Unending happiness is available here and now to anyone who rejects all the ideas that priests, parents and society impose. When you drop every idea you have ever had, you find yourself sitting on the throne of the kingdom of heaven. The ideas and practices that the shepherds impose on you don't help you to get nearer to heaven, they keep you permanently away from it. Don't listen to the shepherds and don't be afraid of the dogs. Be a lion and walk your own path. Don't let anyone impose a belief or a practice on you by saying it will produce results later. If you want the kingdom of heaven, you can have it here and now by dropping every idea and concept in your mind.

This particular talk was given to a Jesuit priest. I don't know if Papaji gave lectures like this on his European tour, but if he did, it is not surprising that some of the monks who listened to him got sick.

After his brief but entertaining stay at Monteveglio, Papaji moved on to Rome, arriving there in late November. Meera said that Papaji enjoyed Rome very much because it was the one place in Europe that reminded him of India.

I was taken to see all the sights of Rome, including St Peter's, the main church there. There were many beautiful paintings and statues all over Rome. I had been taken to galleries and museums in different parts of Europe, and most of them seemed to be full of pictures of naked women. In Rome it was different: most of the statues and paintings depicted naked men. Romans seem to prefer to look at male muscles rather than female curves.

In one place I was shown a picture of a Christian saint who was being crucified upside down. I was told that he voluntarily chose this position because he didn't want to be crucified in an upright position. It's bad enough being crucified. Why impose further suffering on yourself by choosing to do it upside down?

Christianity teaches you that it is good to suffer. The priests tell you, 'The more you suffer in this world, the more you will be happy in the next'.

Because of this, many Christians deliberately seek out environments where they can suffer as much as possible. If you want to learn how to cry and be miserable, Christianity is the best religion for you. I talked to many Christian scholars and priests during my travels in Europe. None of them taught or believed that happiness is the true nature of man. Instead, they preached that man's nature is inherently sinful, and that misery and suffering are an inevitable and unavoidable part of life here on earth. Hinduism teaches exactly the opposite. We say that man's nature is inherently pure, that happiness is the true nature of man, and that this happiness is available here and now in this world, and not in some heavenly realm.

While I was in St Peter's I was taken to see one of the smaller chapels that was under the ground. There were some statues in one corner, and behind them a young couple was hugging and kissing.

I went up to them and asked, 'This is a holy church. Can't you find somewhere else to do your kissing?'

'No,' replied the boy. 'We can't do it in the parks or on the streets or in the restaurants, and we definitely can't do it at home with our parents watching. This is the only place where we can get any privacy.'

'This is also a public place,' I said. 'You also run the risk of being arrested here. If the priests catch you behaving like this in their chapel, they might hand you over to the police.'

'Oh no,' replied the boy, laughing, 'the priests never complain about what we do here. We put on this show for their benefit. They peep through the screens and watch us kissing. All the young couples come here and nobody stops us because we all know that the priests are watching us through the holes in the walls.'

After visiting Rome and attending a mass at the Vatican, Papaji, Joachim and Meera moved on to Assisi, arriving there on 1st December. They checked into a local hotel but soon found themselves in a confrontation with one of their neighbours.

I was sitting in this hotel room in Assisi when I suddenly began to laugh for no reason at all. Once I started, I couldn't stop. It just went on and on for hours. Later that evening I thought I heard someone banging on the door of our room. Joachim was in the room with me at the time, so I asked him to open the door to see who it was.

He said, 'No, Master, it's not someone knocking at the door. It's your neighbour on the other side of the wall. He is banging on the wall and shouting at you, telling you not to make so much noise.'

'I have paid the rent for this room,' I replied. 'If I want to laugh in my room, I will laugh in my room. What's it got to do with him? He can do what he likes in his room, and I will do what I like in my room. And right now, what I like to do is laugh.'

'But he's objecting very strongly. What should I do?'

'Don't do anything,' I replied. 'Let him make his noise and I will make mine.' And I carried on laughing for the rest of the night.

The next morning the manager of the hotel came to see me and said, 'Your neighbour came to me to make a complaint that you were disturbing him the whole night. He claims that your laughing gave him such a headache, he couldn't sleep. I heard you as well, but it didn't bother me. On the contrary, I like to hear people laugh and I like to hear people enjoy themselves. Your joy was very infectious. I also got very happy just listening to it.'

This kind of laughing attack has happened to me on a few

occasions. One time in the 1970s I was giving satsang in a house in Lucknow. I suddenly started laughing and couldn't stop. Everybody in the room joined in. We all spent the whole day, maybe seven or eight hours, laughing and laughing. I remember that there was some water boiling to make tea for everyone. We all forgot about. It boiled away and the pot burned. Nobody noticed. We were all too busy laughing.

Laughing is something that humans are designed to do. We are unique in the animal world. Other creatures bark, moo, bleat, cackle, chirp, etc., but we alone laugh. Why suppress it?

Papaji often remarks that causeless laughter is often an indication that the mind is absent. When thoughts drop away, leaving the joy and happiness of no-mind, this new state often manifests as spontaneous, uncontrollable laughter. I questioned Papaji about this in an interview I had with him in 1993:

David: When all mental problems go, then spontaneously laughter arises?

Papaji: Of course, of course. A person who has got rid of all his problems, he alone laughs, he alone dances. As a solution to all his problems, he only has to dance, he only has to laugh.

Those who don't laugh, they have got minds. They look very serious and have many problems. They have minds because for any problem, for any suffering, you need to have a mind. It's the mind that suffers, you see. So laugh away your problems! If any problem comes, laugh it away! If you laugh, it will go away; it will run away; it will fly away.

There was once a saint who lived on top of a mountain. At midnight, on a full moon night, he started laughing and laughing. All the people of the village woke up wondering, 'What has happened to this monk?'

They went to the top of the hill and asked him, 'Sir, what happened?'

The saint answered, laughing, 'Look! Look! Look! Look! There's a cloud! There's a cloud!'

Many people see clouds, but who laughs at them? Only the one who has no mind. Anything he sees will give him occasion to laugh. Because, as he looks at it, he becomes that thing itself. The cloud is there, the moon is behind it. If you have no mind, this sight alone can make you laugh.

David: So when you see the world you mostly laugh at it. You think it's all a big joke?

Papaji: [laughing] I only joke. What else is there to do? I don't study any *sutras*, I've never studied any *sutras*, nor do I refer to any *sutras*. I only make jokes!

While he was in his hotel room in Assisi Papaji had a dream or a vision that led him to a nearby grave.

During the night I had a very clear dream, so clear it might be more correct to call it a vision. In this dream I saw that a body I had had in another life was nearby. I knew it was from three life-times ago. In the dream I saw exactly where this body was, and I was also given information on how to get to it. I told Joachim, who was staying in the room with me, about it.

'Tomorrow,' I said, 'we will go there and see it. It's not far away.'

'Should we get a guide?' he asked. 'We don't know Italian, and we don't know this area.'

'No,' I said. 'I have a map in my head that is good enough to get us there.'

This had happened to me before in South India. On that occasion a dream had told me where my old ashram and *samadhi* were. The information I had received in that dream had been accurate enough to take me to the right place, even though I had never been to that area before.

The next day the three of us, guided by my dream informa-tion, walked to the chapel where St Francis was buried. I knew that this was the place I had been sent to. As I stood next to his grave I felt as if the body under the ground was my own body, and I felt great pain because I had the distinct feeling that it was being eaten away by insects. The nerves in my present body were feeling the pain of the old body. It was a very strange feeling.

In a written answer he gave me in 1994 Papaji added a little extra information:

During one night at Assisi, I had a dream that my previous body was buried a few miles away. I could trace my grave and found that the body was lying there dead, being eaten by worms. I still felt the pain of the body, such was the attachment even to a dead corpse. Maybe this attachment was the reason for my next birth.

I asked Meera what she remembered of her visit to Assisi with Papaji.

Meera: Assisi is one of those places that seems to be saturated with an atmosphere of *bhakti*. It reminded me a little of Vrindavan. Master also felt this atmosphere. At one point he told me that it reminded him of several holy places in India that he had visited. We walked around the town and saw all the places that tourists go to. On our return to our hotel Master remarked that he somehow felt a very intimate relationship with St Francis. This was after we had been to the chapel where he was buried.

David: What happened while he was standing in front of the grave? What did you see?

Meera: He stood there in silence for a long time. There was a very absorbed look on his face, so I knew something was happening to him. It is a look he only gets when he is having some special experience. He didn't tell us what was happening at the time. It was only when we got back to our hotel room that he told us that he had felt that this was his old body. When he mentioned the pain he had felt there, he seemed very moved by the recollection. I think it was a big experience for him

---

171

David: Was anyone else there with you in the chapel where the body is kept?

Meera: No. We were alone. It was very silent there. When I looked at him there, I thought he must be having some kind of vision because the expression on his face was the same one that he has when he is seeing the gods.

David: Did you have any special experiences there?

Meera: I had had a vision of St Francis while I was staying with Master in Lucknow in 1969. It surprised me at the time because I didn't have a Christian background. I knew about St Francis, but before that vision I didn't have any special interest in him. I have had a few visions in Master's company, but the one of St Francis was extraordinary because it was so unexpected. On other occasions I would just see Hindu gods, but these experiences would usually be in places that were associated with them. Papaji regularly has visionary experiences, and some people who move closely with him seem to have them as well. In his proximity the most amazing things happen. In Assisi I started having visions of Santa Clara, but I didn't attach much significance to them. When one is with Papaji in holy places that are associated with some saint or deity, it is somehow quite natural to start having visions of the saint or the deity who is connected with that place. I felt quite ecstatic in Assisi, and felt that I had some connection with the place, but I have felt like that in other places with Papaji.

David: He seems to have distinct memories of some of his past lives. Did he speak about anything that had happened to him in that life he had in Assisi?

Meera: No. I have heard him speak about the vision at the *samadhi* on several occasions, but I have never heard him mention any memories he has from that life. Once or twice I heard him say, 'He was a true saint,' but I never heard him explain why.

*Papaji and Meera had been living as husband and wife since
1969. Meera intuitively felt that she became pregnant on the night
that followed Papaji's visit to St Francis' tomb. When I asked
Papaji about this, he also agreed that she conceived that night. The
juxtaposition of Papaji's unusual visit to St Francis' tomb, Meera's
visions, and the baby that was conceived the same day, prompted
me to ask Papaji on two separate occasions whether there was
some old karmic connection between himself and Meera that bore
fruit in their union in Assisi. On neither occasion did I receive an
answer.*

*After the momentous events at Assisi, Papaji and his party
headed north. They had been invited to stay in Austria by the
parents of a girl who had stayed with Papaji in Rishikesh. They
spent a day in Padova, seeing the sights, and then drove north
towards the Alps.*

Because it was midwinter, the alpine passes were covered
with deep snow. We didn't have chains on our wheels, so we often
skidded all over the road It was an adventurous ride through beautiful scenery. I noticed that many of the other cars had chains on
their tyres, and that these cars were skidding a lot less than ours. I
pointed this out to Joachim and suggested that we stop to buy some
for our car. We stopped at the next hardware store where Joachim
bought a long length of ordinary chain. He didn't know that the car
tyres needed special chains, and neither did I. We then wrapped the
chains around the tyres of our car and tried to drive off. Of course,
nothing happened. We couldn't move at all. A passer-by pointed
out our mistake to us and we took them off.

Our final destination was Salzburg, but before we got there we
stopped at a large lake that was completely frozen over. The other
people in the car wanted to show me how to skate, but when we
reached the edge of the lake the local people there advised us
against it because the ice was not yet thick enough. They told us a
few gruesome stories about other people who had plunged through
the ice to their death after trying to skate there. That was enough
for us. We admired the scenery for a while and then continued our
journey.

I had the address of a girl, Bettina Baumer, who had visited me in India, but on our arrival in Salzburg we were not able to trace the house from the directions she had given us. After a few futile attempts to locate her, I suggested to my driver that he ask one of the passers-by. The first person he approached was a woman who was walking on the footpath near our car.

Very politely he asked her, 'Can you please tell me where this address is? We can't find it.'

By way of a reply she started abusing him, saying that he should buy a map of the town if he didn't know where he was. This encounter was quite a shock to me. I could not have imagined something like this happening in India. Anyway, we followed her advice and bought a street map of the city in a nearby shop. As we were studying it by the side of the road, we witnessed a serious road accident. A woman with a three-year-old girl had been walking towards her parked car. She was hit from behind by another car and fell down injured. The girl who was with her did not seem to be aware that something serious had happened to her mother. She just gazed silently at the bleeding body on the ground. This surprised me. In India, if a mother had been injured in this way, the children would immediately start to cry.

Many people collected around the woman, but no one seemed to be helping her. She was lying in the middle of the road in the middle of the traffic. Since no one seemed interested in moving her out of danger, I went up to her and tried to lift her. The spectators forcibly prevented me. They told me that an ambulance had already been phoned for and that I shouldn't touch her until expert help arrived because there was a danger of making the injuries worse by moving her. The ambulance eventually arrived and took her off to hospital. In India victims of accidents are rarely fortunate enough to have trained paramedics to help them in situations like this, so we just get them off the road and wait for a doctor to come. It was my second lesson that day that customs and manners differ radically from country to country.

After a brief stay in Salzburg in the home of the parents of Bettina Baumer, Papaji, Meera and Joachim drove back to Köln.

174

The long car ride was over.

Papaji had received an invitation to visit Enrique Aguilar, one of his devotees who lived in Barcelona. Since it was much too far to drive, he flew there in late December. Meera spent a few days with her family in Belgium and then flew to Barcelona to be reunited with Papaji. Joachim stayed in Köln.

I mentioned Enrique Aguilar's story in the 'Mining Manager' chapter. He was the man who had come to India as a Benedictine monk but ended up as a nominal Muslim after brief interludes as a Hindu sadhu and a Buddhist monk.

While I was travelling in Germany and Switzerland, Enrique wrote to me: 'My parents will be very happy if you come and stay with them. I have told them so many things about you.'

I accepted the invitation and went there shortly after my return to Köln. Enrique came to meet me at the airport and took me to his house.

175

After two or three days the mother didn't appear at the break-fast table. Enrique told me that she had suddenly got sick.

'Then let's go and see her,' I said. 'Let's go and see how she is.'

This is the tradition in India. If family or friends get sick, you immediately go and visit them.

'We can't,' replied Enrique. 'We don't have an appointment. If we want to see her, we will have to go to her maid and ask for an appointment. Even I can't get to see her unless I make an appointment in advance with this woman.'

'But you're her son,' I said, disbelievingly. 'Do you need your servant's permission to visit a sick member of your family?'

'Yes,' he said. 'That's the tradition here. I cannot go into her room even when she is healthy unless I have received permission in advance through her maid.'

This European tour was proving to be very educational for me. In India I would never have guessed that western families lived like this. That day Enrique's mother chose to stay alone. Not even her husband got to see her because he couldn't secure the necessary permission from her maid. We found out later, through the servant of course, that she wasn't even very sick. She had just lost her voice and had decided to stay in bed for the day.

I told Enrique about my desire to meet with Christian contem-plative monks. He was a good person to ask because he had spent several years living in a Christian monastery. Enrique had spent his monastic years at Montserrat, a very famous monastery located near Barcelona. He still knew the man in charge and through him he said that he could probably get us an interview with a hermit who lived outside the main community.

We went there and were introduced to a Father Basilio. He surprised me by saying that he had heard about me from several monks who had come into contact with me in India. He said, jokingly I think, that I had been a subversive influence on some of his monks.

'They go to India as good Catholics,' he said, 'but when they come back from seeing people like you, they have *rudraksha malas* round their necks and they are chanting "*Om*" instead of "*Ave Maria*".'

176

I had lunch with the abbot and some of the monks. I remember that a lot of wine was served during the meal. Some was offered to me but I refused. I never drink alcohol. Drinking a lot of wine seems to be part of the monastic tradition in Europe. I was offered wine in almost every monastery I visited.

I asked some of the people I was introduced to, 'Have you at any time seen God? If not physically in your waking state, then in a dream or a vision?'

As I listened to their answers I discovered that no one, not even the head of the monastery, had ever seen God or Jesus, even in a dream. They were a little surprised by my question because they didn't seem to think that seeing God or Jesus was a legitimate spiritual aim.

I asked one of the senior monks, 'You don't seem to attach much importance to seeing God. But if one of your monks reported to you that he was having visions of Jesus, what would your response be? What advice would you give?'

'We have to be careful with cases like this,' he replied. 'They do occur from time to time, but often they happen to people who are psychologically disturbed. Schizophrenics often claim to see God, or even be God, but we can't take their claims seriously because they are mad. In my experience, people who report having visions of Jesus usually have some mental disorder.'

After lunch I was shown around and introduced to some of the monks. There was a beautiful statue of Mary there that I liked very much. During my tour one of the monks approached me and asked with great sincerity whether I could help him to see Jesus Christ.

'I overheard your conversation earlier today about seeing Jesus or God. I have been told that you have seen Jesus yourself even though you are a Hindu. I have always wanted to see Him myself. Can you help me?'

If anyone asks me this question, I always say 'Yes,' because if one has a great desire to see God, and if one has faith that He will appear, then He will manifest. I invited this monk, I think his name was Fernandez, to come to some of the satsangs I was holding in Barcelona. He accepted and was allowed to attend by his superiors.

Montserrat seemed to have a very liberal attitude towards

other religions because when I was finally taken to see Father Estanislau, the hermit I had come to see, I found he had a big '*Om*' on his wall and a photo of Ramana Maharshi on one of his shelves. He lived high above the main monastery in a small house that could either be reached by a cable car or a stairway that had about seven hundred steps. I took the cable car on the way up and the stairs coming down.

Father Estanislau had been told in advance about my visit. As I walked into the room he enquired, 'Is that Poonjaji?'

'Yes,' I replied.

'Good,' he said. 'I wanted to meet you. I had been thinking of coming to India to see you, but now it is not necessary.'

We sat there together for some time and had a very good meeting, a meeting of true silence. I had looked hard and long for a living Christian mystic and I finally found one in this hermitage in Montserrat. I have met many Christians in my life, but this one was undoubtedly the best. We did not stay together very long because it wasn't necessary. After about fifteen minutes I took leave and went back down the hill.

Meera accompanied Papaji up the hill but was not present at the meeting between the two of them because Papaji asked her to stay outside Father Estanislau's hut while he went in. I asked her for her impressions of this visit.

Meera: We went up to see him by cable car, but even after we got out, we still had to walk quite a long way. He was living in a very remote place. When Papaji went inside, I waited outside, about three metres from the hut. I saw the '*Om*' that was hanging on his wall, and I think he also had an '*Om*' on a pendant round his neck.

David: Did Papaji tell you about the meeting as soon as he came out of the hut?

Meera: They came out of the hut together and embraced. There was a radiant, happy smile on both of their faces, so I knew that they had had a good meeting. As Master went into his room I heard

Father Estanislau say, 'Is that Poonjaji?' and I heard Master reply, 'Yes, I have been waiting for you'.

David: What do you think he meant by that?

Meera: The Self was waiting for him. I think this was a meeting that had to happen. Somehow Master recognised this as soon as he saw him.

David: How did Father Estanislau get to hear about Papaji? What did he know about him?

Meera: Master told me later that he had seen a copy of Abhishiktananda's book in the room. Father Estanislau told him that he had read about him in the book but at the time he wasn't certain if Master was still living. When he found out for sure that Papaji was still alive, he made a plan to come to India to meet him, but Papaji found him first. This was their only meeting. Father Estanislau never made it to India. Master told me the whole story of the meeting as we walked down the mountain. He was clearly very moved by the encounter.

David: It seems to have been a short meeting. Afterwards, they never arranged to see each other again. Did you find this strange?

Meera: No. Master told me later that it was one of those extraordinary meetings that only need to take place once. Whatever business they had together was finished in that one brief encounter.

Papaji did try to keep in touch with him by post, but Father Estanislau left the monastery soon afterwards. When Papaji tried to contact him at his Montserrat address, one of the other monks replied, stating that Father Estanislau had left both the monastery and his order and was engaged on a walking pilgrimage to Israel. While I was researching this book I discovered that he had settled down in Japan. I wrote several letters to him, asking for his impressions of his meeting with Papaji. I eventually received a two-line note in Spanish from his secretary: 'Father Estanislau remembers having a very good meeting with Poonjaji, but he cannot give an account of it because he no longer replies to letters.'

After visiting Montserrat, Papaji went back to Enrique's house in Barcelona where he soon found himself in another domestic drama:

There was another son in this family, a psychologist called James. Soon after my arrival his mother started complaining about his bachelor status. Like most mothers, she wanted to get her children married and settled.

'Look at this boy,' she would say, pointing to him. 'Nearly thirty years old and still not married. What's wrong with him? I had my first date when I was eight years old, but this boy is twenty-eight and he still can't find a woman for himself. I never even see him talking to women. Whenever I mention it to him, he tells me he's not interested. "I want to be free," he says. "Let me be free."'

His family was trying to push him into an alliance that he didn't want, and James had responded by saying that he would commit suicide if his family made him go through with the marriage. He had had several bouts of depression and the thought of getting married had brought on several new ones.

Enrique's mother enlisted me in her campaign to get him married. I didn't think it was any of my business but I somehow persuaded him to go through with this marriage.

'After some time,' I told him, 'you will probably find yourself getting attached to your new wife. Marriage is not so bad once you get used to it. Many people have survived it without killing themselves. Some people even manage to enjoy it.'

He withdrew his suicide threat and went ahead with the ceremony. I visited the family again a few years later and found that James and his wife had a baby son. The whole family seemed quite happy.

Papaji gave several satsangs in Barcelona, some of which were attended by monks from Montserrat. I asked Meera how these monks responded to Papaji's message.

Meera: He surprised us all by speaking very eloquently about the Bible and Christianity in general. Many of the people asked for explanations of particular biblical verses. He answered them all very well.

David: Did his answers sound plausible to you? Did they satisfy the monks?

Meera: I thought he answered brilliantly. You could never tell from listening to him that he knew virtually nothing about Christianity. He tried to explain the advaitic dimension of several biblical quotes, particularly those that spoke of God as being 'I am'. It wasn't just the explanations that were impressive. There was an inner fire in Master that somehow communicated itself to the listeners. Many of them had lost their passion for God. Their spiritual fires were not burning as brightly as they once had. Master reignited the flame in several of them. Of course, doubts came up later in many of these people because they couldn't reconcile what Master was saying with the traditional teachings of the Church, but while they were in his presence, listening to his words, they definitely felt something of his inner fire.

During his stay in Barcelona someone told Papaji about St Teresa of Avila. When he expressed a wish to visit that town to see what remained of her presence, Enrique, Meera and a man called Felipe drove him there.

During this trip I made a point of going to see any places that had been associated with great saints. I had heard that Teresa had seen Jesus, and this immediately attracted me. In India we have had many saints who have been able to see God: Mirabai could see Krishna, Tukaram saw his Lord Vitthal, and so on. If you feel intense love towards a form of the deity, then the deity appears to you in that form. It can happen in dreams, and it can also happen in the waking state when these forms appear as visions.

I went to Avila and was shown St Teresa's house. It was a very simple place. Some articles that she had used in her daily life were still there. Since some little Spanish pamphlets were on sale there, I asked Enrique to buy one because I wanted to learn a little more about her life and experiences.

He read out and translated a story about her devotion to a particular form of Jesus. One day that form materialised, came up to her, hugged her and kissed her. She immediately ran off to tell St John of the Cross, who was her spiritual advisor.

'I am so happy!' she exclaimed when she arrived. 'Jesus has finally appeared to me. He laughed at me, he smiled, and then he came up to me and kissed me. I have been wanting Jesus to appear before me for so long. Today it finally happened!'

St John was very sceptical. 'I don't think it was really Jesus,' he said. 'Jesus doesn't laugh, and he certainly doesn't hug and kiss women. It must have been some kind of demon that appeared before you.'

This is a typical Christian response to an experience of joy and happiness. Jesus never laughed or smiled in the Bible, so if a laughing, smiling form of Jesus appears in front of you as a result of your devotion to Him, the priests will tell you, 'It is the devil coming to tempt you'. Because Jesus cried and suffered, it is acceptable to see an image of Him crying and suffering, but if you are a woman and your Jesus appears to you and gives you a big hug and a kiss, don't tell the Church authorities or you will get into trouble.

What is wrong with a God who laughs and smiles and hugs? If God is love itself, why shouldn't He appear to you in a happy, smiling form and give you a big hug?

Many good, devout Christians have been discouraged by priests who teach that this world is a place of suffering. If any are listening to me today, I will tell them, 'Don't be fooled into believing that Jesus was miserable and that you too have to be miserable in order to be like Him. Look into your own Heart and find the truth about God. That Heart doesn't belong to any religion. Go into that Heart and find the peace and the joy of the God who is permanently dwelling there. If you walk into the Heart, you won't find Jesus crying there. Instead, happiness and love will welcome you with a smile. They will kiss you and embrace you so tightly, you will never get out of that place again.'

I travelled all over Europe, meeting Christians and visiting their churches and monasteries. I finally came to the conclusion that no one could see God through Christianity. If you like being chronically depressed, then Christianity is the religion for you. If that's what you want, go to church and learn how to be guilty and miserable. But if you want peace and happiness, throw away all your ideas and walk into the kingdom of heaven that is inside you, in your own Heart.

Papaji clearly did not regard his brief foray into Christianity as a great success. Apart from the meeting with Father Estanislau, he only had two other good meetings with monks – the two he had met at Maria Laach and Niederaltaich.

Papaji was not impressed by any of the institutions he visited. When I asked him what he talked about in these places, and further asked him to evaluate the response, he gave me the following answer:

I visited Christian monasteries in Spain, including Montserrat. I also visited the Maria Laach monastery and other institutions in Germany, Switzerland and Italy. If I was ever asked to speak in these places, I would generally speak about the love of God. The response on all occasions was negative.

Papaji ended his European tour in Barcelona. In January, 1972, he flew back to India, intending to spend some time alone on the banks of the Ganga. Meera returned to Belgium because she wanted to try to get some kind of visa that would enable her stay in India for a long time. The bureaucratic procedures were lengthy and complicated and she didn't receive her papers for several months. By that time she knew for sure that she was pregnant with Papaji's child. Papaji invited her to come to India to have the baby in Lucknow, but Meera had been told that it was not safe for her to fly in an advanced state of pregnancy. She remained in Belgium until the baby was born, but flew to India soon afterwards. Mukti, her new daughter, was twenty days old when the two of them flew into Delhi at the beginning of October, 1972. Papaji met them on their arrival:

We stayed in Delhi with my sister, Sumitra. Meera told me she wanted the baby to be dipped in the holy Ganga, but I said, 'First we must go to Lucknow. My mother wants to see the baby.'

We went to Lucknow where my mother warmly welcomed all of us. It was an unusual situation but my mother went out of her way to make sure that Meera and Mukti felt that they were now part of our family. We stayed in Lucknow for about ten days. Towards the end of this period we were invited to stay in Varanasi for a few days by a devotee of my mother who had a house there. He was a Chief Inspector with the Electricity Board. We accepted his invitation and spent a few days in his house, which was nicely located on the banks of the Ganga near the Kashi Viswanatha Temple. I visited some of my old friends who worked at Benares Hindu University and then bought tickets for us to travel to Hardwar.

When we got off the train in Hardwar I found rooms for us at Kali Kambliwala, which was mostly vacant at that time because the rooms had no windows. The Swarg Ashram Trust looked after these rooms, and one of the trustees kindly allowed us to stay there.

Meera's mother, whom I called Durga, joined us after some time. I had seen her before in both Belgium and Spain. She came to India for the first time to be with me and her new granddaughter. The four of us spent most of the next six months living quietly in Rishikesh. Every day we would go for long walks by the side of the Ganga. Durga had brought a baby stroller with her which made life easier for all of us because Mukti could not walk by herself.

Meera describes the months they spent together that winter:

Meera: We arrived in Hardwar sometime in the first half of October and started off staying in a *dharamsala*. Winter was just beginning. We lived a simple life, hardly meeting anyone. After some time we moved to Vitthal Ashram in Rishikesh because we were expecting my mother to arrive. They had more facilities

Papaji and Mukti, sitting on a log in the Ganga in Rishikesh.

there. My mother eventually came and stayed with us for about six months. We would sometimes have satsangs with foreigners and seekers by the banks of the Ganga, but most of the time we were alone.

David: What did your mother think of Papaji?

Meera: When my mother first saw me after my return from India she was so impressed by the transformation she saw in me, she was ready to believe that I had met a real Master. She herself had been on a spiritual quest but had always thought that she could find the truth within herself without a living teacher. When I brought Master to see her in Belgium, he made a big impression on her. Later, when we were staying in Barcelona, she also came and stayed with us for a few days. She had a house in Portugal where she spent most of her time. That's where she came from when she arrived in Barcelona. In Spain she recognised Papaji as her own Master. That's why she came to visit us in India. She wanted to be in the Master's presence and share our life with him as much as possible. When Master next went to the West in 1974, he stayed for three months at my mother's house in Portugal.

David: Papaji told me once that some yogi tried to seduce her while she was in Rishikesh.

Meera: Oh yes, that was very funny. She had a lot of energy and she was always running around, checking out what was going on. In one ashram a yogi promised her he would teach her some secret *asanas* that would give her a lot of power. He took her down into his basement, closed the door and told her that she had to take off all her clothes to do them. When she refused he tried to grab her.

She pushed him off, saying, 'I am your mother! You must treat me as your mother!'

The yogi didn't want a mother, he wanted something else. Eventually she pushed him away, ran up the stairs and escaped.

David: How old was she when this happened?

Meera: She was in her sixties, but she was still quite good looking. The yogi was at least thirty years younger, but he still found her attractive.

David: Did she spend the whole winter with you and Papaji?

Meera: No, she was always going on expeditions to other places, especially after the first month. She also wanted to see different parts of the Himalayas. For one month she stayed at Phool Chatti and just came to visit us during the day.

David: How long were you with Papaji on this trip to India?

Meera: Till June, 1973. We got two visa extensions, but after that

I couldn't get any more In those days there was a strange rule. If you had been in India for several months as a tourist, you had to be out of India for the same length of time before the government would let you back in. I stayed nine months, so I had to leave India for nine months before I would be allowed back. I left with my mother and Mukti in June and went back to Europe. Master stayed in India.

David: What did you do during those months in Europe?

Meera: When I went back to the West, I was very enthusiastic about Master. I wanted to tell everyone how great he was, and I wanted to tell everyone about the experiences I had had with him. Some friends had given me money, so I was able to travel all over Europe. I met western teachers such as Jean Klein and Wei Wu Wei, told them about Master and encouraged them to meet him on his next trip to the West. I ended up at my mother's place in Portugal and stayed there for a few months, waiting for Master to arrive in Europe. I knew he would soon come, so I didn't bother trying to get back into India. When he informed me of his arrival date in Spain, I went to meet him at the airport and stayed with him throughout his European tour.

Papaji spent the first few months after Meera's departure in Karnataka, meeting devotees in Londa and the surrounding areas. In October he went to Rishikesh and spent most of the winter there. He booked his ticket to Europe in the spring and flew into Barcelona on 10th April, 1974. This trip was sponsored and arranged primarily by Felix Coral Garcia, a Spanish architect who had met Papaji on his previous trip to Europe.

Many people wanted to see me, so satsangs were arranged at a yoga centre run by a man called Anthony Blay. He was a well-known writer and yoga teacher in Spain. His centre was very big and on some days I found myself giving satsang to over 150 people. I also gave satsangs in the apartment of a doctor called Jimmy. That place was full up as well. One time about eighty people were squashed into his sixth-floor flat.

One of the first people to meet Papaji was Carlos Silva, a
student of Krishnamurti who was working at Brockwood Park, a
Krishnamurti school that had been set up in England in 1969. His
encounter with Papaji in 1974 is described in his book, The Fourth
Movement, *from which the following extracts are taken:*

I was told that Poonja had arrived that day. On the very next
day I flew from England to Barcelona. It was a Friday and nobody
except Sofia, my wife, knew about the trip.... Two friends of mine,
Miguel and Ana, were waiting for me at Barcelona airport. They
told me excitedly that I was very fortunate because Poonjaji had
cancelled a meeting in order to be ready when I arrived. He was
actually waiting for me as we entered their home. We shook hands
and sat in silence for twenty minutes or half an hour.

I started to smile. The smile turned to laughter. Then the
laughter grew and developed into a deep belly laugh. I was
laughing openly and without motive. I was laughing in this way
and was immensely happy when I suddenly realised with astonish-
ment that the muscles of my face were not actually moving. My
mouth was closed. The moment I became aware of this, our eyes
met. Happiness was dancing in his gaze. We got up and hugged
tightly, with deep affection. It was a most loving embrace. Poonja
was a big strong man and in his effusiveness he actually picked me
up off the ground. All the time it had been my heart that had been
laughing so very happily. It was 'The Heart'. We finally sat down
and started to talk. At the time I was still trapped in some
'Krishnamurtian reasonings'. I immediately asked him how he had
arrived at the state of being he was currently in.

Papaji responded by telling him the story of his life from the
time when he ignored the mango milk shake in Lahore up till the
time he had his decisive meeting with Ramana Maharshi. Carlos
continues:

It was time to leave the apartment and go to the place where we all met for meditation. It was the study of the philosopher Antonio Blay. I went there to see him every day. We would first stay in silence for an hour and a half and then whoever wanted to could ask questions. We repeated these meetings twice a day and the average size of the group was about twenty-five people. Each time we got together Poonja would ask when I was leaving for London and at what time. It was something systematic and quite curious. I could not understand his repeating the question so many times a day. My answer was always the same: 'On Friday at three o'clock in the afternoon.' The week went by quickly, almost without noticing, and I soon found myself departing for Barcelona airport. As I was hugging my friends goodbye, I began to feel something quite extraordinary. I am ashamed to say it was a 'wave' of immense affection. Why am I afraid to call it Love? It was something so intense that it made me feel hot. I could even see a cloud of very subtle powder....

During the take-off Carlos asked himself, 'Who is the pilot of this plane, and how would he react in a situation of real danger?'

The answer, Carlos says, came as a direct experience, 'instantly... as reality, without any words whatsoever. There was only Seeing, Being.'

Carlos elaborates:

Words are never the facts. Words are symbols, an illusion. When words refer to objects, the image and the object correspond. When we say 'glass', it corresponds to the idea of a glass, but the word 'Seeing' that I use does not refer to an object. It has nothing to do with the actual fact or action of seeing. The word can never be the fact. As I only have words to communicate with in this moment, I will say that the pilot of the plane was God, more precisely, the Divine. The Divinity was the 'pilot of the airplane'. These were not mere words in the brain that I now write down, not at all. I was actually seeing and living this. There was no 'I' as different from the movement of the Divine. I was That. Only That. A golden light 'coloured' everything I looked at, both inside and outside, either with closed eyes or open eyes. What was more astonishing still was the fact that this new state of being or dimension did not leave me. Even amid the commonplace activities of a plane full of passengers, everything continued to be the movement of the Divine. Somehow I felt sorry that the others could not see they were That. Each one 'carried his own luggage' without realising that they were on board 'The Airplane'. One could compare it to someone walking forwards inside an airplane in an attempt to arrive before everyone else. Everyone travelled weighed down by his worries, in an anguished state, full of endless misery and mediocrity. Everyone was carrying bags and more bags of luggage, so very heavy because they were so empty.

We arrived at Heathrow Airport in London after a flight of almost two hours. The intensity of the new state was exactly the same....

As soon as I arrived home [Brockwood Park, two hours drive from London] I typed out everything that had happened since my departure from Barcelona airport. It was really a letter for Poonjaji. Sofia, my wife, translated it into English and then I mailed it to Spain. Though it was quite unnecessary to write to Poonjaji, I felt happy communicating and acknowledging his role in what had happened. I wanted to admit his action had existed and to thank him for his Love-Power gesture, though no words could ever be enough.

The experience lasted for about five hours, after which it subsided into a more general feeling of peace and contentment. While he was waiting for a response from Papaji, he continued with his work at Brockwood Park. One of his daily chores was washing Krishnamurti's car. Krishnamurti himself usually came along and helped.

First he [Krishnamurti] would wet the whole car with the hose pipe. I had prepared the water and the soap beforehand. Krishnaji liked it foamy. I also added some kerosene to the bucket. Then we would start with a sponge, dip it in the soap and wash methodically from the top down. My heart felt like springtime while we were together there. In the middle of this particular washing job we met face to face at one corner of the car.

Without any preamble he asked: 'Why did you go to see another? Don't you have here the "bread" you are looking for?'

He was not reproachful, nor were they simple words. It was real Love. I was struck dumb with surprise, because he could not have known that I had been to Barcelona. I could not utter a word. He continued speaking, not waiting for an answer.

'If another one enlightens you, then you yourself or someone else can put out that light. One has to enlighten oneself. If it is done this way, no one, not even you, will be able to put out that light. It is necessary to use one's own intensity, effort and passion.'

He spoke with deathly seriousness. The Love that flowed from him as he said this was so great, my legs gave way under me.

At the beginning of June Carlos received a reply from Papaji:

My most Beloved Divine Friend:

...Even before I got your letter I was confident that you are absolutely open and intelligent and are perfectly ready to grasp the truth after only hearing IT once. This happens in the case of a few very mature seekers after Truth. They have a clear glimpse of the Truth once and then seek the advice of the Master to stabilise it.

The experience that you have expressed in your above letter is one of very high calibre and is worthy of praise. The method you explain is unique too and very lovingly understandable.

I am most happy with you and hope to keep the link with you so that you get established in the Truth and that the Truth abides in you eternally.

May this silence have a permanent imprint upon your Heart. I send you my love, happiness and congratulations.

Could it be possible to see you before I leave for India? I am going to France around 15th June and I shall write to you about my travels in that country. Till then you can write to me at the above address.

Please keep a note of your experiences in a book and convey them to me once a week when you write because I am sure you will

191

have deeper experiences once the doors of the Heart are pushed. With regards, profound love and embraces.

Your own Self Poonja

As requested, Carlos sent a record of his experiences to Papaji. On 10th June, Papaji, who was then travelling in France, sent him the following reply:

My most Beloved One,

What happiness your letter gave me as I was leaving for France just now. I will write to you in detail when I am there. Also I will inform you when I will be in Paris so that I can meet you. This can be either at Paris, or I could even go to your place for a day.

It is no surprise to me that you have had this most marvellous and highest mystic experience. It is an absolutely abstract experience. I should not call it an experience at all. It is total being, existence itself. I am absolutely happy for you, my beloved son.

You came to see me for what purpose? I knew it very well. I saw it within you, and you saw it when you looked into Me. Though I was talking to other persons, I was with you all the time, even when you left for your place. I was with you at the airport and even in the plane. I AM with you always.

What a wonderful explanation you gave in your letter dated 4th June, 1974, from Brockwood! You have described most efficiently what you actually saw. This experience is not less than any experience that any great sage of any country could have had.

Your friends [Miguel and Ana] are no longer coming to see me at the daily silent meditation at the Institute. Perhaps my way is just too much for them. I don't mind. Anyone is welcome to go his or her own way.

I am so happy to have an account of your experiences. If you permit me I can send it to India to my disciples because they will be very happy to have another brother in our cosmic family. They will write to you.

Papaji then addressed some of the questions that Carlos had raised in his letter:

Papaji in Anthony Blay's Barcelona house: 1974.

'Whatever I did, "That" was there' is an experience of Being.

'I was afraid "That" would go away' and 'I could perceive the fear of seeing the fear', are still marvellous. This explanation is most necessary for constant stabilisation. I will explain when I have more time.

'There was no separation between mind, Heart and body.' On reading this I want to fly at once to embrace you till the end of all time!

Please write more on this subject. You have achieved what is worthy of achievement. Or there was nothing to achieve. It was just Be-ing as you were, and You Are. Worry not, 'I am with you'.

We both must meet. Please write to me if I can see you when I go to Paris.

I send you my love.

Love to whom? To my own Self,
The Self of Carlos,
Poonja

Papaji and Carlos arranged to meet later that summer in Saanen, Switzerland, at the time when Krishnamurti was scheduled to give a series of talks there.

When Carlos read Papaji's comment that he was with him at the airport, he remembered the frequent requests for the time and date of his departure. When he asked Papaji later that year in Switzerland whether he had deliberately chosen that moment to give him the experience, Papaji confirmed that this had been so.

Carlos was not the only person to have a spectacular experience during Papaji's first few days in Barcelona. Because there were so many people coming to see him, Papaji asked Gyaneshwar, one of his Barcelona devotees, to send reports to his devotees in India, since he didn't have time himself. This was his first report:

We are a bit late to announce the arrival of our Holy Master amidst us because of the overcrowded meetings of his disciples and devotees from Europe who have been eagerly awaiting the fortunate day since November, 1973.

The eternal love of the Master is flowing like the Holy Ganga into our hearts. The name of the Lord, His *lilas* [divine plays], the stories of the saints and the stories of the Master's devotees from India are constantly ringing in our hearts.

Many people of España have already received his grace. This is evident from the experience of one of his closest disciples, Nivritti.

The Master will find time in a few days to write to his children in his own hand.

Appended to this note was a first-person account by Nivritti that related the effect Papaji had had on her:

All this world seems faded out from my mind and all people

194

1974: giving satsang in Barcelona.

sleeping. I feel myself alone, floating on a sea of the dead. My spirit is fixed only within you. And when I have no more your physical presence, I feel only the need of weeping, of weeping deeply, and to come near you again.

O Master! You have stolen my heart. I don't know what to do. I can only think of you and cry. I am now in your prison. People talk to me about their occupations, but nothing interests me. I say nothing but smile and remember your love.

But now I am alone and I am crying. My Father! I want nothing more, and nothing is of any importance to me except to be with you. Only speak to me about God. Show Him to me. I want only God, my beloved Master.

You have made me crazy. You have stolen my heart. Don't leave me because I will die if I am left alone. If you wish I will die, but don't leave me, don't leave me!

I FEEL GOD HAS VISITED ME AND HAS TOUCHED MY SOUL. What more do I ask for? I want only to remain with Him. I want to remain with you. I want to die in your arms. My Master!

From now onwards you will be the whole for me, my Father, my Mother, my Wife, my Sons, my Friend, my God.

I am crazy and overwhelmed. You have broken my tastes for normal life, and now I see only you when I speak. When I hear and when I look at anything, you are alone there. I see only you and hear only you.

To be in your presence every evening, what a bliss! To be by your side, living only in your heart, in the heart of God. What a fortune!

Thanks, Master. I am unconditionally your bride. All my being now belongs to you. I want nothing, nothing at all, only to dwell forever in your heart.

Ten days later Gyaneshwar's next report to Papaji's devotees in India contained the following anonymously written account:

This morning I was driving in a car from the residence of the Master to my office. What a marvellous experience do I have! It is fantastic to see with my own eyes that the form of the Master is universally located on all sides, and I suddenly perceived it is becoming greater and greater and I was placed in its centre.

It was not me who was the seer of this cosmic vision, but it was in the opposite way. I was filled entirely *as It Is*. It was my own extended form but subtler and more glorious. It could not be decided that it was interior or exterior.

Thank you, My Lord!

I am living in thee, and what all I see is within thyself.

I am still in the car and suddenly I hear the sound of *OM* from somewhere, neither inside nor outside, spontaneously. This sound was heard with more clarity, oozing out from the source. Then, music flowed automatically from my vocal organ.

It is so evident that everything happens within the Master! Master is unique existence. All the rest is happening within the heart of the Master.

In a moment I perceived that all that has been seen, along with the seer, was the Master. Now, all this became subtler and subtler and disappeared, leaving me in a sad state. Still, my mind was

fixed in the previous vision.
Thank you, thank you, Master! There I am at your disposal. You have enslaved me. I have nothing to ask, and have no desire whatsoever. I am in the orbit of your grace. Thanks, O Master! Having found you, I have added all the rest unto me. THANK YOU.

Kindly excuse my bad English.
I speak Spanish my mother tongue.

Thanks.

At least one other person had a remarkable experience at these early satsangs, although the consequences were rather unfortunate. Papaji was reminded of the story as he was talking about a visit he once made to a mental hospital in Bombay.

As I walked in through the gates I saw many laughing and smiling people there. Some of them came up to me and greeted me with a big welcoming smile. At first I thought that I must have met them somewhere and that I had forgotten who they were because they were greeting me with the kind of smile one reserves for old, dear friends. It was only later that I found out from a psychiatrist that these people had been locked up because they smiled and laughed all the time.

How to tell who is mad and who is not? The psychiatrists will tell you that people who laugh and smile constantly for no reason at all are mad. I disagree. I would say that people who don't check their thoughts are mad. This is the true symptom of madness. This whole universe is one vast mental asylum full of people who are mad because they cannot exercise any control over what goes on inside their heads. Who is truly wise and sane in this world? You may find one or two people if you search the whole world hard enough and long enough. The rest of the people are just inmates in a vast lunatic asylum.

So, going back to these people in the mental hospital in Bombay, I don't know if they were really mad or not, but I do know from personal experience that if one laughs too much in public, and for no reason, one runs the risk of being locked up in a mental hospital. This actually happened to someone who attended one of my satsangs about twenty years ago in Spain.

In those days I was giving talks in a yoga centre that was being run by a man called Anthony Blay. He had met me in Lucknow on one of his visits to India, and while he was here he had given me an invitation to talk at one of his centres in Europe. Some of the Spanish people here may have heard of him. He was quite a famous spiritual teacher in those days. He had written several books and had centres in many places. The one I was giving my talks at was in Barcelona. There was a big hall that held about 180 people. From six to eight every evening I would be there, either giving a talk or conducting a meditation session.

During one of these satsangs a man I had never seen before came and prostrated before me. This in itself was unusual because Europeans don't have this habit. Also, in those days, I used to discourage people from prostrating before me.

When the man stood up he started laughing and shouting. In between his bursts of laughter he would shout, 'I am Jesus! I am Jesus! I am God! I am God!' He didn't stay very long. After a few minutes he ran out of the room, still shouting, 'I am Jesus! I am Jesus!'

At the end of the evening I asked Anthony Blay who this man was.

'I don't know him,' he replied. 'I have never seen him before. He is not a member of our centre. We have a sign outside that says "Everyone is welcome". He probably just saw the sign and walked in.'

I wanted to know who he was because I always like it when someone stands up and proclaims, with authority, 'I am God'. A man who knows who he really is can stand up and proclaim this truth, because it is his own inner experience, but when people behave like this in the West, they get into trouble both with the Church and with the civil authorities. Anyone who persistently proclaims that he has understood that he is identical with God runs the risk of being put in a mental hospital. In India we have no problem with declarations such as these. In fact, our scriptures encourage us to say 'I am *Brahman*' and to experience the truth of this statement.

Since no one knew who this man was, or where he had come from, I had to let the matter drop. However, in the middle of the night I got a phone call from a woman I didn't know.

'My husband told me that he was going to attend a talk that was being given by an Indian man. This talk was supposed to be at 6 p.m. in Anthony Blay's centre. He has still not come home. I called up the centre but no one there knew my husband. The man I spoke to suggested that I call you because you are the one who gave the lecture. He is called Pedro and he is a professor. Did you see him this evening?'

I didn't know anyone called Pedro but I had a feeling that this might be the man who had left abruptly after shouting 'I am Jesus! I am God!' I described this man to the woman on the phone and she agreed that this was probably her husband. I couldn't help her because I had no idea where he had gone after he left the satsang.

Early the next morning she called me again and said, 'I received a call from the police in the middle of the night. I was told they had found a man dancing in the middle of the *autopista*. They said he had abandoned his car in the middle of the road about 120 kilometres from here and that he was dancing around it shouting "I am Jesus! I am God!" He wasn't able to answer any of their questions but they found out who he was by checking his driving license.

'The policeman told me, "He is not able to look after himself. Please come at once to collect him. He is in no condition to drive his car. Bring an extra driver. You will need one person to drive and another to control him."

'When I went to see him I was shocked at the condition he was in. We are a respectable family. My husband is a professor of music in the university, but when I found him, he was dancing like a drunkard on and around his car, screaming to anyone who passed, "I am God!"

'The police wanted me to take responsibility for him since I am his wife, but I told them, "He is not my husband any more. I don't know who this man is. He didn't even recognise me or acknowledge my presence in any way. I don't want to live any longer with someone who behaves like this.'"

'But what happened to him?' I asked. 'He can't be still there, dancing in the road.'

'I refused to take him back to our apartment because he was clearly mad, so I drove him to the local mental hospital and left him there. So far as I know, he is still there.'

I called Mr Blay and told him what had happened. Since Pedro had been abandoned by his wife, I thought that it was up to us to do something about him. I knew he wasn't mad. I knew he was dancing and laughing for an entirely different reason.

Mr Blay told me, 'You can't do anything. They will not allow you into the hospital because you are not a relative. In that place only family members are allowed to see the patients.'

I called the wife again and asked her to go to the hospital because she was the only one who could get to see him. I explained that it was just a temporary experience brought on by intense happiness. When you drink for the first time, if you take more than one or two pegs, and if your body is not used to it, then you will also dance and sing. That's so, isn't it? I offered my services to this woman because I knew that her husband was in a state of shock as a result of being suddenly immersed in an ocean of joy and ecstasy.

She listened to my explanation but was adamant in her refusal to have anything more to do with him.

'I don't care how he got in that state, and I don't want to know the reason. And I don't care if it is just a temporary state or experience. You say that he will soon be back to normal. That may be so, but I will still not take him back. What he did last night was totally unacceptable. I can never allow this man to come back into my house again. His laughing and dancing have demonstrated to me that he is prone to madness. I can never trust him again because I will never know when he will start behaving like this again.'

'But he won't be like this for long,' I said. 'In a couple of days he will be back to normal. Right now he needs someone to look after him. Because you are his wife, you are the only person who can get to see him. You should not abandon him just because he got very excited on account of being so happy.'

She wouldn't listen to me. 'I want nothing more to do with him because I am afraid of him. He never spoke of God before. We loved each other very much. We were married for thirteen years but he never behaved like this before. Now, after attending one meditation class with you, he is screaming in the middle of the road, claiming he is God. I don't want to live with God. I want to live with a man who is normal and who knows how to behave properly. I cannot take him back because I will never know when he will start acting like this again.'

So, this is one of the social laws in the West. If you get so happy that you start laughing and dancing in the street, you will be locked up as a madman, and when you get out you will be shunned by your former friends and relatives. In India we revere people who behave like this, particularly if they have had this direct experience of God, but in the West such people are never accepted by society or by the Church.

Papaji encourages anyone who has a waking-up experience around him to celebrate by singing, by dancing, or by expressing themselves in any way that feels appropriate. His experiences in Europe, where at least two people were arrested after having ecstatic experiences in his presence, have not caused him to modify his views on this subject.

The following remarks were made to a man who had had a profound experience in one of Papaji's satsangs and who was subsequently sitting quietly, in a very introverted way. After telling the man that he should 'learn to celebrate,' Papaji went on to make the following remarks:

Some people dance and some people sing when they have this experience. It is not planned or rehearsed, it just happens by itself because the particular person cannot contain the joy and the peace that has suddenly been revealed to him. It immediately bursts out and expresses itself.

One woman was once driving me from her home to the place in Bombay where I was staying. It was a distance of about twenty miles. She was an Indian woman who lived in Florida. Her son worked in the Gulf as a chartered accountant. Suddenly, as she was driving along, she had this experience. She didn't sit quietly like you. She stopped the car in the middle of the road, got out and started dancing on the roof. This is the real way to celebrate. When your time comes, your experience will compel you to get up and dance. You can't postpone it even for a minute. This woman didn't wait till she got to my house. She stopped the car immediately and started dancing on the roof. When you go into your bedroom with your wife on your honeymoon night, do you say to her, 'Now is not an appropriate time. Let's put it off till later'?

That reminds me of an Englishman called Rod who came to see me in Narhi in the 1980s. He turned up one day with his baggage so I asked my son, Surendra, to arrange for his accommodation in the nearby Hotel Pal. I told him that he could come to my house later to have lunch with us.

He came almost immediately and attended the satsang until it finished at around 1 p.m. During the course of the satsang he said that he had seen many teachers in England and America, and had been told by one of them, a *vipassana* teacher, to come to Lucknow to visit me.

At first he was just asking questions, the sort of questions that most new visitors ask. But then suddenly, for no apparent reason, he stopped asking, stood up and started dancing around the room. He was so ecstatic, he was unable to answer any questions that were put to him. After some time, he ran out of the house and started dancing down the street. He was jumping around, throwing his hands in the air, completely oblivious to everything that was going on around him. In his joy he failed to see an open manhole in the middle of the road. He went straight down the hole and plunged into the sewage below. Not even this experience could slow him down or dampen his ecstatic joy. He crawled out of the manhole, covered with smelly, rotting sewage, and carried on dancing ecstatically down the street. This is how it is when this moment comes. Nothing will quench this joy, not even a total immersion in the sewers of Lucknow.

This drama took place at the beginning of June, 1988. When

Rod had calmed down a little, Papaji asked him to write about his experiences and to keep a diary in which he should write a daily record of what was happening to him. I found a copy of this diary among Papaji's books. These are extracts from what Rod had to say about the experience and its aftermath:

In the morning I told Poonjaji about my experiences before I came to him, of just wanting freedom. He said words to the effect, 'You are very lucky. This only happens to a very few people. If you have found a jewel, you must honour it, treasure it, make a friendship with it.' Then he said, 'Friendship is a misleading term because it implies two where there is only one'.

I feel relaxed and excited at the same time. I want to go to the mountains for a while but Poonjaji tells me not to take the chocolate instead of the $100 He says, 'Going to the mountains will not give you freedom because you will take your old mind with you'.

He looked at me lovingly and said that he could see me shining more and more. I could feel myself that this was true. I expressed my joy at his teaching, and Master said he was very happy with me. Something wonderful and mysterious is happening to me. While it is happening Master lovingly and compassionately touches me, shakes me, and then asks me how I am. He put his hand on my shoulder and gave me a piece of fruit. Wow!...

Master says to me, 'Do you think you can handle the experience of freedom?' I say, 'Yes!' Master then says that it can be a great shock to the system. I don't think he meant to frighten me. He just wanted to say that the body must be able to handle it. Then he said, 'After this experience some go mad, some get stuck in bliss and happiness, and the third group, the best group, stay silent'.

There's nothing left for me to do! I'm the luckiest person in the world! JAI JAI RAM! Destiny places me at the feet of a perfect Master. JAI JAI RAM! This is even more perfect than perfect. This is totally wondrous and incredible. JAI JAI RAM!

I told Master this and his face lit up. This is the kind of thing he wants to hear and read about....

There's the excitement about the ever new and fresh unfolding before me. I feel like jumping, jumping into the unknown. There's nothing for me to do now. No effort for me to make. Nowhere for me to go. Nothing to be remembered. Nothing to be forgotten. My mind clings to nothing. And deep inside I feel something wondrous. I don't feel the need to accomplish or attain anything. No need to move from 'here'. This is the most important thing. The thing which I long for the most. And when I long for Truth, it is Truth itself speaking. I feel most blessed to be sitting at your feet. Where else is there for me to go? A feeling of mystery and wonder. Nothing to be worked out or understood. And I'm totally blessed when truth speaks through my heart. And how can it speak at any other time than 'now'? Only when I stop looking does it appear. There's so much more the feeling of being present – and the fullness of the moment....

As we were walking in the park thoughts are coming, but there's AWARENESS AWARENESS AWARENESS of them. Surrender, surrender, surrender is happening, but then who is there to surrender? There is only the Self. There is a sudden intensity; energy rushes up and then concentrates like an arrow at my third eye. Then it seems my intellect is surrendering. Then I start going into crazy shaking, but you, my divine Master shout 'No!' and immediately I am brought out of the craziness, the uncontrollableness. You say, 'Remain normal, observe the beauty of nature'. Ah! This is unparalleled wondrousness.

So much is happening but I know the work is not yet over. Master says that after one year something will happen. But still I feel the joy of the unknown opening up before me. Such wonder. Such beauty. Such incredibleness.

Master, Rod, Poonjaji and Self are dancing in and out of each other in a divine *Lila*. How to make a formality out of bowing to Poonjaji's feet? But still it is a beautiful custom and a wondrous expression of the Self bowing to the Self. When I bowed to you in the park you said that it was the first real bow I had done.

Thoughts have much less grip on me. I wrote to you earlier that all my thoughts are divine. I still feel this way, which is why they don't bother me.

204

Rod's descriptions indicate long periods of peace interspersed with bouts of ecstasy in which he would occasionally get over-excited and lose control of his body. Writing about these outbursts, Rod remarked, 'Divine craziness is the divine in the body but in an uncontrolled state'. Papaji felt that he needed a break in order to let his body adjust to what had happened.

After observing Rod for some time I decided that it would not be good for him to stay in Lucknow. One day I took him to the Residency because I thought he needed to be outside more and have some exercise. Instead of enjoying the gardens, he started rolling on the grass and screaming. The experience had obviously triggered off a major shock in his nervous system and I thought that a continued stay in Lucknow might make it worse. Thinking that he would benefit from a few days in the Himalayas, I asked my son to take him to the station and buy a ticket for him on the Doon Express. He was planning to go to the mountains anyway. He had already told me that he had come with a lot of warm, water-proof clothes because he had plans to go climbing in Ladakh.

He wrote to me from Leh in Ladakh, saying that he liked the place very much. I wrote back to him, telling him that I would be going to Hardwar in a week, and that he need not come back to Lucknow to see me. After about a month he came to visit me in Hardwar. He stayed with me for a while and then followed me back to Lucknow when I returned. After spending some time with me in Lucknow, I told him to go back to England and speak to his friends about what had happened to him. Sometime later he wrote to me, saying that no one understood him in England. He had been working as a teacher, but in his letter he told me the experience had changed him so profoundly, he could no longer carry on with his work. He said that he needed to spend more time with me and asked if he could come back to India the following winter. I invited him to come. On that visit he just sat quietly and peacefully without exhibiting any of the wild symptoms that characterised his first visit. Since he seemed to have adjusted to the experience quite well, I eventually told him to go to America and tell his previous teachers what had happened to him in Lucknow.

After about two weeks in Barcelona, Papaji accepted an invitation to give satsangs in Madrid. In a letter he wrote to Vinayak Prabhu shortly after his arrival in Madrid, he remarked, 'Many people want to come with me to India but I have no place, nor do I want to make any. The whole universe is my house. I live like an owner wherever I go. The Father of the universe takes good care of me. I am His Son. I am proud of being so.'

An architect from Madrid, Señor Enrique Noriega, attended my satsangs in Barcelona. He invited me to come to Madrid for a few days to give satsangs to devotees there. He told me that his wife Consuelo also wanted to meet me and question me on several topics. I went there and gave satsang in his house. About fifteen people used to come every day.

One day Enrique answered the phone and found himself talking to a Professor Rivera of Madrid University. This man had apparently lectured in India at the invitation of the government of India. He was telephoning to ask if I would come to the university to meet some of the professors and students at 5 p.m. I accepted the invitation because it was an opportunity to meet a large group of people. General Franco had a rule that no more than fifteen people could assemble in a private house for a meeting, so my satsangs in Enrique's flat were limited to that number. But in public premises such as the university, the rule did not apply. Enrique knew this professor and advised me not to go.

'Professor Rivera doesn't like Indians,' said Enrique. 'I have heard him make many rude remarks about India. He is probably only inviting you so that he can abuse you in front of all his students and fellow teachers.'

I don't run away from challenges like this. I went at the appointed hour and found that about a hundred people had come to listen to me. There was a stage with three chairs on it. One was for me, one was for the professor, and the third was for a Spanish woman who had been engaged to translate my answers into Spanish.

The professor stood up to make some introductory remarks. As the Spanish woman translated for me, it became clear to me that

206

Madrid, 1974.

he had a low opinion of India and Indians.

'I do not know anything about this man's background,' he began, 'but I do know that he comes from a poor country that begs for food and money from the West. Let us see if this man from the land of beggars has brought anything that we don't have already.

'I will ask the first question myself. Mr Poonja, who is greater, Buddha or Jesus?'

I realised immediately that he was trying to set a trap for me. He wanted me to offend one of the religions by saying that the other was better. Then the people could get into an argument with me. So, when he asked me this question, 'Who is greater, Buddha or Jesus?' I just looked at him and said, very quietly, 'I'.

In that 'I' neither the Buddha nor Jesus is the greater. 'I' is greater than anything else. This answer somehow stopped his mind and destroyed all his antagonism. He threw his arms around me, hugged me, and kissed me with tears in his eyes.

207

Then he spoke to the other teachers and students, 'This man will be able to answer all your questions. Ask him anything you like.'

I had a good evening, talking to all these new people. They didn't know anything about me, enlightenment or the Indian spiritual traditions, but they still asked some good questions. At the end of the evening Professor Rivera invited me to come and meet his wife the next day. She was also a professor at the university, but she hadn't attended my question-and-answer session.

The next morning I was driven about thirty miles to a beautiful garden that had been made for General Franco. We sat on chairs in the landscaped garden and ate breakfast together. Since they were both professors, they had a lot of intellectual questions, but they must have been satisfied with my answers because they came to see me every day while I was in Madrid. Professor Rivera was writing a book called *Oriente Occidente*. He told me that he would put an account of his meeting with me in this book.

Enrique, the architect, wanted me to stay in Madrid and settle down there. One day during my stay he took me to a place in a forest a short distance from Madrid and told me, 'I want to build a house or an ashram for you here so that you can stay with us permanently'.

I didn't want to be tied down to a particular place so I turned down his offer.

Enrique's wife, Consuelo, was a big follower of Krishnamurti. She knew him personally and had attended many of his talks in different parts of Europe. Consuelo asked me many intelligent questions based on her understanding of Krishnamurti's teachings. She liked my answers and wanted to come to India to spend some time with me there, but she wasn't in a position to travel because she had two small children. Though she was a good woman, with a serious interest in spiritual matters, she had a very unstable personality. One day while I was there she got hysterical and started smashing plates and throwing them out of her kitchen window. No one could control her or make her calm down, not even her husband.

When I first heard Professor Rivera criticise India, I assumed that he was probably a Christian who had a low opinion of Indian religious thought. I found out later, though, that he was deeply disgusted with the methods that western Christians were using to impose their beliefs on third world countries.

One day, after I had gained his confidence, he said to me, 'Poonjaji, I want to show you one of our local theatres. I think you will be very interested in the show they are putting on.'

I replied, 'I am not very fond of theatre performances. I came to Europe for a different purpose. I came to teach meditation and to instruct people how to find out who they really are. That's why I accepted your invitation to speak at the university.'

'This is a different kind of performance,' he said. 'It is not open to the general public. It is a theatre at the university in which missionaries are trained to perform for people in poor countries. I am allowed to go in, partly because I am a professor at the university, and partly because I also lecture in India occasionally. They want to teach people like me how to have the maximum emotional impact on potential converts.'

I accepted his invitation and went to watch these missionaries being trained. It was just as Professor Rivera had said. They were being trained by actors to look and sound convincing as they delivered their message.

At one point the instructor said, 'People in India like spiritual teachers to get very emotional when they give out their message. If you cry while you are reading from the Bible, you will make a much better impression. If this doesn't come naturally to you, put some lemon juice or onion juice in your eyes as you read. When the tears start to flow from your eyes, the audience will be very impressed because they will think that you are in a state of bliss.'

Then he showed them how to keep the lemon hidden in the hand, and how to bring it to the eyes without anyone noticing it. The teacher said that the best way was to put the juice in a handkerchief. No one suspects a man who is mopping his brow or blowing his nose. This is how the missionaries were being taught. They didn't have their own inner experience of God that would make them cry naturally, so they were being taught to cheat.

This is one way to catch new people. Another is to get them

as children when they are very young. In India the Christian organ-
isations take girls from poor, low-caste families and promise to
look after them and educate them. When they are in their teens
they are encouraged to enter a convent abroad for further training.
But when they agree and go to these institutions, they find that they
are mostly used as domestic servants. If the potential converts are
already adults, they are bribed with food. When I worked at Castle
Rock, near Goa, the missionaries handed out sugar, flour and
pulses every week to the people who attended the church services.
This is a religion that depends on cheating and bribery to get
people into its ranks. I don't see any future for a religion like this.
In the West church attendance has been declining for decades.
Many of the people who are seriously interested in finding God or
enlightenment are leaving Christianity and following other religions. I saw this for myself when I travelled in Europe.

*Papaji gave satsangs in Madrid for about two weeks. He
seems to have found a way round the 'no more than fifteen people'
rule, for on May 5th, 1974, he sent the following message to Sri B.
D. Desai:*

Madrid

My Dear Son,
I am staying at Madrid these days but Meera phoned to me to say
that some boys have suddenly come from France to [Barcelona to]
see me. So, tomorrow I have to return. About 100 persons are
attending my talks every day here. They have offered me a permanent big house to use as my residence and as a meditation centre.

The people of this place are very nice. In a couple of days
many of them have had experiences. Gyaneshwar will write to you
in detail from Barcelona.

*While he was in Madrid Papaji met an artist who wanted to
paint his portrait. He describes his encounter with her and then
goes on to talk about other artists he met in Europe:*

A woman approached me after one of my satsangs and asked

if she could paint my portrait.

'I will need to sit with you alone for about six hours,' she said.

I didn't want to waste six hours sitting, doing nothing, while she finished her picture, so I told her, 'We hold satsangs for an hour here every day. You can come then and do your work while I am answering everyone's questions, or while they are meditating.'

She agreed and completed the picture in about a week. Everybody liked it, including me, but she wasn't satisfied.

'A photo shows you what the outside of a person looks like,' she explained, 'but a portrait should reveal what goes on inside. You may like it, but so far as I am concerned, it has been a failure because I never managed to get a feeling of what you are really like inside. Because of this, I couldn't transmit my understanding to the canvas. There is something in you that I couldn't capture. I am not satisfied with it, but you are welcome to have it.'

I accepted it and even had it sent back to India. It now hangs in my house in Lucknow. I liked this woman's attitude to her painting. She was not just trying to copy my face, she was trying to find the reality that lay behind it so that she could transmit some of its essence to the picture. The hourly sessions were a real satsang for her because she was focusing her whole attention on the true nature of the teacher who was in front of her.

I met several other artists during my travels around Europe. During my first trip to Europe I encountered a German artist who told me a very interesting story.

'I went to an exhibition,' he said, 'because some of my paintings were on display. I didn't have a big reputation and my paintings at that time were selling for very small amounts. I would turn them out very quickly and sell them very cheaply. There was one tiny painting of a very ugly woman that I didn't expect to sell for more than DM 10. In fact, it was so ugly, I wasn't really expecting anyone to buy it. One eye was closed, the nose was twisted, and I had deliberately made her look as old, wrinkled and ugly as I could.

'One woman came up to me during the show, emptied her purse in front of me and said, "This is all the money I have with me, except some change in my pocket which I need for the bus fare home. Is it enough to buy this picture?"

'She pointed at the painting of the ugly woman.

'I looked at the pile of money in front of me and replied, "There are hundreds of marks here. You don't need to spend all this money. I will take ten. The rest you can keep."

"'No," she replied. "I want to give you everything I have. I didn't come here intending to buy a picture. I just came to town to do some shopping. I wandered in here out of curiosity. But as soon as I saw this picture I thought to myself, 'This is the best picture of a woman I have ever seen. I like it because I know inside that I am like this, and I like it because I know that inside, all women are like this. This is the ultimate representation of womankind. I must have it, and I want to give everything I have for it because I know that if I do, I will appreciate it even more.'"

'I sold her the picture for this large amount and she went home happy.'

This was a very strange story, one that I still don't know how to explain. Why would this woman want to look at something so ugly? Why did she think it was so accurate, and why was she willing to spend all her money on it when she could have had it for DM 10? I have told this story to several people, but no one has given me an answer that satisfies me.

Another artist, quite a well-known one, invited me to his flat in Paris. He was an art professor who was also a student of Krishnamurti. As I walked into his flat, I saw one of his works hanging on the wall in front of me. I had no idea what it was supposed to be, so I asked him directly, 'What is it?'

'I don't know,' he responded. 'I don't use my mind when I work. There are no ideas or intentions when I work. I am not trying to make anything or accomplish anything. I just let go and let my hands do whatever they want to. When it is done, I cannot say what it means because I didn't put any meaning into it when I made it. It is just a reflection of my state at the moment when my hands did the work.'

I liked this idea of no-mind art but I cannot say that I liked the finished product because all the works he showed me were constructed out of old cigarette ends. In his spare time he wandered the streets of Paris, picking up discarded cigarette butts. When he had enough for a new work of art, he would stand in front of his canvas, turn off his mind and allow his fingers to fix the old cigarettes to it in seemingly random patterns. This man was quite famous, and he even persuaded people to pay lots of money for these works. I couldn't appreciate them because his whole flat stank of stale tobacco. I got out of there as soon as I could.

I found out later that he had switched to wooden blocks. He would take these pieces of wood, which looked like children's building blocks, and arrange them in patterns on the floor. Sometimes he would add a few stones. These arrangements went on display in Paris galleries and many of them were sold for large amounts of money.

Most of the artists I met told me that their paintings were a representation or a reflection of their mental states, but I could rarely see any connection between the two. On my first visit to Europe, for example, I met an artist in Salzburg who showed me some beautiful wildlife pictures he had painted. Flying birds seemed to be his speciality. When he was not painting, he was having violent quarrels with his wife. I met her as well and she told me that he frequently beat her, but there was no trace of his violent nature in the pictures he produced.

I cannot say that I understood or appreciated much of the art I was shown in Europe. Perhaps my tastes are too different. I like dancing and I like singing, but I rarely like works of art. When I was in India, I liked to sing and dance in the rain. I would go to the mountains by myself and express my inherent joy by dancing and singing alone.

Papaji returned to Barcelona in the second week of May and paid a visit to the farm of Enrique Aguilar, the man who had invited him to Barcelona in 1971. He gave an account of his brief visit in a letter to Vinayak Prabhu:

Barcelona

My beloved Divine Son,
Enrique Aguilar and José Tewar, whom you have known in India,

came to take me to their farm. I have returned today after spending a few days with them. They have a very big farm of 700 hectares that is completely mechanised. They grow wheat, maize, barley and cattle fodder. Enrique married a Sinhalese girl who is the younger sister of Ibrahim Chhota, a man who came to see me in Lucknow. She is currently at Pons, in the province of Lerida. José will write to you soon. I gave him your new address. Enrique wants to spend nine months in India with me at Rishikesh and three months at his farm. Nowadays he does not like very much to stay in the society of Christians. I find him completely Aryanised due to his study of the *Vedas*. He teaches Sanskrit in the University twice a week. He is staying with me till I return home. His farm is 200 km from Barcelona.

Many persons are getting ready to accompany me to India. Perhaps they think that I too fall in the category of other spiritual teachers who have big ashrams in India. They visit Europe and then return with a full jetload of sheep. They like to show off their greatness by counting up how many sheep they have persuaded to follow them. I have told them all they must wait till I write to them from India.

While he was in Barcelona Papaji also accepted an invitation to visit the island of Ibiza for a few days:

Some hippies wandered into one of my satsangs in Barcelona, liked what they heard there, and invited me to spend a few days with them in Ibiza. I accepted their invitation because I was curious to see how they lived. In those days almost everyone on the island seemed to be a hippy. They liked it there because the police didn't bother them. Many of them didn't even have visas, but they were left in peace. The people I stayed with explained to me that they were traditional hippies; that is to say, they had established a self-sufficient, communal way of living. They were quite well organised. There was a maternity centre for the women, a school and a care centre for the children. The school was run by a big, fat American girl whom I liked very much. They were young, innocent people who really believed that one day they would rule the world.

I asked Meera why he accepted this particular invitation.

He was very curious about everything that was going on in Europe. He wanted first-hand information on how people were living and thinking. I think he went to Ibiza because he heard that there were many young people there who had left their rich families to live a life of voluntary simplicity and poverty. We didn't stay there long, perhaps only a few days. Papaji gave satsang there but he soon realised that the hippies were not ready for the message he had. We left and went back to Barcelona.

Meera's assessment was possibly a little pessimistic because later that year some of these Ibiza hippies turned up at Saanen in Switzerland where both Papaji and Krishnamurti were holding satsangs.
From Barcelona Papaji travelled north to Paris where he stayed with Sita, the teacher who had come to Rishikesh a few years earlier to search for her 'invisible Master'. Papaji describes the visit:

We arrived at Sita's flat, which was in Palaiseau, about thirty kilometres from Paris, and met both Sita and her boyfriend. He was a follower of Rudolph Steiner and he didn't like some of the things I was saying to Sita.

Whenever I tried to tell her something, he would get out a Rudolph Steiner book and say, 'What you are saying is not correct. Look, Steiner says something completely different.'

After some time I got annoyed with him: 'These satsangs are not for you,' I said. 'If you don't like what I say, you can go somewhere else.'

This just created even more antagonism in him.

Sita and her boyfriend had been living together for many years but they had never had any official wedding ceremony. I soon found out that the boy didn't like the idea of getting married.

I asked Sita, 'You have been living with this boy for years. You must like him or you wouldn't still be living with him. Why don't you get married?'

'He doesn't want to,' she answered. 'He doesn't like the idea of marriage.'

I approached the boy, whom I called Ram because his wife was Sita: 'Why don't you want to marry this girl? You have been living with her for years. You must like living together otherwise you wouldn't have stayed together so long.'

'I have my freedom now,' he replied. 'If I marry her, she will start to dominate me and tell me what to do. Right now, if I want to go out with another girl for a while, I can do it, and she can't complain because we are not married.'

I got very angry with him when I heard that he was behaving like this. We had a big quarrel and I ended up throwing him out of the flat. I was so angry, I forgot it was his flat and not mine, and that I was the guest not the owner. Anyway, I threw him out, slammed the door and locked it so he couldn't get back in.

He was very unprepared for his eviction. It was late at night and he had no warm clothes. He didn't even have the key to his car, so he couldn't drive away and spend the night with friends or relatives.

Sita wanted to help him to stay warm. 'Why don't I at least give him the car keys?' she asked. 'Then he can sit in the car with the heater on, or go somewhere else to spend the night.'

'No,' I replied, 'he has been behaving very badly with you. Let him freeze for a while, and while he is freezing he can think about how he has been treating you.'

I took the car keys to my room and kept them in my pocket so she couldn't give them when I wasn't looking.

'I will give them to you tomorrow morning when it is time for you to go to work. Till then I will keep them with me.'

The next morning she took the keys and went off to work. She was a teacher in a school for children whose various problems meant that they needed some kind of special education.

Later that morning, as I was leaving the flat to go out for a walk, I saw a sign that had been pinned to the door. It said, 'Thank you, Master. We are going to get married now.'

He had spent the whole night shivering on the street, not daring to ask to be allowed back in, even though it was his own flat. When Sita came out to go to work, he apologised and asked her to marry him.

When I met him later that day, all his hostility had vanished. He was even prepared to admit that my teachings had some merit.

'As I was standing outside in the cold,' he said, 'some of your words came back to me and I suddenly realised that there was something in them. What you said began to make sense.'

In India there is a tradition that the Guru can transmit his teachings by look, by word, by touch, or merely by sitting in silence. There is also another way. Sometimes the disciple needs to be given a good kick before he understands what is being told to him. Ram got the import of the teachings after receiving a good kick.

I arranged an Indian ceremony in their own flat. For traditional Indian weddings we make a sacred fire and perform ritual ceremonies called *yagnas* and *homas*. I didn't want the local fire brigade to interrupt the show, so I made Ram and Sita close all the windows and doors while I performed the ceremony. I chanted the appropriate mantras while the couple walked around the fire seven times to complete the ceremony. This all happened over twenty years ago. It turned out to be a good marriage. They are still together and they now have three children.

Meera told me that this was the first wedding ceremony that Papaji ever performed. In subsequent years he married many other devotee-couples in the same traditional way, although nowadays a qualified brahmin priest is engaged to chant the appropriate mantras.

Papaji now narrates some of the drawbacks of the Palaiseau flat:

Wherever I stay I like to go for long walks every day, preferably amid natural scenery. The area I was living in was criss-crossed by metalled roads, with hardly any greenery in sight. I felt like walking somewhere that wasn't covered by continuous stretches of tarmac and cement.

'Is there a park nearby,' I asked, 'somewhere where I can walk in the morning without being poisoned by all the car fumes and deafened by the noise?'

They couldn't think of anywhere local but they promised that they would take me somewhere when they had time off work.

'Next Saturday,' they said, 'we will take you for a walk in the country.'

So, I had to wait several days for my walk. The following weekend I was driven eighty miles to a forest, but when we got out to walk there was a big sign there that read, 'No admission. Anyone who enters this area will be prosecuted.'

'Is this the only place you can find?' I asked. 'Have we driven for hours just to come to a piece of fenced-in private property?'

'No,' they said. 'The place we are taking you to is nearby. It used to be owned by some people who went to America. Now it is vacant and waiting to be sold. We can walk there undisturbed.'

She showed me a tiny plot of land nearby that was only the size of this Satsang Bhavan hall [about fifteen metres by ten]. She took off her shoes and started dancing around this tiny little garden.

'Isn't it wonderful?' she asked. 'Isn't it beautiful to have one's bare feet touching mother earth?'

I had spent my whole life in India, mostly walking barefoot, so I wasn't very impressed. I found it rather sad that these city dwellers had to drive eighty miles at the weekend just to experience the pleasure of walking in a natural place. Modern city dwellers live in an atmosphere of benzene, smoke and smog. They catch cancers and other diseases from living in their so-called civilised cities, and if they want some fresh air, they have to drive for hours in their cars.

There is one other thing that I must mention about my walks in Paris. For the last thirty years or so I have had trouble with my knees. The joints are painful whenever I put my full weight on them. When I go for a walk with devotees, I sometimes lean on the arm or the shoulder of the person who is nearest to me in order to take some of the weight off my painful joints. But when I did this in Paris and put my arm on the shoulder of Sita's husband, he was very shocked.

He pushed it off, saying, 'You can't do that here. Everyone will think that we are homosexuals out for a walk together. Normal men don't put their arms round each other in public in this country. You can put your arm round my wife's shoulders and nobody will mind or think it strange, but don't do it to me. We are well-known in this neighbourhood. If our friends see us behaving like this they will start gossiping about us.'

After a short stay in Paris, Papaji and Meera travelled to the south of France to stay in Ardèche at the home of a French devotee called Maurice Rey. I asked Meera about Papaji's stay there:

Meera: It was an extraordinary place. I got the feeling that Master liked it very much. Maurice had a huge house with extensive gardens. Maybe 'gardens' is the wrong word. It was so big it would be more correct to call it a park. We were made very welcome there. Many French seekers who had known Master in India came to see him. We went back to this place several times on subsequent trips because Master obviously liked it so much.

David: You arranged a meeting with Jean Klein while you were there.

Meera: Yes. He was one of the most famous teachers of *advaita* and enlightenment in the West at that time. I had already told him about Master because I thought he might be interested in meeting him. He lived at nearby Aix en Provence in a small place called St Jean. I think Yvan Amar, who knew Master from his days in Hardwar in the late '60s, actually set up the meeting. It was a sort of dinner party that was attended by Master, Jean Klein and a small group of students from each teacher.

David: What happened?

Meera: The disciples of the two teachers got into a debate about the teachings of their respective Masters, but the two teachers themselves kept mostly quiet. Though Jean Klein taught self-enquiry, there was a lot of difference between his and Master's approach to liberation.

Afterwards Jean Klein advised all his students to stay away from Master, telling them Papaji was a dangerous man with a dangerous teaching. He came up to me afterwards and told me directly that I should leave Master because I would be in great danger if I stayed with him any longer.

Jean Klein's character seemed to undergo a strange change that evening. There was a hostility and a rudeness in him that I had never seen on any of our previous meetings. He seemed to see something in Master that made him afraid. He wouldn't say what it was, but he did go out of his way to tell all the people there that for their own safety they should have nothing more to do with Master. It was a very strange response because he had previously seemed so calm and self-assured. I was very disappointed by his behaviour and by the meeting in general. It was not a success.

While he was in the south of France Papaji accepted an invitation to spend a few days with Frédéric Leboyer, the man who pioneered natural childbirth under water.

I wasn't aware of it at the time, but Dr Leboyer was famous all over the world. His underwater birth techniques had become fashionable among the rich and the famous, and many celebrities were asking him to deliver their babies. His book, *Shantala*, which contained many photos of a Bengali girl giving birth underwater, had become something of a cult classic among young women of the early 1970s.

I went to see him at his house in the south of France and was immediately surprised to see how dirty and untidy it was. I thought that a doctor who was used to performing delicate operations in sterile, tidy conditions ought to know how to sweep and clean his house once in a while.

We got on very well. He had a flat in Paris and he invited us to come and see him next time we were there.

'I can arrange very good food for you,' he said. 'The wife of the Indian ambassador is one of my students. She is from Kerala and knows how to cook good South Indian food. Next time you are in Paris we can all have authentic *iddlies* and *dosas* together.'

When we visited him, he was hard at work on a new book. He showed me a few chapters and they had titles such as 'How to walk', 'How to sit', 'How to stand', and so on.

'People learn this by themselves when they are about two years old,' I said to him. 'Why do they need help from you?'

'They don't learn properly, or they pick up bad habits later,' he replied. 'Many physical problems could be solved if people could be taught how to perform simple actions more efficiently. That's why I am writing this book.'

He was also quite interested in *advaita* and had had a guru in India a few years before. When I spoke to him I discovered that his whole life had been moulded by an unfortunate childhood. His mother had disliked him, and made no secret of her dislike. He went to see Nisargadatta Maharaj in the early 1970s and discussed his psychological problems with him. Their conversation appears in chapter fifty-two of *I Am That*.

I looked up this chapter and found the conversation Papaji referred to. This is an extract from the summary of his life that Leboyer gave Maharaj:

My mother could not give me the feeling of being secure and loved, so important to the child's normal development. She was a woman not fit to be a mother; ridden with anxieties and neuroses, unsure of herself, she felt me to be a responsibility and a burden beyond her capacity to bear. She never wanted me to be born. She did not want me to grow and develop, she wanted me back in her womb, unborn, non-existent. Any movement of life in me she resisted, any attempt to go beyond the narrow circle of her habitual existence, she fought fiercely. As a child I was both sensitive and affectionate. I craved for love above everything else; and love, the simple instinctive love of a mother for her child, was denied me. The child's search for the love of its mother became the leading motive of my life and I never grew out of it. A happy child, a happy childhood became an obsession with me. Pregnancy, birth, infancy interested me passionately. I became an obstetrician of some renown and contributed to the development of the method of painless childbirth.

A long conversation ensued at the end of which Leboyer asked Nisargadatta Maharaj, 'Why was I so unhappy all my life?'

Maharaj replied, 'Because you did not go down to the very roots of your being. It is your complete ignorance of yourself that covered up your love and happiness and made you seek for what you had never lost....'

I asked Meera if she remembered this visit to Leboyer's house:

He came to see us in Ardèche when we were staying in Maurice's house. We had a lot of good satsangs when he was there because he knew how to provoke Master into giving good answers. He had a good intellect and a thorough knowledge of many Indian traditions. People like that were rare at that time in the West. I remember that he was obsessed with his early life and felt that his mother's behaviour had traumatised him. After having several long talks with him, Master more or less agreed with him. The whole pattern of his life had been shaped by these early experiences. He liked Mukti and took many photos of her, saying that he would like to include some of them in his next book. However, I never saw any of them in print.

He didn't manage to transcend his mental problems while he was with Master, but he was impressed enough to recommend him to several of his friends and acquaintances. During our time in the south of France, many people came to see us on Dr Leboyer's recommendation.

After a few weeks in the south of France, Papaji moved on to Switzerland to meet Carlos Silva, the Brockwood Park teacher who had had the remarkable experience on the Barcelona-London flight. Papaji also planned to attend some of the Krishnamurti talks that were being held in Saanen in July that year. Carlos, who

Carlos Silva and Papaji in Saanen, Switzerland, 1974.

had spent the previous three summers in Saanen, describes Papaji's arrival and his first few days there. Most of the new people he mentions were either teachers or students from Brockwood Park.

We had invited Poonjaji to spend a few weeks in Saanen during the time when Krishnamurti gave his talks there. For accommodation we rented a floor in the house of a woman called Mrs von Grunninger. It was the third year in a row we had stayed in her house. By 1974 it felt like having one's own home to live in but without any of the inconveniences.

One afternoon Poonja arrived at the small Saanen train station. It was so good to see him again. Once more I had a friend, someone who would not escape. It was the first time I had seen him since the flight from Barcelona. To me he also meant the opportunity for hard inner work. Poonjaji is a man of power and he uses it generously. He proceeds like an ice-breaking ship and nothing detains him. He will push forward non-stop. He personifies the hour of Truth for the serious and dedicated seeker, and the end of all pretense.

He liked the house very much. It had a beautiful view of the Saanen valley, and because it was high up, one could see all the way to Gstaad. We went to the Krishnamurti talks together sometimes. It was the first time he had listened to him speak. His only comment was: 'Why does he go to all this trouble?' That year the talks lacked strength. One felt he could not 'take off' as usual.

A former mathematics teacher from Brockwood called Jean Michel Laborde came to the house almost every day. Sofia had telephoned the news that Poonja was with us and from the very first day Jean Michel fell in love with him. Jean Michel did not go to the Krishnamurti talks that year. He was a good, gentle and quiet young man and a serious seeker....

At Saanen we would meet with Poonjaji every afternoon: Jean Michel, my wife Sofia, Lais, Carol, Ruben and his mother, Michael, Matthew and some others. We would be silent for hours, in a most natural way. At other times we would take long walks in the valley, following the Saanen River. When we arrived at the airport we would watch the gliders. A couple of airplanes would alternately carry the gliders into the air. At about 1,000 metres they would trigger them free and the glider would float in the sky, free as a bird, and come slowly down, playing with the air currents. This would be repeated endlessly until it was dark....

In Saanen we would work inwardly, passionately with Poonja, without interruptions. It was like a spontaneous bicycle race, with each one's interest alternately pulling the group along. I believe that Poonja was too much for most people: too strong, too powerful, too demanding.

Papaji has his own memories of attending these talks:

I was in Saanen, Switzerland, attending a lecture of Krishnamurti. An Italian man whom I knew was sitting next to me. At the end of each talk Krishnamurti would allow members of the audience to ask questions. This man put up his hand because he had a very important question.

When it was his turn he said, 'This morning, according to the announcement, there are 800 people listening to you inside this tent. Others are sitting outside. Simultaneous translations are going on so that everyone who speaks a major European language can understand what you are saying. My question is: "Who, apart from yourself, has been benefited by your talk today and by all your previous talks?" This is a serious question because I am a serious student of your books I have read all your books and I have listened to you talk in several different countries but I cannot say that I have benefited by listening to you. Furthermore, I have yet to find anyone who has really been transformed by listening to your talks or by reading your books.'

Krishnamurti looked at him for a while but he didn't answer the question, so my friend repeated it again.

'Please let me know if even one person has been truly benefited by your teachings. You have travelled all over the world. You have met and talked to hundreds of people who have studied your words and tried to put them into practice. Has anyone directly experienced the truth of what you are saying?'

This time Krishnamurti said, 'If you have not been benefited, that is not my problem'.

I liked his answer. The true teacher has no intention to accomplish anything. He is not concerned with the consequences of what he is saying. If you have the idea, 'I will teach so that others can become enlightened,' your teachings will never work. They will only be effective when there is no intention to produce results. The true teacher does not care whether people are benefited by what he says. Some power compels him to speak, but that power has no interest in the consequences.

At the end of the talk, as we were walking out, I said to the Italian man, 'What you said was not true. You really have been benefited by listening to these talks.'

'No,' he said, 'I don't feel any benefit at all.'

I tried to make him see it from a different perspective: 'Everybody else here today either thinks that he has been benefited, or hopes that he will be benefited in the future. You alone know that you have not been benefited. That conclusion is the benefit you have derived from listening to all these talks and reading all those books. By listening to these talks you have finally understood that there is no benefit to be gained from listening to talks such as these.'

He laughed and then begrudgingly agreed with me.

This man had studied all these books because he wanted to understand what Krishnamurti was trying to say. However, he had had a lot of trouble.

'Krishnamurti never seems to stay in the same position,' he told me. 'I read one book and I come to the conclusion that my perspective is from point A and Krishnamurti's is from point B, somewhere totally different. So, I make a big effort to move my perspective to point B. But just when I think I am getting there, I read another book and find that his perspective has moved to point C. I never seem to catch up with him or find out where he really is.'

'You're trying to understand him with your mind,' I said to him. 'That's your problem. If you don't try to arrange all his words in your mind in such a way that they make patterns that you can understand and relate to, you might find that you suddenly understand directly what he is talking about. When you listen to a teacher, don't listen with your mind. Let his words fall into that place that is behind the mind.'

'But these are complex ideas,' he objected. 'If I don't think about them, how can I even understand them?'

'I'm telling you to "not understand" them,' I replied. 'Just keep your mind quiet when he speaks and see what happens.'

He was very frustrated by this comment. 'I don't understand Krishnamurti and I don't understand you either,' was his comment. 'Neither of you makes any sense.'

'Very good,' I said. 'Now you are making progress. Stay in that state in which you don't understand.'

He thought I was making fun of him, but it was very serious advice. Early the next morning, at about 6 a.m., there was a knock on my door. I opened it and found the Italian professor there.

'I got it,' he said, very happily. 'You were right. I didn't need to understand anything at all. I don't know what happened but I am very happy now, and I don't understand why. All I know is that it has nothing to do with understanding.'

He laughed and went away.

The house I was staying in was located in a very beautiful area. I went for long walks every day, sometimes in the countryside, and sometimes to Gstaad, the nearby town. One time while I was there I saw Charlie Chaplin walking down the street with his daughter. Sometimes I went to sit near a little church that was in the neighbourhood. One day, as I was sitting outside this church, it began to rain. I asked the priest if I could come inside and meditate.

He surprised me by saying, 'What is meditation?'

I knew that few people in the West at that time knew anything about meditation, but I expected priests to be better informed. I offered to give him a demonstration and a lesson, and he accepted.

We went inside and sat on some of the benches. I introduced him to the sound of '*Om*', which he had never come across before.

'This is like the Christian "Amen",' I told him. 'The two words have the same origin.'

I made the sound '*Om*' for him and then said, 'Hindus believe that this is the primordial sound out of which all creation manifests. Chant this sound for some time and then look inside yourself to see how and where it arises. If you do it properly, you will find yourself being pulled into a silence of the heart. In that place you will find true peace. Try it and see.'

The priest followed my advice and within a few minutes I could see from his face that he had entered a state of deep inner peace.

When he opened his eyes, he said with pleasure and surprise, 'I have never experienced anything like this before. It's so easy.' And then he closed his eyes again to enjoy it.

Nobody goes to church to be quiet, so this priest had never learned how to do it. When you walk into a church you will hear loud music coming from an organ. And if the organ stops it will be replaced by singing, chanting and rituals in which you have to participate. No one leaves you alone so you can find your own inner peace. I went to churches and monasteries all over Europe. They were all full of people with busy minds and busy bodies.

Krishnamurti used to give talks on alternate days. On the days that he was not speaking I would give satsang to anyone who was interested. Most of the people who came were Krishnamurti students, so most of the questions I was asked were about various aspects of Krishnamurti's teaching.

Though Krishnamurti was Indian by birth, he was educated in a very western way. His terminology tended to come from western ideas about psychology, not from traditional Indian sources. Most of the people who came to see him seemed to be western intellectuals who liked to have lots of interesting ideas to play with. Though Krishnamurti encouraged everyone to drop his or her concepts, most of the people I spoke to in Saanen wanted to spend their time playing with ideas and discussing them.

One couple, who used to give talks on behalf of the Krishnamurti Foundation, came to hear to what I had to say.

After listening to my answers and explanations, one of them said, 'You seem to be saying the same thing as Krishnamurti. You use a lot of Indian terms that Krishnamurti never uses, but still, ultimately, you are both saying the same thing. Krishnamurti says that we should empty the mind of all its concepts, and you seem to agree with him.'

Before I could give a reply one of the other people who was present interrupted us and said, 'There is a big difference. Krishnamurti says, "Empty the mind of all concepts and keep it empty". Poonjaji, on the other hand, is saying, "Mind itself does not exist except in your imagination. Instead of emptying the mind, concept by concept, have the direct understanding that there is no such thing as mind. If you have this understanding, where can concepts abide?"'

This was a good explanation. It showed a proper understanding of what I was trying to communicate. As long as you think that the mind is real, you will always be occupied with organising its contents. You will either be looking for pleasures by fulfilling your desires, or you will be looking for peace by trying to throw away, ignore or witness all the thoughts and concepts in your mind. As long as the idea that the mind is real is present in you, you will never have peace, because this idea alone is the cause of all your suffering, all your problems.

There is a famous story about a Zen Master who wanted to appoint a successor. He asked all the monks in his monastery who wanted the job to write a brief poem that would show their understanding of the teachings. One of the monks wrote, 'The mind is a mirror. By frequently and carefully polishing the mirror, we can ensure that it stays clean.'

One of the kitchen workers in this monastery, his name was Hui Neng, saw a group of monks reading this poem that had been written on the wall outside the Master's room. He asked what was going on and was told about the competition. Hui Neng couldn't read or write, so he asked one of the other monks to read out what was written.

After he had listened to the poem Hui Neng said, 'This is not correct. I will dictate my own poem. Please write it underneath.'

The other monks laughed because he was just an illiterate kitchen worker, but to keep him happy one of them agreed to write down his lines.

He said, 'Write this: "Mind is not a mirror. Mind does not exist. Since mind does not exist, where can the dirt land?"'

When the Master read this verse he appointed Hui Neng his successor by giving him his robe and his bowl.

This is how it is. People tend to view the mind as being some kind of vessel that can either be full of thoughts and concepts, or empty of them. But if you smash the vessel, the idea that there is a mind and that it is something real, where will the concepts abide?

Though Papaji did not accept some of the things that Krishnamurti was saying, he still formed a very high opinion of him. In a letter he wrote to Carlos in 1988 he included the following remarks:

I often speak about Krishnaji as a modern Buddha. I have seen him several times, both in India and abroad. I heard him speaking about something that he did not or could not put into words. Yet from his gestures in between the talks and from the talks themselves I could catch that he was one of the few in our century who could speak in a friendly and loving manner about the Truth which will always remain unsaid....

Though Papaji had no doubts about Krishnamurti's state, he felt that he lacked the ability to pass it on to other people. This is what he had to say on the subject in one of his 1993 Lucknow satsangs:

I listened to Krishnamurti speak while I was in Switzerland. I liked him very much because I could find no fault in him. I am a hard person to satisfy but I will say that he was no doubt an enlightened man. But something was missing. The power to transmit that enlightenment to others was not there.

Papaji's assessment, though it seems to be harsh, was shared by Krishnamurti himself. In a book commemorating his birth centenary Evelyne Blau, a long-time associate of his, wrote: 'For fifty years he had taught, spoken and travelled all over the world. Why was not a single person transformed? He [Krishnamurti] was certainly concerned with this problem.'

As Krishnamurti lay dying in Ojai, California, a tape recorder was running to record his final words. Shortly before he died he said, 'Where did I go wrong? No one got it.'

Papaji will give his views on why not all enlightened people have the power to awaken others in the final chapter, 'Guru and Disciple'.

Papaji and J. Krishnamurti were not the only spiritual teachers in Saanen that summer. U. G. Krishnamurti, an iconoclastic figure whom Papaji had previously met in Bombay, was also there. Carlos describes a chance encounter they had on the streets of Saanen:

We were walking down one of the streets in Saanen when I noticed U. G. Krishnamurti coming in the opposite direction.

I thought that Poonjaji did not know who he was, so I pointed him out and said, 'That's U. G. Krishnamurti. He's a famous guru in India.'

'He's not a guru,' said Poonjaji.

Still thinking that Poonjaji did not know who he was, I said, 'It's true. It's true. He has a lot of followers in India. Many people go to listen to him speak.'

This time Poonjaji made no response to my remarks. Instead, he went up to U. G. Krishnamurti, tapped him on the shoulder and said, 'This man says that you are a guru. You are not a guru.'

Then he walked away without waiting for U. G. Krishnamurti's response.

When I asked Papaji how he had first met U. G. Krishnamurti, he told me the story of their meeting in Bombay:

When U. G. Krishnamurti was staying in Bangalore, he met one of my friends who was a coffee planter. After this man had told U. G. Krishnamurti a little about me, he said he would like to meet me. The coffee planter wrote to me in Lucknow and I replied that we could meet in Bombay because I was planning to meet some friends and devotees there in a few days. I gave him my brother's address in Bombay as the place where I could be contacted.

Soon after arriving in Bombay I received a phone call, saying that I could meet U. G. Krishnamurti at the Swiss consulate at 5 p.m. that day. One of his friends worked there.

When I arrived I was received very cordially at the gates by U. G. Krishnamurti himself. I was then taken inside and introduced to a few people who had gathered there to meet us and ask us questions.

At some point during the discussion U. G. Krishnamurti said, 'I don't believe in spiritual experiences,' to which I replied, 'That's because you haven't had any. If you have a real one you will surely believe in it. If someone has a headache, it is a direct and irrefutable experience of pain. Whether you believe in it or not, the pain will still be there. If you say that you don't believe in experiences, what then is the difference between you and a rock?'

Then he said, 'People tell me you are a Guru. I don't believe in Gurus.'

I replied by saying, 'I don't believe in "no Gurus". Gurus are essential.'

The conversation went on in this vein for some time. We couldn't agree with each other about anything because he insisted on negating the value, the usefulness and even the existence of all spiritual experiences. Some of the consulate staff were curious about me and asked a few questions of their own. Unlike U. G. Krishnamurti, they seemed satisfied with the answers.

I have been told by people who have spent a lot of time with him that U. G. Krishnamurti was highly critical of J. Krishnamurti's state and teachings. Many of his talks are on this subject. I was told that he went to Saanen every year in summer just to annoy J. Krishnamurti and his followers.

While I was in Saanen two of my friends took me along to see him. He was staying in a place called Chalet Sunshine with an old Swiss woman who had been looking after him for many years. He didn't seem interested in meeting us. Saying he was very busy, he told us to come back some other time. I never went back.

As Papaji's Switzerland stay drew to a close, he received an unexpected offer:

One day, as I was leaving my house, a man whom I had seen in one of my satsangs came up to me and said, 'Can I come and see you tomorrow?'

I wasn't giving satsang the next day so I said, 'No'.

That didn't seem to perturb him. 'Fantastic! Fantastic!' he exclaimed, looking very happy.

He pointed to a woman who was standing on the road nearby and said, 'That is my wife, Monique. She is Swiss and I am French. My name is Margail. We came here to finalise our divorce, but after listening to you speak we have decided to stay together as husband and wife. We are going to make a new attempt to live together. We will try for one month and then make a decision about whether we want to stay together permanently.'

I stopped to talk to him because he seemed to be in a very happy mood. I like to spend time with happy people. He asked me what my future plans were because he had heard that I would soon be leaving Saanen.

232

'I will soon be leaving for Paris,' I replied, 'and after that I will probably go back to India.'

'Where do you plan to stay in Paris?' he asked.

'I know a couple there who are my devotees. I have already stayed with them once. They have invited me to stay with them again.'

'You can use my flat if you want a place of your own. I will not be going back there for several weeks.'

He went through his pockets and produced a credit card and the key to his flat. 'You can stay in my flat and you can use this credit card to buy petrol at the gas station. I will also write a letter of introduction to my local grocery store, instructing the owner to give you anything you need on credit. I will settle the bills myself when I return home. I want to thank you for making me so happy.'

I accepted his generous offer and stayed in his flat for several days when I returned to Paris.

I was usually accommodated well on my foreign tours because I was mostly staying in the houses of people who had known me before, but this was exceptional hospitality: a complete stranger I had never spoken to before offering me his flat and unlimited credit so that I could enjoy my stay there.

In all the time I was travelling abroad I only had one bad experience with my accommodation, and that was when I was staying for a few days in the south of France. I stayed with a woman there for three days. It was a nice place on the coast and I spent most of each day walking by the sea or sitting on the beach.

After three days the woman said to me, 'We have a tradition here. A guest is only a guest for three days. On the fourth day he has to start paying.'

It was a nice place. I felt like staying a bit longer there so I replied, 'That's all right with me. I like it here. I can contribute some money towards the cost of my expenses here.'

'No,' she said. 'It is not just a question of a donation. On the fourth day you have to start paying the same rate you would be paying if you were living in a good hotel.'

I knew how much the big hotels charged on the south coast of France. It was far more than I could afford.

I told her, 'The weather is very nice. I will go and sleep on the beach. I will buy some food in the local shop and have a picnic by the sea. That way I will spend about one dollar for the night. I will have a good, cheap sleep under the stars. Tomorrow I will go somewhere else.'

I packed my bag and left.

Papaji had one other interesting encounter before he left Switzerland for Paris:

While I was staying in Gstaad I was approached by a man who said that he was a professor of art in Paris. He was in a miserable, depressed state when I first spoke to him.

'I came here to commit suicide,' he began, 'but somehow I cannot summon up the courage to do it. I have a capsule of cyanide with me. Every day I pick it up and bring it to my mouth, but I can't actually put it on my tongue and swallow it. I heard you talk about courage in one of your satsangs. Can you give me the necessary courage to put this pill in my mouth and swallow it?'

'OK,' I said, 'I will give you courage, but first you must tell me why you want to commit suicide.'

'I have a teaching job in Paris. My wife and I lived there for many years. We have a small son. A few weeks ago she left me for one of my students. She took our son and went with this boy to America. I left my flat without even locking the door and came to Switzerland to find a quiet secluded place to commit suicide, but so far I haven't managed to do it. Can you help me?'

'Yes, I can help you,' I replied. 'You give me your cyanide pill for safe keeping and I will give you the courage to take it. When you are ready to take it, you can have it back.'

He thought that this was a good bargain so he handed over his pill to me. When he wasn't looking, I dropped it on the ground and crushed it.

Over the next day or so I spent a lot of time with him. We talked about his life, his family, his interest in art and many other things. Slowly his depression lifted.

When he seemed to be in a better frame of mind, I said to him,

'Your wife left you to find happiness with someone else. Let her be happy. She is not your concern now. Your business is your own happiness. You don't need to spend your time being miserable and depressed, and you don't need to commit suicide. Many people have found happiness again after experiences like this.'

He accepted my advice and gave up his plans to kill himself. Over the next few days he became very attached to me, so much so he wanted to come to India when I returned. I thought it would be good for him to spend some more time with me so I told him that he was welcome to come to Rishikesh to see me when I returned to India.

His wife had run off with most of his money because they were keeping it in a joint account that either of them could use. He decided to sell off his car to raise funds for the trip to India. Because he wanted the money in a hurry, he offered it for sale at a price that was far less than it was actually worth. One of the first people who came to look at it asked him why it was so cheap.

'I need money quickly to buy a ticket to go to India. I want to spend time with my Master there.'

The man paid him the full value of the car when he heard this story.

The professor and I spent a lot of time together in both Hardwar and Rishikesh. Eventually, when I thought that he was completely cured, I recommended that he go to Ramanasramam for a while. A few months later I read an article by him in their magazine, *The Mountain Path*.

Part of the article said: 'I have been most lucky twice in my life. Very lucky. I am the luckiest person in the world. My first piece of luck was meeting a man in Switzerland when I was about to die. He saved my life. He sent me to his Master, Sri Ramana Maharshi, who saved me from all my future deaths, so I shall not have to die again.'

I didn't see him again for a long time. When I did finally meet him again, I discovered that he had found a Vietnamese girl in the south of France who wanted to marry him. I invited them both to Rishikesh and performed a marriage ceremony for them on the banks of the Ganga.

Papaji went back to Paris and stayed for a few days at the flat of the man who had given him his front-door key and credit card. He was beginning to think about returning to India, but more invitations kept appearing from different parts of Europe. The most pressing was from Enrique Noriega, the Spanish architect who still wanted to make a permanent centre for him in Spain.

22nd August, 1974
Paris 75015

My Beloved Vinayak jee,
I read your letter just now. I have decided to wind up my tour in a few days. I have to go to Madrid in España as some people who want to construct an ashram with a school for me want me to attend the foundation ceremony at the Institute before I leave for India. I will see you when I land at Bombay.

Papaji made a brief visit to Spain to attend this function, but when it became clear to the sponsors that he had no intention of settling permanently there, the scheme fell through. He returned to France and stayed there several more weeks, meeting devotees who wanted to see him again. He finally returned to India at the end of October.

When Papaji had been staying in Rishikesh in 1969 he had met a Frenchwoman called Malou Lanvin. When Malou found out that Papaji was visiting France, she invited him to stay with her in her home at St Genis, which is near Lyon. Papaji accepted and spent some time there. Malou had another house in Croix de Vie, Britanny. Papaji stayed in this house for the last few weeks of his visit to France.

Before I focus on the satsangs that took place in Brittany, I must mention an incident that probably took place while Papaji was staying in Malou's house in St Genis. This is Papaji's recollection of what happened:

I was walking along the bank of the River Rhône when I suddenly had this strange feeling that I had lived nearby in one of my past lives. I paused to allow these long-buried memories to rise. As I looked at them I recollected that I had been a Christian priest in this area several hundred years before. I had a strong, clear image of a chapel that was located on the banks of this river. I knew that it was a place I had spent a lot of time in. I stopped an old man who was walking nearby and described the chapel to him. I asked him if he could direct me towards it.

He looked at me very strangely before giving me a reply.

'There used to be a chapel like that, but it was demolished a long time ago. When I was a boy it stood only a few metres from where we are now talking. The government of the day decided to widen this road we are on, so the chapel was demolished. The priest was moved to another chapel on the other side of town.'

I knew that I had been buried in this place, but it wasn't possible to get any further information because there was no trace of either the chapel or the graveyard that I knew had been next to it.

After talking with Meera about her travels with Papaji in France and Switzerland, I have tentatively located this story in St Genis, since this was the only place they stayed that was anywhere near the River Rhône. Papaji himself cannot remember exactly where he was when this story took place.

Papaji, Malou Lanvin and Meera and Mukti travelled to Brittany in the beginning of October. I asked Meera about this period:

Malou was well known all over India because she seemed to spend most her time meeting saints and swamis in various parts of the country. She looked after us very well when we stayed at her house in St Genis. Malou had a strong Christian background, but she was quite sympathetic to the Hindu tradition.

One time, while Malou was meditating, Mukti, who was then only about three years old, went up to her, tapped her on the chest and said, 'It's not in your head. Don't look for it there. It's in your heart.'

This was a very perceptive comment for her to make because

Malou had been bombarding Master with all kinds of intellectual questions. During our stay there Malou invited many people from different religious backgrounds to meet Master. Everyone enjoyed these meetings.

Later we went to her place in Croix de Vie, Brittany. She had rented a beautiful apartment right in front of the ocean. We had many good satsangs there because Malou knew how to provoke Master into giving very interesting replies.

While they were staying in Britanny, Meera began to write down some of the conversations that were taking place in the satsangs. The first entry is a record of one of her own experiences. The remainder are probably conversations between Malou and Papaji.

12th October, 1974

Meera: With the ocean in the background, Master speaks to Malou about distance and separation. He says, 'The Master removes all distance'. In that split second Meera knows that she is free, ready, absolutely open to him.

In that eternal gaze enlightenment springs forth from the meeting of two hearts who in truth are only ONE. I look at me. He looks at himself. He is only himself, both here in me and there in him. When I smile, it is he who is smiling. The gaze is without effort because I am looking at my Self. He has entered me! A full perfect transmission. I am confident in my experience.

17th October, 1974

Papaji: If attaining God is the result of any *sadhana* [spiritual practice] such as counting the beads on a rosary, He is enclosed in time. *Sadhana* can only be done in time. When you are not doing *sadhana,* not repeating God's name, He is as good as dead. God is not there one minute when you think of Him and absent the next when you forget to remember His name. God does not come and go. It is only your thoughts of Him that come and go.

God is actually continuously repeating your own name, your own real name, but you don't listen. You don't hear.

God is not attainable by any *sadhana* because He is outside time.

You are the Divine Son. When the Father is there, the Son is always living in Him. God is. He is the subject, the divine subject, not an object. You are that divine subject.

Question: And who are you?

Papaji: Everything that I am is in you.

Question: What is Jesus for you?

Papaji: Myself.

18th October, 1974

Papaji: For any object to exist for you, it must make an impression on the mind. These impressions make your world. From the smallest to the biggest, all objects are just impressions on the mind. The vast expanse of the world is just a series of mental impressions. But if you drop all ideas, all these impressions that register in the mind, what remains? Drop them all. Drop even the idea of God and tell me what remains.

Question: How to know this knowledge? It is so vast!

Papaji: Drop it! Drop this idea!

Question: There is a place where I stop, where I cannot jump any more. Does the Master come at this point to help?

Papaji: Have you run so far just to stop now? I say, 'Drop everything'. In the dropping you find the Master, but the Master will not do the dropping for you.

Question: You seem so utterly alone. What gives you this aloneness?

Papaji: Aloneness is 'here': only 'here'. Do you understand? In this 'here' the Master comes; spirituality starts in this 'here'; 'here' is the substance that makes the waves move, makes the wind blow; in 'here' and 'here' alone will you experience who I am. In 'here' some other faculty will take care of you. It will pull you deeper and deeper into the silence.

Question: Just now you showed me. Who you are is who I am. Substance, essence. Only now do I start to realise who I am, which is who you are.

19th October, 1974

Question: So the only way is to surrender to the inner presence?

Papaji: If you have this idea, you believe that you are on the outside and that there is something inside that is superior to you. Give up this idea. You are neither inside nor outside.

You don't need to pray to anything or anyone for help. If you start asking for help, you are in duality. Prayer is fear. You think that something bad is happening to you, or will happen to you, so you pray for help. There is only one without a second. When you know this, all fears go, because there is nothing apart from yourself to be afraid of.

Question: So the Master can't help? One shouldn't ask him for help?

Papaji: My Master gave me nothing new, nor did I attain something by myself. If he had given me something I didn't already have, then one day I would lose it. And if I attained it at one point in time, it means that at another point in time I would lose it.

What did my Master do? He showed me my own treasure, and instantly I recognised it.

Question: How to reach God?

Papaji: You cannot attain God through any effort or *sadhana* that begins or ends in time because God is beyond time. You cannot reach Him by any activity that takes place in time. If you think, 'I will attain God by this particular method,' your mind will give you an experience that corresponds to your idea of God. It won't be an experience of God, it will be an experience of your own idea of God.

If you want to know who God is, give up all your experiences, all your expectations, all your mental activities, and keep quiet.

20th October, 1974

Papaji: *Sadhana* can be physical, mental or intellectual. If it is physical, you get physical results; if it is mental, you get mental results; and if it is intellectual, you get intellectual results. God is not physical, mental or intellectual, so whatever you attain by these methods cannot be God.

Realising the Self is something else. There are many subtle states of mind that are mistaken for realisation. In these states there is still an experiencer who experiences the subtle state. When the sun rises, you see it with your own eyes. You, the experiencer, experience the sun as an object of perception. There is a duality in this perception, just as there is a duality in every kind of experience. But if you are the sun itself, you don't experience it as an object. It is your own nature, your own being.

Seeing, without a perceiver who sees and an object that is perceived, is the state of realisation. In that state, seeing and being are the same. It is a fact, but how can it be explained?

Question: So all expressions of what is seen have to be mental. Even a verbal expression of real seeing is mental and conceptual. In order to describe something I have to take words from my memory of the past. I borrow words and ideas from my past experiences. That means I limit my description to something I have experienced in the past.

241

Papaji: Yes, but not expressing it is also your expression. Whatever has been said about this state is a mental description that does not correspond to the actual fact of it.

Words are not totally useless. When the Guru, who is consciousness itself, speaks, there is a power in his words that can transmit an awareness of that consciousness to others.

Question: Can the intellect help in understanding?

Papaji: The intellect is everything you know about the past and everything you can think about from the future. When you stop the mind you free yourself from the burden of past and future thoughts. Creation itself comes to a halt because you are no longer making it out of your thoughts and ideas.

As you think, so you become. It is the mind that makes your world. If you think that you are in bondage and that you need to be free, then bondage becomes your state and you struggle endlessly to escape from it. Your bondage is sustained by movements of your mind. When you stop your mind, bondage ends. And if you can't do it, just have an intense urge for liberation. That will be enough.

Question: I have been praying to God for grace.

Papaji: If you pray to God for anything, you are turning God into an object. He is not an object, He is you, the subject. By praying, you also turn yourself into an object. You think you are the object God is going to bestow His grace on. The object who wants to receive the grace has to dissolve, along with his prayer. This dissolution is the real prayer to God. If you make God an object that you want to pray to for help, you make Him stronger and stronger. And the more strength you give Him, the more fear you have of Him. You give Him control over your life and live in a state of duality and fear.

The true experience is the resurrection to eternal life. It arises out of the death of the mind. But if you go back to thinking about it and trying to describe it in words, you go back to the miserable state of crucifixion. You nail yourself down with thoughts and concepts.

Question: Please help me.

Papaji: The question of help arises in the place from which help is sought. Do you understand? Grace makes you ask the question, and grace comes as an answer. But you still have this dualistic relationship with the one you want help from. Drop the question. Drop the idea that you need help from outside and you will find that you are grace itself.

Question: If God is everywhere, why does suffering exist?

Papaji: Your God is the God of the Bible. You conceive of Him as Good, as Love. To account for evil you invent an opposite and call him the devil. As long as you think of God as being good, you have to have a devil who is opposed to him.

The divine manifests as everything. The things you think are good and the things you think are bad are all manifestations of this divine energy. You suffer and you worry about good and evil simply because you direct your attention to the effects of this energy, not the source.

Search and enquire who you really are. Your search has to be successful. You have to realise who you are as a result of your search. But don't have any preconceived ideas about what you are searching for, or what it will be like when you find the answer, because if you have this attitude you will end up experiencing a mental state that corresponds to your preconceived idea.

21st October, 1974

Papaji: As you differentiate yourself from a dog, separate yourself from your body. You are not the five elements that make up your body, so why do you insist on thinking that you are the body? Reject your identification with anything you can see or perceive or think about. When you have rejected all thoughts, all perceptions as 'not me', there is silence. You cannot reject this silence because this silence is what you really are.

243

Question: There are many obstacles on the way.

Papaji: This is just your idea. People say, 'Christ fell many times on his way to the crucifixion. Likewise, there are many obstacles on the way to God, many holes that one falls into.'

This analogy arises because people think there is a distant goal to be reached, and that the path to it is long and difficult. There is no goal to reach, no path to follow. There is no tripping over obstacles; there is no falling down and no rising again. All you need is correct understanding. You have to know that you have never fallen down. When you know this, you also understand that you don't need to rise up and move on, because there is nowhere to move on to.

A *sadhana* without any goal or desire is realisation itself. Keeping quiet is the *siddhi*, the accomplishment.

Question: Are you returning to India?

Papaji: No, I am going to India. Returning means that you have previously fixed your place somewhere. This is attachment. My rest, my home, is wherever I am. Live wherever you like, but don't prefer to live in one place or another.

Comparison is death. It puts you in past, future and time. The knowledge you use to compare things has been acquired from outside influences. End it.

Question: Some places are sacred and some are not. Is it not better to live in holy places?

Papaji: No place is intrinsically holy or sacred. It is the presence of a saint there that can make it holy.

Several hundred years ago there was a cobbler-saint in India called Raidas. He used to soak his leather pieces in a waterproof leather bag. The water inside, which originally came from the Ganga, was dirty and stained with secretions from the leather. One day he put his hand in the bag and pulled out a diamond necklace from the water. Goddess Ganga had given it to him. No one else was pulling diamond necklaces out of the River Ganga, even though it was pure water and a holy river. The water in Raidas' bag was polluted but it became holy water because Raidas was a saint.

There is a Hindi saying that can be traced back to this miracle: 'If the mind is pure, leather-soaked water becomes the Ganga.'

Don't become attached to one piece of earth. The elements are our servants. Don't become their slave. The mind likes to be enslaved. It says, 'This is my image of God. God lives in this place; therefore this place is holy.'

If you think, 'God is more present in this Siva *linga* than in any other place,' you enmesh yourself in differences and duality. There is only one truly sacred place, and that is the place where no differences or distinctions arise. Identify with That.

Question: Can one reach that place by cultivating the attitude, 'Thy will be done'?

Papaji: I don't believe this will work because who is saying it? It is your will that is saying to God, 'Thy will be done'. You are not allowing God's will to be done. You are still telling Him what to do. That's not surrender.

Keep quiet. Don't think, 'This should happen,' or 'This shouldn't happen'. Don't give God orders. Don't tell Him what He has to do with you.

If you want to do something, find a true saint and have satsang with him. In his presence the fantastic activities of the mind will be destroyed. The true Master is Siva, the God who destroys the universe of the mind and then dances joyfully on the remains.

22nd October, 1974

Papaji: In the *Gita*, Krishna said two things to Arjuna: fight, and don't lose your hold on Me:

Therefore, dedicating all actions to Me, with your

mind fixed on Me, the Self of all, freed from hope
and the feeling of 'mine', and cured of mental fever,
fight. [3.30]

Mentally resigning to Me, and taking recourse to
yoga in the form of even-mindedness, be solely
devoted to Me, and constantly give your mind to Me.
[18.57]

What did he really mean by 'fight'? He meant fight with the idea
of 'I'. Fight the idea 'I am the body'. If you successfully fight the
idea of 'I', you discover the underlying silence that is not
concerned with or connected to any of the three states of waking,
sleeping and dreaming. You find *turiya*, the fourth state that is
beyond these three states.

Question: Yesterday I watched myself going to sleep. I was trying
to find out what was the waking state and what was the sleep state.
I found myself accepting the waking state and accepting that it had
to sleep. But I also realised that I will have to give up all my ideas
about the waking and sleep states if I want to be really aware.

Papaji: In the waking state you see objects. In the dream state you
also see objects. The mechanism is the same in both states. In the
sleep state you see nothing at all because the 'I' who sees is not
present. In sleep there is just a timeless feeling of happiness. When
there is no 'I' looking at objects, there is timeless happiness. That
is why I say, 'Fight the "I" '. Destroy the 'I' in the waking state and
be happy. If you destroy it in the waking state, it will not appear in
any of the other states.

Question: How to tell if a spiritual experience is genuine or not?

Papaji: A genuine experience is one in which there is no one left
to have the experience. All other experiences are intellectual. They
are experiences of the mind.

Question: But how to tell the difference?

Papaji: If you need to hold on to the experience in order to keep it, then it is an experience of the mind. But if the experience takes hold of you, and won't ever let you go whatever you do, it is a real experience.

Question: So a real experience is one in which there is the knowledge that it cannot ever be lost. If I feel, 'I had an experience,' that experience was not a genuine one because it appeared and disappeared in time. Is this correct?

Papaji: In a real experience, mind and intellect leave you. They get lost completely. There is not even a witness left because there is nothing to be witnessed. In that place you can't even call it an experience. There is just an awareness in which knowledge of subjects and objects has been destroyed. It is not reached by effort. It only comes by grace.

23rd October, 1974

Papaji: Don't try to imitate a saint by following his footsteps. Don't follow the tracks of his lifestyle or his career. If you do, you will set up some destination that you have to reach. That destination will be a thought in your mind, and if you reach it you will only experience the thought that was already in your mind.

If you want to follow a saint, identify with what he really is. Identify with his freedom. Not the freedom that is the opposite of bondage, but the freedom that is beyond all comparisons, all opposites.

Question: How can I choose the most favourable circumstances for inner work?

Papaji: Don't choose. For the one who dives deeply into himself, there are no circumstances at all. If you dive deeply and reach the source, your body will no longer be yours. It will belong to destiny. It will react to whatever circumstances it is in, doing whatever it is destined to do.

The circumstances you talk about are just your dream. In your dream you might be living in a cave, or you might be living in a palace. When you are in a palace, you might dream of renouncing the world and going to live in a cave. And while you are in a cave, you might dream of going to live in a palace. But when you wake up you realise that these dream palaces and caves never really existed. Don't worry about which part of your dream world you should inhabit. Dive deeply into yourself and wake up in reality.

Go through all the layers that cover it up: the superficial layers of body consciousness, the deeper levels where past and future are seen simultaneously, and beyond even them to the worldless, bodiless place where you no longer even know where you are. Disconnect yourself from all the false identifications you make at the superficial levels.

Question: Where does the soul go after the death of the body?

Papaji: You think the soul is in the body and that assumption makes you ask what happens to it when the body dies. I say, 'The body is in the soul'. If you understood this, you wouldn't ask the question. Krishna says, 'All beings are in Me, but I am not in them'. All bodies, all beings are in the Self, but you seem to think that the Self is hiding somewhere in the body, and that with the death of the body it goes somewhere else.

Question: Then what is death?

Papaji: Death is an idea that makes you afraid because you are identifying with this body that will one day disappear. The person who asks this question has accepted that he was born and he assumes that he is going to die. When you don't identify with the body, you don't die.

27th October, 1974
At Palaiseau with Sita

Papaji: All your thoughts belong to the past. Everything you do is a reaction based on past experience. Even when you think of the future, the thoughts of your future projection come from the thoughts, memories and experiences of the past. All mental activity comes from stirring up thoughts of the past. The present moment is free from thought, but when thought arises, you are no longer in the present, you are in the past. The thoughtless present moment is peace. It is only the thoughts of the past that make you miserable.

You choose a course of action for the future and assume that it is you who are doing the choosing. Actually, it is the Supreme Power that is giving you the strength to choose. Don't be foolish and think that it is you who are doing the choosing. That power is there all the time, making you do all the things that you do. Instead of trying to organise your future, look at the source of that power and be aware of how it does everything. It makes the body move; it makes the mind move All the things that you imagine you do by yourself are done by this Supreme Power.

You go through life making plans for the future. Give up ideas of succeeding in the future because all such ideas keep you in mental bondage. All thoughts of future plans are ideas from the graveyard of your past ideas. If you want to change in the future, then you are attached to things that change. You are looking for something that is not permanent. Have love for the changeless. Find that unmoving place where you know that the Supreme Power makes you move. In that place you won't make plans and you won't care about the results of your actions.

You become one with whatever you think you are. If you think you are the body and the mind, you will experience yourself as the body and the mind. You will identify with them and that identification will bring you endless trouble and suffering. Keep quiet. In that silence you automatically identify yourself with the peace, the silence and the freedom of the Supreme Power that is looking after everything. When this happens your work is over because, from that moment on, the Supreme Power runs your life for you.

Papaji always insists that he never makes plans. He says that this Supreme Power animates him and makes him do all the things that he does. I got an interesting insight into this when Jaya, his granddaughter, appeared in his house and asked him to participate in one of her projects.

Jaya, who was studying for a degree in Lucknow, had been given, as part of a psychology course she was taking, several copies of a questionnaire to distribute among her friends and relatives. It was a multiple-choice questionnaire that attempted to gauge the respondent's attitude to life, the world and relationships. Papaji was given a copy which he dutifully went through. For many of the questions there were no relevant choices for him, but Jaya insisted that he tick at least one box. When he encountered a question about his friends, he refused point-blank to give a response.

'I haven't got any friends,' he said, 'and I don't want any. Friendships only cause trouble. It is better to be alone, absolutely alone. I have been absolutely alone all my life. That is the only way to be truly happy. Friendships and relationships just get you into trouble.'

Papaji did not appear to take the rest of the questionnaire very seriously. He made jokes about the questions and the choice of answers and seemed deliberately to pick the least appropriate response. One box that he ticked said: 'If I had to live my life all over again, I would plan it differently.' I asked him about this answer later and his reply confirmed that he had not been taking the questions very seriously:

For most of those questions, none of the answers was relevant. However, Jaya made me tick at least one answer, even when I didn't think that there was an appropriate one.

As for the question about planning, I have never planned my

life at all. From my childhood on, there has never been any planning. When you make plans, you make karma for yourself, and when you make karma, you have to be reborn to enjoy or suffer it. I have never made any plans. I have made no new karma, so I will not have to come back again in this age or the next. Plans are desires, and desires cause one to be reborn. It is better not to plan at all.

INDIAN SATSANGS

At the end of October, 1974, Papaji returned to India. Many people wanted to accompany him or join him later, but he put them all off by saying that he would write to them to give details of where and when they could see him. Two of the people he had met in Europe, Carlos Silva and Jean Michel Laborde, did follow him. Papaji treated them very hospitably in Delhi, where they were accommo-dated at the home of his sister. After a short stay there, Papaji took them on a trip to Hardwar, but after a couple of days he disap-peared without trace. This was a fairly common experience for devotees who tried to follow Papaji around India in those days. He kept the crowds away by frequently travelling to new places without telling most of the people who were with him where he was going. On this particular occasion he went to Lucknow to see his family and the devotees who lived there. Meera and Mukti joined him sometime in November.

In those days Papaji was not giving satsangs in either his own house or his mother's house, the two places where he had been meeting Lucknow devotees throughout the 1950s and '60s. He was, instead, meeting people in a separate house that one of his devotees had provided for him.

This is Papaji's account of how he came to be using this house:

The man who let me use this house was an advocate who owned a large tract of land at Karona, near Sitapur. At the time of our meeting he was a disciple of Swami Naradananda Saraswati of Nemisharanya, a famous teacher who had a big ashram and a school for boys.

This advocate, whose name was Shiv Shankar Trivedi, used to come to Lucknow once a week to attend a clinic that was run by a man called Dr S. N. Misra. Trivedi had a stomach ulcer that was so bad, he was only allowed to drink milk, glucose water and rice gruel. Solid foods had been prohibited. He would come to Lucknow the evening before his appointment, spend the night here and then see his doctor the following morning. On one of his evenings in town he was captivated by a photo of me that was hanging on the wall of a shop in Aminabad. It was owned by A. N. Tandon, a devotee of mine.

Finding himself unable to take his eyes off this photo, he asked him, 'Who is this man? Where does he live? I have to see him.'

Mr Tandon told him the address: '522, Narhi. It's near Hazrat Ganj. But don't go there and bother him with all your worldly problems. Either sit quietly or ask spiritual questions.'

He came early the next morning, before his visit to the doctor. He was so early, I hadn't even eaten breakfast. After my wife let him in, he just sat silently in my room. I had never seen the man before, so I was a little surprised that he didn't even bother to introduce himself. He just sat quietly and looked at me.

I thought to myself, 'If this man doesn't want to tell me why he is here, I will have to find out myself'.

I asked him what had brought him to my house and he replied, 'I want to see Lord Ram. Can you show him to me?'

I didn't answer his question. I just sat quietly and watched him for a while. After a few minutes his body began to shake uncontrollably. He made some effort to try to stop the convulsions but he didn't succeed. I didn't interfere. I just kept quiet and watched. While he was still in this state my wife came in and told me that breakfast was ready. Not knowing about his condition, I invited him to eat with us. I took him downstairs where my wife served him a large portion of *parothas* [a chapati-like preparation] that had been stuffed with grated radish and fried in mustard oil. He didn't refuse the food even though his doctor had told him not to eat any heavy, greasy food. I found out later that he had only eaten it because he felt that it was *prasad* that he could not refuse.

He didn't tell me he had a serious stomach problem, nor did he tell me what had happened during the time he had been violently shaking in front of me. At the end of the meal he bowed to me and left without saying a word.

Once he was out on the street, he rushed off to see his doctor to tell him what he had just eaten. He was beginning to feel that maybe it hadn't been such a good idea to eat all that heavy food. The doctor examined his stomach but could find no trace of the ulcer that had been there on his previous visit. Either his experience in my room or the heavy breakfast of *parothas* had effected a complete cure.

The following day he came back with A. N. Tandon. Even then Trivedi did not tell me about either the experience he had had in my room or the stomach ulcer that had mysteriously vanished. I only found out later when Mr Tandon told me the full story.

Trivedi decided that he wanted to move to Lucknow so that he could spend more time with me. He didn't have a house of his own there, so he needed to find somewhere to stay.

'I would like to get a big house,' he said, 'where I can stay and where you can also give satsang. If I find such a place, will you come?'

I agreed on condition that he live there by himself. I didn't want him to bring his whole family along.

'That's all right,' he said. 'I can live independently. I know how to cook and look after myself.'

We found a house that belonged to a man called Dr Chaturvedi. At that time he was the Director-General of Health for Uttar Pradesh. Trivedi bought the house from him and moved into the ground floor. It was a three-storey building. Since there was a lot of space upstairs, I began to hold satsangs there. In those days many government officials used to come regularly. There was Dr M. K. Goel, head of the department of orthopaedics at the King George Medical College; Dr B. C. Gupta, Additional Director of Health; S. R. Sharma, a retired Chief Engineer of the U.P. Electricity Board; S. S. Goel, an inspector in the Electricity Board; S. S. Shukla, Chief Engineer in the Bridge Corporation; a Mr Sherwani, the state Minister of Agriculture; and several M.L.A.s from the U.P. State Assembly.

In the 1960s, when Papaji was still giving satsang in his Narhi house, there was one other regular satsang visitor whom Papaji did not include in this list:

I was conducting satsang in my old house in Narhi. About 35-40 people could be accommodated there. Every day a dog would come and sit in the front row. It would sit there, in front of everyone, with its eyes closed, as if it were in deep meditation. My wife didn't like any dog to come inside the house because she was cooking there and wanted to keep it clean. She complained about this dog coming every day, so I thought I would ask who it belonged to and tell that person not to bring it any more. Or at least he could tie it up outside before he came in.

I asked a friend of mine, a Director of Education who regularly attended the satsangs, who the dog belonged to. He surprised me by saying that it did not belong to anyone in the room.

'It waits in front of the GPO,' he said. 'When it sees a group of people walking towards your house for satsang, it joins the group and follows them into the house. It knows the people who come here regularly. Every day it comes in with a different person or a different group.'

Papaji continues with his account of the house that was bought for him in Lucknow:

The house soon became my main base in Lucknow. Visitors to the city who came to attend my satsangs would be accommodated on the ground floor. Many foreigners ended up staying there for quite long periods. Bettina Baumer, who was teaching at Benares Hindu University, used to come and stay there, as did another girl called Anakutty. She was a French teacher from Kerala.

Once a week Trivedi would go back to Karona, the village in which he used to live. He would buy *dhal*, potatoes and onions very cheaply because they were all grown in the neighbouring fields, and bring them back to Lucknow. These provisions were used to feed the many devotees who used to come to the house.

At first Trivedi exhibited a lot of devotion towards me. He adopted me as his Guru and even washed my feet in a ritual *pada puja*. However, after some time, his ego came up and he began to resent all the attention I was getting. He used to sing good *bhajans*, accompanying himself on the harmonium. He felt that since it was his house, the visitors should also come and visit him to listen to his *bhajan* performances and to his recitations of Valmiki's *Ramayana*. But nobody ever came. Everyone who entered his house would walk straight up the stairs to meet me. Even when he stood at the bottom of the stairs to intercept all the people who were coming in, no one listened to him.

This neglect made him very angry and his original devotion turned to hate. He began to write to all my devotees, both in India and abroad, criticising me and saying that I had a bad character. He was particularly abusive about my relationship with Meera. I found out what he was doing when some of the devotees he had written to forwarded his letters to me. When I found out what was happening, I stopped going to his house and resumed my satsangs at Butler Road, the home of my mother.

After I left he was finally able to fulfil his desire to have an audience for his performances. A few people started to come to listen to him. I had stipulated that he had to live there alone if he wanted me to give satsangs there, but when I left, this restriction no longer applied. He brought his whole family to live with him.

This man was publicly criticising me for a long time afterwards. I sent a message to him, saying that if he wanted to forget the past and come to me again, he would be welcome, but I never received a response.

Shiv Shankar Trivedi's original meeting with Papaji took place in the late 1960s. 'Vrindavan', the house that he lived in and in which Papaji gave satsangs, was a meeting place for Papaji's Lucknow devotees until the mid-1970s.

Om Prakash told me several stories about the devotees who were coming to see Papaji during this period:

During the first few years that I knew him [late 1960s and

early 1970s], Papaji was virtually unknown in Lucknow. The crowds of people that surround him nowadays were not there. Maybe seven to ten people were coming to see him regularly. Rarely more.

Most of these people were local businessmen, engineers or doctors. One of these doctors was particularly attached to him. His name was Dr Minni Goel and he was an orthopaedic surgeon with an international reputation. He would come every evening at about 10 p.m. after he had finished his day's work and spend the whole night sitting in meditation in Papaji's house. At 5 o'clock in the morning he would get up, brush his teeth, take a cup of tea and then go off to his medical college to work.

Satsangs in those days were very informal affairs because Papaji always insisted that people should act in a normal way around him. He particularly didn't like to see people sitting with closed eyes in front of him. He wanted visitors to imbibe his grace as they were going about their ordinary, everyday activities.

In those days if anybody sat in satsang in an eyes-closed meditation posture, Papaji would shake him by the shoulder and rebuke him, often quite harshly.

'What are you closing your eyes for? Get out! Get out of here at once! Don't come to see me if you just want to sit here with your eyes closed. Be normal! Be natural!'

One of the regular visitors in the early 1970s was a man called B. M. Gupta. He was a Director in the Department of Medical Health and he used to come and sit with Papaji nearly every day. During one of his visits this man was reading out some of the questions and answers from Ramana Maharshi's pamphlet *Who am I?* After the first two questions and answers had been read out, there was a power break that left us in darkness. We sat for a while in silence.

Suddenly Papaji called out to Gupta, 'Why did you stop?'

We all laughed because we thought he was joking.

Papaji said, 'No, no, I am serious. Why did you stop? Why didn't you carry on reading?'

This civil servant replied, 'How can I continue? It's completely dark in here. How can I read if I can't see the book?'

'Ah,' said Papaji. 'That explains it. If you read with your inner light, it wouldn't matter if the lights were on or off.'

We all still thought he was joking with us.

The man said, 'Only you can do that. We ordinary mortals have to make do with light bulbs.'

'How do you know that this is true?' demanded Papaji. 'Have you ever tried it? Try it now and see what happens. Maybe you can do it as well. If you don't try, how will you find out whether you can do it or not?'

Then, as we sat there in complete darkness, the man began to read out the entire text of *Who am I?* I knew he was not familiar with the text, so he could not have been reciting it from memory.

At the end of that satsang I went up to him and asked him how he had done it.

He replied, 'At the moment Papaji said, "Try it yourself and see," there was a flash of light in my head after which I saw the whole text illuminated inside me. It was like reading from a lighted screen inside my head.'

This same man was involved in another strange incident with Papaji. They were both very big men, perhaps 85 kg each. One day they were travelling together in a rickshaw when their combined weights caused the back axle of the rickshaw to break. As the axle broke, they both fell crashing to the ground. By a curious coincidence, both of them cracked their kneecaps during their fall. I know this is true because they later had x-rays taken at a local clinic. Though the damage sustained was equal in both cases, the accident seemed to have no effect on Papaji. He walked away from the broken rickshaw with no apparent ill-effects. The civil servant, though, had to spend several weeks with his leg immobilised, waiting for his crack to heal. Though he had not suffered any serious injuries, this incident made Papaji very wary of rickshaws. For the next few years he would always inspect the axle of any rickshaw he was intending to travel in. If it didn't satisfy him, he would go and look for another.

I have already mentioned that I never had any particular reason for going to Papaji. I was addicted to his physical presence, but I could never say that I was ever going there to get anything from him. I had no expectations when I went, no ambitions that I wanted him to help me to fulfil. I wasn't even trying to make spiritual progress. Thoughts like these never arose in me. I went to see him so often because some inner power compelled me to do it, but there was no motive attached to the action. I went because I had to.

Around this time [1970] I had a chance meeting with Ram Mohan Sharma, an electrical engineer who worked for the government. He had known Papaji for many years and he used to come to see him almost every day. I think he had been coming to see him regularly since 1954. His father was also an electrical engineer and a devotee of Papaji.

Before I tell this story about Ram Mohan Sharma I should say that I have rarely come across someone who was such a sincere devotee of Papaji, but he had a passion for results. He had a very clear spiritual goal in his mind and worked very hard to attain it. I wasn't like that at all.

After I had been visiting Papaji for about a year, this man asked me, 'Om Prakash, you are coming to see Papaji every day. I have been observing you for some time. What have you attained through all these visits? What have you got from him?'

'Nothing,' I replied. I didn't think that I had attained anything by going to see him.

'Then what are you coming for?' he asked.

'I don't know,' I said.

I wasn't being evasive. I really didn't know why I was going to see Papaji every day.

'Then you have wasted your time!' exclaimed Ram Kumar Sharma.

'I don't know if I have wasted my time,' I answered.

My inability to answer him coherently was beginning to exasperate him.

'Every time I ask you a question, your answer is "I don't know". If you don't know the answers to any of these questions, what *do* you know?'

'Even that I don't know.'

That was the end of the dialogue. He was so disgusted by my inability to give sensible reasons for my behaviour, he just got up and left.

Though I had answered honestly, his questions had the effect of raising these questions in my mind for the first time. Why was I going to Papaji? Was I getting anything out of these visits? Had I attained anything by going to see him every day? I decided to put all my doubts before Papaji.

The next day at his house I approached him and said, 'Papaji, may I ask you a question? Something is troubling me.'

'Yes, of course. What is it?'

'Papaji,' I began, 'I have to ask you one question which has been bothering me since yesterday. I have been coming to see you for more than a year. As I look back on that period, I cannot see that I have gained anything from you. I don't know what I have received from you. Can you tell me?'

Papaji looked at me and said, 'When we first met, did we enter into any agreement? Was there any commitment? Did I agree to provide you with anything?'

'No,' I answered.

'Did I ask you to come to me?'

'No.'

'Did I ever force you to come?'

'No.'

'Then why are you carrying this garbage in your pocket? This garbage you are carrying is not your own disease. You have picked it up from someone else. If you want my advice, throw it away. Don't have anything to do with it.'

I followed his advice. I stopped worrying about results and just went to see him to satisfy my insatiable craving for his *darshan*.

My lack of interest in getting anything from him was so pronounced, for many years I never even regarded him as my Guru. Once you accept someone as a Guru, inevitably the relationship imposes some kind of expectations on the disciple.

Ram Mohan Sharma had been known to Papaji for almost twenty years when this incident took place. He had initially come as a complete sceptic but soon became an ardent devotee. Papaji himself has described what happened:

In the 1950s I used to conduct satsangs upstairs in my house in Narhi. One day a group of about twenty-five devotees came to see me. They introduced themselves by saying that they were members of the Yogoda Satsang, the organisation which had been founded by Swami Yogananda. Their leader, who was president of one of the branches of this organisation, was an inspector in the electricity department.

After the introductions were over, the president explained the purpose of their visit.

'According to Swami Yogananda, a person who has realised the Self is capable of stopping his heartbeat any time he wants to. We have heard that Poonjaji is a realised person, so we have come to test him. We want to see if you can stop your heart while we have a stethoscope recording the beats.'

I told them, 'I have never claimed to be a Self-realised person'.

This was true then, and it is still true now. This is not a claim I ever make on my behalf. Enlightenment may be there, but if it is, there is no one left who can say, 'I have attained it'.

Although I told them that I had never made this claim, and although I also told them that I was not interested in being tested, they insisted on going ahead with their plan. They had brought a doctor with them to do all the necessary checks.

The doctor attempted to locate my heartbeats both by using his stethoscope and by feeling for my pulse, but he couldn't find any beating anywhere. He was most surprised because he had come with the intention of unmasking me as a fraud. They all wanted to show off the superiority of their teacher and their practices by exposing my inability to pass this test.

I should say at this point that I didn't attempt to stop my heart for this test. All I can say is that their faith that this was a sign of enlightenment may have produced some mental state in them in which they were incapable of hearing the beats. I have had my heart and blood pressure tested countless times by doctors who merely wanted to ascertain the state of my health. None of them ever found that my heart wasn't beating.

The president, Ram Mohan Sharma, was very impressed by

the demonstration.

'How long can you stop the heart for?' he asked. 'How long can you remain in this state?'

'I don't know whether my heart is beating or not,' I replied. 'But what I do know is that I have to go out and post some letters. This is the time of my afternoon walk. I have some letters to post, so I will go to the GPO and post them.'

He offered to drive me there, but I refused, saying that I liked having some exercise in the afternoon. What I really wanted was to get away from this group and their silly tests, but they wouldn't leave me alone.

'Can you walk while your heart has stopped?' he enquired. 'Can we follow you with a stethoscope on your back while you walk to see if you can move around without using your heart?'

I refused, excused myself and left.

I thought I had seen the last of Mr Sharma but he showed up at my house the next day saying that he had decided to hand in his resignation to the Yogoda Satsang Society.

He called together all the members of his branch and publicly announced that he was no longer interested in being a part of the Yogoda Satsang.

'I have found my true Guru,' he told them. 'From now on I will be following Sri Poonjaji. He has demonstrated to my satisfaction that he has attained the supreme heights of yoga.'

He came to see me regularly for several years along with his wife. When he went out in the morning, he would often bring her to my house and drop her there so she could have satsang with me while he was at work.

After many years he became dissatisfied with both me and my teachings and began running after other gurus. He read a Hindi book entitled *Meditation Through Sex* by Rajneesh and decided that he would go to Pune and become a *sannyasin* there. He embraced his new beliefs as ardently as he had embraced all his previous ones. He came back from Pune full of enthusiasm for his new ideas and practices and attempted to pass on the teachings of Rajneesh to his family and friends.

Friends of mine who knew him well told me that, along with

his parents, his wife and his brothers, he would sit in his house
jumping up and down and shouting 'Hoo! Hoo!' as loudly as he
could. This, apparently, was one of the Pune meditations. He was
a dedicated seeker, an earnest practitioner, and for at least a year,
an ardent missionary of the Rajneesh teachings. Many people who
had been attending my satsangs went to be with him instead. After
a year though, when he realised that this new system was not
bringing him any benefits, he left Rajneesh and became a disciple
of Muktananda instead.

Mr Sharma went to Ganeshpuri, the place where Swami
Muktananda had his main ashram, and chanted mantras there for
about two years. When this failed to bring him any satisfaction, he
moved on to Ananda Mayi Ma and went to live at Kankhal with
her. He tried very hard to be a good devotee, but he never developed a taste for the traditional forms of worship that formed a large
part of the activities around her. His next stop was Puttaparthi, the
ashram of Sai Baba. He fell in love with Sathya Sai Baba and when
he eventually returned to Lucknow, he converted his house into a
Sai Baba ashram. On one of his walls he had an enormous picture
of Sathya Sai Baba which became famous because *vibhuti* would
materialise on its surface and fall to the ground. His house and the
picture eventually became a pilgrimage centre. After word of these
miraculous manifestations spread, thousands of people started to
visit his house.

*Om Prakash now continues with his reminiscences about Mr
Sharma:*

Ram Mohan Sharma enjoyed arguing with Papaji about
various philosophical matters, but he couldn't relate to Papaji's
bhakti side. In those days Papaji would often talk about his love for
Krishna and about devotional matters in general, but Mr Sharma
dismissed all these talks about Hindu gods as primitive superstitions. Then, one day, as Mr Sharma was coming to visit Papaji in
Narhi, Krishna and Arjuna appeared before him, riding in a
chariot. He couldn't disbelieve the evidence of his own eyes, so
after that he stopped making fun of all the Hindu gods. Papaji

263

himself just laughed when he was told the story.

Though Papaji himself has been an ardent Krishna *bhakta* all his life, he rarely talks about his devotion. It brings tears to his eyes, and I don't think he likes to be seen crying in public. When it happens nowadays, he changes the subject or looks the other way to hide his tears, but when I first knew him he was far less reticent about displaying his emotions. I once had the privilege of listening to him chant the *Bhagavatam* daily over a period of about two or three months. There were days when he couldn't speak more than half a line without being choked by his devotional tears.

Mr Sharma's wife, Indira, was also an ardent devotee of Papaji for many years. When she had no other work at home, she would come to Papaji's house and do a little work for him. She would sweep his house, clean any kitchen utensils that needed to be washed, and even prepare food for him. After some time she began to neglect the work in her own house in order to spend more and more time with Papaji. At first her husband didn't mind her visits because he thought that she would get some benefit from them, but when she started to neglect him and her household chores, he became less and less enthusiastic about her visits. He was a friend of mine and he told me several times that his wife was neglecting her own work in order to come and see Papaji.

'Om Prakash,' he would say, 'she is always rushing off to that house. The moment I leave for the office, she gives up all the work in our house and goes rushing out to see Papaji. I have told her to stay at home and do more work, but she doesn't listen to me any longer.'

The problem came to a head a few days later when she rushed over as usual in the morning, having forgotten to switch off the gas cylinder in her house. Her thoughts were on Papaji, not on the mundane details of housekeeping in her own home.

A few hours later her father-in-law started banging on Papaji's door. This man, who was a Chief Engineer in the electricity department, was clearly in a very angry mood. He had a stick in his hand which he waved in front of Papaji's nose.

He started abusing Indira in front of everyone. 'This bitch is a useless woman!' he shouted. 'She did not even bother to turn off the gas before she left the house today! There is a smell of gas all over the house! Our whole house might have blown up or burnt down because of her carelessness and her stupidity! Even though nothing serious happened, still I have to pay for a new cylinder because this woman has wasted all the gas in the old one!'

Indira was sitting to one side of Papaji, trembling with fear. Because her father-in-law was waving his stick while he shouted, she probably thought that he would soon start beating her with it.

Papaji listened to all the complaints and then spoke to Indira in a very mild-mannered way.

'You shouldn't be careless like this. You should check on things like this before you leave. Go home with your father-in-law and make sure that there is no danger to your house.'

The two of them left in the same rickshaw that the man had arrived in. On arriving at their house, the father-in-law went in first because he wanted to show Indira that the gas tap was fully open. He didn't want her to go in first and tamper with it. To his utter amazement, when he entered the kitchen, the gas tap was closed and there was no smell of gas in the house.

Indira got some of her courage back and said to him, 'Why are you accusing me of things like this? You think that you can shout at me whenever you like because I come from a poor family, whereas you people are all rich. You can see for yourself that the tap is closed. There is no smell of gas here. If the gas had leaked, there would have been a bad smell all over the house.'

The man wouldn't accept the evidence of his senses. He abused her even more, saying that a whole cylinder of gas had gone to waste because of her carelessness, and that he would have to take it away and have it refilled. He lifted up the gas cylinder to take it out of the house and found, much to his amazement, that it was completely full. That really confused him. When he had discovered the leak earlier that day, he had lifted up the cylinder to see how much was left and he had found that the cylinder was completely empty. He had found some rational explanations for the tap being off and the gas smell being absent, but he couldn't think of any way that the cylinder could have refilled itself in his brief absence.

Ram Mohan Sharma had been doing yoga for many years. Papaji tried to discourage him from doing these practices, but Mr Sharma was very attached to them. It was Papaji's view that none of the traditional spiritual paths was a valid route to enlightenment. He would always say that there is no path and no route to enlightenment. Mr Sharma never really accepted Papaji's teachings, though initially he had a deep respect for him. After some time he stopped visiting Papaji, but we would still occasionally hear news of him. Some of our mutual acquaintances told us that he was criticising Papaji publicly, saying that his teachings were not true.

Years later I received news that he was in Lucknow, that he had had a heart attack, and that he was seriously ill in hospital. I went to see him to find out how sick he really was. I managed to see him for a few minutes at about 10 p.m. on the day I found out about his condition.

When he saw me come in, he folded his hands in a greeting and spoke with tears in his eyes.

'Om Prakash, I don't think that I have much longer to live. I know that you are very close to Poonjaji. I don't think that I will ever see him again. I have one last request to you. If I die here, please go to him and prostrate on my behalf. Tell him that Sharma is bowing before him and apologising for all the things he has done and all the things he has said about him. Please also give him the following message. Tell him that I have wasted my life running around India trying to find the truth in different ashrams. What Poonjaji taught me and what he is still teaching is something that can only be experienced when one throws oneself completely at his feet and surrenders to him. I was never able to do that, so I was never able to experience the fruit of his teaching. I was too interested in discussing theories with him. I wanted to convince him that my beliefs and my ways were better than his. Poonjaji refused to compromise in any way. He told me the truth as he saw and experienced it, and refused to concede that there was any truth in anything that I tried to tell him. I think that he was right and I was wrong. Please tell him all this and send him my belated apologies.'

Mr Sharma's medical prognosis was as inaccurate as his philosophical views. He survived his heart attack and went on to live for several more months. Papaji was not in Lucknow at the time that Mr Sharma had his attack, but he returned a couple of months later. By that time Mr Sharma was terminally ill with other diseases. His liver and kidneys had failed and he was not expected to live for more than a few days. I told Papaji what had happened when I had visited Mr Sharma, and I carried out my promise by prostrating at his feet on his behalf.

Papaji immediately decided to visit him in his house. We went there and Papaji gave him Rs 4,000 as a contribution towards his medical expenses. That was a large amount of money in those days. Papaji displayed no feelings of ill-will towards him at all, even though he knew that Mr Sharma had been publicly criticising him in many ashrams all over India. Because of this visit Mr Sharma was able to offer his apology in person.

'I have been a foolish man.' he said. 'You offered me the supreme wisdom but I rejected it. I have not accepted or honoured your teachings. Instead, I have gone to other teachers looking for the truth. It was my bad karma that disqualified me from receiving and experiencing what you wanted to give me. Please accept my apologies for everything I have done and said against you.'

Papaji graciously accepted his apology.

Papaji himself has described this final visit:

Om Prakash went in to see him first. I overheard him say, 'Poonjaji is here to see you. Do you want to meet him?'

Ram Sharma invited me into the room. He couldn't get out of bed and he could barely speak, but he welcomed me as well as he could. When I asked why he looked so pale, I was told that his liver and his kidneys had virtually stopped functioning. His wife had already been told that he would not live for more than seven days.

He motioned me to come closer so that he could whisper to me. 'Poonjaji,' he said, 'I repent. I have wasted my life going from teacher to teacher, but I have not found peace of mind. Now it is too late. Please bless me because I have not found a teacher like you anywhere in the world.'

He put his palms together on his chest to show his reverence and respect.

I put the Rs 4,000 in an envelope and gave it to his wife. I knew that it seemed to be a hopeless case, but I asked her to spend the money on getting him the best medical treatment that was available.

Nothing more could be done for him. Two days later he passed away.

I began this chapter with a brief account of Papaji's return to India after his second foreign trip. In the weeks that followed, he gave regular satsangs to his Lucknow devotees, mostly at 'Vrindavan', the house that S. S. Trivedi had bought for him. Meera recorded many of these dialogues and talks in her notebook.

Most of these conversations reflected the traditional Hindu background that Papaji's Indian devotees had. In Europe Papaji had flavoured many of his talks on liberation with Christian references, since that was the tradition to which most of his listeners had been exposed. In India he tended to explain his message of freedom by giving analogies and examples from the Ramayana *and from the life and teachings of Krishna. He would also speak very movingly about the path of devotion to God, a subject he rarely broached when foreigners were present.*

Many of his Indian devotees were following sadhanas *that incorporated* nama japa, *repetition of the name of God. Papaji had followed this path himself for twenty-five years, so he was more than qualified to give out expert, first-hand advice on this topic. Usually, when Papaji spoke on this subject he would adopt the line that had been taken by many of Hinduism's most respected saints. Three points would repeatedly be explained:*

1. *The real Name of God is indistinguishable from God Himself.*
2. *When one finds God in the Heart, one finds God's Name, which is one's own real name, repeating itself there, but not in a way that is perceptible by the senses.*

3. God's original unutterable Name is the source of all manifestation.

This is a complex subject that has its roots in the mystical writings of Hindu saints such as Kabir, Tukaram, Namdev and others, all of whom Papaji greatly reveres. The various nuances of the subject will, I hope, become more clear as Papaji explains his position in the following dialogues. All of them were recorded in the first few weeks after Papaji's return to India in 1974.

In the dialogues that follow, the Name (capital 'N') is the source, God Himself, or even the source from which God manifests. The name (lower-case 'n') is the word that can be vocally or mentally repeated.

15th November, 1974

Papaji: Ram put a stone on the ocean to construct the bridge to Lanka, but it fell into the water. When Hanuman tried, his stone floated because the Lord's name was written on it. Even God has his source in the Name. The Name is the source of the Lord's form, and of all other forms.

Ram gave the name 'Eternity' to that monkey Hanuman on account of his love and service. At one point in the *Ramayana* Ram sent Hanuman to search for Sita.

Hanuman asked, 'How can I recognise Sita?'

Ram replied, 'When you hear the constant repetition of the Name, there will be Sita'.

When there are faith and love, the Name is there. Each repetition of the name brings you nearer to the Lord. The name is the foundation of the house for the *sadhak* [spiritual practitioner]. For the *siddha*, the enlightened one, it is the roof.

Wherever your mind is fixed in non-attachment, that place is the abode of the Lord. The Name Itself is the physical vision of God. The experience of the Name in the primal ego is *shanti* [peace].

Question: How to concentrate? I don't know how to do it.

269

Papaji: You are already concentrated. All the time you are concentrating on the idea, 'I am so-and-so'. My advice is to stop concentrating on anything. Be the subject alone.

The state of 'don't know' denotes a real experience. Your memory is full of objective knowledge that you have acquired from outside. Any answer that you find in your memory cannot be a real answer. If you want to know 'Who am I?' you will not find a real answer anywhere in your mind. You will find it in a place where you have nothing to compare it to. It's a quick, sudden experience that has nothing to do with the mind.

If asking 'Who am I?' does not appeal to you, ask 'To whom do I belong?'

21st November, 1974

Papaji: Hanuman brought *sanjivini,* the herb that Ram wanted, by carrying the whole mountain on which it was growing from the Himalayas to Lanka. Hanuman symbolises love and devotion. If you have full faith in your Master, if you have the kind of love and devotion that Hanuman had, no physical feat will be impossible.

While flying to Lanka with the mountain, Bharat, the brother of Ram, accidentally shot Hanuman down with an arrow because he thought that he was an enemy. Bharat represents the subtle ego. Hanuman still had some residual pride that he was a great devotee of Ram. He felt that he was lucky to be serving Him in this way. His pride brought about his downfall, but as he fell through the air he uttered the name 'Ram, Ram' and by the time he reached the ground his pride was gone.

Hanuman is the all-powerful mind. When filled with devotion it can perform great miracles. When its pride goes, when its sense of being the performer of actions disappears, the mountain it is carrying crashes to the ground. What is this mountain? It is the sense of duty: 'I must do this; I must do that.'

Ram is the Name. All names are in this one Name, and all forms come out of it. You can call its form Ram or Krishna, but the Name itself has no form. Its depth is the bluest. The divine drama, the *lila,* is another name of that original Name. It all comes from Ram Himself, from the source.

270

27th November, 1974

Question: Should one repeat the 'Sitaram' mantra instead of 'Ram' alone?

Papaji: It is because of Sita that you can repeat Ram's name.

Question: Are *bhakti* and *jnana* the same?

Papaji: There were four brothers, Sanatkumar, Sanadana, Sanaka and Sanatsujata, the sons of Brahma. They were all *jnanis*, but when they went to Ayodhya to have *darshan* of Lord Ram, they forgot everything. They lost themselves in *bhakti* to the point where they were not aware of anything else.

The *vrittis*, the mental activities, gather information about the world, and they try to understand God in the same way. But when they attach themselves to Him in an attempt to find out who He is, they become absorbed in Him. The experience of absorption is expressed as the emotions of *bhakti*.

Questioner: I find that I cannot hold onto the name tightly enough to be absorbed. My attention wanders.

Papaji: One who pays attention to the repetition of the name accepts that he has not always repeated it. To be attentive to our inattention brings us to awareness.

Creation, the creation of this whole world, arises from inattention. Inattentiveness to the Divine Name that is being repeated in the Heart of all beings brings the world picture into existence. The world is only there when the Divine Name is not consciously heard. We remind ourselves that we are not listening to the Divine Name in the Heart by mentally repeating the name of God.

When I say the name of God, my attention goes to the place that is behind the mind. In that place Hanuman, the mind, and Garuda, the intellect, are constantly repeating my real Name.

Hanuman carries Ram on his shoulders. There Ram endlessly hears His own Name. Ram is myself. His vehicle is the Name.

The Name is the form of the formless. We dwell with descriptions of names and forms and not with that state in which the described is not different from the describer. Descriptions come from the senses, and when we attend to what the senses are telling us, we become absorbed in emotional responses. But when the Name is uttered, when It is heard in the Heart, there is nothing: nothing to be involved in; nothing to get emotional about; nothing to get attached to; nothing to depend on.

Question: How do I reach that state in which I don't depend on anyone, or anything, where I depend on God alone?

Papaji: If you merely say, 'I am going to depend on God alone,' that will be a false statement. You are depending on the intellect that is saying, 'I will depend on God'. This statement does not change anything in your life. If you believe that it does, you are merely fooling yourself. To be truly dependent on God you have to abandon everything, including mind and intellect.

Fighting with the forgetfulness is repeated remembrance.

Papaji's statement in the penultimate answer that he is Ram Himself reminded me of a story I was told while I was preparing this book.

In 1991 an American devotee was sitting with Papaji in the front room of Papaji's Indira Nagar house. In those days, before the big crowds started coming, all the satsangs were held there. This is what the devotee told me:

'I was looking at Papaji, focussing on his eyes. There was a beauty in them I had never seen anywhere else. The intensity of the beauty grew stronger and stronger until I finally had to avert my eyes. This was the only time in my life I ever had to stop looking at something because the beauty of it was too intense. Papaji wasn't looking at me, and I didn't think that he even knew what had happened to me, but as I was leaving the room a few days later, just before I left to go back to my country, he called me up to him.

He picked up a small picture of Hanuman that was displayed near his seat, gave it to me and said, 'Take this. If you are lucky,

Ram may appear to you again.'
Other people have also seen Papaji take the form of Ram. In
the following unusual story, Papaji was taken to be Ram by a deity
in a temple. Before I give Papaji's account of this strange
encounter, I will give a few background details for those readers
who are unfamiliar with the Ramayana.

The incident took place in Bithoor, near Kanpur, at a place
that is believed to be the site of Valmiki's ashram. The sage Valmiki
was the author of the Ramayana.

After the famous battle in Lanka, Lord Ram returned to
Ayodhya with Sita, whom he had rescued from Ravana. Prior to
her release she had spent many years imprisoned in Ravana's
palace. Shortly after her return to Ayodhya, some of the citizens of
that city began to cast doubts on her suitability to be queen of the
kingdom.

'This woman has spent many years in another man's house,'
they said. 'Such a woman is tainted and cannot be acceptable here.
Lord Ram should send her away. He has done his duty in rescuing
her, but now he should send her away because she has spent many
years with another man.'

Sita had retained her chastity throughout her ordeal in Lanka,
but the fact that she had spent so long in a foreign country in
another man's house meant that suspicions about her behaviour
there were inevitable. Ram felt that for the good of the country and
for the good of the monarchy that governed it, she should be sent
away into exile. This decision, one of the most perplexing that Ram
ever made, has never been satisfactorily explained.

Sita accepted her exile and went to live in the ashram of
Valmiki. On the day she was exiled, she was already pregnant with
Ram's twin sons, although Ram was not aware of this at the time.
Sita gave birth to the two sons in Valmiki's ashram and brought
them up there. It was not until many years later that Ram became
aware of their existence.

This is Papaji's description of the visit he made to this ashram
in the 1950s with his two sisters, Tara and Leela:

My sister Tara lived in Kanpur with her family. I had been

invited to her home to attend the thread ceremony of her son. One of my other sisters, Leela, came the next day from Ambala, Haryana. The thread ceremony of a brahmin boy is a big occasion. All the relatives are expected to attend.

During the course of my stay I heard Leela asking Tara, 'Where is Bithoor, the ashram of Brahmarishi Valmiki?'

Tara told her that it was quite near to where we were staying, adding that she didn't know much about it because she had never been there herself. We made some enquiries from the neighbours and found out how to get there. It was a difficult place to reach. The last part of the journey, we were told, had to be completed on a horse cart because there was no other public transport available. Despite the inaccessibility of the place, both sisters wanted to go. They asked me to join them because they didn't want to travel to such a lonely place by themselves. I agreed to go with them because I too had never seen it, even though I had spent many years in Lucknow, which is only a few hours away from the ashram.

We travelled as far as we could by bus and then hired a *tonga* for a few hours to take us to the temple that now marks the location of the old ashram. The temple is fairly near the Ganga. Tara also wanted to visit the river, but she had to go by herself because Leela had arthritis and I didn't want to undertake the long walk in the hot sun.

While she was off visiting the Ganga, Leela and I went into the temple and walked towards the image of Sita. She was represented as suckling her two sons. When we came near to it, the image seemed to melt before our eyes and change into the real form of Sita.

Sita stood in front of me, pointed an accusing finger at me and said, 'Why did you send me away and make me stay here in the forest?'

Then she turned to Leela and demanded, 'What mistake did I make that your brother abandoned me here? Why did he ask his brother Lakshman to abandon me here in the forest? They threw me out, but Valmiki took me in, even though he knew I was pregnant with Ram's children.'

Sita was crying hysterically as she listed all her complaints to Leela and me. Other people came into the temple and they too saw Sita addressing me as Ram and complaining to me about her exile. They all started to prostrate to me. Meanwhile, my sister Leela was acting very strangely. The power of the *darshan* had unhinged her mind a little and she started to shout and scream. She didn't want to leave, so in the end I had to drag her out.

Tara reappeared after her bath in the Ganga. With her assistance I managed to put Leela into the *tonga*. On the drive home Leela became hysterical again. She was crying and fighting with me, demanding to know why I had abandoned Sita and exiled her to the forest. Eventually she lost consciousness.

We got her home safely and after some time her mental state returned to normal. The experience caused her to re-evaluate her relationship with me.

She came up to me, prostrated, and asked, 'I want to sever this brother-sister relationship that we have had up till now. I don't want to regard you as my brother any longer. I want you to be my Guru. While I was in the temple, Sita told me that you are my Guru and not my brother. From now on, that is the only relationship I want to have with you.'

She came with me to Lucknow and stayed with me for a while. After some time her son came and took her back to her family.

Before she left, I gave her a photo of me. She took it home with her and started worshipping it in her *puja* room. Her eldest son, who was then an officer in the Delhi Customs Department, found her doing *puja* to my picture and objected.

'Why are you praying to this photo? Your brother is still alive. You should only do *puja* to a relative's photo after he has died. It is not proper to do it while he is still alive.'

She ignored him, carried on with her *puja* and said, 'He is not my relative; he is my Guru'.

I contacted Leela who still lives in Ambala, and she kindly sent me her own version of what happened on that momentous day. Her reply was written in the form of a letter addressed to 'Dear

*Brother' Papaji. Her version is substantially the same as Papaji's,
but there are a few extra details that Papaji omitted.*

It was the birth anniversary of Valmiki. There was a festival
that day at his ashram. We picked up our sister Tara from Kanpur
and proceeded to Bithoor. I lost my purse during the journey. We
got down at Ganga Ghat. Before taking a dip I put my empty handkerchief below my clothes. When I returned from my bath in the
Ganga, I found, wrapped up in my handkerchief, seven notes of
Rs 100 each. I became nervous on seeing that money and I told the
whole incident to you, dear brother. I also thought that perhaps
God was testing me. I tore up all the currency notes found there
and threw them into the Ganga. Then we all proceeded onwards.
At Bithoor you met and sat near the person whom you had to meet
there. [Presumably she means that Papaji had an appointment with
Sita.] Sita Maharani [the great queen] had a long conversation with
you. She was rapidly shedding tears from her eyes.

Seeing this I asked you, 'Dear brother, what is all this?
Maharani Sita is crying.'

You replied, 'Sister, do you not understand? Don't you know
what this story is?'

*Leela seems to have little or no recollection of the dramatic
events that happened next. Papaji says that she began to dance and
cry ecstatically, so much so that she attracted a large crowd of
pilgrims who somehow, intuitively, recognised her high state and
began to shower her with money. When she returned to normal, she
had no idea what she had been doing or where all the money had
come from:*

I [Leela] too sat down near her [Sita] and closed my eyes.
When I opened them, I found heaps of currency notes. We left
them all there, took leave and returned home.

*I showed Leela's written account to Papaji. Before returning
it to me, he wrote the following comments at the bottom:*

All the devotees who came to the temple for *darshan* started prostrating to Leela and offering her money. Leela became unconscious, so I brought her in a horse cart to Kanpur where my sister Tara lived. For the next three days Leela was shouting, 'I cannot bear this strong rope! This rope is the bondage of feeling that you are my brother! You are no longer my brother! You are my Guru!'

I will return now to the 1974 satsangs in which Papaji was speaking primarily about the Name of God.

2nd December, 1974

Papaji: You cannot see God unless you don't see what is in front of you. This differentiation between what is divine and what is not divine is killing you.

The Name is not uttered. It is the three bodies that repeat the Name endlessly. This is the repetition of that eternal Name.

[The three bodies are the gross physical body, the subtle body of dreams and the so-called causal body, the state of the 'I' during deep sleep.]

The substratum, or the Name, bluish in its transparency, can be called Krishna. Krishna signifies 'attention', attention without an external object to attend to. Then 'intelligence' tries to understand it. Don't understand by the word 'intelligence' the normal functioning of the intellect. It is something beyond the intellect. Call it pure intelligence. When this pure intelligence tries to understand It, the Name, a most subtle and transparent form comes from Krishna Himself. This is Radha [the divine consort of Krishna], a form of consciousness that is attracted by the conscious substratum. Radha is an extension of the original essence that rises from intention, intention to understand. Knowing this is direct seeing, real seeing, because it stays eternally.

3rd December, 1974

Papaji: I see the silence. It even has a form. It is a most active and attracting silence. Where are the eyes of Siva? They are eternally attracted by this. He is constantly meditating on this. This is His work. Understanding this is seeing, and seeing this is understanding. The *Vedas* are a description of it.

You see your face in the mirror. You are face to face with your own reflection. You look for yourself in the mirror. Staring back at you is the Name, repeating Itself.

The comments recorded by Meera on the 2nd and 3rd December were, I think, an attempt to explain the appearance of the manifest in the unmanifest in terms that Krishna bhaktas could relate to. Papaji sometimes asserts that manifestation arises out of an attempt by consciousness to understand itself. I think he was referring to this phenomenon in the comments he made on 2nd December, 1974, in which he stated that Radha, the creative force that makes the universe, arises out of the substratum when the primal intelligence seeks to understand its own nature.

I asked Papaji to give an explanation of the comments he made on these two days, but he declined to expand on them in any way. Since I still think that some of these statements are obscure enough to require some sort of commentary, I will give an answer he gave to me in 1993 when I asked him to explain the difference between silent mind and no-mind.

Silent mind means to keep quiet temporarily. It is simply a suppression of the objects in the mind. It can happen many times, but it will not last. Still mind is also temporary. Meditation or concentration can result in still mind. It is like the flame of a candle. When there is no breeze, the flame will be still. When a wind comes, the candle will flicker and go out. Still mind will be blown away as soon as it encounters the wind of a new thought....

Before we speak about no-mind, we have to see what mind is. Let us start from consciousness. Sometimes you want to look in a mirror to see what you look like. In the same way, consciousness sometimes wants to look at itself to see what it is. A wave will arise in consciousness. It will ask itself, 'Who am I?' This wave that arises in consciousness imagines itself to be separate from the ocean. This wave becomes 'I', the individual self. Once it has become separate, this 'I' degenerates further and starts to create. First there will be space, the vast frontierless emptiness of infinite space. And along with space, time will be created, because wherever there is space, there must be time. This time becomes past, present and future and from these three, attachments arise. All creation arises within the past, the present and the future. This is called *samsara*. *Samsara* means time. *Samsara* is endless past, present and future. Anything which is born in time, which stays in time, will be finished in time. And all this is mind. The 'I' arose and created space, then time, then *samsara*. This 'I' has now become mind, and this mind is 'I'.

Then at some point an intense desire for freedom will arise. The desire will arise from consciousness itself. Originally there was a descent from consciousness – from the 'I' to space to time to *samsara*. Now there will be an ascent. As you ascend, attachment to physical objects will go, then vital, then mental, then intellectual. Finally you return to 'I' alone. This 'I' is still mind.

This 'I' has rejected everything. It exists alone with no attachments. It cannot go back to the world of attachments, to *samsara*. It has a desire for freedom; it wants to return to its original place. The 'I' which rose from consciousness is now returning to consciousness. It takes the decision, 'Become no-mind now', and with that decision the 'I' is gone. The 'I', which is the mind, has been rejected, but there is still something there which is between the 'I' and consciousness. This in-between thing is called no-mind. This in-between entity will merge into consciousness, and then it will become consciousness itself....

When you go from mind back to consciousness, you go through this stage of no-mind. In that state there will be the feeling, the recollection, 'Now I have no-mind'. Gradually, slowly, this no-mind will merge back into the beyond. But how it happens I do not know.

4th December, 1974

Papaji: I once had a vision of Radha and Krishna. What Goswami Tulsidas says about them is true: 'When I see them as one, they are two, and when I see them as two they are one.' The limbs and bodies were intertwined. One part initially looked like two bodies, but as I focussed on it, it turned out to be one. And something that started off looking like one person, on closer inspection turned out to be two.

Questioner: I have experienced Krishna's presence as a kind of blue ether or vibration, but I cannot properly express what I felt. I cannot describe it in the way that you describe your vision.

Papaji: You cannot describe Krishna because He is the describer. He is the one looking at you.

10th December, 1974

Papaji: When you first repeat the name of Ram, you say it with your mouth. It is a sound. Before it became a sound, it was a thought. The thought came from your mind, and the mind came from the Self. Trace it back: from the sound to the thought to the mind and finally to the Self. Go right back to where the original Name is sounding. Let no thought arise from that place. Just let the Name repeat Itself there. Here, in this place, is the true *darshan* of Ram. The Name is the substratum.
Study the mind so that you can separate yourself from it.

Question: How to surrender to the supreme power?

Papaji: By not allowing any thought to rise and by giving up all effort. Hanuman served Ram beautifully because he allowed the divine commands to work in him. The power of Ram enabled him to carry a mountain through the sky, but when the thought arose, 'I am doing this,' the arrow of Bharat shot him to the ground. As he was falling, he surrendered to Ram again by uttering His name. When he again remembered that Name, that state, his power to fly was restored to him. When he was asked how he managed to perform such superhuman feats, Hanuman replied, 'It is all through grace'.

Questioner: I was previously uttering the name of Lord Vishnu. It took some effort to keep it always on the tip of my tongue. But now my mind is peaceful. No thought dares to cross my mind. Now, I don't care about anything. In this peace no outside sound enters my place.

Papaji: The true Name is not said. It is eternally unuttered. Is God a thing that we should give Him a name? He is the one who gives the names to all things. If we give names, we bring objects into existence. You must break all the links in the memory.

Question: Does the process of asking oneself 'Who am I?' help to break the links?

Papaji: If you make a process of self-enquiry, you stay in the mind. You make it a series of linked thoughts. You look outside and remember that you should be looking inside. This is a movement of the mind. Next, you try to turn your mind inwards. You try to look at yourself, or you try to see where your 'I' is coming from. This searching and this looking are just thoughts and perceptions that are attached and linked to each other. The result of such activity will be more thoughts. Thoughts cannot result in no thought. If you have an experience as a result of this kind of enquiry, it can only be an experience of a thought, of a state of mind, not a state of no-mind. So long as you stay in the mind, experiences and thoughts are the same.

You said a few minutes ago that you had a clear, quiet mind. How do you know this? It is because you are comparing it to an active, noisy mind. You judge your mind to be empty, but that is just another thought in your mind. Your mind is still there. You think it is quiet, but it is busy comparing itself to other, less desirable states.

Questioner: I want to be a servant of the divine.

Papaji: To be a servant of the divine, you must have the idea, 'I am a servant of the divine'. That relationship is just an idea in your mind. You are not serving the divine; the divine is serving you. The divine just serves, without the idea that it is doing anything.

Look at Hanuman. First acquire his qualities, his behaviour, his constant love for Lord Ram alone. By doing this you may become Hanuman and have the *darshan* of Ram in the Heart. This is real seeing.

11th December, 1974

Question: I once saw Radha and Krishna, but seeing them I had the feeling, 'Radha is not a lady, nor is Krishna a male'. Is this so?

Papaji: Radha is not a female, nor is Krishna a male. Melted by devotion their forms have merged into a state that is neither one nor the other. It is like those representations of Siva and Shakti in which the two forms have merged into one body. The place of union is neutral. It has neither one sex nor the other.

Question: How to receive Krishna's grace?

Papaji: Several ways are prescribed. You can repeat His name. This is using your will to focus on Him. Secondly, you can attribute all your actions to the Lord. This is allowing the Lord's will to work through you. Thirdly, don't care about the consequences of your acts. The second and third ways need great vigilance. You must be alert to your actions; you must have no feeling that it is you who are performing them; and they must not be done with the expectation of any particular result.

Questioner: I have seen Krishna. I would also like to see Hanuman.

Papaji: Hanuman is very busy, performing service to his Lord. Don't disturb him by your desire to see him. Just make yourself so beautiful that he wants to come and see you himself.

Question: How could Ravana kidnap Sita so easily? How could he run off with God's wife and keep her away from Him for twelve years? Does this mean that God is not omnipotent?

Papaji: When Sita was by Ram's side she had the peace that comes from union with God. But when she left the safe place that He made for her and followed her desire for the golden deer, she lost her union and she lost her peace. Desires for gold and other worldly things take you away from God's side and get you caught up in the world of attachments. In her prison in Lanka she repented. Realising that she had strayed from Ram by disobeying his orders, she decided to get back to Him by repeating His name. Ram heard her call and came all the way to Lanka to rescue her.

God will not interfere if your desires for the world take you away from Him, but when you regret it and call on Him for help, He will rescue you and bring you home.

12th December, 1974

Question: Why does *Om* always introduce a mantra or a scripture?

Papaji: *Om* is the substratum. Without *Om* you cannot utter a mantra or any other word. *Om* is the *prana*, the life-breath itself. Can you speak while you are holding your breath? Try it and see!

Questioner: It's impossible.

Papaji: *Om* is your real nature. You only have to be aware of it.

Questioner: I am in a state of tension. I can't do it.

Papaji: You are in a state of tension because of your in-tention. Just keep quiet. Or observe what is happening in your mind. You are an ex-tension of your thoughts, and wherever there are extensions there are intentions and it is these intentions that are filling you with tension. In a dream the dreamer extends himself into a whole dream world, which he then lives in and enjoys. The same thing happens in the waking state. The world around you is an extension of your thoughts.

Wake up from your waking dream! Roar like a lion and wake up! *Om*!

Question: Where do you place Krishna in the scheme of evolution?

Papaji: In the basement.

Question: Why?

Papaji: He is the substratum. Without Him you cannot utter anything.

Question: What is the experience of Christ for you?

Papaji: In your mind.

Question: And where is my mind?

Papaji: In my extended mind.

Question: In meditation I feel I am a void. What is the difference between my void and the one of the Buddha?

Papaji: Buddha himself must come and ask me this question. If he does, I will give him a reply. As for your own case, this void is not a void since you are aware of it. So avoid it.

15th December, 1974

Papaji: The Lord is always in you, near you. But by repeating His name you push Him away so that you can call Him back to you. If you are standing next to a person, you don't need to chant his name to make him come to you. Repeatedly calling out God's name gives you the mistaken idea that He is far away from you. He is not. He is standing right next to you, softly calling out your own real Name. If you were not so busy calling out His name, you would hear Him.

Whenever you utter someone's name, you have your own Name as its substratum.

Krishna tells us: 'I am the beginning, the middle and the end.' By placing Him far away and by calling Him from that imaginary far-away place you are saying, in effect, 'You are not the beginning, You are not the middle, You are not the end'.

19th December, 1974

Question: How to stop this differentiation between inside and outside?

Papaji: In the *Gita* Krishna says, 'God abides in the heart of all beings'. Vasudeva [one of the names of Krishna] means all-pervasive, everywhere. The divine is everywhere, both inside and outside. Where is this 'someone' who knows or feels something else?

Arjuna once asked Krishna to reveal Himself. At that time Arjuna regarded Krishna as a separate entity, as just a very good friend. Krishna opened His mouth. As Arjuna looked into it he saw the sun, the moon, the whole universe inside it. With this sight Arjuna discovered that he was also a part of the eternal, unbroken whole that Krishna revealed to him. When that knowledge is there, the idea of inside and outside cannot arise.

Question: How does creation arise?

Papaji: Creation never happened. How can there be a creation or a beginning in eternity?

Question: I don't understand. How can you say that creation never happened? We both see it all around us.

Papaji: I must say I don't understand it either. I don't even try to understand it, but I do know that when I speak and say things like

285

this, they are facts. They are spontaneous utterances that reveal the truth. There is a special faculty that speaks these words, and as they are spoken, it knows that they are correct. I don't care if I am understood or not, but I do know that when I speak these words, they are the truth. Don't try to understand this statement. You will not solve this problem through understanding.

In the *Gita* [9.8] Krishna says:

But surely you cannot see Me with these ordinary eyes of yours. Therefore, I vouchsafe to you the divine eye. With this you should behold My divine power.

Arjuna saw separation through his ordinary eyes, so Krishna said to him, 'I will give you My own sight, My own eyes'. With that divine sight Arjuna saw past, present and future as a single instant in that unbroken eternity. With that divine sight comes the knowledge that creation never really happened. Understanding will not help you to see the truth of these words. Divine sight will.

25th December, 1974

Papaji: For me, nothing has ever existed. If you want to know why I keep saying this, you must find out for yourself what creation is: how it arises, how it appears to sustain itself. You must go to the source to find out what is truly real – what exists and what does not exist.

Question: I want to see Hanuman with my own eyes, but when I try, I always see something else. What should I do?

Papaji: This will always happen. But let me ask you a question: when you don't want anything at all, including a *darshan* of Hanuman, what will you see?

Questioner: I think I will lose my ability to perceive.

Papaji: Correct. And if you really lose it, what will remain?

Question: I. I alone.

Papaji: Can you lose your 'I'?

Questioner: Impossible.

Papaji: Everything is included in 'I'. Work on this. When you repeat the name, you create distance and separation between yourself and the object you have named. Once the wave knows that she is not apart from the ocean, she will not call out, 'Ocean! Ocean! Ocean! Please come and give me *darshan*!' First know that you are God Himself. When you have that knowledge, will you spend your days calling out 'God! God! God!'?

As I mentioned earlier, Papaji nowadays does not speak about japa *or the Name of God in his public satsangs in Lucknow, possibly because at least ninety per cent of the audience comprises foreigners who have no background in this tradition. However, he still occasionally speaks on these topics if he finds himself among Hindus who are seriously interested in the repetition of the divine name.*

In October, 1994, Sadhu Rengaraj, a South Indian professor, arrived at his house and asked to meet with him. He had written several booklets extolling the virtue of performing Ram japa *and was on a tour of North India, giving lectures on the glory of repeating Ram's name. After Papaji had glanced at one of the booklets that had been presented to him, he gave a moving talk on the repetition of Ram's name. A few days later I wrote down what I could remember and showed it to him. He read it and seemed to enjoy it.*

As he reached the end of the manuscript he remarked, 'There is one extra story that I forgot to tell him. I will write it on the bottom of the page.'

He picked up the pen, but nothing happened for about thirty seconds. Eventually he said, 'I can't write it now. Something is stopping me. I will write it later.'

The story never got written. In June, 1995, I decided that I would ask Papaji to read out the transcript of this talk in one of his Lucknow satsangs. I wanted to jog his memory about the extra story, and I wanted him to talk about the divine name in general. To give him extra material to talk about, I also appended several questions and quotations.

The indented text is the 1994 talk.

Papaji: This is a talk I gave in my house last year. David asked me to read it out because he has some questions about it.

> I was once travelling to Chitrakoot when I came across a temple that had a plaque outside which announced that under the floor of the temple, in its foundations, there were twelve *crore* [120 million] Ram mantras, all written out by one man. It wasn't just the name of Ram; it was a long mantra with Ram's name in it.
>
> I have done *japa* myself, so I know how many repetitions one can get through in a day. Also, how many mantras one can write in a day. I did some quick calculations and thought to myself, 'This is not possible. Nobody can write twelve *crores* of this mantra. A human life is simply not long enough.'
>
> I decided to go inside to satisfy my curiosity. I had formed a theory that it must be some kind of collective effort, some group that had done the writing between them and then attributed it to one of their members. Perhaps the head of the group that was responsible for building the temple.
>
> I went inside, found someone there, and asked him who had really written all the mantras. I told him, 'I don't believe that it's possible...'

I know this story very well. I don't need to read it out. I can tell it myself.

It was twenty-five *crores*, not twelve, and it was what we call *'likit nam japa',* which means 'written *japa'*. The mantra he had written out was *Om Sri Ram Jai Ram Jai Jai Ram.*

Some of this man's disciples were living on the ground floor of this temple. I did tell them that I didn't think it was possible to write this many mantras in a lifetime, but they reassured me that a single person had been responsible for all these writings.

'From the age of three,' they said, 'he has been obsessed with writing this mantra. When he was a child, if anyone came to his house, he would ask for a pen and paper so that he could write this mantra continuously. Now he is a very old man. All his life has been devoted to the writing of this mantra.'

I thought to myself, 'I must see this man who has spent his whole life writing out this mantra. He must be a very remarkable person.'

I asked if I could go up and see him but his attendant replied, 'Not today, he is very sick. He has acute diarrhoea and his doctors said he shouldn't have any visitors. The pain is very severe.'

It looked as if I had come on the wrong day.

'It doesn't matter,' I told him. 'I am on my way to a village that is about five kilometres from here. I saw the plaque outside and was curious, so I came inside to make some enquiries.'

I left them and began to walk away from the temple, but when I had only gone a short distance, one of the attendants came running after me.

'We have just received a message from Swamiji,' he said. 'He is willing to see you even though the doctor has forbidden him to have visitors.'

I went up to see him and found, as I had been told, that the swami was in much pain Here in India, if you have a severe stomach ache, you are supposed to say, *'O ma! O bapre bap!'* You call on your mother and father and ask them to help you with your pain. That's what I have read. I have seen some people do it in the movies, and I have read about people saying this, but I have never actually seen anyone do it In the West you probably have other names to call out when you are in distress. When I was in America a few years ago, I knew a man who would say the name of his girl-friend if he got a little sick. But if the symptoms got worse, he would start calling out the name of his doctor instead. So, different people call out different names when they get sick. Usually, though, people call out the name that is most dear to them, or the name that they think will do them the most good.

And what was this swami calling out? This *baba* who had written his Ram mantra twenty-five *crore* times was lying on his bed and repeating a sentence in Hindi which can be translated as, 'This demoness will be responsible for my death! This demoness will be responsible for my death!' The demoness was his diarrhoea.

I was amazed that a man who had spent his whole life repeating the name of Ram should abandon it in his hour of need. But this is often the case. If you have really become one with the name, it rises up spontaneously in you, even in the most adverse circumstances. When Mahatma Gandhi was shot, there was no prior warning, but he spontaneously uttered '*Hai Ram*' in the fraction of a second between the entry of the bullet and the moment when he died. This can only happen if the name is always with you.

I wanted to leave this temple and carry on with my journey but the people there insisted that I stay for lunch.

'Today is Ekadasi,' one of them said. 'We observe fasting up till 4 p.m. and then we eat.'

Ekadasi is the eleventh day of the lunar cycle. In India many orthodox Hindus fast on this day. Some people who don't want to observe the fast completely, break it with a light meal in the afternoon.

Not wanting to be a burden to them, I offered to go shopping to buy whatever was necessary for the lunch. I asked what they wanted to eat, thinking that it would be something small and light since it was officially a fast day.

'You can buy potatoes,' one of them said. 'There are about twenty of us here. You should buy about 2 kg for each of us.'

'Is this how you fast?' I asked. 'What do you eat on normal days?'

'Potatoes are not included on the list of prohibited foods for Ekadasi,' one of them said. 'That's why we can eat so many. It is only food such as *pooris* and *khichree* that are prohibited.'

I didn't mind buying all these vegetables because at that time potatoes were only about twenty-five *paise* a kilo. But just before I left one of them said, You can also buy 10 kg of sugar and 2 kg of almonds. We will need some sweets to eat with the meal.'

On Ekadasi some people restrict their diet by only eating food that does not contain cereals and certain vegetables. The idea is to eat less. One should not compensate by eating twice as much of other foods that are not banned.

I did the shopping and the temple devotees did all the cooking. I can eat big amounts of food if I want to, but these so-called fasting *sadhus* amazed me when it was time to eat. I had to leave some of my potatoes on my plate because 2 kg of potatoes, plus sweets, was too much for me, but these devotees all cleaned their plates, and many of them even asked for a second serving.

As I am telling you this story I am reminded of another story that took place when I worked in Goa. This may be the extra story that I was supposed to tell.

I had been invited by a Chief Engineer who had been working in Hubli. He had met me in Goa and wanted to take me around his part of the country because I had never seen it before. We travelled around for a while in his jeep and eventually ended up at an ancient temple. The *pujari* [priest] of this temple was famous because he too was supposed to have recited *crores* and *crores* of Ram *japa*.

The Chief Engineer told me, 'The priest is a very old man now, almost a hundred years old. He is supposed to have repeated twenty *crores* of Ram *japa* during his life. He doesn't look after the temple any more because he is too old. His son has the job now, but the old priest is still alive and lives nearby. If you want to see him, I will drive you to his house.'

I am always interested in meeting people like this, so I agreed to go and meet this man.

We found him sitting in a kind of wheelchair outside his house. He had severe arthritis and couldn't move about much any more. I asked the same question I had asked at the other temple.

'Did you really chant all these mantras? Twenty *crores* is a huge amount to get through.'

'Yes,' he said. 'I am now ninety-eight years old and I have

spent most of my life chanting and writing this mantra. The temple is not a big or busy one, so I had plenty of time to write and chant. All my life, for most of each day I have been chanting the name of God.'

'Have you seen the person whose name you are reciting?' I asked.

Many people recite the name of Ram in the hope of getting a vision of him. I wanted to know if this old man had been successful.

'No,' he said. 'He has never once appeared to me.'

'What about in your dreams?' I asked. 'If He hasn't appeared in a physical form to you, He must at least have come to you in your dreams.'

'No,' he said, 'I haven't even had a single dream of Him.'

I found this hard to believe. If you are obsessed with someone and spend your whole life thinking about Him and repeating His name, He should at least appear in your dreams since the dream world is a place where your desires manifest. If a young girl falls in love with a man and thinks only of him, then at night she dreams about him. This is normal and natural. But here was a man who claimed to have been obsessed with the name of God for all the waking hours of his whole life telling me that he had never once even had a dream of his God.

When I was young, I too was obsessed with the name of God. I spent most of my time repeating it. I would get up at 2 a.m. and chant continuously till 9.30 in the morning. At that hour I had to leave for the office. On the way to work I would sit in one of the Madras tramcars and carry on chanting. I had a small rosary in my pocket that I hid from people both at work and on the way to work. I would chant the name and use the rosary to keep count. I got lost in the name, but my *japa* definitely worked. I would dream about God, and God even appeared to me while I was in the waking state. I have told the story of how Ram and Sita appeared to me in Madras, and of how I went to Chitrakoot afterwards to show my gratitude to Hanuman for bringing them to me. These things will happen if you focus on the name constantly and have love and devotion towards the form it represents. But if there is no love, the repetition is just mechanical. If you don't love God and don't have a strong desire for Him to appear, He won't appear.

Ram *bhaktas* believe that they can attain salvation if they die with the name of Ram on their lips. These two men were probably going to die without the name of Ram on their lips, even though they had been repeating it for decades. They had been repeating the name with their fingers and with their minds. The Name had not been repeating itself in the Heart. If the Name repeats itself in the Heart, then it stays with the man until the moment of his physical death. Even once is enough. Once the Name has uttered itself there, you are free. You no longer need to cling to God because God is now clinging to you. When the name reaches the Heart and merges with it there, God starts to repeat the devotee's name, not the other way round.

Now, what's next on this manuscript?

There is a phrase called '*ulta nam*' that means 'reversed *nam*'. Most Ram *bhaktas* think that this refers to the practice of repeating the two syllables of Ram backwards, as 'Ma-ra', because Valmiki is said to have once followed this practice. But this is not what it refers to. When you do ordinary *japa*, the name is projected outwards from the mind or the lips. The *ulta nam,* or reversed Ram *japa*, takes place when the name goes back into the Heart and merges there. I have done it, but I haven't come across anyone else who has done it. [Speaking to Rengaraj] I challenge you to produce one person from anywhere in the world who can sit in front of me and do the real *ulta* Ram. I don't think you can find such a person anywhere.

The full verse is from the Tulsidas *Ramayana*. It says:

Ulta nam japat jag jaana,
Valmiki bhaye brahman smaana.

It means, 'When I repeated the name in the reverse form, I

understood the world. Valmiki became *Brahman* by repeating the name.'

This is a difficult verse to understand. Nobody knows what Valmiki is really talking about. One man came all the way from Harda to see me because he wanted an explanation of this one verse. It has nothing to do with saying 'Mara' instead of 'Rama'.

Valmiki was a robber, a *dacoit* [bandit] who lived in the forest. He got his money by looting and then killing all the travellers who passed near his house. One day he held up a *sadhu* who was passing through the forest.

The *sadhu* asked him, 'Why are you committing sins like this? You are murdering people and stealing their money. If you live your life like this, you will eventually go to hell. Is that what you want?'

Valmiki replied, 'What else can I do? I have a wife and two sons who are dependent on me for their support. I have no other means of earning a livelihood. This is my ancestral profession. My father was a thief, my grandfather was a thief, and so was his father.'

'You are committing sins just to feed these people. You share all your profits with your wife and family. Are they willing to share all the sins with you? Are they willing to accompany you when you go to hell?'

'Of course,' said Valmiki. 'Wherever I go, they will follow me.'

'But have you ever asked them if they want to go to hell with you? Why don't you go and check first? Maybe they will not be willing to go with you.'

'You are just trying to escape,' said Valmiki. 'You want me to go home so that you will have a chance to escape.'

'No, I'm serious,' said the *sadhu*. 'You can tie me to a tree while you go and come. I will not leave. I am interested to know what your wife's answer will be.'

Valmiki tied him to a tree, went home and asked his wife if she would be willing to accompany him to hell when he died.

'Of course not!' she exclaimed. 'These are your sins, not mine. Why should I suffer on account of them? You must take responsibility for your own actions.'

Valmiki went back to the *sadhu*, untied him and apologised.

'I am giving up my life as a *dacoit*,' he said. 'My wife is not willing to share the consequences of my sins with me, so I no longer have any desire to support her. Please help me.'

The *sadhu* told him that if he repeated the name of Ram he would be freed from the consequences of all his sins. He sat down on that spot and began to do *japa* of the name. Years and years passed but Valmiki remained in the same spot, absorbed in the name of Ram. Over time some ants built a huge anthill over his body until it was completely covered. Valmiki actually means 'anthill'; that's how he got his name. As a result of his intense *tapas* and his one-pointed absorption in the name of Ram, he became a great sage and acquired many powers. He foresaw the future and wrote the whole of the *Ramayana* before Ram had even been born. Things like this can happen if you have intense devotion to the name of God.

Maybe this was the extra story I wanted to tell you. I have forgotten which one it was.

It is rare to find a person in whom the name of God is going on effortlessly and spontaneously. Kabir did it, but not many others have done it. Kabir was a weaver, but the name of God was always on his lips. When his thread broke, he had to lick his finger, moisten the frayed ends, and then twist them together. When he licked his finger, he had to stop repeating the name of Ram. This worried him because he wanted the repetition to be continuous. Eventually Ram himself intervened and told him that he would attend to the broken threads himself so that Kabir would not have to break off his *japa* for even a single second.

This is a story I heard many years ago, but I can't remember where I heard it or read it. Ram appeared in front of him while he was doing his weaving and offered to do all the work himself. Ram sat behind the machine and did the weaving while Kabir sat next to him, chanting His name. What does this mean? It means that if your full attention is continuously on God, it is God and not you who does your work.

Mahatma Gandhi was another person in whom the name of God was repeating itself spontaneously and effortlessly. His lifelong Ram *japa* had so permeated him that when he was shot, without warning, by the assassin's bullet, he spontaneously chanted the name of Ram before falling down dead. The name arose in him at the moment of his death because it was continuously with him during his life. I know this to be true because I met him many times in Madras in 1947.

At this stage of his life Gandhiji had been abandoned by all the political leaders of the Congress Party. All the other leaders wanted to partition India in order to create a separate Muslim state of Pakistan. Gandhi had refused to go along with this.

He had said, 'They can cut my body and partition it if they want to, but they cannot partition India. India is one.'

The other politicians were pragmatists. They wanted Partition because it seemed to them to be the most sensible thing to do. One of these politicians was Rajagopalachari, who later became the last Governor-General of India. I occasionally used to visit him, because he lived quite close to me, and make North Indian food for him because he couldn't get it very easily in Madras.

He once told me, 'Gandhi is a spiritual man, not a politician. He is naive. He doesn't understand the practical realities of politics today. We must give the Muslims a separate state in order to get rid of them. If we let them all stay within India, they will eventually destroy us. It is better to let them go and have their own country.'

I asked Rajaji why he was so in favour of Partition and he answered, 'Hindus and Muslims cannot live together in harmony. There are communal riots going on now which will just get worse and worse if the Muslims are not given their own country. All the politicians except for Gandhi have accepted that this is the only practical solution for the country.'

When I pushed him a little harder on this subject, he voiced a fear that was common among the Hindus in those days: 'If we let them stay, this will eventually become a Muslim country. They ran this country for hundreds of years and they will not rest till they are running it again. It is better to give them a separate state now to avoid conflict later. Even the Viceroy agrees.'

What was his name? I've forgotten.

David: If it was the middle of 1947, it was probably Lord Mountbatten.

Papaji: Yes, everybody had the same opinion in those days. Everybody except Gandhi.

All the big politicians of the day, including Nehru, thought the same way. None of these people was going to see Gandhi any more because they knew that he was so vehemently opposed to Partition.

So, at the time I was visiting Gandhi, there was only a small group around him. Each evening he would conduct a communal chanting of the name of Ram. I went regularly and became an unofficial attendant. Because he was quite old and frail, I would help him to and from the platform, and if there were any announcements to be made, I would make them at the end of the meeting.

On one of these nightly meetings some new person went up to Gandhi to prostrate to him. As he was getting up to leave, he took one of Gandhi's *chappals* [sandals] and ran off with it. I wanted to run after him and catch him, but Gandhi stopped me by saying, 'No! No! Stay here. One is enough.'

At the end of the meeting I made an announcement, asking the person who had stolen the *chappal* to return it. I added, 'If the person doesn't bring it back, Gandhiji will probably walk around with only one *chappal*'. My appeal had no result, for the *chappal* never came back.

I used to talk to him privately as well, but during our conversations he would never look at me eye to eye. He would always be looking down, usually at the *takli* on which he was spinning thread.

Once he told me as he was spinning a thread, 'I got this idea that everyone should spin his own thread many years ago when I was travelling in the Punjab. I saw all the Punjabi women spinning in their spare time and I thought, "This is a good idea. Everyone in India could profitably use their spare time in this way." So I started to encourage people to spin in their spare time everywhere else in India.'

He was a great saint. I could see that just by looking at his body. I didn't need to look into his eyes. He had the most sattvic body I have ever seen. It was copper-coloured, and on a subtle level it was glowing with the light of *Brahman*.

He had a beautiful body. The only body that I have seen that was as beautiful as his was the Maharshi's. Both of their bodies used to shine.

I was once sitting with Gandhi when I heard the sound of 'Ram, Ram' coming from him. His lips were not moving, so I looked to see where the sound was coming from. As I focussed on the source of the sound, I realised that it was emanating from his body. The sound was coming out of the pores of his skin. He didn't need to repeat the name anymore. It was going on continuously inside him and flowing outwards through his skin.

There are several stages of *japa*, and this is a very advanced stage. First the *japa* is repeated with the voice. Then it goes on in the mind. Then, thirdly, it is synchronised with the breath. When this goes on effortlessly and becomes spontaneous and automatic, the name repeats itself all the time, even during sleeping and dreaming because the breath and the name have become one. Without conscious effort, the name is repeated with each incoming and outgoing breath.

Kabir once sang the following verse:

Japa mare ajapa mare
Anha: bhi mar jaye
Surat smani shabd main
Ta ko kaal na khai

This verse says that when *japa* done with effort ends, *ajapa* takes over. *Ajapa* is when the name repeats itself without the person having to say it. Then, the verse says, after *ajapa* the next stage is *anhat*, an awareness of the sound in the Heart. Afterwards the source of the sound merges in consciousness itself. That consciousness cannot be touched or affected by anything in time.

First the sound resolves itself into the silence of the Heart. Then, even the silence goes back to its source and rests there. Before the name of God is chanted, there is only silence. And when the name subsides into the Heart, there is silence again. Why should one extrovert the mind and make it chant the name of God when in the end, one has to make it go back into the silence again? So, I don't tell people to do *japa*, or any other kind of activity. I tell everybody to reject both chanting and non-chanting because these are ideas, concepts, activities of the mind.

When you have rejected everything that appears in consciousness, consciousness merges with its source and remains as That. You cannot get back to this source by any kind of effort. *Japa*, even continuous *ajapa*, will not take you to that place. You have to find a Master who has reached that place and established himself there. If you are pure and holy enough, in the presence of such a being, the source will reveal itself to you and pull you into itself. There is no other way.

We don't have time to chant all day; we have other things to do. So, when people come here and ask me for advice I tell them, 'Don't make any effort. Simply keep quiet. And while keeping quiet, see if any thought comes.'

I explain this every day. Follow thoughts backwards and see where they rise from. Go back to the source of thought. If you find it, you will have peace and happiness. That's all you need to know.

Now, there are some questions from David about *japa* and the name of God.

Question: When I first visited you I asked you why, as a lifelong Krishna *bhakta*, you were often saying *'Hare Ram'* not *'Hare Krishna'*. You said that this had happened spontaneously after you had met Hanuman at Chitrakoot. Has the name of Ram been repeating itself inside you ever since?

Papaji: I have told the story about my visit to Chitrakoot several times. I don't need to repeat it again.

The name of Ram displaced the name of Krishna after Ram Himself appeared to me in Madras. I don't chant the name of God any longer, but if a name spontaneously arises inside me, it is usually the name of Ram.

Question: Though 'Ram' for you is the name of God, you also speak highly of *Om*. For you it is the primordial sound out of which all creation manifests. This is what you said about it two years ago in satsang:

We start our satsang with the word *Om*. When we utter this word, where does it come from? How does it manifest?

It has its own inherent nature concealed within it. As clay has an inherent power, a *shakti*, to become a jar, so *Om* has a latent power to become creation itself. But when we utter the word *Om*, where does it come from? When I heard someone say *Om* at my school, the word sank so deeply into me, it paralysed me for a whole day. Now, when I say *Om*, I know, 'This is Truth, this is *Brahman* Itself'.

It has no meaning; it has no form; it is beyond. It has spread over the three universes, but it is beyond them all.

When I say *Om*, it immediately points to its source. *Om* is both the pointer and the place that is pointed out. Saying *Om* takes you back to your source where you are That Itself.

I found the following five quotes in one of your old notebooks. One is a verse from the *Mandukya Upanishad*, one is from Sankara's commentary on it, and the other three are comments by a modern pandit on the same text:

1. Names are nothing but different modifications of *Om*.
2. All this is *Om*. All that is past, present, future is *Om*. That which is beyond the triple conception of time is *Om*.
3. As the thing is known through its name, so the highest *Brahman* is verily *Om*.
4. When *Om* is uttered there arises the consciousness of *Brahman* in the mind. Therefore it is the nearest symbol to help the mind to the realisation of *Brahman*.
5. Knowledge of *Om* or *Brahman* is identical.

Would you like to comment or expand on any of these statements?

301

Papaji: What more can I say? All this is true. *Om* is everything. *Om* is *Brahman* and *Brahman* is *Om*. All this universe is *Om*. We are having regular readings from the *Yoga Vasishta* nowadays. The nature of *Om* is explained there as well.

If you want to know the real nature of *Om* though, you will not find it in books. Instead, repeat the word *Om* and feel the source from where the word rises. That place is silence, but in that silence *Om* is also repeating itself. This is a very subtle experience that few people have ever had. This is what Kabir was referring to in the verse that I read out a few minutes ago. The sound of *Om* goes back to its source, which is silence, and repeats itself there. If you are very quiet, very silent inside, you can hear and feel this subtle vibration. This vibration is *Om*. It is *Brahman* itself.

Question: The following four verses are from Namdev's *Philosophy of the Divine Name*. Ramana Maharshi often read them out when devotees questioned him about *japa* and the name of God in general.

The Name permeates densely the sky and the lowest regions and the entire universe. Who can tell to what depths in the nether regions and to what height in the heavens it extends? The ignorant undergo the eighty-four *lakh* species of births, not knowing the essence of things. Namdev says the Name is immortal. Forms are innumerable, but the Name is all that.

The Name itself is form; and form itself is Name. There is no distinction between Name and form. God became manifest and assumed Name and form. Hence the Name the *Vedas* have established. Beware, there is no mantra beyond the Name. Those who say otherwise are ignorant. Namdev says the Name is Keshava [God] Himself. This is known only to the loving devotees of the Lord.

The all-pervading nature of the Name can only be

understood when one recognises one's 'I'. When one's own name is not recognised, it is impossible to get the all-pervading Name. When one knows oneself, then one finds the Name everywhere. To see the Name as different from the Named creates illusion. Namdev says, 'Ask the saints'.

None can realise the Name by practice of knowledge, meditation or austerity. Surrender yourself first at the feet of the Guru and learn to know that 'I' myself is that Name. After finding the source of the 'I', merge your individuality in that oneness, which is self-existent and devoid of all duality. That which pervades beyond *dvaita* [duality] and *dvaitatita* [that which is beyond duality], that Name has come into the three worlds. The Name is *Para Brahman* itself, where there is no action arising out of duality.

This seems to encapsulate your own views on the Name and on *japa*. That is to say, in order to find and experience the source of the 'I', one needs to surrender to a Guru. Only then will the real Name be known.

Papaji: Namdev was a great saint who was always repeating the name of God. He lived in Maharashtra, but he was so famous, Kabir, who lived in Varanasi, got to hear about him.

Some devotee went to Kabir and said, 'I met this great saint called Namdev while I was in the South. He is such a great man, even the servant who works in his house is a saint. She is a woman called Janabai.'

Kabir felt a desire to go south and meet this saintly woman who was working in Namdev's house. So, he went there and asked Namdev if he would introduce him to his servant Janabai.

'She's not here right now,' said Namdev. 'She comes in the morning, sweeps my floor and washes my clothes, but she doesn't live here permanently. She only comes when there is some work to do.'

'Where will she be now?' asked Kabir. 'I came here especially to meet her.'

Namdev said, 'She has another job. In the evening she sells cow-dung cakes in the market. You can probably find her there.'

Here in India we use cow dung as a fuel. Women collect it from the streets, shape it into round flat cakes, and then put it out to dry in the sun. Usually, the women who do this use it themselves, but some do it professionally and sell the dung cakes that they make.

Kabir went to the town square and found that there were about twenty-five women there, all selling dung cakes. He asked which one was Janabai.

One of the women sellers pointed to a fight that was going on in another part of the square and said, 'That's Janabai over there. The one fighting with the other woman about the cow dung.'

He still didn't know which one it was, but at least he had narrowed it down to two women.

He approached the two women and asked, 'Which one of you is Janabai?'

One of the two replied, very angrily, 'She is Janabai, and she is a thief!'

Kabir was amazed. He had heard that Janabai was a great saint, but this woman was accusing her of being a thief.

'What are you accusing her of?' asked Kabir. 'What has she stolen from you?'

The woman replied, 'I went off to get a drink of water and while I was away Janabai stole ten of my dung cakes. She has put them in her basket. Look! There they are!'

Janabai retorted, 'No, it's the other way round. She has stolen my cakes. My cakes are in her basket.'

How to settle this dispute? All cow-dung cakes look the same, and each woman was accusing the other of being a thief.

Janabai came up with a solution. 'My cakes are different from hers,' she said. 'If you sit down and listen to them, you will hear what I am talking about.'

Kabir put his ear close to the cakes that Janabai had identified as hers and found that the cow dung was giving off the name of

Ram. Each cow-dung cake was subtly chanting the name of Ram. Then Kabir knew that she was telling the truth.

If your whole being is permeated with the name of Ram, then the things you make will also be filled with the vibration of Ram. You have another question on this subject.

Question: I have heard you say that even inanimate objects can resound with the name of Ram. One of your old devotees in South India wrote to me and told me that you helped to select a house for him and his family many years ago. After rejecting several houses as being unsuitable, you finally picked one for him because you said that the bricks of the house were chanting the name of Ram. How did they get like this, and how many other buildings or objects have you seen that were resonating with the name of God?

Papaji: There have been times when I have heard the name of Ram resounding from everything around me. Even the plants and the stones were singing the name. But not everyone can hear this. You must feel your identity with all the things that are around you. When that identity is there, everything repeats the Name. At that time one enters into the Heart of all the things that one sees. There the Name resounds and repeats itself.

Question: On 6th September, 1982, you wrote the following remarks in your diary:

Early this morning I woke up hearing the Ram mantra and found that someone in my heart was shouting *Om Sri Ram Jaya Ram Jaya Jaya Ram!*

Does this kind of experience happen to you often?

Papaji: The divine name is always repeating itself in the Heart. It permeates the whole universe, just as Namdev said in the verses I read out. When you abide in the Heart, you can always hear the Name repeating itself.

Ram Tirtha also wrote about this. For him the divine name

305

was *Om*. When he listened to the breeze blowing, he heard the sound of *Om*. Sitting next to a waterfall he heard the sound of *Om* as the water came crashing down. As the Ganga flowed by him, he heard her chanting the word *Om*. When you experience your identity with whatever is around you, you always hear the Name being chanted.

Papaji spent most of the final months of 1974 in Lucknow, although he did take short trips to Varanasi, Vrindavan, Mathura and Hardwar. On the way back from Mathura Papaji had a vision of Krishna. Meera recollects the incident:

It was about 4 a.m. and we were returning to Lucknow on the train. We had just been to Mathura, one of the many places associated with Krishna, so thoughts of Krishna may still have been in his mind. Master had been awake for some time. Suddenly he got that particular look that indicated he was having a deep visionary experience. Later that day, when he was back to normal, he told me that Krishna had appeared to him on the train and had communicated the essence of His teachings to him. This must have been a very strong experience because I have heard Master talk about it with awe and wonder on several subsequent occasions.

I asked Papaji for his own version of this vision, since it seemed to be an important one for him, and I received the following answer:

I was returning from Mathura to Lucknow on the Mathura-Lucknow Express. There were very few people on the train. I remember that I was sleeping on the lower berth. Near Kanpur railway station I saw Krishna and heard the *Gita* being recited to me. I have subsequently told this story to several people who are now saying that Krishna recited the *Gita* to me, but this is not what really happened. The verses were actually being chanted by some inner voice that both Krishna and I were listening to. Though the words are attributed to Krishna, as I heard them being recited I knew that these words were coming from the inner voice of the universe, and that Krishna was merely the agent through whom they were being chanted out loud.

I have never read the *Gita* in its original form because I don't know enough Sanskrit. But as I heard these words, chanted in Sanskrit, coming from this inner voice of the universe, I immediately knew and fully understood the meaning of each *shloka* [verse]. After the vision ended, I had a plan to write a commentary on the *Gita* that would incorporate the understanding I had been given during the recitation of the verses, but when I sat down to write, the words would not come. I found that I couldn't translate my understanding into words, so I dropped the project.

The words I heard chanted on the train somehow pointed to and expressed the source from which both Krishna and the *Gita* come. No commentary can ever catch hold of that source and express its essence through words.

In January, 1975, Papaji decided to visit his old devotees in Bombay and Londa. Meera accompanied him and continued to record some of Papaji's replies in her notebook. The dialogues that have 1974 dates took place in Lucknow prior to his departure.

9th December, 1974

Question: I have had experiences that I can only describe by saying that they are 'sweetness' itself. I didn't just feel the sweetness, I *was* the sweetness. After each experience the intellect arises and tries to understand what happened to me. Should I try to forget these experiences? If I want to go further, should I not stop my mind from being fixed anywhere, such as in an experience of the past?

Papaji: Though the experience of sweetness appears to be a state in which the mind is absent, that sweetness is actually a very subtle object in your mind. You become one with it to the extent that you cannot think about or experience anything else. You, the subject, have become one with the object of your thought so completely that nothing else can intrude. When you begin to remember it later, it means that the subject has let go of the experienced object. Whether you are experiencing it or thinking about it later, it all takes place within the mind. Remembering it is mind, and trying to let it go by not dwelling on it is also mind.

The true state is not any of these things. It is not knowledge or devotion or anything in between. It is something that you don't know, and can't ever know.

Question: How to attain it? I understand that I have not attained it.

Papaji: Pay attention to the unattainment. Keep this attention constantly and you will be attention itself.

Question: Why am I not able to catch it?

Papaji: You can make an effort to attain an object, but I am not talking about objects. I am speaking of the subject. You yourself. Effort takes you to objects, but when you give up effort, you remain as the subject. Give up all your efforts and that power will catch hold of you. Give up your body, your senses, your mind, your intellect. Who are you then?

Questioner: I am nothing.

Papaji: As you are becoming nothingness by giving up all these objects, let the power catch hold of that nothingness. Let it catch hold of you. In this way you become one with the power. You will never catch hold of it, but if you allow it, it will catch hold of you.

16th December, 1974

Papaji: Visions are nothing but thoughts.

Question: Are they subtle, astral?

Papaji: This is also a thought. The mind imagines and visualises fantastic images as a result of the outside influences it receives.

The face you see in a vision is a thought that results from a previous external perception. Where else can it come from?

Questioner: When I am tightly united with the divine, even uttering His name seems to be a disturbance.

Papaji: There was once a lover who was separated from his beloved. He found someone who was travelling in her direction to take a message to her. As they were walking along, the lover was telling the messenger how beautiful his beloved was, and how happy he would be when they eventually managed to meet again. The lover gave a long message of love that he wanted the messenger to deliver. The messenger set off but the lover followed him because he hadn't finished describing the greatness of his beloved. He eventually travelled the whole length of the journey with the messenger, and throughout the trip his sole topic of conversation was his beloved.

As they reached the destination the messenger saw the woman first.

'There she is.' he said. 'You can tell her yourself.'

The lover was struck dumb. His tongue was paralysed by the joy he felt. With that one direct sight, all words ended. When you finally glimpse the beloved, you don't need to talk about Her any longer. You just enjoy Her.

When you once experience That, you don't need to talk about it any more. In fact, you can't.

Question: We were talking about visions. What exactly are they?

Papaji: Visions can only exist in time. They come and go because they are in the mind. Whatever is mental comes and goes.

Question: Then what is mind? Is it a kind of seed material out of which everything we see grows?

Papaji: Mind and seed are not different. Take the seed from the mind and what remains?

Question: Does seeing visions require a special spiritual eye, some special kind of sight?

Papaji: The eye that looks at your eyes and through your eyes, and which also looks at and through my eyes is the real spiritual eye.

Radha was once taking water out of the Yamuna. She heard Krishna play a note on His flute and looked in His direction. As their eyes met, all thoughts stopped. She forgot everything except Him. The complete forgetfulness that arises when eyes meet in this way is the spiritual eye in operation.

Questioner: Something comes up in me....

Papaji: Whatever comes up at any time comes up on account of a lack of vigilance.

26th December, 1974

Question: I had a glimpse of Truth, but it was temporary. How can I stabilise in that moment of truth that I once lived?

Papaji: The idea of stabilisation is a disturbance within awareness. Why do you want to fix the awareness? Only because you have accepted that you are unaware. For the awareness itself, what difference does it make whether you are aware or unaware? Is awareness not everywhere, both in attention and in inattention?

Why should you want to remember or stabilise That when it is That Itself which is the power that enables you to remember or stabilise?

Intellect tries to catch That, to give it a name, to make it understandable, but it is beyond the intellect's reach. It is beyond all names and concepts.

Questioner: So I let awareness remain as it is. I just have to live It and not let the intellect touch It.

January 1975
In Bombay with Prabhuji and Sarafji

Papaji: A saint is that one who makes you desireless, who removes all the states of your mind.

Questioner: All this seems to be beyond reason.

Papaji: It is most reasonable, but that doesn't mean that you have to understand it. Look at the sun. It keeps you warm and gives you light whether you understand it or not.

Questioner: It is said that one can only realise through grace.

Papaji: The grace is always there. Let the dis-grace, the idea that you don't have grace, leave you.

Questioner: It is difficult to do.

Papaji: It is very easy. Things are difficult if you have to learn how to do them. To reach a distant goal you have to prepare for the journey and equip yourself with many things. To master a difficult subject you have to use your intellect over a long period of time. But this is something different. It is not travelling to the moon. It is just being what you are. You don't need lessons or understanding for this.

In February, 1975, Papaji was visited in Bombay by a man who asked me to refer to him merely as 'Mr D.', since, he says, he wishes to guard his privacy. Papaji describes the background to his visit:

Carlos Silva, the man who looked after me in Saanen when I attended the Krishnamurti talks, told some of his friends in America about me. One of the people he spoke to passed on the information to Misha Cotler, a South American maths professor. This man in turn mentioned my name to [Mr D.], who was then

311

working as a maths professor in Caracas. So, this information was third or fourth hand by the time it reached [Mr D.]. Though he had never heard of me before, [Mr D.] felt an immediate attraction. He called the airline office and asked for a ticket on the next plane to India. He consulted neither his wife nor his university about this decision. The pull to come was so strong, he just picked up the phone and told the woman on the other end of the line that he wanted to be on the next flight to India.

The woman at the airline office told him that the next flight was fully booked, but she agreed to put him on standby in case somebody cancelled at the last minute.

[Mr D.] then went to see the head of the university and told him that he had to go to India as soon as possible. He hadn't accumulated any leave, and there was no legitimate reason for him to take off so suddenly in the middle of an academic year. [Mr D.] himself knew this, so he offered to resign from his job.

'This is private business,' he said. 'There is a man in India I have to see. He is a spiritual Master I have recently heard about. Something is pulling me to him. I cannot delay this trip. I must go immediately. If you don't let me go, I will resign my job here. Nothing is going to stop me from taking this trip.'

The head of the university didn't want to lose him so he invented some official business for him to do in Bombay.

'If I give you time off for no reason,' he said, 'the other professors will complain, or they will start asking for trips themselves. I will tell them that you have to meet some people at Bombay University. Please don't stay away for too long because this story will only keep them happy for a few weeks.'

A few hours later the woman from the airline office called him up and told him that there had been a last-minute cancellation.

'Go immediately to the airport,' she said. 'If you leave immediately you can get on the plane. If you delay, you will miss it.'

[Mr D.] drove straight to the airport and caught the plane without even telling his wife that he was leaving the country. When the call for freedom comes, you have to follow it, leaving everything behind.

[Mr D.] had been given the address of the Prabhu family in

Bombay. He arrived the following day, with no baggage. His only possessions were the clothes he was wearing.

Papaji was not there on the day Mr D. arrived but the Prabhus and Meera looked after him until Papaji returned. Meera describes what happened:

Master had gone to Lucknow, saying that he would be back within a few days. While we were all waiting for him, this man arrived from Venezuela to meet him. He seemed to be very impatient, but at the same time he was also very shy. He told us about his background, saying that he had flown to India as soon as he heard about Master's existence. Master returned two days after his arrival.

For the first couple of days Master seemed to pay very little attention to [Mr D.]. He hardly seemed interested in him at all. [Mr D.] became very agitated. He had come all the way from Venezuela to see this man but Master didn't seem to care whether he was there or not.

After two days [Mr D.] came up to me and said, 'I can't bear this any more. I am desperate for a Master but this man completely ignores me. If he cannot give me what I want, where else in the world can I find it? I am going back to Venezuela.'

'Please stay one more day,' I told him. 'You have come so far. You should not run away so soon.'

Mr D. confronted Papaji the following day during lunch. This is the exchange, as recorded by Meera in her diary entry for 18th February:

Mr D.: I have not changed from when I was in Caracas. I am not benefited even by your unique and powerful answers.

Papaji: If you say you have not benefited, it is because you are comparing yourself with some state you experienced previously. This comparison is from the past. Dwelling on the past is destruction. If you don't compare, then what?

Mr D.: Yes...Now? [pause] Is it that?

Papaji: Yes, 'now'.

Mr D.: [collapses, laughing, and finally says] You asked me to be serious! [more laughter after which Mr D. begins to dance. Sitting down again he says] It's so simple! It's so simple! It's not knowledge, it's a fact. Enlightenment in one second!

Meera added a few more recollections:

It was such an out-of-character reaction. [Mr D.] had been so shy during the days he had stayed with us, but suddenly he exploded into ecstatic singing and dancing. He was behaving like a madman. In the end he went to the bathroom, locked the door and started laughing hysterically. Every time we knocked on the door he would either burst out laughing or shout, 'I got it! I got it!'

The next day, when he had sobered up, he bowed to Master and said, 'I got it. I got what I came for. I don't need anything else. Now I can go back to Venezuela.'

The following day he went back home. This meeting made a great impression on me. For the first time it struck me that a desire for freedom is enough. I saw someone become a free man without having any spiritual background or any practice. He just had an intense desire to see a Master and to be transformed by his presence. I have known this man for twenty years now and he says that the experience he had that day has never left him. It was a true awakening. The whole episode was a great teaching for me.

Mr D. went back to his job and his family in Venezuela. A few months later another devotee from Venezuela wrote to Papaji and offered him a return ticket to that country. Papaji accepted the offer and went to Venezuela the following year. The story of that particular trip will appear in the next chapter.

In March Papaji and Meera went to Londa to see the devotees who lived in that area. While they were there they were visited by some pandits who wanted to talk to Papaji about Jnaneshwar, one

of India's most famous saints.
Jnaneshwar became enlightened while he was still a small
child. He authored several books, the most famous of which is
Jnaneshwari, *a commentary on the* Bhagavad Gita. *At the age of*
sixteen he voluntarily had himself walled up in a cave. Though this
happened several hundred years ago, his devotees say that he is
still alive, in a state of deep samadhi. *Since the cave has never been*
opened, this claim has not been scientifically tested.
      Meera recorded some of the answers that Papaji gave to the
pandits:

23rd March, 1975

Pandit: What can you say about this *samadhi* state that
Jnaneshwar is supposed to be in? How is it attained?

Papaji: Jnaneshwar says that for liberation several steps are
required:

1. You first sit in *vajra asana* and meditate on the form of the
   Master who is *Om.*
2. You meditate on Siva by repeating *'Soham'* ['I am He'].
3. Concentrate on the tip of the nose when the supreme bliss is felt
   there.
4. If this is done, the great void, *mahasunya,* is experienced.

   When you merge or identify with that *mahasunya,* there is no
separation between you and it. There is complete unity.
   I would say that *vajra asana* and so on are all mental activities. There is no gradual, step-by-step enlightenment. Jnaneshwar
started in the void, the *mahasunya,* and finished in the same place.
All the rest is mind.
   You ask how to get to this state. First you reject manifestation.
And having rejected it, one finds the unmanifest in which one
discovers that all manifestation is Me. For Jnaneshwar, both
manifest and unmanifest have been lost. This is his *samadhi,* his
present state. It has no beginning and it is without end.

Pandit: [Reading out loud from Tukaram] 'I see God outside and inside....'

Papaji: When Tukaram looks out, he sees only Vitthal [the form of Krishna in Pandharpur]. When Vitthal looks at Tukaram, he sees God Himself. Both have forgotten who is who.

Pandit: What is the way of detachment?

Papaji: There is no way. First you have to see if you hate being attached. Who is attached, and what is the attachment? It is the person attached to his body, his mind. You make the body your possession. This is attachment.

The true sage will tell you, 'You have never been bound'. There is no way or path to this understanding. You simply have to give one moment to your own Self. If that one moment of no-thought comes to you, your bondage will be permanently eradicated.

24th March, 1975

Question: How to control the mind?

Papaji: First you must study yourself to see if there really is an entity called mind that needs to be controlled.

Questioner: I am affected by thought. I cannot deny that this is my experience.

Papaji: Who told you, 'I am affected'? I say, 'I am not affected'. That is my experience. You have been brainwashed into believing that your mind is troubling you. Society has imposed this belief on you. You believe it so strongly, it becomes your firm conviction. But I say, 'This is still just your idea'. It is an idea that you can drop once you cease to believe that it is true. Leave this idea alone. Then what?

Questioner: Even when I hear you say, 'I am not affected,' it doesn't change me. I look at myself to see if what you say is also valid for my own experience, and I have to say, 'It is not true. Mind is there and I suffer from it.' That is my irrefutable experience.

Papaji: It is not a fact. It is just a belief, a conviction. Don't allow superstitions like this to arise, and tell me what remains.

You treat your mind as an object that needs to be controlled in some way by you, the subject. Once you have this idea you create distance or separation between you and your mind. What you are doesn't need to be controlled. It always remains as it is whether you are aware of it or not. You cannot see your own Self because it is too close to you. You can only see things that are in front of you. What about this thing that is so near, it is behind your own retina. There is no distance between you and That.

Question: But how to know it?

Papaji: Knowledge is of things that are some distance away from you. When there is no distance involved, there can be no knowledge. By not knowing, by not thinking, by not understanding, you find out something that is no distance away from you.

Papaji and Meera stayed in Karnataka for almost three months. At the beginning of June Papaji accepted an invitation to go to Mysore to visit Mr Neginhal, the Forest Officer who had given him ten acres of land while he was living at Ram Mandir in the 1960s. At the time of the invitation Mr Neginhal was the Chief Conservator of Wildlife for the state of Karnataka. During the visit Mr Neginhal arranged a safari in one of the nature reserves he controlled. Meera describes what happened:

We went to a wildlife park that was somewhere near the border between Karnataka and Kerala. I remember that it was a very remote, wild place. Mr Neginhal accompanied us and arranged elephants for us to ride on. We all had a six-hour elephant ride through the forest. There were many animals to see but the sight that amused Master the most was a group of monkeys stealing eggs out of the nests of some of the birds. The monkeys made their escape by swimming across a river. While they were crossing the river the monkeys held the eggs up in the air to stop them getting wet. Everyone loved the trip, although I think Mukti later caught a case of malaria from being bitten there.

During our stay in Mysore we were visited by a man who said he was the chief pandit of the Maharaja of Mysore. Somehow the Maharaja had found out that Master was a great spiritual being, and that he was in his area. He assumed that this meant Master was a great scholar. The Maharaja passed on this message to his pandit who immediately came to see us because he was having trouble understanding some obscure Sanskrit verses. Master hardly knows any Sanskrit at all, so he couldn't even read the book that the pandit brought for him. Master didn't admit his ignorance because he knew the pandit was depending on him to give good answers. Master told him to read the verses out loud, which the pandit did. At the end of the recitation Master opened his mouth and the most beautiful commentary came out. He gave a whole lecture on the verses without understanding a single word of the original text. The pandit was delighted with the explanation.

This was not the first time I had seen something like this happen. I had seen it in the monasteries in Europe, and I had seen it in Rishikesh when Swami Abhishiktananda came to visit us. People would show him obscure or ambiguous passages from various religious works, and Master would spontaneously give beautiful commentaries on them. After spending a lot of time with him, I realised that he had some innate ability to explain or illumine spiritual texts in a way that would satisfy or even inspire devotees who treated these words as holy scriptures. He never read or studied these books, but when he was asked about them, the Self that produced his words would come up with the most marvellous answers. People who didn't know better would think that he had spent years studying these books.

Though Master could explain texts very well, there were still a few technical, philosophical terms that always seemed to intrigue him. Whenever he encountered learned pandits, such as the one we

Papaji in Mysore, 1975. The photo was taken by
Mr Neginhal.

met in Mysore, he would always ask them for the exact meaning
or import of certain words. There was one word, *sphurana*, that he
seemed to be perpetually fascinated by. It apparently means the
vibration, radiation or pulsation of the Self, but Master was never
content with simple definitions such as these. If scholars were
around in the early 1970s, he would invariably bring up the word
sphurana and begin a discussion of its meaning. I don't think he
was ever satisfied by anyone's explanation.

*The following satsangs were recorded by Meera in Mysore
and Belgaum. The questioner in the first two dialogues is probably
Mr Neginhal himself.*

21st June, 1975

Questioner: People always want realisation to come to them without making any effort. What a joke!

Papaji: In my experience, people want worldly things to come to them without making any effort, but when it comes to realisation, they always want to make a big effort. This is how they get into trouble.

Question: I don't understand. Why are you saying that realisation comes effortlessly? You are always saying things such as, 'Let us work this out together'. Work of any kind needs effort.

Papaji: Yes. I say, 'Work it out for yourself that you don't need to make any effort'. This working out simply means having the right understanding, and right understanding comes from effortlessness.

Question: How can no effort produce results?

Papaji: If you want to go from Hubli to Mysore, you take the train. To make this journey you have to begin at your starting place, Hubli, and then make an effort to journey towards your desired destination. Hubli is not Mysore, so to move from Hubli to Mysore, you have to make some effort. Effort is involved when you have to reach some place that is located at any distance from where you are right now.

I am talking about recognising your own Self. How far do you have to travel to do this? How far away from you is your own Self? You just have to see where you are in this moment and stay there. What effort is required for this? This knowledge, this understanding, is the truth you are seeking.

Is this truth that you are searching for absent at any time? If it is, then you might have to look for it, to see where you might have lost it. But if it has never been absent, what effort do you need to find it? Has this truth ever been away from you, apart from you? No. You are making efforts to attain the truth because you believe that it is something that you don't already have. All you have to do is drop this idea because the truth is there all the time, waiting for you to recognise and acknowledge its presence.

You cannot see the truth because you are making an effort to see it. Your effort is making you look in the wrong direction, because effort is always directed towards external objects. Our real nature is effortlessness. It is only recognised when all effort stops.

Question: But how to stabilise in this state?

Papaji: The idea of stabilisation is just a desire to become something different from what you are right now. If you have the idea that you are not aware of the truth and that you have to make some effort to discover it, you are automatically believing that truth is not present all the time. Whatever is not here all the time is not the truth.

Effort may be needed to attain mental or worldly objects, but for what I am talking about, you only need understanding. Understand what I am aiming at. I am aiming at what you really are.

Questioner: I am having difficulty expressing what I want to say.

Papaji: When you cannot express it, it means that you are That Itself. You can only express something that is other than you. That which you are gives power to all your expressions, but That Itself cannot be expressed.

The *Katha Upanishad* says that the Self reveals Itself to him whom the Self chooses. It is not revealed by the intellect. If the Self chooses you, then Self alone remains. The grace of the Self reveals Itself to Itself.

When you have denuded yourself of all concepts, what happens? The revelation of the Self. You have ideas such as 'my knowledge', 'my experience'. Can't you throw them away for just one second?

Question: You also told me to fight. How to reconcile effortlessness with fighting?

Papaji: They are not opposed to each other. Consciously abiding

321

as the Self is effortlessness. But if the idea 'I am not the Self' arises in you, fight it. Kill that thought as soon as it arises. The moment you kill it, you will remain as you are: the Self.

Reject all concepts. What you are is neither inside you nor outside you. So now tell me what you are.

Questioner: That.

Papaji: 'That' is just an idea you have picked up from outside. Who are you? Where is the 'you' that picked up this concept of That? Where are you now?

Questioner: I am the Self.

Papaji: Who are you saying this to?

Questioner: To the Self.

Papaji: Are there two selves? One to speak and one to hear?

Questioner: Then it cannot be said.

Papaji: Ah, that is better.

22nd June, 1975

Question: How to start *sadhana*?

Papaji: You only need to start if you have a destination that you have to reach. What is this destination that you want to reach?

Questioner: My Self.

Papaji: Then your destination is also your starting point. You are trying to objectify the Self, to make it into an object that you can reach or attain. You cannot own your own Self as a possession, as an object. It can be the possessor, but it can never be possessed.

Your destination is timelessness. When you make effort within time, you keep yourself away from the timeless.

Question: How to preserve awareness of the Self?

Papaji: By not allowing any concept to enter into you. All acquired knowledge comes from outside. You then identify yourself with the acquisition and make trouble for yourself. Return all these acquisitions back to the source from which they came. That includes this person who thinks he possesses them all. What will remain cannot be rejected.

To remain as you are, you need not do anything.

Question: If one studies thoughts, will one ultimately be aware of them?

Papaji: To be aware of them is to hold on to them as objects. If you are simply aware, if you are awareness itself, thoughts will not come.

Questioner: Right now I am holding on to one thought.

Papaji: You say 'one thought' because you have the concept of two or more thoughts to compare it to. Are you not in between the thoughts, in the place where there is no thought at all?

If I am merely myself, and know that I am merely myself, where is the question of a destination or a starting point? I am just myself.

Questioner: It sounds so simple.

Papaji: It is so simple because it is so near to you, so close. If you live in the world of becomings – 'I have become this, I have become that' – you invite death to visit you. Abide as being, without becoming anything, and nothing will ever be able to touch you.

Question: How to retain this in daily work?

Papaji: By giving up the concept, 'I have to retain something'. When you create an intention in your mind, you introduce tension into your mind. This tension produces extensions of thought that make the world you live and suffer in.

Question: Is this the theory of karma yoga, that one should perform acts without having the intention of accomplishing particular goals?

Papaji: Does karma pertain to the body or to the Self? Are you the body or are you the Self? If you say you are the Self, what business do you have in worrying about things that pertain to the body?

Question: All scriptures, all saints say that one must go back to the Self within. The problem is, how to do it?

Papaji: I don't say this. Where are you now? Are you not the Self right now? Why should you set off on some inner journey to reach it? Just be the Self.

Questioner: So the only thing to do is repeat *'Aham Brahmasmi'* [I am *Brahman*] until one convinces oneself that it is true.

Papaji: If you repeat it, you make it an object. I say, 'Understand it and experience it'. Once is enough. Know it and be it.

1st July, 1975
Belgaum

Question: You say, 'Grace is always here,' but at the same time you tell us, 'You must demolish the buildings you have constructed from your concepts by yourself'. Can we really accomplish this by ourselves? Does the destruction of these concepts not require grace?

Papaji: People have been beating this same path for thousands of years. They all think grace is something good that will overcome the badness of the mind. That's not what I am saying.

Grace is always here, always present, but people limit it, saying that it is the power that makes things better. A bud on a rose blossoms into a flower. You can say that this is grace, but why should you stop there? When it wilts the next day, is it not the same grace that is causing it to die? Why do you reject the power that makes the flower die and only accept as grace the power that makes it bloom? You are looking at results all the time, but only if the result is good do you attribute it to grace.

The dog on the street is full of grace; the thief steals by grace, and the saint realises by grace. When I speak about grace I am not speaking about manifested results, I am talking about the cause of causes, the power that makes a seed a seed, the power that makes it bloom into a flower, and the power that makes it wilt the following day. Everything is sustained by grace.

Someone once asked the Maharshi for grace to realise the Self.

He answered, 'You already have the grace. Grace brought you here to see me, and grace motivated you to ask this question, "Please give me grace". How can you say that you still need grace?'

You already have the grace, as much as you need. The grace that makes you ask for grace is the same power that makes the flowers bloom and wilt.

Meera and Mukti left India on 21st July, flying from Bombay to Paris. By then Papaji had already received and accepted an invitation to travel to Venezuela. He wanted to leave soon after Meera's departure, but the bureaucrats in Delhi had other ideas. A state of emergency, recently declared by the Indian government, had made civil servants wary, officious and suspicious of all supplicants coming to their offices. Papaji spent several weeks in Delhi, running from office to office, trying to get the necessary clearances from both his own government and the Venezuelan embassy. While he was there he had his first meeting with Raman, an Australian man who had visited several other ashrams and teachers in India. Raman gives the background to the meeting:

For several years prior to his death in the early 1970s, I had been a disciple of Sri Swami Ram of Ram Kunj, Sapt Sarovar. That place is about three miles north of Hardwar. I found out later that Poonjaji spent a lot of time in a nearby ashram, but at the time I had never heard of him. On one of my visits to Chandra Swami, who lived in a nearby ashram, I met Yvan Amar, a Frenchman who told me about Master's [Papaji's] existence. He gave me a little photo of him, no bigger than my thumbnail, and told me not to show it to anyone else because in those days Master preferred to be incognito. He didn't like people to know who he was or where he was.

I felt an immediate interest in him but at the time I had no idea where to find him. In those days no one who knew him was allowed to tell outsiders where he was or where he was going next. After Swami Ram died, I didn't want to stay in his ashram any longer, but I did feel a strong desire within me to meet this Master whom Yvan had told me about.

For more than a year I searched for him all over India. Knowing that he had been a disciple of Ramana Maharshi, I started at Ramanasramam, but no one there had even heard of him. That was a big surprise for me. I stayed in Tiruvannamalai for some time and while I was there I went to Tirukoilur to meet Swami Gnanananda, an old yogi who was supposed to be more than 150 years old. I found out later that Master had visited him many years before and that he had enjoyed his company. Gnanananda initially wanted me to stay with him, but after a couple of weeks there I realised he wasn't what I had been looking for.

While I was there a devotee of Gnanananda's asked me to show him my palm. He had a reputation for being a great astrologer and palmist.

After looking at my palm for some time, he said, 'You have a great Master, a great Guru'.

'Yes,' I answered, 'his name is Swami Ram. He passed away a few months ago.'

'No,' said the palmist, 'he is not your Guru, and neither is Swami Gnanananda. You haven't met this Master yet. He is much greater than Gnanananda. You don't need to stay here with him.'

This was an unusually candid reading from a man who seemed to regard Gnanananda as his own Master.

I went back to Tiruvannamalai and began to make plans to continue my search. I knew a man called Madhu Saraf who had a big house in Belgaum, Karnataka. I knew that he had met Master, and I knew that Master had even visited him in his house in Belgaum. I thought that I might be able to pick up the trail there. I had met Madhu Saraf through Swami Ram. At one time we had both been his devotees.

I wrote to Mr Saraf to tell him that I was interested in meeting Master. I also asked for his impressions of Master since he was one of the few people I knew who had met him. In his reply Madhu Saraf told me that I would not be disappointed when I met Poonjaji because he had all the qualities I was looking for in a Master. However, he didn't know where he was, nor did he know when he would come to Karnataka again.

Having no alternative, I went to Londa and Belgaum to see if any of the people there had information on Master's whereabouts. Nobody knew, or if they did, none of them was willing to tell me.

Having temporarily come to a dead end, I decided to go to Bombay to spend some time with Nisargadatta Maharaj instead. Maurice Frydman, the man who edited *I Am That,* was an old friend of mine. We had both lived together in Almora at a time when Maurice had been a big follower of Krishnamurti. I stayed with Maurice in Bombay and each day we went to see Nisargadatta Maharaj together. Though I visited Maharaj every day, I was also asking all the devotees I met there if they had ever heard of Master. Eventually I found Carlos Silva, a visitor who had come from South America. Carlos had actually accompanied Master on his return from Europe and had gone with him to Hardwar a few days later. Unfortunately, though, Carlos had lost track of him. Both of us wanted to see him, but neither of us knew where he could be found.

I can't remember how it happened, but eventually I was

introduced to B. D. Desai, one of Master's Bombay devotees. I explained to him that I had been unsuccessfully looking for Master all over India. Desai gave me the address of a Dr Gupta in Delhi, but as he was giving it to me, he begged me not to reveal the source of the information.

'If Master asks you how you got this information, don't tell him that you got it from me. He gets very angry if people give away his address without first getting his permission. You have been searching all over India for him. You can make up some good story about some stranger giving it to you.'

As soon as I received the information I packed my bags and left for Delhi. I knew that Maharaj was great teacher, but at the same time I also knew that he wasn't the man I needed to see. I had had a dream of Master just before Desai gave me the information. This dream *darshan* made me even more determined to find his physical form as soon as possible.

All the trains from Bombay to Delhi were booked up for days to come, so I went by bus. Every day I would find a bus that was heading in the general direction of Delhi. I would sleep in hotels at night and resume my journey the following day. It took me several days and many, many buses to get there.

In Delhi I stayed in the house of Mr G. V. Gode, who was then the manager of the American Express Bank in Delhi. I knew him because he too was a fellow disciple of Swami Ram. Incidentally, this was not the famous Swami Ram who went to America to have his yogic powers tested. He was a lesser-known swami of the same name.

I unpacked my bags in Mr Gode's house, cleaned myself up and then went to the address that Desai had given me. Dr Gupta opened the door when I knocked.

'I have been told that Mr Poonja is staying here,' I began. 'May I come in and see him?'

Dr Gupta looked at me in a very suspicious way.

'How do you know he is here? Who told you? And why do you want to see him?'

He listened to the story I had made up for him and then disappeared back into the house. A few minutes later I was invited in.

Master had seen me through the window and had recognised me as being one of his neighbours from Hardwar.

After I had been ushered into his presence, he informed me that he knew who I was.

'I used to be one of your neighbours in Hardwar,' he explained. 'I saw you working in Swami Ram's garden. I also noticed you buying milk at the shop outside the ashram where I used to stay myself. I saw you while I was drinking tea in the same place. I knew then that you would one day come to see me.'

'But why didn't you tell me then who you were?' I asked, more than a little aggrieved. 'I have just spent over a year, running all over India looking for you. When I started out on my journey, you might have been sitting just a few yards away.'

'I never interfere if someone is with another teacher,' he answered. 'As long as you were with Swami Ram, I kept quiet. When he died, you came looking for me.'

Then he changed the subject. 'How long have you been meditating?'

'Twelve years,' I answered.

He seemed to be impressed. 'In that case,' he said, 'you deserve some kind of reward. Let's go!'

He took me to the house of Phool Singh, another devotee of his who had a house in Delhi. This house was one of the many illegal constructions that were springing up all over the Delhi suburbs. In those days no one cared much about planning permission. It was an unbelievably noisy house. I couldn't understand why Master would choose to stay in a place like this.

Phool Singh had added an extra room to his house, saying that it would be reserved for Master's exclusive use. On the day we arrived it was full of deerskins because Phool Singh had a business exporting them. Master immediately objected.

'I am not a hunter,' he complained. 'I don't want all these dead animals here. Take them away!'

In addition to being a devotee of Master's, Phool Singh also had some connection with Baba Haridas, a yogi who used to keep silence and write on a slate. Haridas went to America and picked up quite a big following there.

Phool Singh was a prosperous businessman. Apart from his deerskin business, he used to recycle plastic, converting old bags and bottles into sandals. I was presented with a pair, but they were so hard, they cut my feet to pieces. Phool Singh recycled his recycling profits by buying copies of the *Ramayana* and sending them to Baba Haridas in America. He would go to Hardwar on a pilgrimage, buy up every single copy of the *Ramayana* he could find, and then ship them all to America at his own expense. I think the deerskins were also being shipped to America so that Haridas' American devotees could sit on them while they meditated.

When Master invited me to stay in this room with him, I immediately accepted. I didn't care how noisy it was. It was a rare chance to spend time in his company. During one of these early meetings I showed him a copy of *I Am That* I had picked up in Bombay while I had been staying with Nisargadatta Maharaj. He took it from me, but he didn't even look at it. I never saw the book again because he told me that I shouldn't read while I was with him. He had nothing against this particular book; he just didn't want me to read anything while he was working on me. I finally got to read the book about fifteen years later, after I had been told that Master had recommended it to some of his devotees.

After a few days in Delhi he decided to take me to Hardwar. We bought our tickets, travelled to Hardwar, and then checked into the Arya Nivas. That was the place Master liked the most in those days. He used to give it as his Hardwar address, and all his mail went there. For the next few days we were alone together. I was asking a lot of spiritual questions and getting very good answers, but at the same time it felt like a relaxed and casual visit to the town.

My former Guru, Swami Ram, had been a tantric yogi. His own Master had been a *siddha* who had lived in the famous Amarnath Cave in Kashmir. I had been practising *kundalini* yoga with Swami Ram and had had many good experiences. I really thought that I was becoming an accomplished yogi, but in retrospect I can see that I was just stuffed full of concepts and ideas. During our time in Hardwar Master was trying to wash these concepts out of my head, but he wasn't very successful because I

Raman and Papaji, sitting in Papaji's Narhi
home sometime in the 1980s.

was still very attached to them.

While we were in Hardwar I got the feeling that Master was working quite hard on me, but at the same time I was also aware that I was missing the point of what he was trying to show me. Instead of experiencing the truth of what he was saying, I ended up debating ideas and concepts with him. Master wanted to show me the Self, but his words didn't get any further than my head. One time, while I was asking him questions about *kundalini*, he just looked at me and put me into a kind of trance in which I could no longer think, speak or even move. I was aware, in a distant sort of way, of what was going on around me, but I couldn't think or formulate any more questions.

When he saw what he had done, Master laughed and said, 'Where's your *kundalini* now? Tell me all about it.'

I couldn't respond in any way. I was totally paralysed, both physically and mentally.

Though Master conceded that the rising of the *kundalini* could produce blissful states and experiences in which the normal functioning of the mind appeared to be absent, the state he was continually pointing at was, he said, something beyond and prior to all experiences. I had had many experiences in which I appeared to go into a kind of *samadhi* in which I was not aware of anything at all, but they were never permanent. Sometime later I would 'wake up' from them and return to normal.

One day I went into one of these *samadhis*, but instead of returning to my ordinary state, I emerged into a conscious, thoughtless state which I knew was beyond the mind.

Master saw it happen, but before I could make any comment on it, he began to speak about one of his own recent experiences.

'This morning I caught a glimpse in the tiniest fraction of a second of something else that is beyond even the undercurrent of the waking, dream and sleep states. Beneath this substratum there is something indescribable, beyond words, beyond description, beyond non-description even.'

As I got to know Master better, I found that these tantalising glimpses of something that was beyond the *turiya* substratum were the starting point of his continuing investigations into himself and into the nature of ultimate reality.

'It's not just a question of seeing that the snake is just a rope,' he told me once. 'The rope is the substratum that makes the appearance of the snake possible. Everyone says, "Stay with the substratum and don't get fooled by the appearances in it". I say, "Throw away the rope as well". There is real purity when the substratum has also gone.'

On this first trip to Hardwar there was one key incident that I particularly remember. Master tried to show me who I really am, but he failed. I missed the chance, and I knew that I had missed it. Afterwards I apologised for my stupidity.

'I'm sorry, Master. I missed it, and I know I missed it. I don't seem able to experience what you are trying to show me.'

He seemed disappointed.

'Maybe one in a million gets it, maybe none. I've done my best. Tomorrow I'm leaving. I'm going to Delhi.'

Before he left he made me write the following two cryptic lines in my notebook:

INATTENTION BELONGS TO NO ONE
That Which Is Beyond Subject and Object

I felt like a schoolboy who had been told to write out an exercise as a punishment for failing to understand a lesson properly.

Master tried to leave me in Hardwar but I followed him to Delhi. I knew that he was going to stay with his daughter, and I also knew her address. I wasn't going to let him escape.

When I walked into Sivani's house and found him there, I immediately prostrated and apologised for being so stupid. While I was still on the floor, his mood suddenly improved.

'That,' he remarked, meaning, I think, our time together in Hardwar, 'was bad, but this is much better.'

From that moment on he allowed me to spend all day with him. In the mornings and evenings we would sit outside on a stone bench that was located in a tiny garden behind Sivani's house. Lajpat Nagar, the area where Sivani lived, was a big commercial market. This tiny garden seemed to be the only quiet, uncrowded place in the neighbourhood. While we were sitting there I would have the most amazing experiences. I had had many wonderful *kundalini* experiences with Swami Ram, but they were nothing compared to the states that Master was putting me in. Some days I felt as if I was in an elevator that kept going up and up and up. There was no top floor. I just kept on going higher and higher, with no apparent end in sight. He was also working on me during the night, while we were sleeping in separate rooms. I would meet him in my dreams and he would continue to show me all these different realms and states. When we met again the following morning, he would know exactly where he had got to in our nighttime encounter. He would mention what we had been doing together during the night and just carry on from where we left off. I once asked him how he managed to do this.

'I don't know,' was his reply. 'I can enter other minds at will, but I have no idea how I do it. I have not so far come across any good explanation of how this happens.'

During office hours Master had a lot of business in various parts of the city because he was still trying to get permission to go to Venezuela. His passport had expired and he was trying to get it renewed. I went with him on these trips. Master called them 'bus *sadhana*'. Every day we would spend several hours crisscrossing Delhi in hideously overcrowded public buses. Once, while we were waiting in line for a bus, a complete stranger came up to us and started to prostrate at Master's feet. Master tried to stop him but the man would not be put off.

When we asked him who he was and why he was prostrating, he replied, 'My own Guru pointed you out to me in a vision. He said you would be standing here at this bus stop at this particular time. He said that you were a great being, so I have come to pay my respects to you.'

I travelled a lot with Master in the succeeding years. Weird things like this happened wherever we went.

The offices we needed to visit were located in different parts of the city. There didn't seem to be direct buses between any of them. Each time we went to a new place, we had to change buses at least once. Inside the offices there would be the usual chaotic scene. Everyone would be trying to push his or her way to the front of a queue. Fights and quarrels would break out every few minutes, and the officials were the sort one would expect to find in such places: lazy, indifferent to visitors' needs, and generally corrupt.

Master could fight and quarrel as well as anyone else in the queue. No one ever succeeded in depriving us of our rightful place in the endless lines that we waited in. Once, when there was a lull in the fighting, I entered a state of utter peace. A new understanding dawned on me.

I turned to Master and said, 'You are in this state all the time, aren't you? Even when you are fighting and quarrelling, you are still in this state.'

He smiled and said, 'Of course, it's the only state there is'.

I was still full of ideas about *kundalini* and yoga. I also had a serious interest in Zen. As we travelled from office to office by bus, we would have conversations about whatever topic I was interested in on that particular day. We both made ourselves hoarse because we had to speak very loudly to make ourselves heard above the competing noises of the bus engine and our fellow passengers. Master slowly wore me down. After endless days of shouted dialogues on the Delhi buses, he finally made me realise that the *kundalini* experiences and the visions I had had were not going to result in enlightenment. I began to pay more attention to his own teachings and to the teachings of his Master, Sri Ramana Maharshi.

I had been introduced to Ramana Maharshi during a long stay in Almora. For about a year I regularly visited Sunya Baba, a Danish devotee of the Maharshi who lived there. As soon as I saw the photo of Sri Ramana that was displayed in his room, I felt attracted to it. I didn't even know who it was the first time I saw it, but the attraction was still there.

My former teacher, Swami Ram, had also recognised that I had a connection with Ramana Maharshi. During the years I had stayed in his ashram, the devotees there had tried to give me all kinds of Indian names. Swami Ram did not accept any of them. He would always say that they were not appropriate. Then, one day, he announced to everyone that he would give me a new name the next day. We had an elaborate name-giving ceremony the following day at the end of which he announced to everyone that in future everyone should call me 'Raman'.

When one of the devotees asked him why he had picked this name, he replied, 'Because I can see that he has a strong connection with Ramana Maharshi'.

I had been a well-respected devotee of Swami Ram. Many of the devotees there expected me to stay on after Swami Ram's death to teach yoga. Swami Ram, though, knew I was destined for other things.

'I am not your Master,' he told me. 'You have a strong connection with the Maharshi. After I die you will find your true Guru.'

I mentioned this to Master during one of our early talks. Afterwards, in the conversations we had, I detected in his voice

335

and his attitude a new respect for Swami Ram.

The 'bus *sadhana*' period lasted about six weeks. During that period I stayed with Mr Gode, the manager of the American Express Bank in Delhi.

One day Mr Gode asked, 'Where do you go every day? You disappear in the morning and reappear at night, but you never tell us what you are doing.'

I hadn't told him that I was visiting Master, partly because Master didn't like people to know where he was, and partly because I knew that Mr Gode was a devotee of Swami Ram. He was extending his hospitality to me because I was a longtime devotee of his own teacher. I didn't want him to think that I was just using his house as a convenient hotel while I visited other teachers. However, when he asked me directly what I was doing, I felt obliged to tell him.

'I have met this great saint,' I said. 'I am going for his *darshan* every day.' Since we both knew Madhu Saraf from our days in Hardwar, I also mentioned that he too had formed a very high opinion of him.

Mr Gode wasn't at all disappointed that I was visiting other teachers. 'You must bring him here for a visit,' he said. 'Why should you keep him all to yourself? Please tell him that I personally invite him to my house.'

I don't think Mr Gode had any idea what he was letting himself in for when he issued the invitation. I think he was expecting a traditional-looking swami who would talk about the scriptures, but that was not what he got.

Master accepted the invitation and we went there together in a car that Mr Gode had provided for us. It was late afternoon and tea was served to us when we arrived. Mr and Mrs Gode were present, along with Mrs Gode's brother and Mr Gode's brother-in-law.

After Mr and Mrs Gode had chatted with Master for a few minutes, the brother-in-law took up the conversation.

'I am an atheist and a socialist,' he said. 'I don't believe in religion at all. It's all superstitious nonsense.'

Master was quite polite with him. 'So what do you believe in?

I don't mean your political beliefs. I am asking "Who or what do you think you are? With what do you identify? Are you this body that I see in front of me, or are you something else?"'

The brother-in-law conceded that he was not the body.

'Then are you the mind or the intellect?' asked Master. 'Or are you something beyond them that merely uses them as tools?'

The brother-in-law thought about this for a while before deciding that his essential nature existed independently of his mind and his intellect. Master then began a remorseless series of questions that were clearly aimed at pushing this man into an experience of that which is prior to the intellect.

I really thought that he was going to get it, but at one point the brother-in-law stopped and said, 'What you say may be true but...'.

That was as far as he got. When Master is bearing down on a devotee like this, he doesn't like to hear the word 'but' being mentioned. It indicates doubt and it indicates that the mind is trying to negate the experience that Master is trying to give.

Anyway, when the word 'but' came out of the man's mouth, Master slammed his fist down on the table in front of him and roared, 'You will never have another chance like this in a thousand lifetimes! This is your one chance and you are throwing it away!'

There was a shocked silence in the room. All the Godes looked at each other, wondering what to do next. They had invited this man, thinking that he was some sort of pious pandit, but he had repaid their hospitality by screaming abuse at one of them, apparently for no reason at all. We all finished our tea in silence and a few minutes after that we were back in their car, being driven home.

Master had not said a word since the explosion in the house, but when we were about halfway home he turned to me and asked, very sweetly, 'Do you think they enjoyed their tea?' Then he burst out laughing and carried on giggling and chuckling till the car pulled up at Sivani's house.

When I went back to the Godes to see how they were taking it, I found that they didn't want to talk about the visit. Master's name was never mentioned again, and he received no more invitations to their home.

I continued to stay there. They didn't seem to hold me responsible for Master's outburst. A few days later I had an interesting experience while I was sitting quietly in Mr Gode's garden. It was a beautiful, lush oasis in the city, full of roses, trees and squirrels. As I sat there, feeling quiet and empty, I suddenly realised that I could communicate with the birds and trees around me. As I looked at them, I could understand their thoughts and feelings, and I found I could even transmit my own thoughts to them with the knowledge that I was being understood. It was a wonderful discovery that made me feel and experience my oneness with all the nature around me.

When I next saw Master, I told him about the experience and concluded by saying, 'Now I know what the mystics know'.

Master wasn't at all impressed by my experience. His only response was, 'That was the mist of the mystics. They were all misty-eyed. They couldn't see what was really happening.'

As he forcefully delivered this comment, the bubble of my experiences exploded, leaving me with nothing to hold on to or own as 'mine'. Master had an uncanny knack of negating the validity of all experiences, and all identification with them.

'In the Self,' he would say, 'there is no experiencer and nothing experienced. If there is still an experiencer, whatever he experiences cannot be reality. Reality is only revealed when all experiences have disappeared.'

A few days later Master took me back to Hardwar with him. He was still determined to show me who I really was. We had a quiet time together, just walking, bathing, sitting and talking. He told me many stories and gave me many teachings, but I never had the experience he was continually pointing at. I felt quite stupid at times because I never seemed to get the point of what he was saying. My mind would understand his words, but I could never go back to that place where he said the mind came from. Sometimes I would have little glimpses, but they wouldn't stick.

One day, for example, we were sitting in his favourite *chai* [tea] shop on the banks of the Ganga. He was reading his morning newspaper while I was sitting next to him, mulling over some of the words that he had spoken to me. Suddenly, without any effort on my part, the thoughts stopped and were replaced by a great clarity and peace.

Before I had a chance to say anything, Master looked at me over the top of his newspaper and said, 'That's it. Now keep it.' And then he went back to reading his paper again. As with all my other experiences, this one just came and went.

There must have been some special bond, some special connection between Master and me that made him put so much energy into me. Most of the people he met in those days were given one or two chances. The scene I described at the Gode's house was not unusual. If new visitors came to see Master, he would work on them for a couple of days, and if by then nothing had happened, he would send them away and never see them again. It was my great luck or my destiny to have Master pound away at my stubborn mind week after week, month after month. Some people never got to see him at all. On this second visit to Hardwar, a group of French people came all the way from France to see him. They checked into the Tourist Bungalow in Hardwar and then sent a message, saying that they wanted to have satsang with him. Master secretly observed them while they were walking up and down outside the Tourist Bungalow, but he must not have liked what he saw.

'Go and tell them that I have left for Delhi,' he told me. 'I don't want to see them.'

These people had come all the way from France to meet Master, but they never even got past his front door. Incidents like these made me realise how lucky I was to be spending all my days in Master's company.

It was not surprising that people were willing to travel halfway round the world to spend time in Master's presence. There was an intense, transforming energy in his satsangs. Everyone who spent time in his company felt his peace or had some sort of extraordinary experience. I once asked Master why this happened.

'I've felt this special energy around several great saints. It's what I feel when I am with you. What is it? Why do people feel so peaceful and happy when they are in your presence? How do you do it?'

'When the Ganga is in spate,' he replied, 'there is so much

water, it pours out over her banks. This is how it is with the divine energy of the saints. It overflows onto the people who are around them. But don't depend on them for this energy. Dive into your own Ganga!'

This last remark was delivered with such force, it felt like a physical kick. It stopped my mind and put me back into silence again.

A few days later we went back to Delhi and ended up staying at Phool Singh's house.

I had spent several months with Master, but I knew my time with him was running out. He had accepted an invitation to go to Venezuela and I knew I couldn't accompany him. I had a return ticket to Australia that would soon run out, and I didn't have enough money to travel anywhere else. I was getting desperate for the experience that Master said I was continually missing, because I knew that I might never get another chance again. I had known him long enough to realise that at any moment he might send me away, and that afterwards I might never see him again.

One day, after we had eaten lunch at Dr Gupta's, I started pestering Master with questions. It was the time he normally went to sleep, but I was so desperate I was prepared to risk his wrath by keeping him awake as long as possible. He tolerated it for a while, but after a few minutes he exploded in anger. I have no idea what he said because in the first moment he got angry, everything inside me stopped. There were no thoughts, no feelings, no sensations, and no world, but at the same time I was still fully aware. It must have looked as if I had blacked out because I was told afterwards that I wasn't responding to anyone's questions, but I never lost consciousness. In fact, consciousness was all that remained.

Raman has no memory of what happened next, so I asked Papaji to tell me what occurred after Raman's apparent collapse. This was his reply:

He closed his eyes and sat quietly without moving. When it became clear that he was not going to ask any more questions, Dr Gupta went up to him and said that he could rest in one of the

Har-ki-Pairi, Hardwar.

nearby rooms until 5 p.m., at which time there would be a regular satsang. Raman gave no sign of hearing what he had said. I gave him a close look and discovered that he had entered into *nirvikalpa samadhi*. I mentioned this to the doctor and told him that he should not be disturbed until he came back to his former state.

'Well, we can at least put him in a nearby room,' suggested Dr Gupta. 'If we leave him here, other people who don't know what has happened may pass this way and try to wake him up.'

After I had agreed to this proposal, the doctor went to Raman to pick him up. He soon discovered, though, that Raman had completely stopped breathing. This is something that occasionally happens in *nirvikalpa samadhi*. It is not a problem because the body can maintain itself without breathing while it is in this state, but Dr Gupta was not aware of this.

'I can't have a foreign man dying in my house,' he said. 'The police are very officious nowadays. If he dies in my house, we will all get into trouble. We may even be arrested. Let us put him in a taxi and send him back to Mr Gode's house. If he dies there, it will be his own landlord's problem, not mine.'

I tried to reassure him. 'He's not sick and he's not dying. He has just had a very profound spiritual experience. After some time he will come out of it by himself.'

I went over to Raman and started to massage his heart and neck. Within a few minutes his body's suspended functions started again. It took quite some time to get him back to normal. With the help of the people in the house I made him walk up and down the room so that he would not go back into this *samadhi* state. I also got hold of a bottle of drinking water, and every few minutes I forced him to swallow some. Within a couple of hours he was back to normal. When he could talk coherently, he approached me with a look of wonder in his eyes.

'I have never experienced anything like that before,' he said. 'What happened?'

I explained to him that his mind had suddenly become very quiet after it had received a satisfactory answer to one of the questions it was asking. Raman had had a strong desire for answers to his questions, and these questions had kept his mind busy. After the desires were fulfilled, for a short space of time his mind stopped because it had nothing new to occupy itself with. *Samadhi* ensued.

Even though Raman made a full recovery, and even though Papaji had explained to his hosts that Raman's experience had been a deep, spiritual one, not a medical emergency, Papaji's hosts were still unwilling to keep Raman in their house. Raman continues:

In the early days of the Emergency, there was a lot of paranoia in India about foreigners. The government was constantly putting out propaganda that the country was full of foreign spies. Dr Gupta argued that if the government found a dead foreigner in his house, he might be accused of harbouring a spy. To placate Dr Gupta and his family, Master put me in a taxi and told me to go to Hardwar for a couple of days and then come back. I don't remember anything about going there, staying or coming back, but I do remember sitting at Master's feet a few days later.

He looked at me and said, 'That's what the Buddha saw'.

That's my last memory of this period in India with Master. A few days later I went to Calcutta and flew back to Australia.

Years later Master told me what it was like for him to see a major awakening like this.

'When this moment comes, when reality reveals itself, the aura completely changes. I love to see this change, and I love to see the light that streams out of the aura when it happens. When I speak to a person who has just had this experience, I am talking to their subtle body, to the light that is streaming out of them. I am not talking to the person at all.'

Before his departure Raman invited Papaji to visit him in Australia. Papaji accepted and promised to come after his visit to South America.

Although I have no exact dates, Raman's stay with Papaji probably took place between September and December, 1975. At the end of December Papaji embarked on a major foreign tour that kept him in Europe and South America for almost a year. He was, therefore, not able to visit Raman in Australia until the beginning of 1977.

While Papaji was travelling, he maintained contact with Raman by post. This is Papaji's reply to the first letter Raman wrote:

Caracas
8th January, 1976

...Your letter dated 20th December arrived here this morning. I have been waiting for it ever since you left because I wanted to see how you had maintained your own natural state. I wanted to read how you express the inexpressible fact that has been surrounding you, beyond all time. I am happy to read your letter because it does not show any kind of achievement or attainment or enlightenment whatsoever.

Enlightenment means some kind of happening, and everything that happens can only be within the scope of time. A happening cannot be realisation because realisation is beyond time. So, nothing happened.

You sat before me in a great, deep SILENCE: eyes wide open, with an unbeating heart, like a picture painted on its own substratum. What beauty, tranquillity and love I saw embraced in that single mass of statue that sat before my eyes! My LOVE, by itself, embraced your inner SELF...

The next letter from Papaji to Raman was written in France several months later:

3rd August, 1976

...You write in your letter dated 20th July, 'Make sure that I don't get a foothold anywhere'.
There is NO foot. There is NO ground.
What will alight where?

You ask me where I am staying this year. You will not believe me when I say that I do not stay anywhere.

Do you remember the Delhi buses, hitchhiking every day from office to office and Nagar to Nagar [suburb to suburb]? I could not give rest to my darling. I still don't allow him to rest, even though he is beyond the other, other banks of the ocean, where the unrest cannot cross....

The events of Papaji's 1975-76 foreign tour will be described in the next chapter. Before that, though, I will put the clock forward a little and allow Raman to narrate some of the stories that took place on his many subsequent visits to India. Before he begins, I should explain that I showed him some of the chapters of this book prior to its publication because I thought that he might be able to add extra details to some of the stories. His first comments refer to an answer Papaji gives in the chapter, 'Guru and Disciple'.

I read an answer in David's manuscript that really struck me. Master said that a Guru can transmit an enormous amount of power and grace, enough to kill the body, but not the latent tendencies of the mind. I think this is what happened in my case. The experience

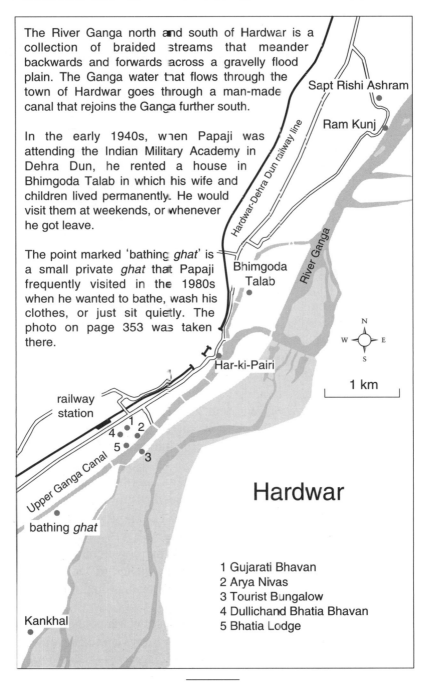

The River Ganga north and south of Hardwar is a collection of braided streams that meander backwards and forwards across a gravelly flood plain. The Ganga water that flows through the town of Hardwar goes through a man-made canal that rejoins the Ganga further south.

In the early 1940s, when Papaji was attending the Indian Military Academy in Dehra Dun, he rented a house in Bhimgoda Talab in which his wife and children lived permanently. He would visit them at weekends, or whenever he got leave.

The point marked 'bathing *ghat*' is a small private *ghat* that Papaji frequently visited in the 1980s when he wanted to bathe, wash his clothes, or just sit quietly. The photo on page 353 was taken there.

Sapt Rishi Ashram

Ram Kunj

Hardwar-Dehra Dun railway line

River Ganga

Bhimgoda Talab

N
W E
S

1 km

Har-ki-Pairi

railway station

4
1
2
5
3

Upper Ganga Canal

Hardwar

bathing *ghat*

Kankhal

1 Gujarati Bhavan
2 Arya Nivas
3 Tourist Bungalow
4 Dullichand Bhatia Bhavan
5 Bhatia Lodge

Master gave me in Delhi almost killed me. Dr Gupta told me afterwards that he thought I was dead because both my heart and breathing had stopped. Even Master told me, years later, that he thought I might have died.

'You must have had very strong nerves to survive an experience like that,' he said.

My mind disappeared for a while but eventually the 'latent tendencies' that Master talked about reasserted themselves. I knew that my work was not done.

Master had once quoted a proverb of his mother: 'You can't put tiger's milk into pigskins.' I knew that I hadn't been ready enough or pure enough for the final liberating experience.

While I was in Australia I had met a woman called Jasmine and had introduced her to Master. She had a profound experience in Master's presence that left her in tears for days. We became close friends and eventually got married.

When Jasmine's experience also wore off, we both knew we had to return to India to be with Master again. A few months after his 1977 Australian visit ended, we travelled to India and managed to stay with him for almost twelve months. In the succeeding years, the late 1970s and early 1980s, we came to see him almost every year. We would write in advance, ask for permission to come, and then wait for his reply. We both knew that we had to get his approval. Without it, trying to track him down would be a hopeless task. Even when we had an official invitation, it was still sometimes hard to get to see him. On one of our visits we waited at the appointed meeting place for months before he finally showed up.

In those days Master always seemed to be in transit. Sometimes he would tell us to come to Lucknow, sometimes to Londa, and sometimes to Hardwar. Hardwar was definitely his favourite place, but he didn't like crowds of people coming to see him there. If people in Londa or Bombay wanted to see him, he would usually go to their own homes, rather than invite them to Hardwar.

In the years we stayed with him in Hardwar, he either stayed at Sapt Rishi Ashram or Bhatia Bhavan. Whenever we arrived for a visit, he would book us into rooms in a nearby ashram. Master had a lovely little *kutir* [hut] in Sapt Rishi Ashram where he lived by himself for long periods. In the mornings he would sweep out his hut, wash his clothes and then just sit by the Ganga for hours at a stretch.

During our stays in Hardwar we would eat with Master and go for long walks with him almost every day. Around seven or eight in the morning, if he wanted company for the day, he would come to have a cup of tea with us. Afterwards, he would either go to one of the ashram libraries to read the morning paper, or we would go for a long walk with him up the river. In those days there was still a lot of dense forest by the Ganga. Sometimes we would leave the river bank and walk through the trees. At other times Master would find a nice spot and just sit by the Ganga for hours at a time. Master had a deep interest in nature. He would point out the various birds and describe their behaviour to us.

One time he said, 'The ancient *rishis* laid down rules that Hindus should go on long, frequent pilgrimages. Most people in this country don't like to wander aimlessly in natural surroundings. They prefer to stay indoors. The ancient *rishis* made these rules because it was the only way to make most people go for long walks in the open air.'

Since I was still very interested in Buddhism, I would take some of the short, classic texts with me on these walks. If Master seemed to be in a talkative mood, I would show him passages from the *Heart Sutra*, the *Sutra of Hui Neng* or Huang Po's dialogues, and ask him to comment on them. He would read them out loud very appreciatively, and then give his own comments.

He liked the classic Mahayana texts and the teachings of the old Zen Masters, but he wasn't so enthusiastic about some of the Tibetan Buddhist teachings that I discussed with him. I asked him once about the *bodhisattva* tradition that maintains that Masters postpone their final liberation so that they can incarnate again and again to help successive generations of disciples.

His only comment was, 'If they really knew, they wouldn't come back. When you once have the direct experience that there is no entity that can be reborn, you cannot come back. It's not possible. If you are reborn, you are not a Master, and if you are not a Master, you can't give any real help to people who desire freedom.'

On many occasions he told me, 'Teaching is the last trap of the ego. If a teacher is not realised, his teachings just spread confusion.'

I tried to look for a copy of the *Diamond Sutra* in the ashram libraries in Hardwar, but no one had a copy. When I mentioned my failure to Master, he laughed and replied, 'No one will have an ashram if he has a *sutra* like this. He will be out on the road like the Buddha, with a begging bowl in his hand.'

One day, while we were sitting together, he read out a biography of the Buddha that I had given him. There was one part in which the Buddha was attempting to describe *nirvana* to one of his monks.

'It is neither coming nor going, neither stopping nor starting.'

The sentence had a great impact on me. The words stayed with me for hours afterwards. Each time I recollected them, I felt myself falling or diving into a state of silence. I told Master about this experience the following day while we were out walking. He seemed to think that I had missed the point of the sentence.

'*Nirvana* is neither coming nor going, neither stopping nor starting,' he repeated. Then he added, 'Nor is it diving or falling'.

His words had such a terrific effect on me, I think I almost lost consciousness. I have a vague memory of being helped back to my room in Ram Kunj by Master and Jasmine, but I don't remember much else about that afternoon or evening. Master went back to Sapt Rishi Ashram but he returned at around 9 p.m. to see how I was.

He studied me for a few seconds, turned to Jasmine and remarked, 'I just thought I would come and check to see if he had gone mad. Experiences such as these can often drive people insane.'

The following letter is an interesting record of some of the philosophical points that Raman and Papaji were discussing. Papaji had gone to Lucknow for a few days, leaving Raman in Hardwar. The book that Papaji quotes extensively from in his letter is a published doctoral thesis. It was written by a South Indian professor of philosophy whom Papaji had met both in Madras and Tiruvannamalai. Gaudapada, the philosopher-sage whose ideas are being discussed, was one of the earliest expounders of advaita. He upheld the radical ajata position that nothing has ever been created. Papaji too maintains that this is the highest teaching and the highest truth, but he prefers to express it by saying, 'Nothing has ever happened. Nothing has ever existed.'

Lucknow
25th March, 1982

Dear Raman,

I have just received your letter, dated 22nd March. I have recently found a book: *Gaudapada, a Study in Early Advaita*, by T. M. P. Mahadevan. It is very interesting to have a comparative study between *advaita* and Buddhism, and in particular between Gaudapada and the Buddha. I have culled some extracts from the book which I am sending to you because we often speak on this subject. We have had several discussions on how they differ. Do you remember when I asked you at Bhumananda Ashram, Sapt Sarovar, 'What is the difference between *Brahman* and *Sunya*?'

These are some of the points that are mentioned in chapter nine. [These are mostly taken verbatim from the book, but Papaji occasionally skips sentences or paraphrases.]

There has been a persistent charge levelled against *advaita* that it is pseudo-Buddhism and its leaders have been characterised by their critics as propagandists for Buddha views under the guise of [Hindu] orthodoxy. Even the great Sankara has been accused of preaching the Buddha doctrine under the false name of '*mayavada*' [the path of *maya*].'

One of the main grounds on which Sankara is branded as a veiled Buddha is that his philosophical progenitor, Gaudapada, was *en rapport* with Buddhism. Louis De La Vallée Poussin writes, 'One cannot read the Gaudapada *Karika* [his commentary on the *Mandukya Upanishad*] without being struck by the Buddhist character of the leading ideas and of the wording itself'. ...Hermann Jacobi holds that Gaudapada has used the very same arguments as the Buddhists to prove the unreality of the external objects of our perceptions, and that there is a near relation, amounting almost to identity, between the epistemology of the Sunyavadins [on the one hand] and Gaudapada's *mayavada* on the other. Surendranath Gupta believes that there is sufficient evidence in the *Karika* for thinking that Gaudapada was possibly himself a Buddhist and considered that the teachings of the *Upanishads* tallied with those of the Buddha. He writes, 'Gaudapada assimilated all the Buddhist Sunyavada and Vijnanavada teachings, and thought that these held good of the ultimate truth preached by the *Upanishads*.'

By far the most searching and detailed examination of the question of Gaudapada's indebtedness to Buddhism has been made by Prof. V. Bhattacharya in the introduction to the *Karika*, ... fourth *prakarana* [section]. It is his view that Gaudapada has accepted and approved of the Buddha doctrines and advocated them throughout the *Karika*. The first evidence that is adduced by him to prove that Gaudapada has borrowed from the Buddha writers [is that Gaudapada] has quoted almost fully, partially or substantially from works of some celebrated Buddhist teachers who flourished between 200 A.D. and 400 A.D. Nagarjuna, Aryadeva, Maitreyanatha or Asanga and possibly Yasomitra would seem not only to have supplied Gaudapada with philosophic thoughts to adopt, but also with model verses to follow in the composition of the *Karika*. The idealistic schools of Buddhism, Vijnanavada and Madhyamika must have appealed to him as sponsoring views very much like his own...

The main thing that Gaudapada teaches in the *Karika* is the unreality of the world and its absolute non-origination (*ajata*). The former is advocated by Vijnanavadins and the latter is proved by Madhyamikas. Gaudapada has fully utilised these lines of thought and has expressed his complete agreement with their views.

The doctrine that there is no external reality is common [says Bhattacharya] to both Gaudapada and Vijnanavadins. The world, according to both, is a figment of the imagination (*kalpita*). There is no difference between the world of waking and the world of dreams. Both are *samvrita*, enclosed within the body. Just as things imagined in the dream are seen inside the body, the objects of the waking world also are inside the body for they are equally the product of imagination. Their appearance outside of us is but an illusion.

The external world is *citta-spandita*, a vibration of the mind. The doctrine of non-origination (*ajata*) which Gaudapada advocates is essentially a Madhyamika view.

Nagarjuna's *Madhyamakakarika* begins with the words, '*anirodham anutpadam*' (there is neither suppression nor origination). This doctrine is accepted by Gaudapada and he commends it to his followers.

The state of mind which is called *nirvana* by the Buddhists is known as *Brahman* in *Vedanta*. This is the *summum bonum* of both the Buddhists and the Vedantins.

Gaudapada pays homage to Buddha in his works. He also agrees with the Madhyamika conclusion that *ajata* is the highest truth. All this is possible because the difference between *Vedanta* and Buddhism is very slight. Buddhism itself owes much to the *Upanishads*. Such is the view of Professor Bhattacharya.

I will bring the book along with me when I come to Hardwar.

Raman continues his account by describing their daily routine when Jasmine and he were in Hardwar with Papaji:

Our walks would normally last a couple of hours. Usually, we would come back to Hardwar in time to cook lunch for ourselves. Wherever we were, Master always picked the menu. He taught us how to cook simple Punjabi dishes, but often we would just have boiled vegetables or a boiled cereal. Sometimes the meals were so simple, we didn't even add salt or seasonings. When the food was ready, we would take it down to the banks of the Ganga and have a picnic on the shore. About once a week Master would take us to the Gujarati Bhavan, a restaurant in Hardwar, and buy us a full meal. At other times he would buy snacks from the street carts that lined the streets. *Pakoras* and carrot *halwa* seemed to be his favourites.

When I first met Master in Hardwar and saw how he was

living, I just assumed that he was a natural ascetic. It was only after I had travelled with him a few times that I realised he utilised his stays in Hardwar to lose some weight. Whenever he went to see devotees in Bombay or Londa, he would be fed enormous meals. On his return to Hardwar he would be about 10 kg overweight. He would go on a crash diet, and whoever was with him had to eat the same way. One time we lived on unsalted, boiled potatoes for a week.

Each time they were put on his plate, Master would make some approving remarks such as, 'Very good! Very simple, clean food. This is the way to live.' As he was encouraging us to eat this pure, wholesome food, he would never mention that he had just spent three months eating oily, spicy food all over India.

Master was on one of his periodic diets when I first met him in Delhi. I thought that this was the way he liked to live and eat because I had never seen him live any other way. It was only later that I realised how much he enjoyed good food. When I invited him to Australia, I made a point of serving him very simple, almost tasteless food. Master must have thought that I was being a very bad host because I never offered him anything tasty.

When Master wanted to abandon his diet, he would never admit it directly. He would never say, 'I feel like eating some good food today. Let's go out for a meal.' Instead, he would invent some pretext or excuse.

On one of my first visits to Hardwar he looked at me and said, 'You look very thin, and you also look a little sick. You need better food. Come with me and I'll get you something nourishing to eat.'

He took me to town and made me sit by a street stall that sold buffalo milk with extra cream on top. Buffalo milk is much thicker and creamier than cow's milk. The owner was skimming the cream off simmering buffalo milk and adding it to the drinks that he was serving in his stall. Master ordered a litre for me, and then, as an afterthought, he ordered a litre for himself. He wasn't sick, and he certainly wasn't malnourished.

The following morning Master asked, 'Did you sleep well? Are you feeling better?'

'Yes,' I replied. 'I slept well.'

Papaji bathing in the Ganga south of Hardwar. Pilgrims who are having a ritual bath in the Ganga adopt these hand positions before fully immersing themselves.

I was initially touched by his solicitude, but I soon realised that he had another reason for asking.

He laughed and said. 'I didn't sleep at all. I had indigestion all night from drinking so much buffalo milk.'

The afternoons in Hardwar would often be a repetition of the mornings. After a long post-lunch nap, Master would get up and invite us for another walk along the river. On our return we would eat dinner and then sit with him for about an hour in his *kutir.*

Sometimes he would take us into town to show us what was happening in some of the ashrams. He would always bow very respectfully to whichever swami was in charge. Then, if he was feeling mischievous, he would ask spiritual questions that no one ever seemed able to answer. He would do this with a sweet, innocent look on his face that would always convince the swami that he was a spiritual novice who had come for advice. In none of these places did Master ever announce that he was a teacher himself. He seemed to know all the ashrams and all the swamis in Hardwar, but very few people in these places had any idea who he really was.

Master never maintained an image that anyone would associate with a spiritual teacher. Although he would often wear a *dhoti* when he was sitting in his room, if we went out visiting, he would wear shirts and pants that I think were left over from his working days in the mines. He could always pass himself off as a tourist, a businessman, or a householder-pilgrim.

However, although Master was polite and respectful when he was in the presence of other teachers or swamis, in private he could be scathingly critical of their activities. In the years that I was with him I heard him make derogatory remarks about virtually all the famous teachers in India.

'I have my standards,' he would say. 'I have lived with the Maharshi. No one can be favourably compared to him.'

During the early 1980s, when I was spending a lot of time with Master in Lucknow, the favourite target of his criticism was Osho. He would read articles in the morning paper or in the weekly magazines that chronicled Osho's teachings, his lifestyle, and the wild habits of his followers. These reports would always provoke Master into delivering a harsh and often angry lecture whose focus would usually be the damage Osho was doing to the minds of the people who were associating with him.

When I came to see him in the early 1990s, after a break of several years, I found him surrounded by former Osho *sannyasins.*

With some amusement I asked him, 'How do you feel about all these people coming to you after what you were saying about Osho and his disciples ten years ago?'

He scowled and replied, 'Osho is sending me faxes from hell'.

Master's only previous contact with large numbers of Osho's devotees had been in Londa. The railway station there was a junction where many Pune-bound travellers had to change trains. In the afternoon, if he had nothing else to do, Master would often go down to the station, sit on the platform and watch the Pune *sannyasins* change trains. He found their behaviour, their dress and their antics very entertaining. On the days when I accompanied him he would always be amused by their appearance and behaviour. Sometimes the encounters would be more interactive. He would say something such as, 'I can't tell if that one is a boy or a girl. Go and find out.' Then I would have to approach one of them on Master's behalf so that his curiosity could be satisfied. He made no attempts to keep his voice down while he made his derogatory remarks, so the *sannyasins* must have heard what he was saying. Master enjoyed these encounters enormously, but there were occasions when I definitely found them to be a little embarrassing.

In the early 1980s Papaji would often stay up at night in order to investigate various spiritual phenomena that were intriguing him. He was particularly interested in the process whereby the manifest appeared in the unmanifest. He would go deeply into the Self in order to witness the whole process of creation within himself. Papaji described some of these nocturnal expeditions in a diary that he always kept with him. Many of his reports are printed in the 'Diaries' chapter.

Raman, who spent many months with Papaji in Hardwar while these investigations were being conducted, describes what Papaji was like during this period:

Master would spend hours at night in what seemed to be deep, meditative trances. The next morning, when he came to have tea with us, he would often give long, detailed reports on all the states and realms he had been in during the night. Some mornings he would be like an excited child who has to tell someone about a big adventure that has just happened.

One morning he appeared for tea with a note in his hand.

'I pinned this to my door last night,' he said. 'I didn't know whether I would survive the experience, so I left instructions about what to do with my body if I died during the night. Some of the states I enter are so subtle, so totally unconnected with the body, there is a possibility that I may not be able to survive them. But something is compelling me to go on with these journeys.

'Last night I left my door open. I didn't want to inconvenience anyone. If I die during the night with the door locked, somebody

---

355

will have to break it down in the morning.'

The same thing happened on a subsequent occasion when we were both staying in the Bhatia Bhavan. When he didn't appear in the morning for tea, I went looking for him and found his door slightly open. There was another note pinned to the door, giving information on whom to inform if he passed away during the night.

I once asked him what it was like to go on these internal journeys.

'The experience of the Self is always constant,' he replied, 'but there are no limits to what one can discover if one dives deeply enough into it. It is like an endless range of mountains. You reach the top of one and find another in the distance. You reach the top of that one and find yet another beyond it. In the subtlest levels of being one can go deeply into the structure of a single atom, one can go to the farthest reaches of the universe, or one can go into and even beyond that place where all creation manifests.'

Papaji alluded to these investigations in a letter he wrote to Raman in 1981:

Lucknow,
20th January, 1981

...I am very happy to find myself in difficulty when I reach a frontier of my expectation. I arrive there and look forward to a vast dimension that is still undiscovered. So, I move along again. Continuously moving forward is a game that I like. Perhaps I never will arrive at a destination. And if I could do it, perhaps I would not accept it. You are welcome to join me. Let us see how it works.

In a letter written the following year Papaji describes what happened when he decided to go to Rishikesh from Lucknow to continue with this intense inner work:

Lucknow
3rd May, 1982

Dear Raman and Jasmine,
As you are aware, I was going to Rishikesh on a definite project. I

Raman and Jasmine with Papaji in
Londa, sometime in the early 1980s.

was thinking that it might engage me for at least six months, if not
more. I wanted to solve the timeless, unsolved mystery.

All at once, an understanding came to me. I don't call it an
attainment, an achievement, realisation or even enlightenment. It is
so rare to face such a situation. I have never known, heard, read or
experienced anything like this before. Even my bones received a
tremendous and utterly strange shock. I can't call it freedom,
moksha or *nirvana.* There is nothing to compare it to. I cannot
define it, yet still I would like to describe it.

Some kind of vibration that I can call an inner cyclone gripped
my soul, mind and intellect, relieving me of the concept of time
and my convictions about the waking reality. I had previously been
convinced that all these phenomena were alternating before an
entity which was immobile and which I identified with
consciousness.

Now, I will go to the Himalayas to play, not to do any kind of
work.

Though Papaji mentioned that his previous convictions or experiences had been somehow invalidated in this state, he gave no further details of what they were replaced by. Many similar descriptions and investigations will appear in the 'Diaries' chapter.

Raman now continues with his account:

Though Master seemed to spend hours each night absorbed in these deep, inner states, he didn't encourage others to do any kind of formal meditation. He liked people to behave in a natural, normal way around him. When I first met him, I was still very much attached to formal meditation practices. On one occasion Master called me 'a meditation addict', an accusation I knew to be true. However, Master let me meditate in front of him because he knew I enjoyed it. Sometimes he would even pretend to meditate himself, but it was just a game for him. If there were children around, he would have fun playing with their toys; if there were meditators with him, he would play at meditation with them, just to keep them happy. I once sat with him in meditation for a couple of hours at Ram Mandir in Londa. At least I thought we were meditating together. When I opened my eyes and looked at him, he was still sitting there, cross-legged, with his eyes closed, but he was holding a transistor radio to one ear so that he could listen to the cricket commentary.

Master would let me indulge in my passion for meditation only as long as it didn't produce any interesting results. Occasionally, I would go into ecstasies or trances. If Master saw this happening to me, he would shake me by the shoulder, make me get up, and then take me out for a walk. In Hardwar these sobering-up walks would be quite nice, but if he did this to me in Narhi, Lucknow, I would have to go out into the noisy, crowded bazaar with him. If I was in a particularly quiet or sensitive state, this would be quite a jarring experience for me.

Master explained this behaviour by saying, 'Don't seek experiences and become attached to them. You are trying to grasp something that cannot be grasped. Be normal. Be natural. Don't become attached to blissful states. If you do, you will just create more desires.'

After reading this account, Om Prakash made the following comments:

In those days Papaji didn't usually allow people to sit in front of him with closed eyes. Raman was an exception. He would go into these *samadhis* or yogic trances regularly, and Papaji would permit him to stay in them for hours at a time. Raman may have lost track of time when he was in these states because he gives the impression that Papaji brought him out of them as soon as he entered them. My memory is that he regularly stayed in them for hours at a time. As Raman has said, Papaji would eventually intervene to bring him back to normal. He would press a point on the top of Raman's head and within a few minutes Raman would be back to normal.

One time Papaji said, after he had brought him back to his usual state, 'That's enough for today. You can carry on tomorrow.'

I didn't get the feeling that Papaji was discouraging Raman from entering these states. He just didn't want him to remain too long in them.

Raman continues with his story:

Master was ruthless when it came to sweeping away concepts or experiences. Though I have many fond memories of his love and compassion, when I think back to those years I spent with him, my abiding memory is of a hard, tough destroyer who was always ready to smash any trace of duality he encountered in a disciple. Nowadays, people call him 'Papaji' and relate to him as a kind, loving grandfather. I never had that image. For me he was and always will be 'The Master', with all the awesome, authoritative connotations that this term denotes. A French disciple once told me that Master's nickname in France in the 1970s was 'the butcher' because of the way he ruthlessly chopped away all pretensions, all ideas, all relationships.

On some of our later visits to India we were invited by Master to stay with him in Lucknow. After the big open spaces of Hardwar, Narhi was a big shock for us. Master's family house was in the middle of a teeming bazaar. The narrow alleyways, barely wide enough for a car to drive down, would be perpetually packed with a seething, noisy mass of pedestrians, rickshaws, carts, traders and beggars.

We felt honoured to be allowed to stay in his house because there was barely enough room for Master and his family. Jasmine and I slept in the downstairs front room, which was a living room during the day. Master's wife usually slept in the kitchen on the floor. Master himself had a private room upstairs, while Surendra [Papaji's son], his wife Usha and their children occupied the rest of the house. In summer we would all go outside and sleep on mats on the roof because the heat inside would be unbearable. The concrete of the house would absorb the fierce heat of the sun during the day and then radiate it into the rooms during the night. There were ceiling fans, but they didn't make much of a difference.

Though we often spent months in this house, we hardly had any dealings with Master's family. We would sit with Master in his room while the rest of the family conducted their business else-where. It was only years later that we got to know Surendra and Usha well. Some of Master's Lucknow devotees would come in the evenings, but for most of the rest of the day we would be alone with him, just sitting silently in his presence. His main indoor activity was reading. Each morning he would carefully go through the morning paper and any letters that had been written to him. During the day, if he felt in the mood, he might pick up a spiritual book and read parts of it to us. If we were lucky, he would add his own commentary.

Even though Master lived for long periods in the house with his wife, son, daughter-in-law and grandchildren, he didn't seem to have many interactions with them. Surendra would sometimes come to speak to him for a few minutes in the morning, but that was all. For the rest of the day he would spend hours sitting in his room, neither speaking nor moving. His eyes would be open, and though he would apparently be looking at the wall in front of him, I don't think he was seeing anything at all.

One time while we were there, his wife said to him, 'You will go mad if you spend all day just staring at the wall. Why don't you go out and get a job? You could get a job pumping petrol at the petrol station on Ashok Marg. You need to get out and meet people and talk to them. It's not good for you to sit all day staring at the wall and saying nothing.'

When Master told us this, we couldn't believe it. We thought we were lucky to be sitting in satsang with a great enlightened Master, but his wife seemed to regard him merely as a candidate for the lunatic asylum.

'Doesn't she know who you really are?' I asked him, incredulously. 'Doesn't she have any understanding of what you are doing to all these people who come to see you?'

He shrugged and answered, 'In this house I am just another member of the family. The people here have always seen me as a relative. They are too close to see anything else.'

Master had a special pass that enabled him to walk in the nearby zoo before it officially opened. We would go there almost every morning for a walk. It was more of a park than a zoo because there were lots of empty green spaces and trees. Sometimes we would go instead to a little park that was by the main post office. We always welcomed these walks in summer because they were the only opportunity we had to get away from the stifling heat of the Narhi house.

Master had had high blood pressure for years. During one of our stays in Narhi he conducted experiments on himself to see how different types of food affected his score. He said he wouldn't accept the conventional medical opinion on this matter until he had proved that it was valid for his own body. Master decided to check the accuracy of the medical advice he had been given by eating foods that were supposed to be bad for him. Afterwards he would check the results for himself.

He would start by eating a big meal that had been cooked in plenty of oil, finish it off with a few sweets, and then call for his blood-pressure machine. For the rest of the day he would have us take his blood pressure every half hour to see what the food was doing to his body. The experiment would be repeated each day with slightly different combinations of salt, oil and sugar. I don't know whether he had a genuine scientific interest in these tests or whether he was just using them as an excuse to eat large amounts of tasty food.

In the end he had to admit that medical science had got it right: when he ate the prohibited foods, he got sick, and when he avoided them, or only ate them in very small amounts, he stayed healthy.

Master liked to travel and he also liked to eat large amounts of good food but he had to balance the two activities because if he ate the wrong food in the wrong amount, he would get so sick he couldn't travel. Sometimes he would diet and travel; sometimes he would indulge in eating and stay at home.

During the early 1980s Raman and Jasmine made frequent visits to India, interspersed with long stays in Australia. While they were in Australia they kept in touch with Papaji by post. Here are a few of Papaji's replies from this period:

Lucknow
16th March, 1982

I am very happy to read your shout: 'Any word or a bird now seems to throw me beyond mind completely. It's an amazing phenomenon. I will really enjoy sharing my stay with this phenomenon forever.'
What is this ENJOYING, SHARING, STAYING, PHENOMENA, FOREVER?
IT IS NOT THE SAME AS

WORD - BIRD - THROW - BEYOND
AMAZING - PHENOMENA

Now, when we meet again, we will work upon this utterance. All is fine here. How is Mrs Jasmine? She has done well silently. Let her take it easy.
IT UNFOLDS ITSELF BY ITSELF
when we have no concept.
Then we see it and BE IT.

With great LOVE and AFFECTION

Lucknow,
23rd February, 1983

Dear Raman and Jasmine,
I was most happy to read your fantastic description of the indescribable, the inconceivable, who is seen, felt and known by even the pores of the body. Such is the beauty queen, the untouched awareness.

I was not happy with your sixty-day stay in India this time but the quantum of work that we three got through was tremendous. After assessing it, I can say that it was huge. Now I am certain that when we meet, we will not meet as strange personalities. We will be three in one and one in three, a unique arithmetic.

Take good care of your health. Good aspirations will make a good bonfire of a good mind. Tell Raman to write down immediately whatever words drop from your lips. Otherwise you will miss hearing what you speak. Reading these words will be like looking at one's own appearance in the looking glass and appreciating one's own Self. I AM with you wherever you are, either at home or in Hardwar.

You are so close to me, so beloved by me, I cannot find a phrase to describe the relationship we have. What an attachment and what a unique understanding there is between us! I don't think there is any other such relationship in the world.

Now, regarding me, I am in absolutely good, sound health. B.P. 130/80, even though I am eating spicy, salty, pungent, greasy and bulky food. I gained 4 kg between the 4th and the 22nd February. Never mind for the weight or the no weight or the abnormal sleep. I do not know when I am awake.

I no longer mind the loud sounds of TV, radios, cassettes, hawkers and shouting. My noise problem has gone after staying twenty-five years with me. I don't see my body as me, nor do I see it as not me. There is no otherness, just a fantastic love with no other separate personality.

Sometimes I miss you a lot and want to speak to you. At other times we are one and the same. Write to me about your ear trouble. You must have consulted some specialists by now. Now I know why Buddha was chattering for half a century.

May I send the letter of Jasmine to Shashikala, a middle-aged Bombay lady who had a similar experience at Bombay with me and is still keeping it. She is roaring like a tiger, 'I AM enlightened by the grace of Masterji'.

She speaks beautiful words.

Shashikala's experience will appear in a later chapter.

Lucknow
7th July, 1983

...for the first time in my life I read [in your letter] something I have never read or heard from any other quarter: neither human nor god, neither in the present nor in the past. This was the secret I mentioned in one of my letters from Hardwar, not knowing that it had been already unlocked and sent to Oman. [Raman's letter was forwarded from there.]

I cannot comment much on your letter that lies before me today, nor do I even like to read it again to enjoy the new language you got hold of for the first time, because this is what I am. This is what I experience, feel, comprehend and know, not in the sense of any unity or diversity, but just as it is.

Now is the time to live and now is the time to die.

NO death, NO life, NO attainment, NO Loss. NO light, NO darkness, NO freedom, NO bondage, NO thought, NO sun. I am happy you have fulfilled the purpose of life. All is over, dear Raman.

I congratulate you on behalf of all the enlightened ones of the past, present and future. I have full knowledge that the language I have just been speaking is faulty. I just speak to express myself in a common way.

Generally, I destroy letters before I reply. This one I will keep. The dictation is good, and the dictator is a non-entity...

Hardwar
24th December, 1983

...The aerogrammes you left here were handy. I picked one up to tell you immediately about the fantastic sleep I just slept. I hurry because I have to convey to you instantly lest it slips. I reject *nirvana* and I reject *samsara*. It is difficult to hold on in between, to tell you instantly, 'Now you are there,' because there, there is no word to tell.

I can keep away *samsara* and return to *nirvana* whenever I want to.

What is it like? It is wrong if I say 'tremendous light' because we already have an idea in the mind about the light of the sun. If I say 'knowledge', we impose the concept of sleep. Sleep or knowledge are both out of date, not present. It is a very new newness, ever alive. Oneness, no twoness.

I am attached to you. My intention [to help you] brands me with the personality of a *bodhisattva*, whatever it is. I am not concerned with either Buddha or sentient beings, of course, but there is a Poonja-Raman role to play, just as Buddha had a role in Buddha-Ananda.

Many things are missed out when I write. We both spoke, right up to the moment of your return flight, but nothing is held in the memory. I meant to convey something to you in words but I can't, yet you have missed nothing.

You are the only person to keep me in my body for a mutual transaction, a bargain. I want to talk, and you want to listen. Never mind. All is over.

Lucknow
24th February, 1984

...How to comment on the letters from you and dear Jasmine? My hand is just a quarter of an inch away from the aerogramme, waiting for a command from the mind to proceed to write what I have understood and smelt in your letters. But the mind doesn't do justice. Instead, she writes what I am now writing, and that is all she can write. You are the only person who has written to me in this way. I am full of joy. Even my eyes express their gratitude to some phenomenon unknown or unseen to them. The eyes usually respond when they see some beautiful object, but in this case they don't see either an outer or an inner object, yet still they shine forth and look happy. I feel that when man is free from thoughts and envelopments, the whole world sits around to see the beauty.

One such free man was walking along in the woods. He sat down under a tree. The tree blossomed out of season and showered flowers on him. Celestial beings came and prostrated to him because they had never had a satsang like this in the heavens.

Lucknow
29th February, 1984

...I have full confidence that you are the only ONE among the four billion who has crossed beyond the BEYOND. I have much to tell you. Catch my unsaid word about the ungraspable, unknown and unspoken 'unentity'. Tears well up in my eyes when I speak like this. My dear own oneness, my twin personality. Let us talk more together beyond the circular time. Love to you. Love to Jasmine...

Apropos Papaji's remarks in the first sentence, I have come across letters to other devotees that say substantially the same thing. Such statements should not be taken too literally. When Papaji gets excited by the experiences of a particular devotee, in his enthusiasm he somehow seems to forget all the similar experiences that other devotees have had. One could also say that his letter-writing style tends to hyperbole, particularly when outstanding experiences are reported to him.

Papaji occasionally admits that when he speaks, his words are not stored in his memory. It is possible that his mental processes function in such a way that records of devotees' states and experiences are also not stored in the usual manner. Papaji can give detailed descriptions of encounters that happened decades ago, but such memories never seem to surface when he

finds himself reading an account from someone who has just experienced a no-mind state.
   Papaji's letters continue:

Lucknow
2nd April, 1984

...I cannot write about what I want to tell you. It is not possible in normal waking consciousness. I often get into that particular moment that is not waking, dreaming or sleeping. Maybe *turiya* or beyond. What a beautiful phenomenon! My dear darling Raman, get right into IT. And right now I AM THAT. STARE AT IT. Love to Raman. Love to Jasmine.

Londa
3rd August, 1984

Dear Raman.

After reading your letter, redirected from Lucknow, I could only stare into the Beyond from where RAMAN stares at ME! I alone could kiss the nothingness to express my ecstasy. To respond to the letter some ONE could still write in the convenient human language, that language being none other than my own Beingness.

   This has just happened, and no one could ever do it as beautifully as this. It happened spontaneously, from beyond the nameless entity.

   Your letter is a most adequate expression of the nature of the seer, better than most people have expressed it before. The Buddha's finger is lined up, pointing at that which is beyond the void. The Ultimate Truth, though, has ever remained unuttered and unattained. It is unattainable and unknown.

   STOP. I cannot write any more. I saw a mark on the 'w' of 'unknown' that was not mine. Who did it? What does it mean? I know but I cannot name it. In knowing, I lost the means of writing.

   I AM thrown out of waking consciousness into a state of absolute sensationlessness. Now, it rules over me. My Heart, thrown into stillness, is still writing. Once more I make up my mind to complete this letter. I had so much to write, but now I hunt for words...

Lucknow
21st September, 1984

Dear Raman,
I returned here last evening. Immediately on arrival I found your letter among my post and read it. I could never believe that any other person save Raman could convey this through the traditional medium of words. It comes from the other shore. You left behind the mind and the intellect, and even the paper and the pen. It was as if you left them all in your bag before embarking on this journey. It is an utter void, yet we are speaking to each other, as one non-entity to another. Is it not a wonder that we remain what we were, denuded of every possible possession that the mind could possess?

Now our real work begins. That is how I am all the time. Involved, but for no reason. There is no search, no emptiness. What would you call it?

Raman, after reading your letter, I could only react by kissing it. I licked it as a most beloved, non-personal entity.

Let us meet wherever possible, but please inform me early if you plan to come.
Love to you and love to dear Jasmine.

Lucknow
12th March, 1985

Dear Jasmine,
Your letter dated 4th March arrived on 12th March. I remember very well the 21st February incident. Everything that happened there happened in an instant out of time. This is a point where quite a few returned back; one or two stood there bewildered and started enjoying the beauty of nothingness, love and tremendous joy; but a rare one, once in an eon or a *kalpa,* leaps into the immortal ocean of the unknown realm beyond. At this juncture I left you alone to do the rest by yourself at Ram Kunj. If you couldn't do it, never

368

mind. There is no return from here. There is no map to leap into the beyond. No guide or suggestions from any quarter will help. So, I withdrew, leaving you alone.

I will soon be joining you. Thank you.

Love to you and dear Raman.

Jasmine sent me the following note about her experiences with Master during this period:

Master was tireless in working with us. In every minute of the day he was grace beyond measure. I must have had heaps of good *samskaras* to merit living with the Master. I wanted freedom. That was my one and only desire. I knew that I had no other desire whatsoever. Nothing else existed, just the desire for freedom. And I was ever thankful for the grace of being so close to the Master. I am still amazed at my great good fortune. When I first met Master, my limited idea of enlightenment was a quiet mind. Working with Master showed me the limitless, the fathomless. The ever-expanding nature of this universe can truly never be contained or described by our limited brain. And to me that is the joy of living. It can't be described or known. The sheer beauty of the elusiveness of being has never been touched. You can choose any description, but has anyone ever caught a description of it?

Most of the information Raman has given so far came from several sources: a long letter he wrote to me a couple of years ago, Papaji's replies to his letters, some notes he made in his diary in the 1970s, personal conversations in Lucknow, and a taped interview he recently gave to Mira, a devotee of Papaji who lives near him in Australia.

The final question of this interview was, 'What effect has Master had on your life?'

This was Raman's reply:

I can say that the effect has been total. Master worked so hard on me and gave me so much. When I first met him I was totally addicted to meditation and concepts. By the 1980s he had liberated me from these attachments so successfully, I couldn't tell who was Master and who was me. He destroyed the concepts that had made me believe that I was separate and different from him. But somehow, this only seemed to happen when I was with him. In his presence I experienced a full sense of communion with what he really is, but when I went back to Australia, ideas about differences would start to arise again.

On one of my visits in the 1980s he said, 'A young sapling cannot grow under the shade of a big tree. You have to go away and be by yourself for some time.'

I felt like a baby bird being thrown out of the nest, but at the same time I recognised the necessity of what he was doing. Knowing that I had to learn to fly by myself, I didn't see him for several years after that.

What could I do in his physical absence? I couldn't meditate because he had convinced me of the futility of striving. I couldn't do any kind of practice because I could see very clearly that all practices involve seeking results and grasping for experiences. Thrown back on my own resources, I had to give up seeking and keep quiet. When I finally abandoned the effort of trying to attain something, I discovered that the peace and communion I had enjoyed in his presence could be found and enjoyed anywhere. I learned that when one does not look for results, grace is everywhere.

I came back to see him with Jasmine in 1989. It was a quiet time with two or three other people in Hardwar. On our next visit in 1992, everything had changed because over a hundred people were attending his satsangs every day. We were warned in Delhi about this new development by Sivani, Master's daughter. She showed us a magazine that was featuring Master as its cover story. He had suddenly become famous.

When we walked up to greet him in his living room in Indira Nagar, he laughed and said, 'You never expected to see me like this, did you?' As he was saying this, he was pointing out the packed rows of people on his floor and the large group at the gate outside.

Then he got up, put one arm around my shoulder and his other arm around Jasmine's, walked us to the door and said, 'Let's go for a walk down the Ganga'.

Jasmine and I walked down the street with him, enfolded in his huge arms. I think all three of us were pretending that we were back in Hardwar, walking by the side of the Ganga.

I hardly visited him at all on this trip because the craving to be in his company all the time was no longer there. I attended all his public satsangs, but I only went to see him in his house a couple of times. I think the bird he had thrown out of his nest had learned to fly and fend for itself. There was also a feeling that it was now other people's turn to get what they could from his physical presence. Having spent years sitting virtually alone with him, I felt it would be selfish and greedy of me to take up space in his crowded room when there were so many other new people begging for *darshan*.

One morning I was musing on something he had told me many years before: 'There is no relationship with the Master.'

As this thought revolved within me while I was sitting on my bed, another thought arose: 'What is my own relationship with the Master?'

As I was pondering over this question some great force seemed to throw me forward, face down, on the bed. There was no one else in the room, but this power was so strong, I felt as if I had been physically hit from behind. As I lay there, I had what can best be described as a divine, cosmic vision. I saw innumerable universes arising out of and disappearing into That which Master is. There was a direct knowledge that the Master, the Self, was the source and support of everything, but at the same time there was also the knowledge that Master, as the Self, had no relationship with anyone or anything. I explain this as best I can, knowing that nothing I say can convey the awesome directness of this experience. It was nothing to do with thought or mind. Beyond all perceiving and conceiving, it was the unmanifest Self showing me directly that it had no relationship with manifestation. I was shown directly that the Self was the essence of manifestation without being the cause of it.

The experience left me with no questions and no thoughts. I

knew that there never had been any distance or any relationship between Master and me. I knew that duality and separation, essential components of all relationships, had never existed.

I have nothing else to say except *'Hari Om Tat Sat!'*

Raman's concluding quote is untranslatable, except to say that each of the four words denotes the Absolute. In this context it is a declaration of identity: 'Self alone exists and I am That.'

SOURCES AND NOTES

The stories that Papaji tells in this book can rarely be attributed to a single source. During the course of my research I collated all the available versions of each story and ended up producing composites that included all the details I could collect.

The following abbreviations indicate some of the sources I have used:

L ('letters') – when the date and the recipient of the letters have been given in the text, I have not duplicated the information here. With very few exceptions, the originals of all the letters written by Papaji are in the possession of the devotees they were addressed to.

MD ('Meera's diary') – teaching dialogues from the mid-1970s, recorded by Meera Decoux in her diary.

MEE ('Meera') – an interview with Meera Decoux, 1st October, 1995.

OMP ('Om Prakash Syal') – an interview with Professor Om Prakash Syal, 1st December, 1994.

PI (*'Papaji Interviews'*) – extracts from *Papaji Interviews*, published by Avadhuta Foundation, 1993. The numbers in **PI**, **PMS** and **TTI** entries are page numbers.

PMS ('Papaji manuscript') – in 1994 I submitted a 120-question questionnaire to Papaji about all aspects of his life. He responded by writing out 234 pages of answers in three foolscap notebooks.

SAT ('satsang audio tape') – from 1991 onwards, Lucknow satsangs were recorded on ninety-minute audio tapes. In my attributions I have given the tape number, rather than the date, since satsangs from different days often appear on the same tape. Copies of these tapes can be ordered from Poonjaji Tapes, Boulder, Colorado.

TTI (*'The Truth Is'*) – though this is primarily a collection of teaching dialogues, Papaji includes many personal stories in his answers.

UT ('unrecorded talks') – many supplementary details came from comments Papaji made in his house, or on other occasions when there were no facilities for recording what he said.

The attributions have the following format:
1. Page number or numbers.
2. The first three and last three words of the material that is being cited. For ease of reference, the quoted words either begin or end a paragraph.
3. Sources of the material.
4. I have occasionally added supplementary notes.

Papaji read out about two thirds of my completed manuscript during his 1996 Lucknow satsangs. The other third he read and checked privately. Before the page-number attributions for each chapter begin, I have given the **SAT** numbers for the days Papaji read out all or part of that chapter.

HARDWAR, RISHIKESH
SAT 973, 974, 975, 976

5-6 For most of ... was his headquarters. **SAT** 278, 638; **PMS** 25-9.

6 For some time ... in eating me. **SAT** 460.

7-8 I was sitting ... a similar experience. **PI** 60-1; **SAT** 211, 474, 693.

8-9 I was living ... it to manifest. **PMS** 37.

9-11 When I was ... Sri Ramanasramam instead. **PMS** 9-10.

11-21 I once read ... to Jagannath Puri. **PMS** 88, 95-9, 127-8; **SAT** 206, 394, 441, 509, 578; **TTI** 393, 409.

21-2 *Papaji embarked on ... to do so.'* **PMS** 102; this is the only major spiritual encounter in Papaji's life that I have never personally heard him narrate. This version comes from Prof Om Prakash Syal, who heard it from Papaji about twenty years ago. I twice asked Papaji to narrate the full story, but on both occasions he declined to say anything. Eventually, I wrote out Om Prakash's version and asked him if it was accurate. He read it, said that it was true, but added no comments of his own.

22-3 Dr Dattatreya Bakre ... or the *rishis.* **PMS** 169-78.

24-8 I had a ... the Ganga again. **MEE.**

29 *When the subject ... to her meditation.'* **PMS** 64-73.

29-30 He still wouldn't ... together in Rishikesh. **MEE.**

30-1 When I saw ... to have changed.' **L** dated 9th December, but no year was given.

31-2 That day when ... us to Vrindavan. **MEE.**

32-3 There was another ... in our rooms. **PMS** 64-73.

34-6 He took me ... and then depart. **MEE.**

37 I once travelled ... everything is here.' **SAT** 663.

37-8 I showed Meera ... us a room. **PMS** 64-73.

38-9 We had moved ... miracle can happen.' **MEE.**

39 *I asked Meera ... the squash family.* I got the story of Papaji dancing in Rishikesh second-hand from a friend of mine who in 1995 talked to Balayogi on my behalf about the latter's memories of Papaji's years in Rishikesh. The two were apparently quite close in the 1970s, so much so that Balayogi tried, unsuccessfully, to interest Papaji in starting an ashram in which they would both teach. It seems that Papaji initially showed some interest, but he eventually rejected the plan.

40-1 From early childhood ... of expressing it. **PMS** 112-3; **SAT** 261, 479, 660; **TTI** 483.

42-3 When we arrived ... book was finished. **MEE.**

43-4 *There are several ... in our rickshaws.* Both of these stories, neither of which

I had heard before, emerged in a conversation I had with Raman Ellis in 1996. Raman was present during the 'missing tapes' episode, and heard the story of the Muslim yogis directly from Papaji when the two of them were living together in Hardwar in the 1980s.

44 After we had ... never had before. **MEE.**

45 *Though Vidyavati must ... her household needs.* My comments on Vidyavati's opinion of Papaji and Ramana Maharshi come from a conversation I had with Om Prakash Syal, who spent many years watching the domestic dramas in Papaji's Narhi home.

45-6 **Question:** What did ... even more angry. **PMS** 145-6; I was given a very similar answer by Papaji shortly after Vidyavati's death in 1992. I asked him what his wife had thought of his peripatetic lifestyle, and he replied that she always complained about it.

46-7 We decided to ... act of consecration. Papaji wrote out this answer in response to a brief questionnaire I gave him on the subject of his marital life with Meera.

48 There is nothing ... cannot be touched. **UT.**

48-54 In the late ... a free room.' **PMS** 54-9; **SAT** 334, 400, 443, 487.

54-7 He was very ... became good friends. **MEE.**

57-60 In 1970 I ... happen many times. **PMS** 54-9; **SAT** 202, 248, 27th October, 1990. **SAT**s for 1990 do not have numbers since they belong to the era before official recordings began.

60-2 I was planning ... absorption, very still. **PMS** 31-3; **SAT** 188.

63-6 This encounter happened ... back to normal. **PMS** 25-6, 51.

66-8 We were walking ... this cure again. **MEE.**

69-70 We were staying ... back to Hardwar. **PMS** 74-6.

70-2 We were living ... a Ganga *prasad.* **MEE; PMS** 64-73.

72 Papaji and I ... it came from. Personal conversation with Arno, 1995.

73 I sometimes wondered ... eventually they stopped. **UT.**

73-83 I first encountered ... this boy's father.' **OMP.**

83-5 I met him ... narrated the story. **MEE.**

85 *Swami Abhishiktananda was ... this cosmic form.* Swami Abhishiktananda, his *life told through his letters,* by James Stuart, published by ISPCK, Delhi 1989. In a letter to Bettina Baumer (page 268) Abhishiktananda wrote: 'A friend [Papaji] who is a real advai in last month had a shattering vision of Christ, feet on earth, arms and head above the heavens, with arms held out "as if to hold me". I am looking forward to meeting this friend, to speak of it with him.' On page 272 there is an extract from a 26th January, 1971, letter to Sister Sara Grant: 'It is the same man who had two months ago an overwhelming vision of the cosmic Christ, encompassing the whole universe, yet coming to *him* with open arms.... All my theology and rationalism is put to the test by this vision.'

85-6 Abhishiktananda was actually ... his Christian ideas. **MEE.**

86 I have known ... *AUM* or *AMEN.* **L** dated 2nd November, 1970.

86-7 Swami Abhishiktananda and ... have just described. **SAT** 484; **L** from Papaji to Gabri, 18th March, 1985; **UT.**

88 I was sitting ... are viewing me.' **OMP.**

88-9 Who can bear ... etc. have disappeared. *Swami Abhishiktananda, his life told through his letters* by James Stuart, published by ISPCK, Delhi 1989, pp. 348-9.

89-91 That's a very ... the American medicine. **SAT** 346, 669; **PI** 239-40. Father Shigeto Oshida was a Japanese Christian who was brought to Papaji by Swami Abhishiktananda in January 1971. See *Swami Abhishiktananda,* p. 271.

92 I was walking ... since meeting Papaji. **MEE.**

92-102 For the last ... people around us. **PMS** 56-7; **SAT** 120, 201, 202, 230, 237, 255, 265, 322, 326, 333, 349, 369, 430, 456, 467, 473, 476, 478, 486; **TTI** 361. Stories of Papaji's meetings with foreigners in Rishikesh during the late 1960s and early 1970s were a recurring feature of his Lucknow satsangs in the early 1990s. These **SAT** numbers are only a small fraction of the total number of sources.

102-5 Some of my ... for several days. **SAT** 144, 757; Papaji also wrote out a full version of the story for me when I asked him for extra details.

106-7 *In 1995 I ... Devi Temple instead.'* Interview with B. D. Desai, December, 1994.

107-8 I was happy ... case of typhoid. See the note for pp. 102-5; I also gathered details of the bus crash and its aftermath from B. D. Desai and Ravi Bakre.

109-10 Though I am ... of their lives.... **L** dated 7th March, 1971, 18th May, 1972, and two letters for which the years are not available: 13th January and 23rd March. I am assuming that they belong to the same period.

110-1 As has been ... Him in detail. This widely circulated letter had no date, but I would guess from some of the contents that it was circulated during Papaji's 1971 trip to Europe.

111-2 I was once ... this offer also. **PMS** 202-3.

112 In the 1970s ... place at all. **MEE.**

112 I was invited ... looking for me. **SAT** 123.

113-7 In the early ... was his wife. **PMS** 60-4.

117-9 Yes, we were ... of being quiet. **MEE.**

119-20 I once went ... an authoritative answer. **PMS** 196; **SAT** 196, 240; **UT.**

120-4 When Papaji was ... do it anymore. **OMP.**

124-7 I was staying ... Self reveals it. **PMS** 33-5; **SAT** 137, 232, 235; **TTI** 471.

128-9 Master accompanied me ... I was coming. **MEE.**

129-31 One day, after ... restored to health. **PMS** 27-9.

131-4 In 1971 Papaji's ... divine cosmic form. **OMP.**

134-6 After my father ... great I was. **PMS** 143-5.

136-8 My younger brother ... effort into it. **PMS** 145-6.

FOREIGN TRIPS 1971-74
SAT 986, 987, 989, 990, 991

141-2 Many people I ... great enlightened beings. **SAT** 252.

143-6 Joachim showed me ... health and cleanliness. **PMS** 219; **SAT** 243, 450, 486, 705.

146-50 One man who ... by their parents. **SAT** 225, 336, 454, 475, 548, 669, 690.

151 My nephew had ... is not allowed. **SAT** 123, 160, 201, 274, 484; the story of the 'night in Berlin' is also entertainingly retold by Papaji in the video documentary *Call Off The Search.*

153 We were walking ... happiness and ecstasy. **MEE.**

154 I told him ... were giving them. **PMS** 37-40.

154 We met the ... in Master's presence. **MEE.**

156 That one Christian ... are, by HIM. **L**, Meera to B. D. Desai, 20th December, 1971.

156-60 When I lived ... peaceful and quiet. **PMS** 37; **SAT** 273, 454, 683.

160-5 As I was ... a Christian saint. **PMS** 46-8; **SAT** 652; **UT**; **TTI** 371. The Italian account of Papaji's life must have been based on an article by Swami Abhishiktananda entitled 'Un ermite de l'Inde, Harilal' that appeared in *Revue Monanchin*, May 1970 (Volume III, no. 5, pp. 2-14). This was substantially the same account that appeared years later in *Souvenirs d'Arunachala* and *The Secret of Arunachala*, neither of which had been published when Papaji was shown this account.

165-6 Virtually everyone in ... in your mind. **SAT** 652; **UT.**

166-8 I was taken ... in the walls.' **PMS** 49-50; **SAT** 258, 267, 670.

168-9 I was sitting ... Why suppress it? **SAT** 271, 297, 326. When Papaji narrates this story, he sometimes says that it happened in either Washington or Bologna. However, Meera (**MEE**) remembers the incident well and says that it happened in Assisi.

169-70 **David:** When all ... only make jokes! **PI** 241-2.

170-1 During the night ... my next birth. **PMS** 46; **SAT** 670. I have found Papaji's remarks on this previous life to be very ambiguous. When I asked him in 1994 if he wanted to go on record as saying that he was St Francis in a previous birth, he replied (**PMS** 46), 'I did not say that I was St Francis'. I found this comment to be a curious one since he has never denied being guided to the saint's grave by a vision, and when he talks about the body that was being eaten away by insects, he always says that it was his own body in a previous birth. I thought that perhaps he was standing in front of another tomb in Assisi, so I asked Meera exactly where he was when he had this experience. She replied that she was standing near him, and that Papaji was definitely positioned right in front of St Francis' tomb. I would therefore interpret his 'I did not say that I was St Francis' quote to mean that he was not keen to proclaim it publicly. This is definitely true. In all the years I have known him, I have never once heard him publicly admit that he was St Francis in a previous life, although I have heard him tell the story of his visit to the tomb several times. However, two people have told me that Papaji very clearly said to them many years ago that he was St Francis in a previous life. When one of them asked him why he had to be reborn after such a life, Papaji replied, 'I was too attached to the beauty of the world'.

When I gave him this section to read and check, I was hoping that he would confirm or deny its underlying claim. However, he read and approved it for publication without making any additional comments.

171-2 **Meera:** Assisi is ... him explain why. **MEE.**

173 *Papaji and Meera ... receive an answer.* **MEE**; Papaji wrote out a short account of his relationship with Meera in response to a brief questionnaire I gave him. The questions were based on the version of events that Meera had given me.

173-4 Because it was ... country to country. **PMS** 49-50.

175-8 While I was ... down the hill. **SAT** 476, 507; **PMS** 37-40, 115-6; **TTI** 52-3.

178-9 **Meera:** We went ... one brief encounter. **MEE.**

180 There was another ... seemed quite happy. **SAT** 690; **PMS** 37-40.

181 **Meera:** He surprised ... his inner fire. **MEE.**

181-3 During this trip ... your own Heart. **PMS** 37-40; **SAT** 484, 457; **UT.**

183 I visited Christian ... occasions was negative. **PMS** 207.

184 We stayed in ... walk by herself. **PMS** 64-73.

184-7 **Meera:** We lived ... his European tour. **MEE.**

187-8 Many people wanted ... sixth-floor flat. **PMS** 25-6.

188-92 I was told ... own Self   Poonja. *El Cuarto Movimento*, by Carlos Silva, published by the author in Uruguay, 1995, pp. 35-44, 122-3.

194-7 We are a ... mother tongue. Thanks. These two accounts come from typed reports on the note paper of Felix Corral Garcia. The first was undated, but the second was written on 26th April, 1974.

197-201 As I walked ... by the Church. **SAT** 83, 200, 243, 256, 267, 434, 661.

201-5 Some people dance ... him in Lucknow. **PMS** 10-1; **SAT** 205; Swami Ramanananda Giri, who was present during some of these events, clarified the sequence for me.

206-10 An architect from ... travelled in Europe. **PMS** 69-70; **SAT** 127, 560, 658.

210-3 A woman approached ... and singing alone **SAT** 261, 348, 383, 428.

213 *Papaji returned to ... to Vinayak Prabhu.* No date is available for the letter that follows.

214-5 Some hippies wandered ... rule the world. **PMS** 223; **SAT** 357.

215 He was very ... back to Barcelona. **MEE.**

215-7 We arrived at ... have three children. **SAT** 506, 702.

217-9 Wherever I stay ... gossiping about us. **SAT** 319; **UT.**

219-20 **Meera:** It was ... not a success. **MEE.**

220-2 I wasn't aware ... *had never lost....'* **SAT** 650, 658; *I am That*, edited by Maurice Frydman, published by Chetana, Bombay, India.

222 He came to ... Dr Leboyer's recommendation. **MEE.**

223-4 We had invited ... powerful, too demanding. *El Cuarto Movimento*, by Carlos Silva, published by the author in Uruguay, 1995, pp. 49-52; **SAT** 666.

224-9 I was in ... the concepts abide? **PMS** 224-5; **SAT** 131, 430, 454, 457.

229-30 I often speak ... always remain unsaid.... **L** to Sofia and Carlos, 25th February, 1988.

230 I listened to ... one got it.* SAT 237; *Krishnamurti, 100 years*, published by Joost Elfers, 1995, p. 142. I don't know what happened to the 'no one got it' tape. I was told by Krishnamurti insiders that there was a big fight over the tape after Krishnamurti's death. One group wanted to destroy the tape, but the wishes of the people who wanted to preserve it finally prevailed.

230-1 We were walking ... G. Krishnamurti's response. Personal conversation with Carlos Silva.

231-2 When U. G. ... never went back. SAT 356; PMS 108-10.

232-4 One day, as ... bag and left. SAT 134, 440, 459, 616; PMS 224-5.

234-5 While I was ... of the Ganga. SAT 123, 258, 332, 352, 439.

236-7 I was walking ... next to it. PMS 37-40.

237-8 Malou was well ... very interesting replies. MEE.

238-50 **Meera:** With the ... life for you. MD.

250-1 For most of ... plan at al. PMS 146-7.

INDIAN SATSANGS
SAT 1024, 1025, 1026, 1027, 1028

252 *At the end ... sometime in November.* Personal conversation with Carlos Silva. Papaji's return to India is also briefly mentioned in his book, *El Cuarto Movimento* [The Fourth Movement], published by the author in Uruguay, 1995.

252-6 The man who ... received a response. PMS 26-7; Papaji also wrote a more detailed version for me when the subject of Trivedi came up in his house in 1996; UT.

256-60 During the first ... on the disciple. OMP.

261-3 In the 1950s ... visit his house. PMS 76-9; TTI 52-3.

263-7 Ram Mohan Sharma ... accepted his apology. OMP.

267-8 Om Prakash went ... he passed away. PMS 26-7.

269-72 **Papaji:** Ram put ... is repeated remembrance. MD.

272-3 About five years ... to you again. Personal conversation with a devotee who wishes to remain anonymous.

273-5 My sister Tara ... is my Guru. PMS 129-31.

277-8 **Papaji:** You cannot ... Name, repeating itself. MD.

278-9 Silent mind means ... do not know. PI 263-5.

279-87 **Papaji:** I once ... 'God! God! God!'? MD.

288-306 **Papaji:** This is ... Name being chanted. SAT 743.

306 It was about ... several subsequent occasions. MEE.

306-7 I was returning ... essence through words. PMS 137-8.

307-11 **Question:** I have ... understanding for this. MD.

311-3 Carlos Silva, the ... he was wearing. PMS 210-4.

313-4 Master had gone ... teaching for me. MEE; MD.

315-7 **Pandit:** What can ... away from you. MD.

317-9 We went to ... by anyone's explanation. MEE.

319-25 **Questioner:** People always ... bloom and wilt. MD.

326-72 For several years ... *I am That.*' Raman's account has come from several sources: an interview with him conducted by Mira in Australia on 21st August, 1996; a long letter Raman wrote to me in 1995; several conversations I had with him in 1996 and 1997; a diary he kept in the late 1970s and early 1980s. Papaji's account of Raman's first major experience (pp. 340-2) is from **PMS** 84-7. I also had several conversations with Jasmine about the years she spent with Raman and Papaji in India, particularly the time they spent together in Papaji's Narhi home.

INDEX

The index is in two parts. In the first section, which I have entitled 'Papaji Stories', all the events that Papaji was personally involved in are listed in the order in which they appear in the book. The initial number or numbers identify the page or pages where the story can be found. The second part of the index is an alphabetical listing of proper nouns, technical terms and other key words by which stories and events can be identified. If a page number following a person's name in the alphabetical listing appears in **bold**, it indicates that a photo of him or her can be found on that particular page. If the page number of a place name appears in this way, it shows that a map featuring this place can be found on that page.

PAPAJI STORIES

ALPHABETICAL LISTING OF PEOPLE, PLACES, TECHNICAL TERMS AND OTHER KEY WORDS

389

GLOSSARY

The definitions of technical philosophical terms given here are not exhaustive. They merely indicate how the terms have been used in this book. Words followed by an asterisk (*) are defined elsewhere in the glossary. If a letter is bracketed within a word, e.g. *linga(m)*, it shows that the word can be spelt either with or without the bracketed letter. Indian languages terminate the same word in different ways. In the above example, *ling* would be Hindi, *linga*, Sanskrit, and *lingam*, Tamil.

Adi-Sankara – see Sankara.

advaita – literally 'not-two'; non-duality or absolute unity; pure monism. A school of *Vedanta**, one of the six orthodox schools of Indian philosophy; specifically the non-dualistic, non-theistic interpretation of the *Upanishads** and *Brahma Sutras* given by Sankara* (788-820 AD). Its central teaching is the identity of the individual soul with *Brahman**. It affirms that what is, is only *Brahman,* the Ultimate Reality. It also affirms the unreality of the world and the empirical self.

aham Brahmasmi – 'I am *Brahman.*' Located in the *Brihadaranyaka Upanishad**, this famous dictum is one of four such 'great sayings' (*mahavakyas**) from the *Upanishads,* each of which asserts the identity between the individual (*jiva**) and the supreme (*Brahman**).

ajapa – 'involuntary *japa'**; the state in which repetition of the divine name continues without any effort by the practitioner.

ajata – see Gaudapada.

Amarnath Cave – located at 13,700 feet, 145 km from Srinagar in Kashmir, it is the focus of a major pilgrimage each year around the full moon that falls between mid-July and mid-August. The goal is to have *darshan** of a natural ice-*lingam** that forms inside the cave. It is a five-day walk, and about 25,000 pilgrims complete the pilgrimage each year.

ananda – bliss.

Ananda Mayi Ma (1896-1982 AD) – literally, 'bliss-permeated mother'; a celebrated Bengali saint who had many ashrams, including one in Kankhal, Hardwar.

Arjuna – one of the five Pandava* brothers married to Draupadi and the greatest archer of ancient India. Lord Krishna* acted as his charioteer in the Pandavas' war with the Kauravas, which forms the subject matter of the *Mahabharata**. Krishna transmitted the teachings of the *Bhagavad Gita** to Arjuna on the Kurukshetra battlefield just prior to the climactic battle.

396

Arya Samaj – literally, 'Society of Nobles'; a Hindu social and religious reform movement started by Swami Dayanand (1824-1883 AD) as a reaction to western influences upon Hinduism.

asanas – physical postures, the regular performance of which is a standard feature of many yoga* practices.

ashram – a forest retreat, dwelling place of sages, yogis, and their students and disciples.

Atma(n) – in *Vedanta*, the immortal real Self of all beings, identical with *Brahman*, but used more specifically to refer to *Brahman* as individuated within the person.

avatar(a) – literally, 'descender'; an incarnation or 'descent' of a deity, especially one of the ten incarnations of Vishnu*, who include Ram* and Krishna*.

aum – see *Om*.

baba – a term of respect for *sadhus** and ascetics. See Babaji.

Babaji – a respectful term of address for a *sadhu** or holy man; also applied in families for father, grandfather and child. The person of this name whom Papaji tried to find north of Badrinath was the founder of the yogic lineage made famous by Paramahamsa Yogananda*. This Babaji is said to be several thousand years old, but still occupies a very young body.

Badrika – see Badrinath.

Badrinath – also known as Badrika; the main temple in this famous Himalayan pilgrimage centre was supposedly established by Adi-Sankara*. Traditionally, it is one of the four *dhamas* ('kingdoms of God') visited by Hindus who are seeking Self-realisation.

banian – a T-shirt, usually worn as an undergarment by Indian men.

Bhagavad Gita – literally, 'Song of God' or 'Celestial Song'; composed about 400-300 BC, it is the most famous sacred text of Hinduism. Found in the sixth chapter of the *Mahabharata**, it consists of the teachings given to the Aryan prince Arjuna* by Lord Krishna* on the battlefield at Kurukshetra. It attempted to synthesise many strands of Indian philosophy (e.g. *Vedanta**, *Yoga**, *Samkhya**) as well as recommending personal worship of Krishna.

Bhagavatam – also known as *Bhagavata Purana* and *Shrimad Bhagavatam*. Composed around 750 AD and attributed to Vyasa*, it contains extensive stories about Krishna's* early life.

Bhagirathi – the name of the River Ganga before it joins the Alaknanda River. It is named after the sage Bhagirath who originally persuaded Ganga to come down from the heavens and flow on earth.

Bhagwat – see Eknath.

bhajan – from the Sanskrit* root *bhaj*, 'to love, adore, worship'; a devotional song or hymn.

bhakti – 'loving devotion to God'; the ideal religious attitude according to theistic Hinduism.

bhiksha – food received as alms; the giving of such food; the act of going out to beg for it.

Bodhisattva – in Mahayana* Buddhism, a *Bodhisattva* is a highly evolved being who postpones his own entry into *nirvana** in order to help others attain enlightenment.

Brahma – In Hindu cosmology, God as creator, the first conscious mind in the universe and the first created being.

Brahma Loka – the highest heaven of some Hindu traditions. According to some schools, enlightened beings inhabit this realm after their physical death until the moment of *mahapralaya**.

Brahman – The designation in Hinduism for the impersonal Absolute Reality, ultimate truth, existence-knowledge-bliss; the one, formless, non-dual, Absolute, substratum of all that exists; identical with *Atman**.

brahmin – a member of the highest Hindu caste; a member of the priestly class, having the duties of learning, teaching, and performing rites *(pujas*)* and sacrifices *(yagnas*)*.

brahmin thread – a circular string, about two feet in diameter; looped over the left shoulder and around the waist, it is worn next to the skin by many brahmins.

Brihadaranyaka Upanishad – 'The Great Forest *Upanishad**'; written down in the 8th century BC, it contains the earliest clear presentations of the doctrines of rebirth and *moksha**.

chapati – round , flat, unleavened bread; a ubiquitous presence in all North Indian meals.

chillam – a baked, earthenware pipe, often used for smoking *ganja**.

Chitrakoot – The place where Ram* and Sita* spent eleven of their fourteen years of exile. Ram stayed on Kamad Giri, which means, 'the hill that can fulfil all desires'. Other places near Chitrakoot that are mentioned by Papaji are (1) Sati Anasuya: sixteen kilometres upstream on the Mandakini River, it is the ashram of the sage Atreya and his wife Anasuya, whose three sons were incarnations of Brahma*, Vishnu* and Siva*. (2) Gupt Godavari: located eighteen kilometres from the town, it has two caves in which Ram and his brother Lakshman* are said to have held court. (3) Hanuman Dhara: a spring, said to have been created by Hanuman after he returned from setting Lanka on fire. (4) Sita Rasoi: Sita's kitchen, located on top of a nearby hill. (5) Bharat Koop: a well where Bharat, the brother of Ram, is said to have stored water collected from all the pilgrimage places in India.

darshan – from the Sanskrit* root, *drs*, meaning 'to see'; sight of a holy person or temple deity, especially when the eyes meet; to be in, or be received into, the presence of a saint.

deva – a celestial being, a god; an inhabitant of the Hindu heavens. The female is *devi*.

Devanagari – the script in which Hindi*, Sanskrit*, Marathi and some other North Indian languages are written.

Devaprayag – the confluence of the Bhagirathi* and Alaknanda rivers, after which the two streams officially become the Ganga. Spiritually, it is the second most important confluence in India after Prayag in Allahabad.

devi – see *deva*.

dharamsala – a wayside shelter where pilgrims may stay for the night, either free of cost or at a nominal rate. Such places are common on major pilgrimage routes.

dharma – literally, 'that which bears, supports'; 1) the eternal principal of right action; 2) moral duty; 3) virtue; 4) divine law; 5) religious tradition.

dhoti – a rectangular piece of cloth worn by Indian men. Draped around the waist, it resembles a skirt.

Dogri – the language spoken by the Dogra ethnic group that lives mostly in Jammu and Kashmir.

dosa – a South Indian sourdough pancake, commonly eaten for breakfast or supper.

Durga – literally, 'The inaccessible or unfathomable'; one of the oldest and most widely-used names for the Divine Mother (Devi) in Hinduism; the consort of Siva. Usually depicted as a ten-armed woman riding a tiger, she wields the power to punish or confer grace. Her annual festival (Durga Puja) is held around October and is the premier religious festival in Bengal.

Ekadasi – the eleventh day of the lunar cycle; a fasting day for many orthodox Hindus.

Eknath (1533-99 AD) – A Marathi saint who edited *Jnaneshwari* and wrote poems of his own, along with commentaries on the *Bhagavad Gita** and the *Bhagavatam**. His *Bhagavatam* commentary, which Papaji calls *'Bhagwat'*, is a commentary on the eleventh canticle of the *Bhagavatam*.

Gangotri – A small town near the source of the Ganga. The Ganga itself begins at Gaumukh, about twenty kilometres upstream, when it emerges from the base of a glacier.

ganja – dried marijuana leaves; in India they are usually smoked in a *chillam**.

Garuda – in Hindu mythology, a demi-god in the form of an eagle, king of birds and destroyer of serpents the sacred mount of Lord Vishnu* and his consort, Lakshmi*.

Gaudapada – the greatest name in pre-Sankara* *advaita** *Vedanta**, he probably lived in the sixth century AD. Held traditionally to be the preceptor of Sankara's Guru*, Govindapada, Gaudapada is credited with writing a commentary on the *Mundakya Upanishad** called the *Mundakya Karika* in which he expounds a variation of *advaita* called *ajatavada*, the doctrine that nothing has ever happened and that nothing has ever been created.

ghat – stepped terraces on the side of a river; any steep embankment.

Gita – see *Bhagavad Gita*.

gopis – also known as *gopikas*; the female cowherders of Vrindavan who left their chores and homes to play and dance with Sri Krishna*; they are held to be paradigms of loving devotion. The chief *gopi* was Radha*. More generally, the term can nowadays mean any devotee of Krishna.

Gujarati – The language of a region north of Bombay, mostly contiguous with the state of Gujarat; a person who speaks this language as his mother tongue.

guru – literally, 'remover of darkness'; a spiritual teacher or preceptor, qualified to initiate disciples into a spiritual tradition. As capitalised in this book, either as Guru or *Sadguru**, it refers to the true Guru who has the power to show disciples who they really are.

Guru Purnima – 'Guru full-moon'; an annual festival celebrated on the day of the July full moon, in which devotees worship or felicitate their spiritual Masters.

Hai Ram – literally, 'O God'; however, the phrase does not have the same connotation as the English expression. In Hindi* and Sanskrit* it is a form of addressing God that indicates nearness, closeness and reverence. This is the phrase that Mahatma* Gandhi uttered as he was shot.

Haidakhan Baba – also spelt Hairakhan Baba, he is named after the hamlet on the banks of the Gautam Ganga in Kumaon where he was first seen. The original Haidakhan Baba disappeared in the 1920s. The one whom Papaji met in the early 1970s was claiming to be the same man.

Hanuman – the monkey-god, renowned as the devoted servant of Ram*. Helped Ram retrieve Sita* from captivity in Lanka. The story is recounted in Valmiki's Sanskrit* Ramayana* and its Hindi bhakti-cult version, the Ramacharitmanas*.

Hare – see Hari.

Hari – 'the one who captures'; a name for Vishnu* and His avatars*. The rules of Sanskrit* grammar change 'Hari' to 'Hare' when it is followed by a name, e.g., 'Hare Ram, Hare Krishna'.

Heart – a term frequently used by both Papaji and Sri Ramana Maharshi, it is a translation of the Sanskrit word hridayam, which literally translates, according to Sri Ramana Maharshi, as 'this is the centre'. When capitalised in this book, it is synonymous with the Self*. It denotes the spiritual centre of one's being and the place from which all thoughts and material phenomena originally manifest.

Hindi – the native language of most North Indians; the most widely spoken language in India.

homa – a yagna* in which consecrated offerings to a god are ritually thrown into a sacred fire.

iddly – a South Indian sourdough cake, made of rice and black gram; commonly eaten for breakfast or supper.

Jai Sitaram – 'Victory' or 'Glory to Sitaram*'.

jalebi – a sticky, deep-fried sweet.

Janabai – a servant and disciple of Namdev*, she was an accomplished mystical poet and a passionate devotee of Vitthal*, the image of Krishna* in Pandharpur. She and Muktabai, sister of Jnaneshwar*, are considered to be the two foremost women saints of Maharashtra.

japa – literally, 'uttering'; the scientific repetition, usually after initiation, of a word or words (mantra*), or name of God. It is repeated as a means of invoking grace, a vision of a deity, or Self-knowledge.

Jee – see ji.

ji – a Hindi* and Sanskrit* honorific suffix added to a name to denote respect; a respectful term of address, short for jiva*.

jiva – philosophical term denoting the individual embodied human soul, especially when unenlightened. Indian schools of thought differ on what degree of reality it has In *advaita**, it has formal, relative reality only until one is enlightened, after which it is seen to be not-separate or one with all that is.

jivanmukta – 'a liberated soul'; traditionally, one who is liberated while still alive, as opposed to a *videha mukti**, one who is liberated at the moment of death.

jnana – knowledge, wisdom, especially knowledge which is incontrovertible and permanent; absolute knowledge.

Jnaneshwar (*circa* 1281-1296 AD) – the founder of the *bhakti** movement in Maharashtra, the author of the *Jnaneshwari*, a verse translation-and-commentary on the *Bhagavad Gita**, and one of the greatest Marathi saint-poets. He is also known as Jnandev.

jnani – literally, 'one who knows'; a person who has *jnana**; a liberated or enlightened one. It is not an experience of true knowledge, it is knowledge itself. 'There are no *jnanis*, there is only *jnana*.' – Sri Ramana Maharshi*.

John of the Cross, Saint (1542-1591 AD) – Spanish mystical Carmelite saint and poet. Author of the mystical poem, *The Dark Night of the Soul*. Associated with Saint Teresa* of Avila, his senior contemporary.

Kabir (*circa* 1440-1518) – celebrated medieval saint, poet and mystic of Varanasi. An illiterate weaver by trade, his poetry and mystic teachings still form the focus of a popular sect in modern India. Kabir was above caste and class distinctions, against ritualism and idolatry, and equally disposed to Hindus and Muslims. The *Bijak*, an anthology of his poems, is the sacred text of the Kabir Panth, a group that reveres Kabir as a God. The book is divided into the *Raimini*, the *Sabdas* and the *Sakhi*.

Kali – also known as Devi; the wife of Siva*; though depicted in a horrific form, she is the primal creative force behind manifestation and she also bestows the grace that destroys egos.

Kannada – the native language of most people in Karnataka state.

Karika – see Gaudapada.

karma – literally 'action', 'rite', 'work'; the law of retributive action, the retributive moral force generated and accompanying all performance of action, held to bring back upon the doer good or evil according to the doer's motive, in this or a future life.

Katha Upanishad – composed around 500 BC, it teaches Yoga* philosophy and Samkhya* through a dialogue between Yama, the Hindu god of death, and his student, Nachiketas.

Kauravas – see *Mahabharata*.

Kedarnath – one of the four major Himalayan pilgrimage centres for Hindus; its main attraction is a Siva* temple supposedly built by the Pandavas to atone for the sins they incurred in the *Mahabharata** war. It is also claimed that Sankara* passed away there.

khichree – a dish whose principal (and sometimes only) ingredients are boiled rice and *dhal*.

Krishna – literally, 'One who attracts or wins over'; the cowherd-god whose flute

playing and sportive ways enchanted the *gopis**; His instructions to Arjuna*
on the battlefield during the great *Mahabharata** war form the text of the
*Bhagavad Gita**. The eighth *avatar** of Vishnu*, He is considered to be an
incarnation of love and is worshipped in His own right.

kundalini – 'the serpent power'; a psychospiritual force that lies dormant at the
base of the spine until activated by yogic practices. Conceived as a coiled
snake by yogis*, it uncoils and rises progressively up the spine through
various *chakras* (literally, 'wheels'), which can be visualised as spinning
vortices of energy and which are located in the subtle body in the centre of
the trunk and head. The *chakras* are the *muladhara* ('root-foundation
wheel') located at the anus, *swadhishthana* ('wheel of the self-base') located
at the genitals, *manipura* ('wheel of the jewelled city') located at the navel,
anahata ('wheel of the unstruck sound') located at the heart, *vishuddha*
('pure wheel') located at the throat, *ajna* ('command wheel') located in the
centre of the head, behind the point between the eyebrows, and the *sahasrara* ('thousand-spoked wheel') at or above the crown of the head.
According to Yoga* philosophy, when the *kundalini* reaches the *sahasrara
chakra, samadhi** ensues.

kurta – a long-sleeved, collarless men's shirt.

Kurukshetra – the battlefield on which the *Mahabharata** war was fought.

kutir – a small cottage or hut, especially one used as a hermitage.

lakh – one hundred thousand.

Lakshman(a) – Faithful brother of Ram*; He accompanied Ram and Sita* into
exile in the forest; the Hindu ideal of the devoted brother.

Lakshmi – wife of Vishnu* and goddess of wealth and good fortune.

lila – literally, 'sport', 'play'; held by the Vaishnavas* to be the divine purpose
behind the creation of the manifest universe.

linga(m) – literally, 'sign' or 'emblem'; a vertical column of stone with a rounded
top; the symbol of the unmanifest Siva*, it is worshipped in the inner shrines
of all Saivite* temples.

lota – a brass or copper pot, used to contain drinking water.

Madhyamika – see *Madhyamika Karikas*.

Madhyamika Karikas – a philosophical work by Nagarjuna (*circa* 150-250 AD);
it attempts to refute logically the positions of all other religious philosophies
and it forms the basis the Madhyamika school of Buddhist philosophy, also
known as Sunyatavada, 'the doctrine of emptiness'. Madhyamika is the first
of the two great divisions of Mahayana* Buddhism, the other being
Yogacharya or Vijnanavada*.

maha – a prefix meaning great or large.

Mahabharata – 'Great Bharata'; composed between 200 BC and 200 AD, it is a
massive poetical compilation of myths and legends about the Hindu gods. Its
centrepiece is a narrative describing the struggle between two families, the
Kauravas and the Pandavas, for control of Bharata (North India).

mahapralaya – the great dissolution; the moment when the manifest universe
disappears at the end of each *kalpa*.

mahatma – literally, 'great soul'; a fully-realised saint; a title given to Mohandas Gandhi (1869-1948), leader of India's Independence movement.

mahavakya – literally, 'great saying'; term used to refer to one of the four great sayings of the *Upanishads**, one from each *Veda**, which express in different ways the fundamental truth – the equation of *Atman** with *Brahman**.

Mahayana – literally, 'great vehicle'; one of the two great divisions of Buddhism, the other being the Hinayana (Lesser Vehicle) or Theravada (Doctrine of the Elders).

mantra – a sacred word or phrase given to a disciple by his Guru*; the repetition of the mantra *(mantra-japa)* is one of the most common forms of *sadhana**.

maya – literally, 'that which is not'; illusion; the unreal appearance of the world; the power that makes one believe in the reality of unreal appearances.

Mira(bai) (1498-1546 AD) – celebrated North Indian princess, saint and poet; her poems and songs, expressing her devotion to Krishna, are even today known and sung by ordinary Hindus all over India. The shoemaker-saint Ravidas* was her Guru*.

moksha – 'liberation', 'freedom'; in Indian philosophy, the emancipated state of the *jiva** or individual soul; freedom from the round of rebirths *(samsara*)*; Self-realisation.

Namdev (1270-1350 AD) – a Marathi tailor-saint who was a contemporary of Jnaneshwar*. He travelled extensively in India, extolling the virtues of repeating God's name.

Narada – one of the seven great *rishis** of ancient times, he is lord of the *gandharvas*, the heavenly musicians, and the inventor of the *veena*, a stringed instrument. He is an eternal being who has the power to roam at will through this world and other heavenly realms.

Narayana – literally, 'the son of Nara', meaning, 'the son of a man'; a very early, traditional name of the supreme being in Hinduism. By a syncretistic process common in Hindu mythology, Narayana's name came to refer to either Vishnu* or Krishna*.

Nemisharanya – 'the Nemisha Forest'; located near Sitapur in North India, it was famous in puranic times for several reasons: a major *yagna** lasting twelve years was conducted there, and was attended by thousands of *rishis**; according to some sources Suka*, the son of Vyasa*, gave the first recitation of the *Mahabharata** there; Krishna's* discus, the *sudarshan chakra*, landed there at the end of the *Mahabharata* war. The place where it landed is now a place of pilgrimage.

nirvana – 'extinction'; a Buddhist term denoting the state of enlightenment in which all desires have been extinguished.

Nirvana Sutra – the one Papaji read was probably the *Mahaparinirvana Sutra*, a Mahayana* text that states, among other things, that all beings are eligible for enlightenment, and that Buddha-nature is not other than the Self*.

nirvikalpa samadhi – the *samadhi** in which no differences arise or are perceived; the supreme superconscious state; the formless, intensely blissful *samadhi* of non-dual union with *Brahman**, the highest state of consciousness according to *Vedanta** and Yoga*.

Om – according to Hinduism it is the primordial sound from which all creation springs. It is the most important element in all mantras*.

Om shanti, shanti, shanti – '*Om**, peace, peace, peace'; an ancient vedic benediction concluding the prayer mantras* that introduce many of the classical *Upanishads**; a common form of benediction after the recital of a mantra, or at the conclusion of ritual worship (*puja**). For several years Papaji began all his satsangs with this mantra.

pa(a)n – a preparation of chopped arecanut, lime and occasionally other ingredients wrapped in a betel leaf and chewed. It colours the gums and teeth a characteristic red.

pada puja – Ritually worshipping the feet of a God or a Guru* as an act of veneration and respect.

padmasana – 'lotus posture'; in classical and *hatha* yoga*, the full-lotus posture in which the body is seated with the legs folded over the thighs, left ankle over right, spine and neck straight. Properly mastered, it allows the body to remain for long periods in trance or *samadhi** without falling.

paise (also *paisa*) – a unit of currency now equal to 1/100th of a rupee. Before independence there was a different division of the rupee: it was divided into sixteen *annas*, with each *anna* having four *paise*.

pakora – a preparation of chopped vegetables coated with batter, and deep fried.

Pandavas – see *Mahabharata*.

pandit – a Hindu scholar; one who writes about, researches or teaches subjects whose authority is derived from sacred Hindu texts.

Parvati – the wife or consort of Siva*.

Patanjali – writing around the 2nd century AD, he compiled and systematised the existing knowledge of Yoga* and gave it a sound philosophical base.

pooris – made of white-wheat-flour dough, they resemble chapatis* except that they are deep-fried and have a smaller diameter.

prana – vital energy; life breath; the common basis of breath and mind.

pranayama – yogic exercises that control or regulate the breath. Since Yoga* philosophy maintains that the breath and the mind are linked, controlling the former is supposed to control the latter.

prasad – a sanctified present; food offered to a Guru* or deity becomes *prasad* when some or all of it is publicly distributed or returned to the devotee who offered it.

puja – ritualistic worship; adoration and decoration of a deity or saint with mantras, *yantras**, hymns and offerings of light, water, flowers, sandalpaste, food, gifts, etc.

Radha – chief of the *gopis**, the female cowherds of Vrindavan who were the favourite lovers and playmates of Sri Krishna*.

Ram Tirtha, Swami (1873-1906 AD) – famous North Indian saint and mystical poet whose lyrical celebrations of the pristine advaitic state in Hindi*, English, Persian and Urdu rank among the best of their genre. A contemporary of Swami Vivekananda*, whose talks he arranged in Lahore, he also travelled to the United States (1902-4), meeting President Theodore Roosevelt, before returning to India where he retreated to the high Himalayas. He was drowned in the Ganga at Tehri, Garhwal, in 1906. Ram Tirtha was the maternal uncle of Papaji.

Ram(a) – the seventh *avatar** of Vishnu*, said to be the incarnation of *dharma**. He is the eponymous hero of one of India's great national epics, the *Ramayana**, which recounts the story of his rescue of Sita*, his queen, from her capture by Ravana*, the demon king of Lanka.

Ramana Maharshi (1879-1950 AD) – Guru* of Papaji and one of the most acclaimed spiritual figures of modern times. He spent all his adult life in Tiruvannamalai, at the foot of Arunachala. His clear presentations of *advaita**, his saintly lifestyle and his innovative method of self-enquiry attracted followers from all over the world.

Ramayana – one of India's great national epics, it recounts the story of Ram*. The original version was composed in Sanskrit* by Valmiki. The *bhakti*-cult version was composed in Hindi* by Tulsidas* (1532-1623 AD) and is called *Ramcharitmanas**. It is the most popular scripture in modern India.

Ramcharitmanas – 'The Sacred Lake of the Deeds of Ram*'; the title of the Hindi *Ramayana** written by Tulsidas* between 1574 and 1584 AD. Though the basic theme is the same as Valmiki's Sanskrit* version, Tulsidas places more emphasis on devotion to Ram.

ras lila – a drama enacted by devotees of Krishna* in which they dress up as Krishna and His *gopis** and then, through music and dancing, implore Krishna to manifest before them.

rasam – a spicy, watery soup consisting primarily of boiled pepper and tamarind.

Ravana – ruler of Lanka and the principal villain of the *Ramayana**. By kidnapping Sita*, the wife of Ram*, he triggered a major war, which he eventually lost.

rishi – literally, 'a seer'; one who through inner vision sees the truth of himself, or of spiritual texts.

Rudra – the name of an early vedic deity who later evolved into Siva*; one of the names of Siva.

Rudraprayag – the confluence of the Mandakani and Alaknanda rivers, seventy kilometres upstream from Devaprayag*.

rudraksha – literally, 'Rudra-eyed'; Rudra is a name of Siva*. *Rudraksha* seeds, often strung and worn as a necklace, usually have five faces, supposedly corresponding to the five faces of Siva.

Sadguru – literally, 'truth teacher'; the Self or *Atman** manifesting through a human form. See guru.

sadhak – one who practises spiritual exercises or *sadhana**.

sadhana – from the Sanskrit* root *sadh*: 'to go straight to the goal, be successful'; conscious spiritual exercise; that which produces success (*siddhi*) or the result sought; spiritual practice.

sadhu – an ascetic holy man; one who does *sadhana**, especially as a way of life.

Sai Baba, Sathya – born in 1925, he is probably India's most famous living spiritual teacher. His ashram at Puttaparthi attracts millions of visitors each year.

Sai Baba, Shirdi – Maharashtra saint of unknown origin who lived at Shirdi and died there in 1918. Well known for his miraculous powers, he still has a major following in western India.

Saivite – a follower or a devotee of Siva*.

sakti – divine power or energy; the cosmic force that allows manifestation to take place, and the energy that bestows grace and enlightenment.

samadhi – literally, 'to bear or support together'; 1) an intensely blissful, super-conscious state or trance; the highest condition of human consciousness in which the seer-seen, subject-object distinction is transcended; 2) the tomb of a saint.

sambar – a spicy, South Indian sauce, it is the standard accompaniment to all South Indian rice meals.

Samkhya –derived from a word meaning 'number', its doctrines are based on the twenty-five *tattvas*, or 'categories of existence'. Most of them pertain to or classify different levels of manifestation. In practical terms *Samkhya* teaches a gradual renunciation of everything that is not *Purusha*, the *Samkhya* term for the Self*. The literature of the school evolved more than 2,000 years ago. Though it is still listed as one of the six major schools of Indian philosophy, it has been in a state of decline for at least 1,000 years.

samsara – the empirical world of names and forms, especially as it appears to the unenlightened mind; the continuous cycle of death and rebirth to which the *jiva** is subject till liberated.

Sankara (Adi-Sankaracharya) (788-820 AD) – the great Hindu scholar-saint and reformer whose commentaries on the classical *Upanishads**, *Bhagavad Gita** and *Brahma Sutras* revived orthodox Hinduism at a time when it was stagnating under ritualistic brahminism. He established *advaita Vedanta** on an impregnable popular footing, rendering it proof against the onslaught of Mahayana* Buddhism, especially the Madhyamika* School of Nagarjuna, which subsequently died out in India.

Sankaracharyas – Honorific title given to the heads or pontiffs of the five principal monastic institutions established by Adi-Sankara*: Joshi Math, near Badrinath; Kanchipuram, southwest of Madras; Puri, on the east coast near Cuttack; Dwarka, in western Gujarat; Sringeri, in south-west Karnataka. Each of these monasteries (*maths*) traces its lineage back to either one of Adi-Sankaracharya's four direct disciples (Sureshwaracharya, Padmapada, Trotakacharya and Hastamalaka) or to Adi-Sankara himself. The prefix 'Adi' means 'original'. It is used to distinguish the first and original Sankaracharya from his successors.

sannyasa – renunciation, specifically the monastic rite enacting the vow to renounce; the last and highest stage of Hindu life when one leaves worldly cares and responsibilities for the wandering life of a monk, living on alms, having freedom (*moksha**) as the sole aim of life.

sannyasin – one who has taken *sannyasa vrata*, the vow of renunciation; a renouncer.

Sanskrit – No longer widely spoken, it is the language in which Hinduism's sacred texts were composed.

Saraswati – wife of Brahma* and the Hindu goddess of learning.

Sastras – from the root *sas*, to enjoin, teach, instruct; strictly, a manual or compendium of rules or instructions containing the authoritative teaching on a subject or tradition, especially a religious treatise, sacred text or scripture of divine authority; sometimes applied collectively to whole departments of knowledge, e.g., the *Dharma Sastras*, or law texts, or to refer to the whole corpus of Indian orthodox, religious philosophical literature.

satsang – literally, 'fellowship or company with truth'; the conversation and/or company of a realised saint; the group of disciples or seekers who form such a company; conversation which leads one towards truth; a sacred and essential component of spiritual life for all traditions in orthodox Hinduism.

sattva – purity, harmony; many Hindu sects maintain that nature consists of three 'qualities' or 'strands', never at rest, called *sattva* (harmony, purity, brightness), *rajas* (agitation, activity, passion) and *tamas* (inertia, darkness, ignorance), one of which is always predominant. The mutual interaction of the *gunas* accounts for the quality of all change in both manifestation and consciousness.

Satyananda, Swami – a *sannyasin* disciple of Swami Sivananda* of Rishikesh, he established the Bihar School of Yoga* in Monghyr, Bihar, and achieved renown as an exponent of *hatha* yoga and *tantra**.

Self – the term adopted in English, when capitalised, for the *Atman**.

shakti – See *sakti.*

shanti – peace.

shloka – a type of Sanskrit* verse, especially from a sacred text, of four half lines containing, usually, praise or precept; a literary form in modern Hindi applied to many types of verses.

shraddh(a) – an annual ceremony in which Hindus feed the spirits of their ancestors.

siddha – an enlightened being one who has mastered many *siddhis**; an indiginous form of Indian medicine; a practitioner of that form.

Siddha Loka – a heavenly realm inhabited exclusively by enlightened beings. See Brahma Loka.

siddhi – from the Sanskrit* root *sidh*, 'to be accomplished, succeed'; Superhuman powers or attainments, usually achieved through the practice of yoga*. The *ashtadha siddhi,* the eight major accomplishments, vary from text to text, but the following are the most commonly cited: 1) *anima* – the ability to shrink the body to a minute, even atomic, size. 2) *mahima* – enlarging the body to a gigantic size, enabling the adept (*siddha**) to witness cosmological processes such as the formation of stars. 3) *laghima* – weightlessness, used to levitate the body. 4) *prakamya* – to have one's wishes regarding the location and size of the body fulfilled merely by willing them. 5) *garima* – making the body as heavy as one wishes. 6) *isitva* – lordship or dominion over all beings and substances. Through this *siddhi* the adept can either create new beings or order living entities or inanimate objects to appear and disappear. 7) *vasitva* – universal mastery; an adept with this faculty can make any creature act as he wishes, and he can also change the course of nature, since he has control over the wind, the rain, and other elements. 8) *prapti* – the ability to accomplish everything desired, or a state in which nothing remains to be desired.

Sita – daughter of Janaka, King of Videha, wife and consort of Ram*, the seventh incarnation of Vishnu*. Their story is told in the *Ramayana*.

Sitaram – the gods Sita* and Ram* treated as a joint, divine entity.

Siva – the god of destruction in Hindu mythology; also, by extension, the god who destroys the egos of his devotees.

Sivananda, Swami (1887-1963 AD) – a popular North Indian swami who founded the Divine Life Society in Rishikesh. His world tours and his more than 300 books did much to popularise *hatha* yoga* and meditation in the 1960s and '70s in India and the West.

Smt – short for Srimati; a respectful form of address for married Hindu women; approximately equivalent to 'Mrs'.

Sri – literally, 'the auspicious one'; often used as an honorific prefix, it also denotes Devi, the Divine Mother, or Lakshmi*, the consort of Vishnu*.

Sri Ramanasramam – the ashram of Sri Ramana Maharshi* in Tiruvannamalai. Founded in 1922, Sri Ramana spent the last twenty-eight years of his life there.

sudarshan chakra – an irresistible, discus-like weapon wielded by Krishna*.

Suk(a)dev – see Suka.

Suka – also known as Sukdev, he was the son of Vyasa, to whom is attributed authorship of the *Mahabharata*and the *Brahma Sutras*. Suka was the narrator of the *Bhagavat Purana*, also known as the *Bhagavatam*.

Sumeru – also known as Meru; a mythical mountain, the central point of the universe according to Hindu cosmology.

Sunyatavada – see *Madhyamika Karikas*.

sutra – literally, 'a thread, a suture'; a short, pithy, aphoristic statement in Sanskrit* religious or philosophical literature. Because they are often meant to function as a mnemonic device, *sutras* frequently need further explanation or commentary.

swami – literally, 'one's own'; strictly, 'one's own Master'; a person who has realised the Self; a spiritual preceptor, guru*; often used as a respectful term of address for senior monks, approximately equivalent to 'sir'.

takli – small metallic device, resembling a spinning top, on which followers of Mahatma* Gandhi used to spin cotton.

tantra – an esoteric religious movement and literature, of obscure origin, which arose in India after the Gupta period (3rd to 4th centuries AD) as a successor to vedic brahminism. It identified *nirguna Brahman* (unmanifest, formless *Brahman**) with Siva* and exalted the worship of Devi, or the Divine Mother, which was identified with *saguna Brahman* (*Brahman* with form or attributes) as the active feminine principle of cosmic power or divine energy responsible for all change.

tapas – literally, 'heat'; asceticism or ascetic practice; one of the adjuncts to
   sadhana* for the Yoga* school; *Vedanta** too has its counterpart. It is a deep-
   rooted notion in Hinduism that some form of restraint or discipline (psychological heat) is needed for transformation.
Teresa of Avila, Saint (1515-82 AD) – medieval Spanish Christian Carmelite mystic.
   She experienced a spiritual marriage with Christ and helped St John of the
   Cross* to found a monastic order.
tilak – a coloured dot, applied to the forehead either as a decoration or at the
   culmination of a Hindu religious ceremony.
tonga – a small, covered, two-wheeled cart, pulled by a horse. Formerly a major
   form of public transport in many Indian cities.
Tukaram (1608-1649 AD) – a Marathi poet-saint who lived near Pune,
   Maharashtra. Author of many devotional poems addressed to Ram*.
Tulsidas (1532-1623 AD) – the most celebrated name in Hindi literature, his
   Ramcharitmanas* is the most influential religious text in northern and
   central India. A brahmin* of Uttar Pradesh, he belonged to a lineage that can
   be traced back to Ramananda, the Guru* of Kabir*. Other details of his life
   are scanty and probably legendary.
Upanishads – literally, 'sitting close to'; the later 'knowledge portion' of the
   Vedas* which incorporate the profound speculations and teachings,
   originally secret, of the ancient Aryan seers of Hinduism. Since these
   teachings came later, after the ritualistic portion of the *Vedas*, as a group they
   are called the *Vedanta**, or 'end of the *Veda*'. Traditionally, the *Upanishads*
   number 108. They are the fundamental authorities for the Hindu teachings
   on reincarnation, karma* and the doctrine that the Self* and *Brahman** are
   identical.
Urdu – The language produced by the confluence of Hindi* and Persian during
   Mughal rule. Similar to Hindi in grammar, it is written with a Persian-Arabic
   script and contains numerous Persian, Arabic and Turkish words. It is the
   national language of Pakistan.
Vaishnava – a follower of Vishnu*. See Vaishnavism.
Vaishnavism – one of the three great divisions of modern theistic Hinduism (the
   other two being Saivism and Shaktism) which identifies Vishnu* – or one of
   his incarnations, Ram* or Krishna* – with *Brahman**, the Supreme Being.
Vaishno Devi – a cave-temple in Kashmir where three major goddesses are
   worshipped, it is located at an altitude of 5,100 feet, sixty-one kilometres
   north of Jammu (Kashmir) and fourteen kilometres from Katra. Over a
   million pilgrims attend the main festivals in March/April and
   September/October.
Vasishta – see *Yoga Vasishta*.
Vedanta – literally, 'end of the *Vedas*'; the system of Hindu thought based on
   the *Upanishads**, *Bhagavad Gita** and *Brahma Sutras*, and holding
   primarily the doctrines of pure non-dualism (*advaita**) and qualified non-
   dualism (*visistadvaita*).
Vedas – literally, 'knowledge, wisdom'; the highest, oldest and most sacred

scriptures of Hinduism and the oldest written religious texts in the world. The earliest portions are about 4,000 years old.

vibhuti – ash from a sacred fire that is subsequently used for worship. It is applied to the body and sometimes swallowed as *prasad**.

Viceroy – 'Deputy Emperor'; the title given to the seniormost British official in India during colonial times.

videha mukti – 'disembodied liberation'; generally understood to be the post-mortem state of enlightened beings. Papaji, with some scriptural authority, takes it to be a pre-death state, a condition of perfect identity with the Absolute, in which all body consciousness has been lost.

Vijnanavada – also called Yogacharya; the 'mind-only' school of Mahayana* Buddhism which denies the independent real existence of perceptible objects in the phenomenal world, holding that no external objects exist except either as ideas in the mind or within the universal storehouse consciousness (*alaya-vijnana*).

vipassana – literally, 'insight' or 'intuitive cognition'; one of the main forms of meditation in Theravada Buddhism. Called 'Insight Meditation', it is said to be the practice by which the Buddha himself attained enlightenment. It analyses sensations in the body-mind field, leading into insight into the true nature of things as being empty and void of all self-content.

Vishnu – 'the strider', 'the pervader'; in the Hindu trinity, the Lord of preservation and appearance. He is the ruler of *maya** and the guardian of *dharma**. As his *avatars** Ram* and Krishna*, he descended from his celestial abode in order to defeat various demons plaguing humanity and to uphold the eternal human aims of *dharma** and *moksha**.

Vitthal – the name of Krishna* as He appears in the temple at Pandharpur, Maharashtra.

Vivekachudamani – 'the Crest Jewel of Discrimination'; a popular advaitic work, traditionally attributed to Sankara* (788-820 AD).

Vivekananda, Swami – dynamic successor of Ramakrishna Paramahamsa, he was, in 1893, one of the first Indian swamis to take the message of Hinduism to the West. Through his lectures, his books, and through the organisation he founded, he promoted a major revival of Hindu culture and philosophy.

Vyasa – a generic term meaning 'the arranger' or 'the compiler', it is applied to the author or authors of various important Sanskrit* works, especially to Veda-Vyasa, the arranger of the *Vedas**. He is listed as the author of the *Mahabharata**, the *Bhagavatam** and the eighteen major *Puranas**. Some texts mention as many as twenty-eight Vyasas who have appeared on earth at various times to compile and disseminate vedic knowledge.

yagna – a sacrificial fire; a ritualistic sacrifice, especially one that follows vedic prescriptions.

Yamunotri – the official source of the Yamuna River, although it actually emerges in a hard-to-reach glacial lake further upstream.

yantra – a sacred geometrical design; the empowerment of *yantras* and their subsequent ritual worship are a central element of *tantra**.

yatra – a pilgrimage.

Yoga – literally, 'to yoke, harness, unite'; the orthodox system of Indian philosophy associated with the *Yoga Sutras* of Patanjali (1st or 2nd century AD). It comprises the eight-limbed path set out in the *Yoga Sutras**: moral observance (*yama*); self-discipline (*niyama*); physical postures (*asanas*); breath control (*pranayama*), restraint of the senses *(pratyahara)*, concentration (*dharana*); meditation (*dhyana*); and *samadhi** in which the subject and object of meditation have become one.

Yoga Vasishta – a Sanskrit* work of 32,000 lines; composed between the 9th and 13th centuries AD, it is classified as an epic (*itihasa*). It contains the teachings on liberation given to Lord Ram* by his Guru*, the sage Vasishta. Although there are many long teaching parables and occasional digressions into various yogic techniques, its main message, that the Self* alone exists, is uncompromisingly advaitic. The author is unknown.

Yogananda, Paramahamsa (1893-1952 AD) – a Bengali yogi* who popularised Indian spirituality in the West through his best-selling book, *Autobiography of a Yogi*. His lineage, founded by Babaji*, propagated *kriya* yoga, a simplified but secret form of *raja* yoga*.

yogi – one who practises yoga*; one who strives earnestly for union with God, particularly by the path of *raja* yoga; one who has achieved *siddhi** (success) in yoga; one who has become 'harmonised' or 'yoked' in *Brahman**; a spiritually advanced or freed soul.

yuga – a subdivision of a *kalpa*; in Hindu cosmology, a *kalpa* is a period of time corresponding to 4,300 million years. Known as a 'day of Brahma*', a *kalpa* is the period that the manifest universe lasts prior to its dissolution. After another *kalpa* in which there is no manifestation at all, Brahma, the Hindu god of creation, creates a new universe that lasts for another *kalpa*. The creation and dissolution cycle is endless. Each *kalpa* is divided into four *yugas*: the *satya*, the *treta*, the *dvapara* and the *kali*. We are currently about 5,000 years into the *kali yuga*, which is due to end in about 427,000 years time.

David Godman, Papaji, and a rented snake on a bridge in
Hardwar, sometime in March, 1993.

David Godman has been living in India since 1976, mostly at the
ashram of Sri Ramana Maharshi. He has written or edited four
other books about Sri Ramana and his direct disciples: *Be As You
Are*, *No Mind – I am the Self*, *Papaji Interviews*, and *Living by the
Words of Bhagavan*. From 1993-7 he resided in Lucknow,
researching and writing this book and attending Papaji's satsangs.

If you are interested in obtaining books, audio tapes and videos on
Papaji, please contact the Avadhuta Foundation, 2888 Bluff Street,
Suite 390, Boulder, Colorado 80301 USA.
     e-mail: mail@avadhuta.com
   Telephone: 001-303-473-9295
       Fax: 001-303-473-9284